MASS CALENDAR

The Value of a Missal

"Hand Missals which are drawn up according to the requirements of the modern liturgical renewal and which contain not only the Ordinary of the Mass but a version of all the liturgical texts approved by the competent authority are still necessary for more perfect understanding of the total mystery of salvation celebrated during the liturgical year, for drawing meditation and fervor from the inexhaustible riches of the liturgical texts, and for facilitating actual participation.

"This demands not only that the Word of God be proclaimed within the gathered community and attentively listened to by it, but also that the holy people respond to the Word of God which they have received and celebrate the Sacred (Mysteries) by singing or reciting the parts of the Ordinary and Proper [of the Mass], hymns and Psalms.

[Missals are] especially necessary for . . . those who participate in daily Mass, or who desire to live and pray every day in the spirit of the liturgy; those who because of sickness or inconvenience or other similar reasons cannot assemble with their own liturgical community, so that they may be joined to their prayer more truly and intimately; children who are to be initiated progressively into the mystery of the liturgy."

Postconciliar Commission for the Implementation of the Constitution on the Sacred Liturgy.

This Missal belongs to

....

Cyle B
For 2002 - 2003

New *Saint Joseph*
SUNDAY MISSAL
PRAYERBOOK AND HYMNAL

This new Missal has been especially designed to help you participate at Mass . . . in the fullest and most active way possible.

How easy it is to use this Missal

- Refer to the Calendar inside the front cover for the page of the Sunday Mass (the "Proper").
- This arrow (↓) means continue to read. This arrow (→) indicates a reference back to the Order of Mass ("Ordinary") or to another part of the "Proper."
- Boldface type always indicates the people's parts that are to be recited aloud.

VIRGINIA BRODERICK

*The People of God together with Christ worship
the heavenly Father*

New . . . St. Joseph
SUNDAY MISSAL
PRAYERBOOK AND HYMNAL

For 2002-2003

THE COMPLETE MASSES FOR SUNDAYS, HOLYDAYS, and the EASTER TRIDUUM

With the People's Parts of Holy Mass
Printed in Boldface Type
and Arranged for Parish Participation

WITH THE "NEW AMERICAN BIBLE" TEXT
FROM THE REVISED SUNDAY LECTIONARY,
SHORT HELPFUL NOTES AND EXPLANATIONS,
AND A TREASURY OF POPULAR PRAYERS

Dedicated to St. Joseph
Patron of the Universal Church

CATHOLIC BOOK PUBLISHING CO.
New Jersey

NIHIL OBSTAT: Sr. M. Kathleen Flanagan, S.C., Ph.D.
Censor Librorum

IMPRIMATUR: ✠ Frank J. Rodimer, J.C.D.
Bishop of Paterson

The St. Joseph Missals have been diligently prepared with the invaluable assistance of a special Board of Editors, including specialists in Liturgy and Sacred Scripture, Catechetics, Sacred Music and Art.

In this new Sunday Missal Edition the musical notations for responsorial antiphons are by Rev. John Selner, S.S.

The Scriptural Readings and Responsorial Psalms are taken from the *Lectionary for Mass, Vol. 1* © 1998, 1997, 1970 by Confraternity of Christian Doctrine, Washington, D.C. All rights reserved.

The poetic English translations of the sequences of the Roman Missal are taken from *The Roman Missal* approved by the National Conference of Catholic Bishops of the United States © 1964 by the National Catholic Welfare Conference, Inc. All rights reserved.

English translation of the Roman Missal, Rites for Holy Week, original texts of The Alternative Opening Prayers, Invitatories, and the Penitential Rites; The Rite of Marriage; The Rite of Penance; The Rite of Christian Initiation of Adults; titles, responsorial psalms and alleluia verses of the Lectionary for Mass, Copyright © 1969, 1970, 1973, 1974, 1981, 1985, 1997, International Committee on English in the Liturgy, Inc. All rights reserved.

All other texts and illustrations © Copyright by Catholic Book Publishing Co., N.J.

(T-2003)

PREFACE

IN the words of the Second Vatican Council in the *Constitution on the Sacred Liturgy*, the *Mass* "is an action of Christ the priest and of his body which is the Church; it is a sacred action surpassing all others; no other action of the Church can equal its efficacy by the same title and to the same degree" (art. 7). Hence, the Mass is a sacred sign, something visible which brings the invisible reality of Christ to us in the worship of the Father.

The Mass was first instituted as a meal at the Last Supper and became a living memorial of Christ's sacrifice on the cross:

"At the Last Supper, on the night when he was betrayed, our Savior instituted the Eucharistic sacrifice of his body and blood. He did this in order to perpetuate the sacrifice of the Cross throughout the centuries until he should come again, and so to entrust to his beloved spouse, the Church, a memorial of his death and resurrection: a sacrament of love, a sign of unity, a bond of charity, a Paschal banquet in which Christ is eaten, the mind is filled with grace, and a pledge of future glory is given to us.

"The Church, therefore, earnestly desires that Christ's faithful, when present at this mystery of faith, should not be there as strangers or silent spectators; on the contrary, through a good understanding of the rites and prayers they should take part in the sacred action conscious of what they are doing, with devotion and full collaboration. They should be instructed by God's word and be nourished at the

7

table of the Lord's body; they should give thanks to God; by offering the immaculate Victim, not only through the hands of the priests, but also with him, they should learn also to offer themselves; through Christ the Mediator, they should be drawn day by day into ever more perfect union with God and with each other, so that . . . God may be all in all" (art. 47-48).

Accordingly, this new Sunday Missal has been edited, in conformity with the latest findings of modern liturgists, especially to enable the people to attain the most active participation.

To insure that "each . . . layman who has an office to perform [will] do all of, but only, those parts which pertain to his office" (art. 28), a simple method of instant identification of the various parts of the Mass, has been designed, using different type faces:

(1) **boldface type** — clearly identifies all people's parts for each Mass.

(2) lightface type — indicates the priest's or lector's parts.

In order to enable the faithful to prepare for each Mass AT HOME and so participate more actively AT MASS the editors have added short helpful explanations of the new scripture readings geared to the spiritual needs of daily life. A large selection of hymns for congregational singing has been included as well as a treasury of private prayers.

We trust that all these special features will help Catholics who use this new St. Joseph Missal to be led—in keeping with the desire of the Church—"to that full, conscious, and active participation in liturgical celebrations which is demanded by the very nature of the liturgy. Such participation by the Christian people as a chosen race, a royal priesthood, a holy nation, a redeemed people (1 Pt 2, 9; cf. 2, 4-5), is their right and duty by reason of their baptism" (art. 14).

PLAN OF THE MASS

INTRODUCTORY RITES
1. Entrance Antiphon (Proper)
2. Greeting
3. Blessing and Sprinkling Water
4. Penitential Rite
5. Kyrie
6. Gloria
7. Opening Prayer (Proper)

LITURGY OF THE WORD
8. First Reading (Proper)
9. Responsorial Psalm (Proper)
10. Second Reading (Proper)
11. Alleluia (Proper)
12. Gospel (Proper)
13. Homily
14. Profession of Faith (Creed)
15. General Intercessions

(Preparation of the Gifts)
16. Offertory Song
17. Preparation of the Bread
18. Preparation of the Wine
19. Invitation to Prayer
20. Prayer over the Gifts (Proper)

(Eucharistic Prayer)
21. Introductory Dialogue
22. Preface
23. Sanctus

LITURGY OF THE EUCHARIST
Eucharistic Prayer
1, 2, 3, 4
Children 1, 2, 3
Reconciliation 1, 2

(Communion Rite)
24. Lord's Prayer
25. Sign of Peace
26. Breaking of Bread
27. Prayers Before Communion
28. Reception of Communion
29. Communion Antiphon (Proper)
30. Silence After Communion
31. Prayer After Communion (Proper)

CONCLUDING RITE
32. Greeting
33. Blessing
34. Dismissal

THE ORDER OF MASS

Options are indicated by A, B, C, D in the margin.

INTRODUCTORY RITES

Acts of prayer and penitence prepare us to meet Christ as he comes in Word and Sacrament. We gather as a worshiping community to celebrate our unity with him and with one another in faith.

1 ENTRANCE ANTIPHON `STAND`

If it is not sung, it is recited by all or some of the people.

Joined together as Christ's people, we open the celebration by raising our voices in praise of God who is present among us. This song should deepen our unity as it introduces the Mass we celebrate today.

→ `Turn to Today's Mass`

2 GREETING (3 forms)

When the priest comes to the altar, he makes the customary reverence with the ministers and kisses the altar. Then, with the ministers, he goes to his seat. After the entrance song, all make the sign of the cross:

Priest: **In the name of the Father, ✠ and of the Son, and of the Holy Spirit.**

PEOPLE: **Amen.**

The priest welcomes us in the name of the Lord. We show our union with God, our neighbor, and the priest by a united response to his greeting.

A ————————————————————

Priest: **The grace of our Lord Jesus Christ and the love of God and the fellowship of the Holy Spirit be with you all.**

PEOPLE: **And also with you.**

B ———————— OR ————————

Priest: **The grace and peace of God our Father and the Lord Jesus Christ be with you.**

PEOPLE: **Blessed be God, the Father of our Lord Jesus Christ.**

or:

And also with you.

C ———————— OR ————————

Priest: **The Lord be with you.**

PEOPLE: **And also with you.**

[Bishop: **Peace be with you.**
People: **And also with you.**]

3 RITE OF BLESSING and SPRINKLING HOLY WATER

The rite of blessing and sprinkling holy water may be celebrated in all churches and chapels at all Sunday Masses celebrated on Sunday or Saturday evening. See pp. 72-74.

4 PENITENTIAL RITE (3 forms)

(Omitted when the rite of blessing and sprinkling holy water has taken place or some part of the liturgy of the hours has preceded.)

Before we hear God's word, we acknowledge our sins humbly, ask for mercy, and accept his pardon.

Invitation to repent:

After the introduction to the day's Mass, the priest invites the people to recall their sins and to repent of them in silence:

A As we prepare to celebrate the mystery of Christ's love,
let us acknowledge our failures
and ask the Lord for pardon and strength.

B Coming together as God's family,
with confidence let us ask the Father's forgiveness,
for he is full of gentleness and compassion.

C My brothers and sisters,
to prepare ourselves to celebrate the sacred mysteries,
let us call to mind our sins.

Then, after a brief silence, one of the following forms is used.

A

Priest and **People:**

> **I confess to almighty God,**
> **and to you, my brothers and sisters,**
> **that I have sinned through my own fault**

They strike their breast:

> **in my thoughts and in my words,**
> **in what I have done,**

and in what I have failed to do;
and I ask blessed Mary, ever virgin,
all the angels and saints,
and you, my brothers and sisters,
to pray for me to the Lord our God.

B ————————— OR —————————

Priest: Lord, we have sinned against you:
Lord, have mercy.
PEOPLE: Lord, have mercy.
Priest: Lord, show us your mercy and love.
PEOPLE: And grant us your salvation.

C ————————— OR —————————

Priest or other minister:
You were sent to heal the contrite:
Lord, have mercy.
PEOPLE: Lord, have mercy.

Priest or other minister:
You came to call sinners:
Christ, have mercy.
PEOPLE: Christ, have mercy.

Priest or other minister:
You plead for us at the right hand of
the Father:
Lord, have mercy.
PEOPLE: Lord, have mercy.

(Other invocations may be used as on pp. 75-77.)

Absolution:

At the end of any of the forms of the penitential rite:

Priest: May almighty God have mercy on us,
forgive us our sins,
and bring us to everlasting life.

PEOPLE: Amen.

5 KYRIE

Unless included in the penitential rite, the Kyrie is sung or said by all, with alternating parts for the choir or cantor and for the people:

℣. Lord have mercy.

℟. **Lord, have mercy.**

℣. Christ, have mercy.

℟. **Christ, have mercy.**

℣. Lord, have mercy.

℟. **Lord, have mercy.**

6 GLORIA

As the Church assembled in the Spirit we praise and pray to the Father and the Lamb.

When the Gloria is sung or said, the priest or the cantors or everyone together may begin it:

**Glory to God in the highest,
and peace to his people on earth.**

**Lord God, heavenly King,
almighty God and Father,
we worship you, we give you thanks,
we praise you for your glory.**

Lord Jesus Christ, only Son of the Father,
Lord God, Lamb of God,
you take away the sin of the world:
   have mercy on us;
you are seated at the right hand of the Father:
   receive our prayer.

For you alone are the Holy One,
you alone are the Lord,
you alone are the Most High,
   Jesus Christ,
   with the Holy Spirit,
   in the glory of God the Father. Amen.

7 OPENING PRAYER

The priest invites us to pray silently for a moment and then, in our name, expresses the theme of the day's celebration and petitions God the Father through the mediation of Christ in the Holy Spirit.

Priest: **Let us pray.**

➜ Turn to Today's Mass

Priest and people pray silently for a while. Then the priest says the opening prayer and concludes:

Priest: **For ever and ever.**
PEOPLE: **Amen.**

LITURGY OF THE WORD

The proclamation of God's Word is always centered on Christ, present through his Word. Old Testament writings prepare for him; New Testament books speak of him directly. All of scripture calls us to believe once more and to follow. After the reading we reflect on God's words and respond to them.

As in Today's Mass   **SIT**

8 FIRST READING

At the end of the reading: Reader: The word of the Lord

PEOPLE: **Thanks be to God.**

9 RESPONSORIAL PSALM

The people repeat the response sung by the cantor the first time and then after each verse.

10 SECOND READING

At the end of the reading: Reader: The word of the Lord.

PEOPLE: **Thanks be to God.**

11 ALLELUIA (Gospel Acclamation)   **STAND**

Jesus will speak to us in the Gospel. We rise now out of respect and prepare for his message with the alleluia.

The people repeat the alleluia after cantor's alleluia and then after the verse. During Lent one of the following invocations is used as a response instead of the alleluia:

(a) **Glory and praise to you, Lord Jesus Christ!**
(b) **Glory to you, Lord Jesus Christ, Wisdom of God the Father!**
(c) **Glory to you, Word of God, Lord Jesus Christ!**
(d) **Glory to you, Lord Jesus Christ, Son of the Living God!**

(e) **Praise and honor to you, Lord Jesus Christ!**
(f) **Praise to you, Lord Jesus Christ, King of endless glory!**
(g) **Marvelous and great are your works, O Lord!**
(h) **Salvation, glory, and power to the Lord Jesus Christ!**

12 GOSPEL

Before proclaiming the Gospel, the deacon asks the priest: Father, give me your blessing. *The priest says:*

The Lord be in your heart and on your lips
that you may worthily proclaim his gospel.
In the name of the Father, and of the Son, ✛ and of
the Holy Spirit. *The deacon answers:* Amen.

If there is no deacon, the priest says inaudibly:

Almighty God, cleanse my heart and my lips that
I may worthily proclaim your gospel.

Deacon (or Priest):
> The Lord be with you.

PEOPLE: And also with you.

Deacon (or Priest):

✛ A reading from the holy Gospel according to N.

PEOPLE: Glory to you, Lord.

At the end:

Deacon (or priest):
> The Gospel of the Lord.

PEOPLE: Praise to you, Lord Jesus Christ.

Then the deacon (or priest) kisses the book, saying inaudibly: May the words of the Gospel wipe away our sins.

13 HOMILY `SIT`

God's word is spoken again in the homily. The Holy Spirit speaking through the lips of the preacher explains and applies today's biblical readings to the needs of this particular congregation. He calls us to respond to Christ through the life we lead.

14 PROFESSION OF FAITH (CREED) `STAND`

As a people we express our acceptance of God's message in the scriptures and homily. We summarize our faith by proclaiming a creed handed down from the early Church.

All say the profession of faith on Sundays.

NICENE CREED

We believe in one God,
 the Father, the Almighty,
 maker of heaven and earth,
 of all that is seen and unseen.
We believe in one Lord, Jesus Christ,
 the only Son of God,
 eternally begotten of the Father,
 God from God, Light from Light,
 true God from true God,
 begotten, not made, one in Being with the Father.
 Through him all things were made.
 For us men and for our salvation
  he came down from heaven:
 by the power of the Holy Spirit
  he was born of the Virgin Mary, } bow
  and became man.
 For our sake he was crucified under Pontius Pilate;
  he suffered, died, and was buried.
  On the third day he rose again
   in fulfillment of the Scriptures;
  he ascended into heaven
   and is seated at the right hand of the Father.
 He will come again in glory to judge the living and
   the dead,
  and his kingdom will have no end.
We believe in the Holy Spirit, the Lord, the giver of life,
 who proceeds from the Father and the Son.
  With the Father and the Son he is worshiped and
   glorified.
 He has spoken through the Prophets.
 We believe in one holy catholic and apostolic Church.

We acknowledge one baptism for the forgiveness
  of sins.
We look for the resurrection of the dead,
  and the life of the world to come. Amen.

OR ————— APOSTLES' CREED —————

*In celebrations of Masses with Children, the Apostles'
Creed may be said after the homily.*

I believe in God, the Father almighty,
  creator of heaven and earth.

I believe in Jesus Christ, his only Son, our Lord.
  He was conceived by the power of the Holy Spirit
    and born of the Virgin Mary.
  He suffered under Pontius Pilate,
    was crucified, died, and was buried.
  He descended to the dead.
  On the third day he rose again.
  He ascended into heaven,
    and is seated at the right hand of the Father.
  He will come again to judge the living and the dead.

I believe in the Holy Spirit,
  the holy catholic Church,
  the communion of saints,
  the forgiveness of sins,
  the resurrection of the body,
  and the life everlasting. Amen.

15 GENERAL INTERCESSIONS (Prayer of the Faithful)

As a priestly people we unite with one another to pray for
today's needs in the Church and the world.

*After the priest gives the introduction the deacon or
other minister sings or says the invocations.*

PEOPLE: Lord, hear our prayer.

(or other response, according to local custom)
At the end the priest says the concluding prayer:

PEOPLE: Amen.

LITURGY OF THE EUCHARIST

Made ready by reflection on God's Word, we enter now into the eucharistic sacrifice itself, the Supper of the Lord. We celebrate the memorial which the Lord instituted at his Last Supper. We are God's new people, the redeemed brothers and sisters of Christ, gathered by him around his table. We are here to bless God and to receive the gift of Jesus' body and blood so that our faith and life may be transformed.

PREPARATION OF THE GIFTS

16 OFFERTORY SONG `SIT`

The bread and wine for the Eucharist, with our gifts for the Church and the poor, are gathered and brought to the altar. We prepare our hearts by song or in silence as the Lord's table is being set.

While the people's gifts are brought forward to the priest and are placed on the altar, the offertory song is sung.

17 PREPARATION OF THE BREAD

Before placing the bread on the altar, the priest says inaudibly:

Blessed are you, Lord, God of all creation.
Through your goodness we have this bread to offer,
which earth has given and human hands have made.
It will become for us the bread of life.

If there is no singing, the priest may say this prayer aloud, and the people may respond:

PEOPLE: Blessed be God for ever.

18 PREPARATION OF THE WINE

When he pours wine and a little water into the chalice, the deacon (or the priest) says inaudibly:

20

By the mystery of this water and wine
may we come to share in the divinity of Christ,
who humbled himself to share in our humanity.

Before placing the chalice on the altar, he says:
Blessed are you, Lord, God of all creation.
Through your goodness we have this wine to offer,
fruit of the vine and work of human hands.
It will become our spiritual drink.

*If there is no singing, the priest may say this prayer
aloud, and the people may respond:*
PEOPLE: Blessed be God for ever.

The priest says inaudibly:
Lord God, we ask you to receive us
and be pleased with the sacrifice we offer you
with humble and contrite hearts.

Then he washes his hands, saying:
Lord, wash away my iniquity;
cleanse me from my sin.

19 INVITATION TO PRAYER

Priest: Pray, brethren, that our sacrifice may be
acceptable to God, the almighty Father.
PEOPLE: STAND
**May the Lord accept the sacrifice at your hands
for the praise and glory of his name,
for our good, and the good of all his Church.**

20 PRAYER OVER THE GIFTS

The priest, speaking in our name, asks the Father to bless
and accept these gifts.

➔ Turn to Today's Mass

At the end, **PEOPLE: Amen.**

EUCHARISTIC PRAYER

We begin the eucharistic service of praise and thanksgiving, the center of the entire celebration, the central prayer of worship. We lift our hearts to God, and offer praise and thanks as the priest addresses this prayer to the Father through Jesus Christ. Together we join Christ in his sacrifice, celebrating his memorial in the holy meal and acknowledging with him the wonderful works of God in our lives.

21 INTRODUCTORY DIALOGUE

Priest: The Lord be with you.

PEOPLE: And also with you.

Priest: Lift up your hearts.

PEOPLE: We lift them up to the Lord.

Priest: Let us give thanks to the Lord our God.

PEOPLE: It is right to give him thanks and praise.

22 PREFACE

As indicated in the individual Masses of this Missal, the priest may say one of the following Prefaces (listed in numerical order).

23   ACCLAMATION

Priest and **People:**

Holy, holy, holy Lord, God of power and might, heaven and earth are full of your glory.
Hosanna in the highest.
Blessed is he who comes in the name of the Lord.
Hosanna in the highest. `KNEEL`

Then the priest continues with one of the following Eucharistic Prayers.

EUCHARISTIC PRAYER ....Choice of nine

EUCHARISTIC PRAYER No. 1

The Roman Canon

(This Eucharistic Prayer is especially suitable for Sundays and Masses with proper "Communicantes" and "Hanc igitur.")

[The words within brackets may be omitted.]

[Praise to the Father]

We come to you, Father,
with praise and thanksgiving,
through Jesus Christ your Son.
Through him we ask you to accept and bless
these gifts we offer you in sacrifice.

[Intercessions: For the Church]

We offer them for your holy catholic Church,
watch over it, Lord, and guide it;
grant it peace and unity throughout the world.
We offer them for N. our Pope,
for N. our bishop,
and for all who hold and teach the catholic faith
that comes to us from the apostles.
Remember, Lord, your people,
especially those for whom we now pray, N.
  and N.

Remember all of us gathered here before you.
You know how firmly we believe in you
and dedicate ourselves to you.
We offer you this sacrifice of praise
for ourselves and those who are dear to us.
We pray to you, our living and true God,
for our well-being and redemption.

In union with the whole Church*
we honor Mary,
the ever-virgin mother of Jesus Christ our Lord
   and God.
We honor Joseph, her husband,
the apostles and martyrs
Peter and Paul, Andrew,
[James, John, Thomas,
James, Philip,
Bartholomew, Matthew, Simon and Jude;
we honor Linus, Cletus, Clement, Sixtus,
Cornelius, Cyprian, Lawrence, Chrysogonus,
John and Paul, Cosmas and Damian]
and all the saints.
May their merits and prayers
gain us your constant help and protection.
[Through Christ our Lord. Amen.]

Father, accept this offering*
from your whole family.
Grant us your peace in this life,
save us from final damnation,
and count us among those you have chosen.
[Through Christ our Lord. Amen.]

Bless and approve our offering;
make it acceptable to you,
an offering in spirit and in truth.
Let it become for us
the body and blood of Jesus Christ,
your only Son, our Lord.
[Through Christ our Lord. Amen.]

*See page 90 for Special Communicantes and Hanc
Igitur.

1 *[The Lord's Supper]*

The day before he suffered
he took bread in his sacred hands
and looking up to heaven,
to you, his almighty Father,
he gave you thanks and praise.
He broke the bread,
gave it to his disciples, and said:

Take this, all of you, and eat it:
this is my body which will be given up for you.

When supper was ended,
he took the cup.
Again he gave you thanks and praise,
gave the cup to his disciples, and said:

Take this, all of you, and drink from it:
this is the cup of my blood,
the blood of the new and everlasting covenant.
It will be shed for you and for all
so that sins may be forgiven.
Do this in memory of me.

[Memorial Acclamation]

Priest: Let us proclaim the mystery of faith.

PEOPLE:

A Christ has died,
Christ is risen,
Christ will come again.

B Dying you destroyed our death,
rising you restored our life.
Lord Jesus, come in glory.

C **When we eat this bread and drink this cup,**
we proclaim your death, Lord Jesus,
until you come in glory.

D **Lord, by your cross and resurrection**
you have set us free.
You are the Savior of the world.

[The Memorial Prayer]

Father, we celebrate the memory of Christ,
your Son.
We, your people and your ministers,
recall his passion,
his resurrection from the dead,
and his ascension into glory;
and from the many gifts you have given us
we offer to you, God of glory and majesty,
this holy and perfect sacrifice:
the bread of life
and the cup of eternal salvation.
Look with favor on these offerings
and accept them as once you accepted
the gifts of your servant Abel,
the sacrifice of Abraham, our father in faith,
and the bread and wine offered by your priest
  Melchisedech.
Almighty God,
we pray that your angel may take this sacrifice
to your altar in heaven.
Then, as we receive from this altar
the sacred body and blood of your Son,
let us be filled with every grace and blessing.
[Through Christ our Lord. Amen.]

[For the Dead]

1 **R**emember, Lord, those who have died
and have gone before us marked with the sign
   of faith,
especially those for whom we now pray, N. and N.
May these, and all who sleep in Christ,
find in your presence
light, happiness, and peace.
[Through Christ our Lord. Amen.]

For ourselves, too, we ask
some share in the fellowship of your apostles
   and martyrs,
with John the Baptist, Stephen, Matthias, Barnabas,
[Ignatius, Alexander, Marcellinus, Peter, Felicity,
Perpetua, Agatha, Lucy, Agnes, Cecilia, Anastasia]
and all the saints.
Though we are sinners,
we trust in your mercy and love.
Do not consider what we truly deserve,
but grant us your forgiveness.
Through Christ our Lord.

Through him you give us all these gifts.
You fill them with life and goodness,
you bless them and make them holy.

Through him,   *[Concluding Doxology]*
with him,
in him,
in the unity of the Holy Spirit,
all glory and honor is yours,
almighty Father,
for ever and ever.
All reply: **Amen.** *Continue with the Mass, as on p. 66.*

EUCHARISTIC PRAYER No. 2

*(This Eucharistic Prayer is particularly suitable on
Weekdays or for special circumstances)*

STAND

℣. The Lord be with you.

℟. **And also with you.**

℣. Lift up your hearts.

℟. **We lift them up to the Lord.**

℣. Let us give thanks to the Lord our God.

℟. **It is right to give him thanks and praise.**

PREFACE   *[Praise to the Lord]*

Father, it is our duty and our salvation,
always and everywhere
to give you thanks
through your beloved Son, Jesus Christ.

He is the Word through whom you made the
    universe,
the Savior you sent to redeem us.

By the power of the Holy Spirit
he took flesh and was born of the Virgin Mary.

For our sake he opened his arms on the cross;
he put an end to death
and revealed the resurrection.

In this he fulfilled your will
and won for you a holy people.

And so we join the angels and the saints
in proclaiming your glory
as we sing (say):

29

2 SANCTUS   *[First Acclamation of the People]*

Holy, holy, holy Lord, God of power and might,
heaven and earth are full of your glory.
> **Hosanna in the highest.**
Blessed is he who comes in the name of the Lord.
> **Hosanna in the highest.**

KNEEL

[Invocation of the Holy Spirit]

Lord, you are holy indeed,
the fountain of all holiness.

Let your Spirit come upon these gifts to make
    them holy,
so that they may become for us
the body and blood of our Lord, Jesus Christ.

[The Lord's Supper]

Before he was given up to death,
a death he freely accepted,
he took bread and gave you thanks.
He broke the bread,
gave it to his disciples, and said:

Take this, all of you, and eat it:
this is my body which will be given up for you.

When supper was ended, he took the cup.
Again he gave you thanks and praise,
gave the cup to his disciples, and said:

Take this, all of you, and drink from it:
this is the cup of my blood,
the blood of the new and everlasting covenant.
It will be shed for you and for all
so that sins may be forgiven.
Do this in memory of me.

2

[Memorial Acclamation]

Priest: Let us proclaim the mystery of faith.

PEOPLE:

A **Christ has died,**
Christ is risen,
Christ will come again.

B **Dying you destroyed our death,**
rising you restored our life.
Lord Jesus, come in glory.

C **When we eat this bread and drink this cup,**
we proclaim your death, Lord Jesus,
until you come in glory.

D **Lord, by your cross and resurrection**
you have set us free.
You are the Savior of the world.

[The Memorial Prayer]

In memory of his death and resurrection,
we offer you, Father, this life-giving bread,
this saving cup.
We thank you for counting us worthy
to stand in your presence and serve you.

[Invocation of the Holy Spirit]

May all of us who share in the body and blood
   of Christ
be brought together in unity by the Holy Spirit.

2 *[Intercessions: For the Church]*

Lord, remember your Church throughout the
  world;
make us grow in love,
together with N. our Pope,
N. our bishop, and all the clergy.*

[For the Dead]

Remember our brothers and sisters
who have gone to their rest
in the hope of rising again;
bring them and all the departed
into the light of your presence.

[In Communion with the Saints]

Have mercy on us all;
make us worthy to share eternal life
with Mary, the virgin Mother of God,
with the apostles, and with all the saints
who have done your will throughout the ages.
May we praise you in union with them,
and give you glory
through your Son, Jesus Christ.

Through him,   *[Concluding Doxology]*
with him,
in him,
in the unity of the Holy Spirit,
all glory and honor is yours,
almighty Father,
for ever and ever.
All reply: **Amen.** *Continue with the Mass, as on p. 66*

---

* *In Masses for the Dead the following may be added:*

Remember N., whom you have called from this life.
In baptism he (she) died with Christ:
may he (she) also share his resurrection.

(This Eucharistic Prayer may be used with any Preface and preferably on Sundays and feast days)

KNEEL

[Praise to the Father]

Father, you are holy indeed,
and all creation rightly gives you praise.
All life, all holiness comes from you
through your Son, Jesus Christ our Lord,
by the working of the Holy Spirit.

From age to age you gather a people to yourself,
so that from east to west
a perfect offering may be made
to the glory of your name.

[Invocation of the Holy Spirit]

And so, Father, we bring you these gifts.
We ask you to make them holy by the power of
    your Spirit,
that they may become the body and blood
of your Son, our Lord Jesus Christ,
at whose command we celebrate this eucharist.

[The Lord's Supper]

On the night he was betrayed,
he took bread and gave you thanks and praise.
He broke the bread, gave it to his disciples, and
    said:

Take this, all of you, and eat it:
this is my body which will be given up for you.

3 **W**hen supper was ended, he took the cup.
Again he gave you thanks and praise,
gave the cup to his disciples, and said:

Take this, all of you, and drink from it:
this is the cup of my blood,
the blood of the new and everlasting covenant.
It will be shed for you and for all
so that sins may be forgiven.
Do this in memory of me.

[Memorial Acclamation]

Priest: Let us proclaim the mystery of faith.

PEOPLE:

A **Christ has died,**
   Christ is risen,
   Christ will come again.

B **Dying you destroyed our death,**
   rising you restored our life.
   Lord Jesus, come in glory.

C **When we eat this bread and drink this cup,**
   we proclaim your death, Lord Jesus,
   until you come in glory.

D **Lord, by your cross and resurrection**
   you have set us free.
   You are the Savior of the world.

[The Memorial Prayer]

Father, calling to mind the death your Son
   endured for our salvation,
his glorious resurrection and ascension into
   heaven,
and ready to greet him when he comes again,
we offer you in thanksgiving this holy and living sacrifice.

3

Look with favor on your Church's offering,
and see the Victim whose death has reconciled
us to yourself.

[Invocation of the Holy Spirit]

Grant that we, who are nourished by his body
and blood,
may be filled with his Holy Spirit,
and become one body, one spirit in Christ.

[Intercessions: In Communion with the Saints]

May he make us an everlasting gift to you
and enable us to share in the inheritance of your
saints,
with Mary, the virgin Mother of God;
with the apostles, the martyrs,
(Saint *N.*) and all your saints,
on whose constant intercession we rely for help.

[For the Church]

Lord, may this sacrifice,
which has made our peace with you,
advance the peace and salvation of all the world.
Strengthen in faith and love your pilgrim
Church on earth;
your servant, Pope *N.*, our bishop *N.*,
and all the bishops,
with the clergy and the entire people your Son
has gained for you.
Father, hear the prayers of the family you have
gathered here before you.
In mercy and love unite all your children
wherever they may be.*

[For the Dead]

Welcome into your kingdom our departed
brothers and sisters,

* *See p. 36 for special prayer for Mass for the Dead.*

3 and all who have left this world in your friendship.

We hope to enjoy for ever the vision of your
 glory,

through Christ our Lord, from whom all good
 things come.

[Concluding Doxology]

Through him,
with him,
in him,
in the unity of the Holy Spirit,
all glory and honor is yours,
almighty Father,
for ever and ever.

All reply: **Amen.**

Continue with the Mass, as on p. 66

---

*In Masses for the Dead the following is said:

Remember N.
In baptism he (she) died with Christ:
may he (she) also share his resurrection,
when Christ will raise our mortal bodies
and make them like his own in glory.
Welcome into your kingdom our departed brothers
 and sisters,
and all who have left this world in your friendship.
There we hope to share in your glory
when every tear will be wiped away.
On that day we shall see you, our God, as you are.
We shall become like you
and praise you for ever through Christ our Lord,
from whom all good things come.
Through him, etc., *as above.*

EUCHARISTIC PRAYER No. 4 | 4

℣. The Lord be with you. **STAND**
℟. **And also with you.**
℣. Lift up your hearts.
℟. **We lift them up to the Lord.**
℣. Let us give thanks to the Lord our God.
℟. **It is right to give him thanks and praise.**

PREFACE

Father in heaven,
it is right that we should give you thanks and
  glory:
you are the one God, living and true.
Through all eternity you live in unapproachable
  light.
Source of life and goodness, you have created
  all things,
to fill your creatures with every blessing
and lead all men to the joyful vision of your light.
Countless hosts of angels stand before you to do
  your will;
they look upon your splendor
and praise you, night and day.
United with them,
and in the name of every creature under heaven,
we too praise your glory as we sing (say):

SANCTUS   *[First Acclamation of the People]*

**Holy, holy, holy Lord, God of power and might,
heaven and earth are full of your glory.**
  Hosanna in the highest.
Blessed is he who comes in the name of the Lord.
  Hosanna in the highest.

37

4   *[Praise to the Father]*   KNEEL

Father, we acknowledge your greatness:
all your actions show your wisdom and love.
You formed man in your own likeness
and set him over the whole world
to serve you, his creator,
and to rule over all creatures.
Even when he disobeyed you and lost your
    friendship
you did not abandon him to the power of death,
but helped all men to seek and find you.
Again and again you offered a covenant to man,
and through the prophets taught him to hope for
    salvation.
Father, you so loved the world
that in the fullness of time you sent your only
    Son to be our Savior.
He was conceived through the power of the
    Holy Spirit,
and born of the Virgin Mary,
a man like us in all things but sin.
To the poor he proclaimed the good news of sal-
    vation,
to prisoners, freedom,
and to those in sorrow, joy.
In fulfillment of your will
he gave himself up to death;
but by rising from the dead,
he destroyed death and restored life.
And that we might live no longer for ourselves
    but for him,
he sent the Holy Spirit from you, Father,
as his first gift to those who believe,

4

to complete his work on earth
and bring us the fullness of grace.

[Invocation of the Holy Spirit]

Father, may this Holy Spirit sanctify these offerings.
Let them become the body ✠ and blood of Jesus
   Christ our Lord
as we celebrate the great mystery
which he left us as an everlasting covenant.

[The Lord's Supper]

He always loved those who were his own in the
   world.
When the time came for him to be glorified by
   you, his heavenly Father,
he showed the depth of his love.
While they were at supper,
he took bread, said the blessing, broke the bread,
and gave it to his disciples, saying:

Take this, all of you, and eat it:
this is my body which will be given up for you.

In the same way, he took the cup, filled with
   wine,
He gave you thanks, and giving the cup to his
   disciples, said:

Take this, all of you, and drink from it:
this is the cup of my blood,
the blood of the new and everlasting covenant.
It will be shed for you and for all
so that sins may be forgiven.
Do this in memory of me.

[Memorial Acclamation]

Priest: Let us proclaim the mystery of faith:

PEOPLE:

A Christ has died,
   Christ is risen,
   Christ will come again.

B Dying you destroyed our death,
   rising you restored our life.
   Lord Jesus, come in glory.

C When we eat this bread and drink this cup,
   we proclaim your death, Lord Jesus,
   until you come in glory.

D Lord, by your cross and resurrection
   you have set us free.
   You are the Savior of the world.

[The Memorial Prayer]

Father, we now celebrate this memorial of our
   redemption.
We recall Christ's death, his descent among the
   dead,
his resurrection, and his ascension to your right
   hand;
and, looking forward to his coming in glory, we
   offer you his body and blood,
the acceptable sacrifice
which brings salvation to the whole world.

Lord, look upon this sacrifice which you have
   given to your Church;
and by your Holy Spirit, gather all who share
   this one bread and one cup
into the one body of Christ, a living sacrifice of
   praise.

4

[Intercessions: For the Church]

Lord, remember those for whom we offer this
    sacrifice,
especially *N.*, our Pope,
N., our bishop, and bishops and clergy everywhere.
Remember those who take part in this offering,
those here present and all your people,
and all who seek you with a sincere heart.

[For the Dead]

Remember those who have died in the peace of
    Christ
and all the dead whose faith is known to you alone.

[In Communion with the Saints]

Father, in your mercy grant also to us, your
    children,
to enter into our heavenly inheritance
in the company of the Virgin Mary, the Mother
    of God,
and your apostles and saints.
Then, in your kingdom, freed from the corrup-
    tion of sin and death,
we shall sing your glory with every creature
    through Christ our Lord,
through whom you give us everything that is good.

[Concluding Doxology]

Through him,
with him,
in him,
in the unity of the Holy Spirit,
all glory and honor is yours,
almighty Father
for ever and ever.
All reply: **Amen.**   *Continue with Mass, as on p. 66.*

EUCHARISTIC PRAYER FOR MASSES WITH CHILDREN I

℣. The Lord be with you.   STAND
℟. **And also with you.**
℣. Lift up your hearts.
℟. **We lift them up to the Lord.**
℣. Let us give thanks to the Lord our God.
℟. **It is right to give him thanks and praise.**

God our Father,
you have brought us here together
so that we can give you thanks and praise
for all the wonderful things you have done.

We thank you for all that is beautiful in the
world
and for the happiness you have given us.
We praise you for daylight
and for your word which lights up our minds.
We praise you for the earth,
and all the people who live on it,
and for our life which comes from you.

We know that you are good.
You love us and do great things for us.
[So we all sing (say) together:

**Holy, holy, holy Lord, God of power and might,
heaven and earth are full of your glory.
    Hosanna in the highest.]**

Father,
you are always thinking about your people;
you never forget us.

You sent us your Son Jesus,
who gave his life for us
and who came to save us.
He cured sick people;
he cared for those who were poor
and wept with those who were sad.
He forgave sinners
and taught us to forgive each other.
He loved everyone
and showed us how to be kind.
He took children in his arms and blessed them.
[So we are glad to sing (say):

**Blessed is he who comes in the name of the Lord.
    Hosanna in the highest.]**

God our Father,
all over the world your people praise you.
So now we pray with the whole Church:
with *N.,* our pope and *N.,* our bishop.
In heaven the blessed Virgin Mary,
the apostles and all the saints
always sing your praise.
Now we join with them and with the angels
to adore you as we sing (say):

People:

**Holy, holy, holy Lord, God of power and might,
heaven and earth are full of your glory.
    Hosanna in the highest.
Blessed is he who comes in the name of the Lord.
    Hosanna in the highest.**

C1

KNEEL

God our Father,
you are most holy
and we want to show you that we are grateful.

We bring you bread and wine
and ask you to send your Holy Spirit to make these gifts
the body ✠ and blood of Jesus your Son.
Then we can offer to you
what you have given to us.

On the night before he died,
Jesus was having supper with his apostles.
He took bread from the table.
He gave you thanks and praise.
Then he broke the bread, gave it to his friends, and said:

Take this, all of you, and eat it:
this is my body which will be given up for you.

When supper was ended,
Jesus took the cup that was filled with wine.
He thanked you, gave it to his friends, and said:

Take this, all of you, and drink from it:
this is the cup of my blood,
the blood of the new and everlasting covenant.
It will be shed for you and for all
so that sins may be forgiven.
Then he said to them:
do this in memory of me.

We do now what Jesus told us to do.
We remember his death and his resurrection

and we offer you, Father, the bread that gives us
　　life,
and the cup that saves us.
Jesus brings us to you;
welcome us as you welcome him.

Priest: Let us proclaim our faith:

PEOPLE:

A **Christ has died,**
　Christ is risen,
　Christ will come again.

B **Dying you destroyed our death,**
　rising you restored our life.
　Lord Jesus, come in glory.

C **When we eat this bread and drink this cup,**
　we proclaim your death, Lord Jesus,
　until you come in glory.

D **Lord, by your cross and resurrection**
　you have set us free.
　You are the Savior of the world.

Father,
because you love us,
you invite us to come to your table.
Fill us with the joy of the Holy Spirit
as we receive the body and blood of your Son.

Lord,
you never forget any of your children.
We ask you to take care of those we love,
especially of N. and N.;
and we pray for those who have died.

C 1 **R**emember everyone who is suffering from pain or sorrow.
Remember Christians everywhere
and all other people in the world.

We are filled with wonder and praise
when we see what you do for us
through Jesus your Son,
and so we sing:

Through him,
with him,
in him,
in the unity of the Holy Spirit,
all glory and honor is yours,
almighty Father,
for ever and ever.

The people respond: **Amen.**

Continue with the Mass, as on p. 66.

EUCHARISTIC PRAYER FOR
MASSES WITH CHILDREN II

℣. The Lord be with you.

℟. **And also with you.**

℣. Lift up your hearts.

℟. **We lift them up to the Lord.**

℣. Let us give thanks to the Lord our God.

℟. **It is right to give him thanks and praise.**

God our loving Father,
we are glad to give you thanks and praise
because you love us.
With Jesus we sing your praise:

All say

Glory to God in the highest.

> *or:*

Hosanna in the highest.

Because you love us,
you gave us this great and beautiful world.
With Jesus we sing your praise:

All say:

Glory to God in the highest.

> *or:*

Hosanna in the highest.

Because you love us,
you sent Jesus your Son
to bring us to you
and to gather us around him
as the children of one family.

47

C 2

With Jesus we sing your praise:

All say:

Glory to God in the highest.

> *or:*

Hosanna in the highest.

For such great love
we thank you with the angels and saints
as they praise you and sing (say):

All say:

**Holy, holy, holy Lord, God of power and might,
heaven and earth are full of your glory.**
> **Hosanna in the highest.**

Blessed is he who comes in the name of the Lord.
> **Hosanna in the highest.**

Blessed be Jesus, whom you sent
to be the friend of children and of the poor.

He came to show us
how we can love you, Father,
by loving one another.
He came to take away sin,
which keeps us from being friends,
and hate, which makes us all unhappy.

He promised to send the Holy Spirit,
to be with us always
so that we can live as your children.

All say:

Blessed is he who comes in the name of the Lord.
> **Hosanna in the highest.**

God our Father,
we now ask you
to send your Holy Spirit
to change these gifts of bread and wine
into the body ✠ and blood
of Jesus Christ, our Lord.

The night before he died,
Jesus your Son showed us how much you love
    us.
When he was at supper with his disciples,
he took bread,
and gave you thanks and praise.
Then he broke the bread,
gave it to his friends, and said:
Take this, all of you, and eat it:
This is my body which will be given up for you.

All say:
Jesus has given his life for us.

When supper was ended,
Jesus took the cup that was filled with wine.
He thanked you, gave it to his friends, and said:
Take this, all of you, and drink from it:
this is the cup of my blood,
the blood of the new and everlasting covenant.
It will be shed for you and for all
so that sins may be forgiven.

All say:
Jesus has given his life for us.

Then he said to them:
do this in memory of me.

C 2

And so, loving Father,
we remember that Jesus died and rose again
to save the world.
He put himself into our hands
to be the sacrifice we offer you.

All say:

We praise you, we bless you, we thank you.

Lord our God,
listen to our prayer.
Send the Holy Spirit
to all of us who share in this meal.
May this Spirit bring us closer together
in the family of the Church,
with *N.*, our pope,
N., our bishop,
all other bishops,
and all who serve your people.

All say:

We praise you, we bless you, we thank you.

Remember, Father, our families and friends (. . .),
and all those we do not love as we should.
Remember those who have died (. . .).
Bring them home to you
to be with you for ever.

All say:

We praise you, we bless you, we thank you.

Gather us all together into your kingdom.
There we shall be happy for ever
with the Virgin Mary, Mother of God and our
  mother.

**C
2**

There all the friends
of Jesus the Lord
will sing a song of joy.

All say:
We praise you, we bless you, we thank you.

Through him,
with him,
in him,
in the unity of the Holy Spirit,
all glory and honor is yours,
almighty Father,
for ever and ever.

The people respond: **Amen.**

Continue with the Mass, as on p. 66.

℣. The Lord be with you. **STAND**
℟. **And also with you.**
℣. Lift up your hearts.
℟. **We lift them up to the Lord.**
℣. Let us give thanks to the Lord our God.
℟. **It is right to give him thanks and praise.**

Outside Easter season:

We thank you,
God our Father.
You made us to live for you and for each other.
We can see and speak to one another,
and become friends,
and share our joys and sorrows.

During Easter Season:

We thank you
God our Father.
You are the living God;
you have called us to share in your life,
and to be happy with you for ever.
You raised up Jesus, your Son,
the first among us to rise from the dead,
and gave him new life.
You have promised to give us new life also,
a life that will never end,
a life with no more anxiety and suffering.

**C
3**

And so, Father, we gladly thank you
with every one who believes in you;
with the saints and the angels,
we rejoice and praise you, saying:

**Holy, holy, holy Lord, God of power and might,
heaven and earth are full of your glory.**
> **Hosanna in the highest.**

Blessed is he who comes in the name of the Lord.
> **Hosanna in the highest.**

Yes, Lord, you are holy;
you are kind to us and to all.
For this we thank you.
We thank you above all for your Son, Jesus
  Christ.

Outside Easter season:

You sent him into this world
because people had turned away from you
and no longer loved each other.
He opened our eyes and our hearts
to understand that we are brothers and sisters
and that you are Father of us all.

During Easter season:

He brought us the good news
of life to be lived with you for ever in heaven.
He showed us the way to that life,
the way of love.
He himself has gone that way before us.

He now brings us together to one table
and asks us to do what he did.

C 3 **F**ather,
we ask you to bless these gifts of bread and wine
and make them holy.
Change them for us into the body ✠ and blood
   of Jesus Christ, your Son.

On the night before he died for us,
he had supper for the last time with his disciples.
He took bread
and gave you thanks.
He broke the bread
and gave it to his friends, saying:
Take this, all of you, and eat it:
this is my body which will be given up for you.

In the same way he took a cup of wine.
He gave you thanks
and handed the cup to his disciples, saying:
Take this, all of you, and drink from it:
this is the cup of my blood,
the blood of the new and everlasting covenant.
It will be shed for you and for all
so that sins may be forgiven.
Then he said to them:
do this in memory of me.

God our Father,
we remember with joy
all that Jesus did to save us.
In this holy sacrifice,
which he gave as a gift to his Church,
we remember his death and resurrection.

**C
3**

Father in heaven,
accept us together with your beloved Son.
He willingly died for us,
but you raised him to life again.
We thank you and say:

All say:
Glory to God in the highest.
(Or some other suitable acclamation of praise.)

Jesus now lives with you in glory,
but he is also here on earth, among us.
We thank you and say:

All say:
Glory to God in the highest.
(Or some other suitable acclamation of praise.)

One day he will come in glory
and in his kingdom
there will be no more suffering,
no more tears, no more sadness.
We thank you and say:

All say:
Glory to God in the highest.
(Or some other suitable acclamation of praise.)

Father in heaven,
you have called us
to receive the body and blood of Christ at this
    table
and to be filled with the joy of the Holy Spirit.

**C
3**

Through this sacred meal
give us strength to please you more and more.

Lord, our God,
remember N., our pope,
N., our bishop, and all other bishops.

Outside Easter season:

Help all who follow Jesus
to work for peace
and to bring happiness to others.

During Easter season:

Fill all Christians with the gladness of Easter.
Help us to bring this joy
to all who are sorrowful.

Bring us all at last
together with Mary, the Mother of God,
and all the saints,
to live with you
and to be one with Christ in heaven.

Through him,
with him,
in him,
in the unity of the Holy Spirit,
all glory and honor is yours,
almighty Father,
for ever and ever.

The people respond: **Amen.**

Continue with the Mass, as on p. 66

EUCHARISTIC PRAYER FOR MASSES OF RECONCILIATION I

℣. The Lord be with you. STAND
℟. **And also with you.**
℣. Lift up your hearts.
℟. **We lift them up to the Lord.**
℣. Let us give thanks to the Lord our God.
℟. **It is right to give him thanks and praise.**

Father, all-powerful and ever-living God,
we do well always and everywhere to give you
   thanks and praise.
You never cease to call us
to a new and more abundant life.

God of love and mercy,
you are always ready to forgive;
we are sinners,
and you invite us
to trust in your mercy.

Time and time again
we broke your covenant,
but you did not abandon us.
Instead, through your Son, Jesus our Lord,
you bound yourself even more closely to the
   human family
by a bond that can never be broken.

Now is the time
for your people to turn back to you
and to be renewed in Christ your Son,
a time of grace and reconciliation.

57

R 1 You invite us
to serve the family of mankind
by opening our hearts
to the fullness of your Holy Spirit.

In wonder and gratitude,
we join our voices with the choirs of heaven
to proclaim the power of your love
and to sing of our salvation in Christ:

All say:

**Holy, holy, holy Lord, God of power and might,
heaven and earth are full of your glory.**
> **Hosanna in the highest.**

Blessed is he who comes in the name of the Lord.
> **Hosanna in the highest.**

Father,
from the beginning of time
you have always done what is good for man
so that we may be holy as you are holy.

Look with kindness on your people
gathered here before you:
send forth the power of your Spirit
so that these gifts may become for us
the body ✠ and blood of your beloved Son,
  Jesus the Christ,
in whom we have become your sons and daughters.

When we were lost
and could not find the way to you,
you loved us more than ever:
Jesus, your Son, innocent and without sin,
gave himself into our hands
and was nailed to a cross.
Yet before he stretched out his arms between
   heaven and earth
in the everlasting sign of your covenant,
he desired to celebrate the Paschal feast
in the company of his disciples.

While they were at supper,
he took bread and gave you thanks and praise.
He broke the bread, gave it to his disciples, and
   said:

Take this, all of you, and eat it:
this is my body which will be given up for you.

At the end of the meal,
knowing that he was to reconcile all things in
   himself
by the blood of his cross,
he took the cup, filled with wine.
Again he gave you thanks,
handed the cup to his friends, and said:

Take this, all of you, and drink from it:
this is the cup of my blood,
the blood of the new and everlasting covenant.
It will be shed for you and for all
so that sins may be forgiven.
Do this in memory of me.

RPriest: Let us proclaim the mystery of faith:
1 **PEOPLE:**

A **Christ has died,**
Christ is risen,
Christ will come again.

B **Dying you destroyed our death,**
rising you restored our life.
Lord Jesus, come in glory.

C **When we eat this bread and drink this cup,**
we proclaim your death, Lord Jesus,
until you come in glory.

D **Lord, by your cross and resurrection**
you have set us free.
You are the Savior of the world.

We do this in memory of Jesus Christ,
our Passover and our lasting peace.
We celebrate his death and resurrection
and look for the coming of that day
when he will return to give us the fullness of joy.
Therefore we offer you, God ever faithful and
    true,
the sacrifice which restores man to your friend-
    ship.

Father,
look with love
on those you have called
to share in the one sacrifice of Christ.
By the power of your Holy Spirit
make them one body,
healed of all division.

Keep us all
in communion of mind and heart
with N., our pope, and N., our bishop.
Help us to work together
for the coming of your kingdom,
until at last we stand in your presence
to share the life of the saints,
in the company of the Virgin Mary and the
    apostles,
and of our departed brothers and sisters
whom we commend to your mercy.

Then, freed from every shadow of death,
we shall take our place in the new creation
and give you thanks
with Christ, our risen Lord.

Through him,
with him,
in him,
in the unity of the Holy Spirit,
all glory and honor is yours,
almighty Father,
for ever and ever.

The people respond: **Amen.**

Continue with the Mass, as on p. 66.

EUCHARISTIC PRAYER FOR
MASSES OF RECONCILIATION II

℣. The Lord be with you.   STAND
℟. **And also with you.**
℣. Lift up your hearts.
℟. **We lift them up to the Lord.**
℣. Let us give thanks to the Lord our God.
℟. **It is right to give him thanks and praise.**

Father, all-powerful and ever-living God,
we praise and thank you through Jesus Christ
  our Lord
for your presence and action in the world.

In the midst of conflict and division,
we know it is you
who turn our minds to thoughts of peace.
Your Spirit changes our hearts:
enemies begin to speak to one another,
those who were estranged join hands in friendship,
and nations seek the way of peace together.

Your Spirit is at work
when understanding puts an end to strife,
when hatred is quenched by mercy,
and vengeance gives way to forgiveness.

For this we should never cease
to thank and praise you.
We join with all the choirs of heaven
as they sing for ever to your glory:

All say:

Holy, holy, holy Lord, God of power and might.
Heaven and earth are full of your glory.
   Hosanna in the highest.
Blessed is he who comes in the name of the Lord.
   Hosanna in the highest.

God of power and might,   **KNEEL**
we praise you through your Son, Jesus Christ,
who comes in your name.
He is the Word that brings salvation.
He is the hand you stretch out to sinners.
He is the way that leads to your peace.

God our Father,
we had wandered far from you,
but through your Son you have brought us back.
You gave him up to death
so that we might turn again to you
and find our way to one another.

Therefore we celebrate the reconciliation
Christ has gained for us.

We ask you to sanctify these gifts
by the power of your Spirit,
as we now fulfill your Son's ✠ command.

While he was at supper
on the night before he died for us,
he took bread in his hands,
and gave you thanks and praise.
He broke the bread,
gave it to his disciples, and said:

Take this, all of you, and eat it:
this is my body which will be given up for you.

R 2 At the end of the meal he took the cup.
Again he praised you for your goodness,
gave the cup to his disciples, and said:

Take this, all of you, and drink from it:
this is the cup of my blood,
the blood of the new and everlasting covenant.
It will be shed for you and for all men
so that sins may be forgiven.
Do this in memory of me.

Priest: Let us proclaim the mystery of faith:

PEOPLE:

A   **Christ has died,**
    Christ is risen,
    Christ will come again.

B   **Dying you destroyed our death,**
    rising you restored our life.
    Lord Jesus, come in glory.

C   **When we eat this bread and drink this cup,**
    we proclaim your death, Lord Jesus,
    until you come in glory.

D   **Lord, by your cross and resurrection**
    you have set us free.
    You are the Savior of the world.

Lord our God,
your Son has entrusted to us
this pledge of his love.
We celebrate the memory of his death and resur-
    rection
and bring you the gift you have given us,
the sacrifice of reconciliation.

R
2

Therefore, we ask you, Father,
to accept us, together with your Son.

Fill us with his Spirit
through our sharing in this meal.
May he take away all that divides us.

May this Spirit keep us always in communion
with N., our pope, N., our bishop,
with all the bishops and all your people.
Father, make your Church throughout the world
a sign of unity and an instrument of your peace.

You have gathered us here
around the table of your Son,
in fellowship with the Virgin Mary, Mother of
    God, and all the saints.

In that new world where the fullness of your
    peace will be revealed,
gather people of every race, language, and way
    of life
to share in the one eternal banquet
with Jesus Christ the Lord.

Through him,
with him,
in him,
in the unity of the Holy Spirit,
all glory and honor is yours,
almighty Father,
for ever and ever.

The people respond: **Amen.**

COMMUNION RITE

To prepare for the paschal meal, to welcome the Lord, we pray for forgiveness and exchange a sign of peace. Before eating Christ's body and drinking his blood, we must be one with him and with all our brothers and sisters in the Church.

24 LORD'S PRAYER

STAND

Priest:

A Let us pray with confidence to the Father in the words our Savior gave us:

B Jesus taught us to call God our Father, and so we have the courage to say:

C Let us ask our Father to forgive our sins and to bring us to forgive those who sin against us.

D Let us pray for the coming of the kingdom as Jesus taught us.

Priest and **PEOPLE**:

> **Our Father, who art in heaven,**
> **hallowed be thy name;**
> **thy kingdom come;**
> **thy will be done on earth as it is in heaven.**
> **Give us this day our daily bread;**
> **and forgive us our trespasses**
> **as we forgive those who trespass against us;**
> **and lead us not into temptation,**
> **but deliver us from evil.**

Priest: Deliver us, Lord, from every evil, and grant us peace in our day.

66

In your mercy keep us free from sin
and protect us from all anxiety
as we wait in joyful hope
for the coming of our Savior, Jesus Christ.

PEOPLE: **For the kingdom, the power, and the glory are yours, now and for ever.**

25 SIGN OF PEACE

The Church is a community of Christians joined by the Spirit in love. It needs to express, deepen, and restore its peaceful unity before eating the one Body of the Lord and drinking from the one cup of salvation. We do this by a sign of peace.

The priest says the prayer for peace:

Lord Jesus Christ, you said to your apostles:
I leave you peace, my peace I give you.
Look not on our sins, but on the faith of your Church,
and grant us the peace and unity of your kingdom
where you live for ever and ever.

PEOPLE: **Amen.**

Priest: The peace of the Lord be with you always.

PEOPLE: **And also with you.**

Deacon (or priest):
Let us offer each other the sign of peace.

The people exchange a sign of peace and love, according to local custom.

26 BREAKING OF THE BREAD

Christians are gathered for the "breaking of the bread," another name for the Mass. In communion, though many we are made one body in the one bread, which is Christ.

Then the following is sung or said:

PEOPLE:

Lamb of God, you take away the sins of the world:

  have mercy on us.

Lamb of God, you take away the sins of the world:

  have mercy on us.

Lamb of God, you take away the sins of the world:

  grant us peace.

The hymn may be repeated until the breaking of the bread is finished, but the last phrase is always: "Grant us peace."

Meanwhile the priest breaks the host over the paten and places a small piece in the chalice, saying inaudibly:

May this mingling of the body and blood of our
  Lord Jesus Christ
bring eternal life to us who receive it.

`KNEEL`

27 PRAYERS BEFORE COMMUNION

We pray in silence and then voice words of humility and hope as our final preparation before meeting Christ in the eucharist.

Before communion, the priest says inaudibly one of the following prayers:

Lord Jesus Christ, Son of the living God, by the will of the Father and the work of the Holy Spirit your death brought life to the world. By your holy body and blood free me from all my sins and from every evil. Keep me faithful to your teaching, and never let me be parted from you.

OR

Lord Jesus Christ, with faith in your love and mercy
I eat your body and drink your blood. Let it not bring
me condemnation, but health in mind and body.

28 RECEPTION OF COMMUNION

*The priest genuflects. Holding the host elevated slightly
over the paten, the priest says:*

Priest: This is the Lamb of God
who takes away the sins of the world.
Happy are those who are called to his supper.

Priest and **People** (once only):
**Lord, I am not worthy to receive you,
but only say the word and I shall be healed.**

Before receiving communion, the priest says inaudibly:

May the body of Christ bring me to everlasting life.
May the blood of Christ bring me to everlasting life.

He then gives communion to the people.

Priest: The body of Christ. Communicant: **Amen.**

Priest: The blood of Christ. Communicant: **Amen.**

29 COMMUNION SONG or ANTIPHON

*The Communion Psalm or other appropriate Song or
Hymn is sung while Communion is given to the faithful.
If there is no singing, the Communion Antiphon is said:*

→ **Turn to Today's Mass**

*The vessels are cleansed by the priest or deacon or
acolyte. Meanwhile he says inaudibly.*

Lord, may I receive these gifts in purity of heart.
May they bring me healing and strength, now and for
ever.

30 PERIOD OF SILENCE or Song of Praise

After communion there may be a period of silence, or a song of praise may be sung.

31 PRAYER AFTER COMMUNION `STAND`

The priest prays in our name that we may live the life of faith since we have been strengthened by Christ himself. Our *Amen* makes his prayer our own.

Priest: Let us pray.

Priest and people may pray silently for a while. Then the priest says the prayer after communion.

→ `Turn to Today's Mass`

At the end, PEOPLE: **Amen.**

CONCLUDING RITE

We have heard God's Word and eaten the body of Christ. Now it is time for us to leave, to do good works, to praise and bless the Lord in our daily lives.

32 GREETING `STAND`

After any brief announcements (sit), the blessing and dismissal follow:

Priest: The Lord be with you.

PEOPLE: **And also with you.**

33 BLESSING

🅐 Simple form

Priest: May almighty God bless you
the Father, and the Son, ✠ and the Holy Spirit.

PEOPLE: **Amen.**

On certain days or occasions another more solemn form of blessing or prayer over the people may be used as the rubrics direct.

B Solemn blessing

Texts of all the solemn blessings are given on pp. 92-99.

Deacon: **Bow your heads and pray for God's blessing.**

The priest always concludes the solemn blessing by adding:

May almighty God bless you
the Father, and the Son, ✠ and the Holy Spirit.

PEOPLE: Amen.

C Prayer over the people

Texts of all prayers over the people are given on pp. 99-103.

After the prayer over the people, the priest always adds:

May almighty God bless you,
the Father, and the Son, ✠ and the Holy Spirit.

PEOPLE: Amen.

34 DISMISSAL

Deacon (or priest):

A Go in the peace of Christ.

B The Mass is ended, go in peace.

C Go in peace to love and serve the Lord.

PEOPLE: Thanks be to God.

If any liturgical service follows immediately, the rite of dismissal is omitted.

RITE OF BLESSING AND

SPRINKLING HOLY WATER

When this rite is celebrated it takes the place of the penitential rite at the beginning of Mass. The Kyrie is also omitted.

After greeting the people the priest remains standing at his chair. A vessel containing the water to be blessed is placed before him. Facing the people, he invites them to pray, using these or similar words:

Dear friends,
this water will be used
to remind us of our baptism.
Let us ask God to bless it,
and to keep us faithful
to the Spirit he has given us.

After a brief silence, he joins his hands and continues:
A.

God our Father,
your gift of water
brings life and freshness to the earth;
it washes away our sins
and brings us eternal life.

We ask you now
to bless ✠ this water,
and to give us your protection on this day
which you have made your own.
Renew the living spring of your life within us
and protect us in spirit and body,
that we may be free from sin
and come into your presence
to receive your gift of salvation.
We ask this through Christ our Lord. ℟. **Amen.**

B. Or:

Lord God almighty,
creator of all life,
of body and soul,
we ask you to bless ✠ this water:
as we use it in faith
forgive our sins
and save us from all illness
and the power of evil.

Lord,
in your mercy
give us living water,
always springing up as a fountain of salvation:
free us, body and soul, from every danger,
and admit us to your presence
in purity of heart.
Grant this through Christ our Lord.

C. Or (during the Easter season):

Lord God almighty,
hear the prayers of your people:
we celebrate our creation and redemption.
Hear our prayers and bless ✠ this water
which gives fruitfulness to the fields,
and refreshment and cleansing to man.
You chose water to show your goodness
when you led your people to freedom
through the Red Sea
and satisfied their thirst in the desert
with water from the rock.
Water was the symbol used by the prophets
to foretell your new covenant with man.
You made the water of baptism holy
by Christ's baptism in the Jordan:
by it you give us a new birth
and renew us in holiness.
May this water remind us of our baptism,
and let us share the joy

of all who have been baptized at Easter.
We ask this through Christ our Lord.

*Where it is customary, salt may be mixed with the holy
water. The priest blesses the salt, saying:*

Almighty God,
we ask you to bless ✠ this salt
as once you blessed the salt scattered over the water
by the prophet Elisha.
Wherever this salt and water are sprinkled,
drive away the power of evil,
and protect us always
by the presence of your Holy Spirit.
Grant this through Christ our Lord.

Then he pours the salt into the water in silence.

*Taking the sprinkler, the priest sprinkles himself and
his ministers, then the rest of the clergy and people. He
may move through the church for the sprinkling of the
people. Meanwhile, an antiphon or another appropriate
song is sung.*

*When he returns to his place and the song is finished, the
priest faces the people and, with joined hands, says:*

May almighty God cleanse us of our sins,
and through the eucharist we celebrate
make us worthy to sit at his table
in his heavenly kingdom.

The people answer: **Amen.**

When it is prescribed, the Gloria *is then sung or said.*

PENITENTIAL RITE

ALTERNATIVE FORMS FOR C (p. 13)

ii

Priest or other minister:
Lord Jesus, you came to gather the nations
into the peace of God's kingdom:
Lord, have mercy.

People: **Lord, have mercy.**

Priest or other minister:
You come in word and sacrament to strengthen us in
   holiness:
Christ, have mercy.

People: **Christ, have mercy.**

Priest or other minister:
You will come in glory with salvation for your people:
   Lord, have mercy.

People: **Lord, have mercy.** (→ p. 13)

iii

Priest or other minister:
Lord Jesus, you are mighty God and Prince of peace:
Lord, have mercy.

People: **Lord have mercy.**

Priest or other minister:
Lord Jesus, you are the Son of God and Son of Mary:
Christ, have mercy.

People: **Christ, have mercy.**

Priest or other minister:
Lord Jesus, you are Word made flesh and splendor of
   the Father:
Lord, have mercy.

People: **Lord, have mercy.** (→ p. 13)

iv

Priest or other minister:
Lord Jesus, you came to reconcile us
to one another and to the Father:
Lord, have mercy.

People: **Lord have mercy.**

Priest or other minister:
Lord Jesus, you heal the wounds of sin and division:
Christ, have mercy.

People: **Christ, have mercy.**

Priest or other minister:
Lord Jesus, intercede for us with your Father:
Lord, have mercy.

People: **Lord, have mercy.**   (→ p. 13)

v

Priest or other minister:
You raise the dead to life in the Spirit:
Lord, have mercy.

People: **Lord have mercy.**

Priest or other minister:
You bring pardon and peace to the sinner:
Christ, have mercy.

People: **Christ, have mercy.**

Priest or other minister:
You bring light to those in darkness:
Lord, have mercy.

People: **Lord, have mercy.**   (→ p. 13)

vi

Priest or other minister:
Lord Jesus, you raise us to new life:
Lord, have mercy.

People: **Lord have mercy.**

Priest or other minister:
Lord Jesus, you forgive us our sins:
Christ, have mercy.

People: **Christ, have mercy.**

Priest or other minister:
Lord Jesus, you feed us with your body and blood:
Lord, have mercy.

People: **Lord, have mercy.**   (→ p. 13)

vii

Priest or other minister:
Lord Jesus, you have shown us the way to the Father:
Lord, have mercy.

People: **Lord, have mercy.**

Priest or other minister:
Lord Jesus, you have given us the consolation of the
  truth:
Christ, have mercy.

People: **Christ, have mercy.**

Priest or other minister:
Lord Jesus, you are the Good Shepherd,
leading us into everlasting life:
Lord, have mercy.

People: **Lord, have mercy.**   (→ p. 13)

viii

Priest or other minister:
Lord Jesus, you healed the sick:
Lord, have mercy.

People: **Lord, have mercy.**

Priest or other minister:
Lord Jesus, you forgave sinners:
Christ, have mercy.

People: **Christ, have mercy.**

Priest or other minister:
Lord Jesus, you give us yourself to heal us and bring us
  strength:
Lord, have mercy.

People: **Lord, have mercy.**   (→ p. 13)

PREFACES

ADVENT I (P 1)

The Two Comings of Christ
(From the First Sunday of Advent to December 16)

Father, all-powerful and ever-living God,
we do well always and everywhere to give you thanks
through Jesus Christ our Lord.

When he humbled himself to come among us as a man,
he fulfilled the plan you formed long ago
and opened for us the way to salvation.

Now we watch for the day,
hoping that the salvation promised us will be ours
when Christ our Lord will come again in his glory.

And so, with all the choirs of angels in heaven
we proclaim your glory
and join in their unending hymn of praise: → No. 23, p. 23

ADVENT II (P 2)

Waiting for the Two Comings of Christ
(From December 17 to December 24)

Father, all-powerful and ever-living God,
we do well always and everywhere to give you thanks
through Jesus Christ our Lord.

His future coming was proclaimed by all the prophets.
The virgin mother bore him in her womb
with love beyond all telling.
John the Baptist was his herald
and made him known when at last he came.

In his love Christ has filled us with joy
as we prepare to celebrate his birth,
so that when he comes he may find us watching in prayer,
our hearts filled with wonder and praise.

And so, with all the choirs of angels in heaven
we proclaim your glory
and join in their unending hymn of praise: ➜ No. 23, p. 23

CHRISTMAS I (P 3)

Christ the Light

(From Christmas to Saturday before Epiphany)

Father, all-powerful and ever-living God,
we do well always and everywhere to give you thanks
through Jesus Christ our Lord.

In the wonder of the incarnation
your eternal Word has brought to the eyes of faith
a new and radiant vision of your glory.
In him we see our God made visible
and so are caught up in love of the God we cannot see.

And so, with all the choirs of angels in heaven
we proclaim your glory
and join in their unending hymn of praise: ➜ No. 23, p. 23

CHRISTMAS II (P 4)

Christ Restores Unity to All Creation

(From Christmas to Saturday before Epiphany)

Father, all-powerful and ever-living God,
we do well always and everywhere to give you thanks
through Jesus Christ our Lord.

Today you fill our hearts with joy
as we recognize in Christ the revelation of your love.
No eye can see his glory as our God,
yet now he is seen as one like us.

Christ is your Son before all ages,
yet now he is born in time.
He has come to lift up all things to himself,
to restore unity to creation,
and to lead mankind from exile into your heavenly kingdom.
With all the angels of heaven
we sing our joyful hymn of praise: ➜ No. 23, p. 23

CHRISTMAS III (P 5)

*Divine and Human Exchange in the
Incarnation of the Word*
(From Christmas to Saturday before Epiphany)

Father, all-powerful and ever-living God,
we do well always and everywhere to give you thanks
through Jesus Christ our Lord.

Today in him a new light has dawned upon the world:
God has become one with man,
and man has become one again with God.

Your eternal Word has taken upon himself our human
    weakness,
giving our mortal nature immortal value.
So marvelous is this oneness between God and man
that in Christ man restores to man the gift of everlasting life.

In our joy we sing to your glory
with all the choirs of angels: → No. 23, p. 23

LENT I (P 8)

The Spiritual Meaning of Lent

Father, all-powerful and ever-living God,
we do well always and everywhere to give you thanks
through Jesus Christ our Lord.

Each year you give us this joyful season
when we prepare to celebrate the paschal mystery
with mind and heart renewed.
You give us a spirit of loving reverence for you, our Father,
and of willing service to our neighbor.

As we recall the great events that gave us new life in Christ,
you bring the image of your Son to perfection within us.

Now, with angels and archangels,
and the whole company of heaven,
we sing the unending hymn of your praise: → No. 23, p. 23

LENT II (P 9)

The Spirit of Penance

Father, all-powerful and ever-living God,
we do well always and everywhere to give you thanks.

This great season of grace is your gift to your family
to renew us in spirit.
You give us strength to purify our hearts,
to control our desires,
and so to serve you in freedom.
You teach us how to live in this passing world
with our heart set on the world that will never end.

Now, with all the saints and angels,
we praise you for ever: → No. 23, p. 23

EASTER I (P 21)

The Paschal Mystery

(Easter Vigil, Easter Sunday and during the octave and season)

Father, all-powerful and ever-living God,
we do well always and everywhere to give you thanks
through Jesus Christ our Lord.

We praise you with greater joy than ever
on this Easter night (day) (in this Easter Season),
when Christ became our paschal sacrifice.

He is the true Lamb who took away the sins of the world.
By dying he destroyed our death;
by rising he restored our life.

And so, with all the choirs of angels in heaven
we proclaim your glory
and join in their unending hymn of praise: → No. 23, p. 23

EASTER II (P 22)

New Life in Christ

Father, all-powerful and ever-living God,
we do well always and everywhere to give you thanks
through Jesus Christ our Lord.

We praise you with greater joy than ever in this Easter season,
when Christ became our paschal sacrifice.

He has made us children of the light,
rising to new and everlasting life.
He has opened the gates of heaven
to receive his faithful people.

His death is our ransom from death;
his resurrection is our rising to life.

The joy of the resurrection renews the whole world,
while the choirs of heaven sing for ever to your glory:

→ No. 23, p. 23

EASTER III (P 23)

Christ Lives and Intercedes for Us for Ever

Father, all-powerful and ever-living God,
we do well always and everywhere to give you thanks
through Jesus Christ our Lord.

We praise you with greater joy than ever in this Easter season,
when Christ became our paschal sacrifice.

He is still our priest,
our advocate who always pleads our cause.
Christ is the victim who dies no more,
the Lamb, once slain, who lives for ever.

They joy of the resurrection renews the whole world,
while the choirs of heaven sing for ever to your glory:

→ No. 23, p. 23

EASTER IV (P 24)

The Restoration of the Universe through the Paschal Mystery

Father, all-powerful and ever-living God,
we do well always and everywhere to give you thanks
through Jesus Christ our Lord.

We praise you with greater joy than ever in this Easter season,
when Christ became our paschal sacrifice.

In him a new age has dawned,
the long reign of sin is ended,
a broken world has been renewed,
and man is once again made whole.

The joy of the resurrection renews the whole world,
while the choirs of heaven sing for ever to your glory:

→ No. 23, p. 23

EASTER V (P 25)
Christ Is Priest and Victim

Father, all-powerful and ever-living God,
we do well always and everywhere to give you thanks
through Jesus Christ our Lord.

We praise you with greater joy than ever in this Easter season,
when Christ became our paschal sacrifice.

As he offered his body on the cross,
his perfect sacrifice fulfilled all others.
As he gave himself into your hands for our salvation,
he showed himself to be the priest, the altar, and the lamb of sacrifice.

The joy of the resurrection renews the whole world,
while the choirs of heaven sing for ever to your glory:

→ No. 23, p. 23

ASCENSION I (P 26)
The Mystery of the Ascension
(Ascension to the Saturday before Pentecost inclusive)

Father, all-powerful and ever-living God,
we do well always and everywhere to give you thanks.

[Today] the Lord Jesus, the king of glory,
the conqueror of sin and death,
ascended to heaven while the angels sang his praises.

Christ, the mediator between God and man,
judge of the world and Lord of all,
has passed beyond our sight,
not to abandon us but to be our hope.
Christ is the beginning, the head of the Church;
where he has gone, we hope to follow.

The joy of the resurrection and ascension renews the whole world,
while the choirs of heaven sing for ever to your glory:

→ No. 23, p. 23

ASCENSION II (P 27)

The Mystery of the Ascension

(Ascension to the Saturday before Pentecost inclusive)

Father, all-powerful and ever-living God,
we do well always and everywhere to give you thanks
through Jesus Christ our Lord.

In his risen body he plainly showed himself to his disciples
and was taken up to heaven in their sight
to claim for us a share in his divine life.

And so, with all the choirs of angels in heaven
we proclaim your glory
and join in their unending hymn of praise: → No. 23, p. 23

SUNDAYS IN ORDINARY TIME I (P 29)

The Paschal Mystery and the People of God

Father, all-powerful and ever-living God,
we do well always and everywhere to give you thanks
through Jesus Christ our Lord.

Through his cross and resurrection
he freed us from sin and death
and called us to the glory that has made us
a chosen race, a royal priesthood,
a holy nation, a people set apart.

Everywhere we proclaim your mighty works
for you have called us out of darkness
into your own wonderful light.

And so, with all the choirs of angels in heaven
we proclaim your glory
and join in their unending hymn of praise: → No. 23, p. 23

SUNDAYS IN ORDINARY TIME II (P 30)

The Mystery of Salvation

Father, all-powerful and ever-living God,
we do well always and everywhere to give you thanks
through Jesus Christ our Lord.

Out of love for sinful man,
he humbled himself to be born of the Virgin.

By suffering on the cross
he freed us from unending death,
and by rising from the dead
he gave us eternal life.

And so, with all the choirs of angels in heaven
we proclaim your glory
and join in their unending hymn of praise: → No. 23, p. 23

SUNDAYS IN ORDINARY TIME III (P 31)
The Salvation of Man by a Man

Father, all-powerful and ever-living God,
we do well always and everywhere to give you thanks.

We see your infinite power
in your loving plan of salvation.
You came to our rescue by your power as God,
but you wanted us to be saved by one like us.
Man refused your friendship,
but man himself was to restore it
through Jesus Christ our Lord.

Through him the angels of heaven offer their prayer of
    adoration
as they rejoice in your presence for ever.
May our voices be one with theirs
in their triumphant hymn of praise: → No. 23, p. 23

SUNDAYS IN ORDINARY TIME IV (P 32)
The History of Salvation

Father, all-powerful and ever-living God,
we do well always and everywhere to give you thanks
through Jesus Christ our Lord.

By his birth we are reborn.
In his suffering we are freed from sin.
By his rising from the dead we rise to everlasting life.
In his return to you in glory
we enter into your heavenly kingdom.

And so, we join the angels and the saints
as they sing their unending hymn of praise: → No. 23, p. 23

SUNDAYS IN ORDINARY TIME V (P 33)
Creation

Father, all-powerful and ever-living God,
we do well always and everywhere to give you thanks.

All things are of your making,
all times and seasons obey your laws,
but you chose to create man in your own image,
setting him over the whole world in all its wonder.
You made man the steward of creation,
to praise you day by day for the marvels of your wisdom
    and power,
through Jesus Christ our Lord.

We praise you, Lord, with all the angels in their song of
joy: → No. 23, p. 23

SUNDAYS IN ORDINARY TIME VI (P 34)
The Pledge of an Eternal Easter

Father, all-powerful and ever-living God,
we do well always and everywhere to give you thanks.

In you we live and move and have our being.
Each day you show us a Father's love;
your Holy Spirit, dwelling within us,
gives us on earth the hope of unending joy.

Your gift of the Spirit,
who raised Jesus from the dead,
is the foretaste and promise
of the paschal feast of heaven.

With thankful praise,
in company with the angels,
we glorify the wonders of your power: → No. 23, p. 23

SUNDAYS IN ORDINARY TIME VII (P 35)
Salvation through the Obedience of Christ

Father, all-powerful and ever-living God,
we do well always and everywhere to give you thanks.

So great was your love
that you gave us your Son as our redeemer.
You sent him as one like ourselves,

though free from sin,
that you might see and love in us
what you see and love in Christ.
Your gifts of grace, lost by disobedience,
are now restored by the obedience of your Son.

We praise you, Lord, with all the angels and saints
in their song of joy: → No. 23, p. 23

SUNDAYS IN ORDINARY TIME VIII (P 36)
The Church United in the Mystery of the Trinity

Father, all-powerful and ever-living God,
we do well always and everywhere to give you thanks.

When your children sinned
and wandered far from your friendship,
you reunited them with yourself
through the blood of your Son
and the power of the Holy Spirit.

You gather them into your Church,
to be one as you, Father, are one
with your Son and the Holy Spirit.
You call them to be your people,
to praise your wisdom in all your works.
You make them the body of Christ
and the dwelling-place of the Holy Spirit.

In our joy we sing to your glory
with all the choirs of angels: → No. 23, p. 23

HOLY EUCHARIST I (P 47)
The Sacrifice and Sacrament of Christ

Father, all-powerful and ever-living God,
we do well always and everywhere to give you thanks
through Jesus Christ our Lord.

He is the true and eternal priest
who established this unending sacrifice.
He offered himself as a victim for our deliverance
and taught us to make this offering in his memory.
As we eat his body which he gave for us,
we grow in strength.
As we drink his blood which he poured out for us,
we are washed clean.

Now, with angels and archangels,
and the whole company of heaven,
we sing the unending hymn of your praise: → No. 23, p. 23

HOLY EUCHARIST II (P 48)
The Effects of the Holy Eucharist

Father, all-powerful and ever-living God,
we do well always and everywhere to give you thanks
through Jesus Christ our Lord.

At the last supper,
as he sat at table with his apostles,
he offered himself to you as the spotless lamb,
the acceptable gift that gives you perfect praise.
Christ has given us this memorial of his passion
to bring us its saving power until the end of time.

In this great sacrament you feed your people
and strengthen them in holiness,
so that the family of mankind
may come to walk in the light of one faith,
in one communion of love.
We come then to this wonderful sacrament
to be fed at your table
and grow into the likeness of the risen Christ.

Earth unites with heaven
to sing the new song of creation
as we adore and praise you for ever: → No. 23, p. 23

CHRISTIAN DEATH I (P 77)
The Hope of Rising in Christ

Father, all-powerful and ever-living God,
we do well always and everywhere to give you thanks
through Jesus Christ our Lord.

In him, who rose from the dead,
our hope of resurrection dawned.
The sadness of death gives way
to the bright promise of immortality.

Lord, for your faithful people life is changed, not ended.
When the body of our earthly dwelling lies in death
we gain an everlasting dwelling place in heaven.

And so, with all the choirs of angels in heaven
we proclaim your glory
and join in their unending hymn of praise: → No. 23, p. 23

CHRISTIAN DEATH II (P 78)
Christ's Death, Our Life

Father, all-powerful and ever-living God,
we do well always and everywhere to give you thanks
through Jesus Christ our Lord.

He chose to die
that he might free all men from dying.
He gave his life
that we might live to you alone for ever.

In our joy we sing to your glory
with all the choirs of angels: → No. 23, p. 23

CHRISTIAN DEATH III (P 79)
Christ, Salvation and Life

Father, all-powerful and ever-living God,
we do well always and everywhere to give you thanks
through Jesus Christ our Lord.

In him the world is saved,
man is reborn,
and the dead rise again to life.

Through Christ the angels of heaven
offer their prayer of adoration
as they rejoice in your presence for ever.
May our voices be one with theirs
in their triumphant hymn of praise: → No. 23, p. 23

CHRISTIAN DEATH IV (P 80)
From Earthly Life to Heaven's Glory

Father, all-powerful and ever-living God,
we do well always and everywhere to give you thanks.

By your power you bring us to birth.
By your providence you rule our lives.
By your command you free us at last from sin
as we return to the dust from which we came.
Through the saving death of your Son
we rise at your word to the glory of the resurrection.

Now we join the angels and the saints
as they sing their unending hymn of praise: → No. 23, p. 23

CHRISTIAN DEATH V (P 81)

Our Resurrection through Christ's Glory

Father, all-powerful and ever-living God,
we do well always and everywhere to give you thanks
through Jesus Christ our Lord.
Death is the just reward for our sins,
yet, when at last we die,
your loving kindness calls us back to life
in company with Christ,
whose victory is our redemption.

Our hearts are joyful,
for we have seen your salvation,
and now with the angels and saints
we praise you for ever: → No. 23, p. 23

PROPER COMMUNICANTES
AND HANC IGITUR
FOR EUCHARISTIC PRAYER I

Communicantes for Christmas

In union with the whole Church
we celebrate that day (night)
when Mary without loss of her virginity
gave this world its savior.
We honor Mary,
the ever-virgin mother of Jesus Christ, our Lord and God,
    etc., p. 25.

Communicantes for the Epiphany

In union with the whole Church
we celebrate that day
when your only Son,
sharing your eternal glory,
showed himself in a human body.
We honor Mary, etc., p. 25.

Communicantes for Easter

In union with the whole Church
we celebrate that day (night)
when Jesus Christ, our Lord,
rose from the dead in his human body.
We honor Mary, etc., p. 25.

Hanc Igitur for Easter

Father, accept this offering
from your whole family
and from those born into the new life
of water and the Holy Spirit,
with all their sins forgiven.
Grant us your peace in this life,
save us from final damnation,
and count us among those you have chosen.
[Through Christ our Lord. Amen.]

→ Canon, p. 25: Bless, etc.

Communicantes for Ascension

In union with the whole Church
we celebrate that day
when your only Son, our Lord,
took his place with you
and raised our frail human nature to glory.
We honor Mary, etc., p. 25

Communicantes for Pentecost

In union with the whole Church
we celebrate the day of Pentecost
when the Holy Spirit appeared to the apostles
in the form of countless tongues.
We honor Mary, etc., p. 25.

SOLEMN BLESSINGS

The following blessings may be used, at the discretion of the priest, at the end of Mass, or after the liturgy of the word, the office, and the celebration of the sacraments.

The deacon gives the invitation, or in his absence the priest himself may also give it: Bow your heads and pray for God's blessing. *Another form of invitation may be used. Then the priest extends his hands over the people while he says or sings the blessings. All respond:* Amen.

I. Celebrations During the Proper of Seasons

1. ADVENT

You believe that the Son of God once came to us;
you look for him to come again.
May his coming bring you the light of his holiness
and free you with his blessing. ℟. **Amen.**

May God make you steadfast in faith,
joyful in hope, and untiring in love
all the days of your life. ℟. **Amen.**

You rejoice that our Redeemer came to live with us as man.
When he comes again in glory,
may he reward you with endless life. ℟. **Amen.**

May almighty God bless you,
the Father, and the Son, ✠ and the Holy Spirit. ℟. **Amen.**

2. CHRISTMAS

When he came to us as man,
the Son of God scattered the darkness of this world,
and filled this holy night (day) with his glory.
May the God of infinite goodness
scatter the darkness of sin
and brighten your hearts with holiness. ℟. **Amen.**

God sent his angels to shepherds
to herald the great joy of our Savior's birth.
May he fill you with joy
and make you heralds of his gospel. ℟. **Amen.**

When the Word became man,
earth was joined to heaven.

May he give you his peace and good will,
and fellowship with all the heavenly host. ℟. **Amen.**

May almighty God bless you,
the Father, and the Son, ✠ and the Holy Spirit. ℟. **Amen.**

3. BEGINNING OF THE NEW YEAR

Every good gift comes from the Father of light.
May he grant you his grace and every blessing,
and keep you safe throughout the coming year. ℟. **Amen.**

May he grant you unwavering faith,
constant hope, and love that endures to the end. ℟. **Amen.**

May he order your days and work in his peace,
hear your every prayer,
and lead you to everlasting life and joy. ℟. **Amen.**

May almighty God bless you,
the Father, and the Son, ✠ and the Holy Spirit. ℟. **Amen.**

4. EPIPHANY

God has called you out of darkness
into his wonderful light.
May you experience his kindness and blessings,
and be strong in faith, in hope, and in love. ℟. **Amen.**

Because you are followers of Christ,
who appeared on this day as a light shining in darkness,
may he make you a light to all your sisters and brothers.
℟. **Amen.**

The wise men followed the star,
and found Christ who is light from light.
May you too find the Lord
when your pilgrimage is ended. ℟. **Amen.**

May almighty God bless you,
the Father, and the Son, ✠ and the Holy Spirit. ℟. **Amen.**

5. PASSION OF THE LORD

The Father of mercies has given us an example of unselfish
    love
in the sufferings of his only Son.

Through your service of God and neighbor
may you receive his countless blessings. ℟. **Amen.**

You believe that by his dying
Christ destroyed death for ever.
May he give you everlasting life. ℟. **Amen.**

He humbled himself for our sakes.
May you follow his example
and share in his resurrection. ℟. **Amen.**

May almighty God bless you,
the Father, and the Son, ✠ and the Holy Spirit. ℟. **Amen.**

6. EASTER VIGIL AND EASTER SUNDAY

May almighty God bless you on this solemn feast of Easter, and may he protect you against all sin. ℟. **Amen.**

Through the resurrection of his Son
God has granted us healing.
May he fulfill his promises,
and bless you with eternal life. ℟. **Amen.**

You have mourned for Christ's sufferings;
now you celebrate the joy of his resurrection.
May you come with joy to the feast which lasts for ever.
℟. **Amen.**

May almighty God bless you,
the Father, and the Son, ✠ and the Holy Spirit. ℟. **Amen.**

7. EASTER SEASON

Through the resurrection of his Son
God has redeemed you and made you his children.
May he bless you with joy. ℟. **Amen.**

The Redeemer has given you lasting freedom.
May you inherit his everlasting life. ℟. **Amen.**

By faith you rose with him in baptism.
May your lives be holy,
so that you will be united with him for ever. ℟. **Amen.**

May almighty God bless you,
the Father, and the Son, ✠ and the Holy Spirit. ℟. **Amen.**

8. ASCENSION

May almighty God bless you on this day
when his only Son ascended into heaven
to prepare a place for you. ℟. **Amen.**

After his resurrection, Christ was seen by his disciples.
When he appears as judge
may you be pleasing for ever in his sight. ℟. **Amen.**

You believe that Jesus has taken his seat in majesty
at the right hand of the Father.
May you have the joy of experiencing
that he is also with you to the end of time,
according to his promise. ℟. **Amen.**

May almighty God bless you,
the Father, and the Son, ✠ and the Holy Spirit. ℟. **Amen.**

9. HOLY SPIRIT

(This day) the Father of light
has enlightened the minds of the disciples
by the outpouring of the Holy Spirit.
May he bless you
and give you the gifts of the Spirit for ever. ℟. **Amen.**

May that fire which hovered over the disciples
as tongues of flame
burn out all evil from your hearts
and make them glow with pure light. ℟. **Amen.**

God inspired speech in different tongues
to proclaim one faith.
May he strengthen your faith
and fulfill your hope of seeing him face to face. ℟. **Amen.**

May almighty God bless you,
the Father, and the Son, ✠ and the Holy Spirit. ℟. **Amen.**

10. ORDINARY TIME I
Blessing of Aaron (Num 6:24-26)

May the Lord bless you and keep you. ℟. **Amen.**

May his face shine upon you,
and be gracious to you. ℟. **Amen.**

May he look upon you with kindness,
and give you his peace. ℞. **Amen.**

May almighty God bless you,
the Father, and the Son, ✠ and the Holy Spirit. ℞. **Amen.**

11. ORDINARY TIME II *(Phil 4:7)*

May the peace of God
which is beyond all understanding
keep your hearts and minds
in the knowledge and love of God
and of his Son, our Lord Jesus Christ. ℞. **Amen.**

May almighty God bless you,
the Father, and the Son, ✠ and the Holy Spirit. ℞. **Amen.**

12. ORDINARY TIME III

May almighty God bless you in his mercy,
and make you always aware of his saving wisdom. ℞.
Amen.

May he strengthen your faith with proofs of his love,
so that you will persevere in good works. ℞. **Amen.**

May he direct your steps to himself,
and show you how to walk in charity and peace. ℞. **Amen.**

May almighty God bless you,
the Father, and the Son, ✠ and the Holy Spirit. ℞. **Amen.**

13. ORDINARY TIME IV

May the God of all consolation
bless you in every way
and grant you peace all the days of your life. ℞. **Amen.**

May he free you from all anxiety
and strengthen your hearts in his love. ℞. **Amen.**

May he enrich you with his gifts of faith, hope, and love,
so that what you do in this life
will bring you to the happiness of everlasting life. ℞.
Amen.

May almighty God bless you,
the Father, and the Son, ✠ and the Holy Spirit. ℞. **Amen.**

14. ORDINARY TIME V

May almighty God keep you from all harm
and bless you with every good gift. ℞. **Amen.**

May he set his Word in your heart
and fill you with lasting joy. ℟. **Amen.**

May you walk in his ways,
always knowing what is right and good,
until you enter your heavenly inheritance. ℟. **Amen.**

May almighty God bless you,
the Father, and the Son, ✠ and the Holy Spirit. ℟. **Amen.**

II. Celebrations of Saints

15. BLESSED VIRGIN MARY

Born of the Blessed Virgin Mary,
the Son of God redeemed mankind.
May he enrich you with his blessings. ℟. **Amen.**

You received the author of life through Mary.
May you always rejoice in her loving care. ℟. **Amen.**

You have come to rejoice at Mary's feast.
May you be filled with the joys of the Spirit
and the gifts of your eternal home. ℟. **Amen.**

May almighty God bless you,
the Father, and the Son, ✠ and the Holy Spirit. ℟. **Amen.**

16. PETER AND PAUL

The Lord has set you firm within his Church,
which he built upon the rock of Peter's faith.
May he bless you with a faith that never falters. ℟. **Amen.**

The Lord has given you knowlege of the faith
through the labors and preaching of St. Paul.
May his example inspire you to lead others to Christ
by the manner of your life. ℟. **Amen.**

May the keys of Peter, and the words of Paul,
their undying witness and their prayers,
lead you to the joy of that eternal home
which Peter gained by his cross, and Paul by the sword.
℟. **Amen.**

May almighty God bless you,
the Father, and the Son, ✠ and the Holy Spirit. ℟. **Amen.**

17. APOSTLES

May God who founded his Church upon the apostles
bless you through the prayers of St. *N.* (and St. *N.*). ℟.
   Amen.

May God inspire you to follow the example of the apostles,
and give witness to the truth before all men. ℟. **Amen.**

The teaching of the apostles has strengthened your faith.
May their prayers lead you
to your true and eternal home. ℟. **Amen.**

May almighty God bless you,
the Father, and the Son, ✠ and the Holy Spirit. ℟. **Amen.**

18. ALL SAINTS

God is the glory and joy of all his saints,
whose memory we celebrate today.
May his blessing be with you always. ℟. **Amen.**

May the prayers of the saints deliver you from present evil.
May their example of holy living
turn your thoughts to service of God and neighbor. ℟. **Amen.**

God's holy Church rejoices that her saints
have reached their heavenly goal,
and are in lasting peace.
May you come to share all the joys of our Father's house.
   ℟. **Amen.**

May almighty God bless you,
the Father, and the Son, ✠ and the Holy Spirit. ℟. **Amen.**

III. Other Blessings

19. DEDICATION OF A CHURCH

The Lord of earth and heaven
has assembled you before him this day
to dedicate this house of prayer
(to recall the dedication of this church).
May he fill you with the blessings of heaven. ℟. **Amen.**

God the Father wills that all his children
scattered throughout the world
become one family in his Son.

May he make you his temple,
the dwelling-place of his Holy Spirit. ℟. **Amen.**

May God free you from every bond of sin,
dwell within you and give you joy.
May you live with him for ever
in the company of all his saints. ℟. **Amen.**

May almighty God bless you,
the Father, and the Son, ✠ and the Holy Spirit. ℟. **Amen.**

20. THE DEAD

In his great love,
the God of all consolation gave man the gift of life.
May he bless you with faith
in the resurrection of his Son,
and with the hope of rising to new life. ℟. **Amen.**

To us who are alive
may he grant forgiveness,
and to all who have died
a place of light and peace. ℟. **Amen.**

As you believe that Jesus rose from the dead,
so may you live with him for ever in joy. ℟. **Amen.**

May almighty God bless you,
the Father, and the Son, ✠ and the Holy Spirit. ℟. **Amen.**

PRAYERS OVER THE PEOPLE

*The following prayers may be used, at the discretion of
the priest, at the end of the Mass, or after the liturgy of
the word, the office, and the celebration of the sacraments.*

*The deacon gives the invitation, or in his absence the
priest himself may also give it:* Bow your heads and
pray for God's blessing. *Another form of invitation may
be used. Then the priest extends his hands over the people
while he says or sings the prayer. All respond:*
Amen.

After the prayer, the priest always adds:

May almighty God bless you,
the Father, and the Son, ✠ and the Holy Spirit. ℟. **Amen.**

1. Lord,
   have mercy on your people.
   Grant us in this life the good things
   that lead to the everlasting life you prepare for us.
   We ask this through Christ our Lord.

2. Lord,
   grant your people your protection and grace.
   Give them health of mind and body,
   perfect love for one another,
   and make them always faithful to you.
   Grant this through Christ our Lord.

3. Lord,
   may all Christian people both know and cherish
   the heavenly gifts they have received.
   We ask this in the name of Jesus the Lord.

4. Lord,
   bless your people and make them holy
   so that, avoiding evil,
   they may find in you the fulfillment of their longing.
   We ask this through Christ our Lord.

5. Lord,
   bless and strengthen your people.
   May they remain faithful to you
   and always rejoice in your mercy.
   We ask this in the name of Jesus the Lord.

6. Lord,
   you care for your people even when they stray.
   Grant us a complete change of heart,
   so that we may follow you with greater fidelity.
   Grant this through Christ our Lord.

7. Lord,
   send your light upon your family.
   May they continue to enjoy your favor
   and devote themselves to doing good.
   We ask this through Christ our Lord.

8. Lord,
   we rejoice that you are our creator and ruler.

As we call upon your generosity,
renew and keep us in your love.
Grant this through Christ our Lord.

9. Lord,
we pray for your people who believe in you.
May they enjoy the gift of your love,
share it with others,
and spread it everywhere.
We ask this in the name of Jesus the Lord.

10. Lord,
bless your people who hope for your mercy.
Grant that they may receive
the things they ask for at your prompting.
Grant this through Christ our Lord.

11. Lord,
bless us with your heavenly gifts,
and in your mercy make us ready to do your will.
We ask this through Christ our Lord.

12. Lord,
protect your people always,
that they may be free from every evil
and serve you with all their hearts.
We ask this through Christ our Lord.

13. Lord,
help your people to seek you with all their hearts
and to deserve what you promise.
Grant this through Christ our Lord.

14. Father
help your people to rejoice in the mystery of redemption
and to win its reward.
We ask this in the name of Jesus the Lord.

15. Lord,
have pity on your people;
help them each day to avoid what displeases you
and grant that they may serve you with joy.
We ask this through Christ our Lord.

16. Lord,
    care for your people and purify them.
    Console them in this life
    and bring them to the life to come.
    We ask this in the name of Jesus the Lord.

17. Father,
    look with love upon your people,
    the love which our Lord Jesus Christ showed us
    when he delivered himself to evil men
    and suffered the agony of the cross,
    for he is Lord for ever.

18. Lord,
    grant that your faithful people
    may continually desire to relive the mystery of the
        eucharist
    and so be reborn to lead a new life.
    We ask this through Christ our Lord.

19. Lord God,
    in your great mercy,
    enrich your people with your grace
    and strengthen them by your blessing
    so that they may praise you always.
    Grant this through Christ our Lord.

20. May God bless you with every good gift from on high.
    May he keep you pure and holy in his sight at all times.
    May he bestow the riches of his grace upon you,
    bring you the good news of salvation,
    and always fill you with love for all men.
    We ask this through Christ our Lord.

21. Lord,
    make us pure in mind and body,
    that we will avoid all evil pleasures
    and always delight in you,
    We ask this in the name of Jesus the Lord.

22. Lord,
    bless your people and fill them with zeal.
    Strengthen them by your love to do your will.
    We ask this through Christ our Lord.

23. Lord,
    come, live in your people
    and strengthen them by your grace.
    Help them to remain close to you in prayer
    and give them a true love for one another.
    Grant this through Christ our Lord.

24. Father,
    look kindly on your children who put their trust in you;
    bless them and keep them from all harm,
    strengthen them against the attacks of the devil.
    May they never offend you
    but seek to love you in all they do.
    We ask this through Christ our Lord.

Feasts of Saints

25. God our Father,
    may all Christian people rejoice in the glory of your
        saints.
    Give us fellowship with them
    and unending joy in your kingdom.
    We ask this in the name of Jesus the Lord.

26. Lord,
    you have given us many friends in heaven.
    Through their prayers we are confident
    that you will watch over us always
    and fill our hearts with your love.
    Grant this through Christ our Lord.

CHRISTMAS

EASTER

ORDINARY TIME

ADVENT

VIRGINIA BRODERICK

"Holy Mother Church is conscious that she must celebrate the saving work of her divine Spouse by devoutly recalling it on certain days throughout the course of the year. Every week, on the day which she has called the Lord's day, she keeps the memory of the Lord's resurrection, which she also celebrates once in the year, together with his blessed passion, in the most solemn festival of Easter.

"Within the cycle of a year, moreover, she unfolds the whole mystery of Christ, from the incarnation and birth until the ascension, the day of Pentecost, and the expectation of blessed hope and of the coming of the Lord.

"Recalling thus the mysteries of redemption, the Church opens to the faithful the riches of her Lord's powers and merits, so that these are in some way made present for all time, and the faithful are enabled to lay hold upon them and become filled with saving grace" (Vatican II: Constitution on the Sacred Liturgy, no. 102).

OUR CHURCH'S YEAR OF PRAYER

Advent

We prepare for the coming of Jesus,
who is here and yet to come

Christmas season

We celebrate the gift of our Father's love:
Jesus is our brother and our Lord

Ordinary Time

With Jesus
we enter into the work of his body, the Church

Lent

In our daily life and prayer
we die with Christ to sin, and live for God

Easter triduum

We celebrate Jesus' dying and rising
and our sharing with him through baptism

Easter season

Sharing in the new life of Christ
we are filled with his Spirit

Ordinary time

Guided by the Spirit of Jesus
we build the kingdom of God by our lives.

"What I say to you, I say to all: 'Watch!'"

DECEMBER 1, 2002

1st SUNDAY OF ADVENT

ENTRANCE ANT. Ps 25:1-3   **[Hope]**

To you, my God, I lift my soul, I trust in you; let me never come to shame. Do not let my enemies laugh at me. No one who waits for you is ever put to shame.

→ No. 2, p. 10 (Omit Gloria)

OPENING PRAYER   **[Welcome for Christ]**

Let us pray
  [that we may take Christ's coming seriously]
All-powerful God,
increase our strength of will for doing good
that Christ may find an eager welcome at his coming
and call us to his side in the kingdom of heaven,
where he lives and reigns with you and the Holy
  Spirit,
one God, for ever and ever. ℟. **Amen.** ↓

ALTERNATIVE OPENING PRAYER   [Longing for Christ]

Let us pray
  [in Advent time
  with longing and waiting
  for the coming of the Lord]
Father in heaven,
our hearts desire the warmth of your love
and our minds are searching for the light of your
  Word.
Increase our longing for Christ our Savior
and give us the strength to grow in love,
that the dawn of his coming
may find us rejoicing in his presence
and welcoming the light of his truth.
We ask this in the name of Jesus the Lord. ℟. **Amen.** ↓

FIRST READING Is 63:16b-17, 19b; 64:2-7 [God Our Redeemer]

> **God is our Father. We are sinful, and you, O God, are hidden from our eyes. We are the work of your hands.**

A reading from the Book of the Prophet Isaiah

YOU, LORD, are our father,
  our redeemer you are named forever.
Why do you let us wander, O LORD, from your ways,
  and harden our hearts so that we fear you not?
Return for the sake of your servants,
  the tribes of your heritage.
Oh, that you would rend the heavens and come down,
  with the mountains quaking before you,
while you wrought awesome deeds we could not hope
  for,
  such as they had not heard of from of old.
No ear has ever heard, no eye ever seen, any God but you
  doing such deeds for those who wait for him.
Would that you might meet us doing right,
  that we were mindful of you in our ways!

Behold, you are angry, and we are sinful;
 all of us have become like unclean men,
 all our good deeds are like polluted rags;
we have all withered like leaves,
 and our guilt carries us away like the wind.
There is none who calls upon your name,
 who rouses himself to cling to you;
for you have hidden your face from us
 and have delivered us up to our guilt.
Yet, O LORD, you are our father;
 we are the clay and you are the potter:
 we are all the work of your hands.
The word of the Lord. ℟. **Thanks be to God.** ↓

RESPONSORIAL PSALM Ps 80   [Come To Save Us]

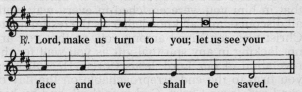

℟. Lord, make us turn to you; let us see your face and we shall be saved.

O shepherd of Israel, hearken,
 from your throne upon the cherubim, shine forth.
Rouse your power,
 and come to save us.

℟. **Lord, make us turn to you;**
 let us see your face and we shall be saved.

Once again, O LORD of hosts,
 look down from heaven, and see;
take care of this vine,
 and protect what your right hand has planted,
 the son of man whom you yourself made strong.

℟. **Lord, make us turn to you;**
 let us see your face and we shall be saved.

May your help be with the man of your right hand,
 with the son of man whom you yourself made strong.

Then we will no more withdraw from you;
  give us new life, and we will call upon your name.

℟. **Lord, make us turn to you;**
  let us see your face and we shall be saved. ↓

SECOND READING 1 Cor 1:3-9   [Fellowship with Christ]
  Jesus gives us faith and the strength to persevere. God
  calls his followers into the fellowship of Christ.

A reading from the first Letter of Saint Paul
to the Corinthians

Brothers and sisters: Grace to you and peace
from God our Father and the Lord Jesus Christ.
I give thanks to my God always on your account for
the grace of God bestowed on you in Christ Jesus,
that in him you were enriched in every way, with
all discourse and all knowledge, as the testimony to
Christ was confirmed among you, so that you are
not lacking in any spiritual gift as you wait for the
revelation of our Lord Jesus Christ. He will keep
you firm to the end, irreproachable on the day of
our Lord Jesus Christ. God is faithful, and by him
you were called to fellowship with his Son, Jesus
Christ our Lord.—The word of the Lord. ℟. **Thanks**
be to God. ↓

ALLELUIA Ps 85:8   [Mercy and Love]

℟. **Alleluia, alleluia.**
Show us, Lord, your love;
and grant us your salvation.
℟. **Alleluia, alleluia.** ↓

GOSPEL Mk 13:33-37   [On Guard]
  Be on guard always. We do not know what time or hour
  God will come.

℣. The Lord be with you. ℟. **And also with you.**
✠ A reading from the holy Gospel according to Mark.
℟. **Glory to you, Lord.**

JESUS said to his disciples: "Be watchful! Be alert! You do not know when the time will come. It is like a man traveling abroad. He leaves home and places his servants in charge, each with his own work, and orders the gatekeeper to be on the watch. Watch, therefore; you do not know when the lord of the house is coming, whether in the evening, or at midnight, or at cockcrow, or in the morning. May he not come suddenly and find you sleeping. What I say to you, I say to all: 'Watch!' "— The Gospel of the Lord. ℟. **Praise to you, Lord Jesus Christ.**   → No. 14, p. 18

PRAYER OVER THE GIFTS   [Promise of Eternal Life]

Father,
from all you give us
we present this bread and wine.
As we serve you now,
accept our offering
and sustain us with your promise of eternal life.
Grant this through Christ our Lord.
℟. **Amen.**   → No. 21, p. 22 (Pref. P 1)

COMMUNION ANT. Ps 85:13   [A New World]

The Lord will shower his gifts, and our land will yield its fruit. ↓

PRAYER AFTER COMMUNION   [Love for Heaven]

Father,
may our communion
teach us to love heaven.
May its promise and hope
guide our way on earth.
We ask this through Christ our Lord.
℟. **Amen.**   → No. 32, p. 70

Optional Solemn Blessings, p. 92, and Prayers Over the People, p. 99

"Prepare the way of the Lord...."

DECEMBER 8

2nd SUNDAY OF ADVENT

ENTRANCE ANT. See Is 30:19, 30   [Lord of Salvation]
**People of Zion, the Lord will come to save all nations,
and your hearts will exult to hear his majestic voice.**
→ No. 2, p. 10 (Omit Gloria)

OPENING PRAYER   [Receiving Christ]
Let us pray
  [that nothing may hinder us
  from receiving Christ with joy]
God of power and mercy,
open our hearts in welcome.
Remove the things that hinder us from receiving
  Christ with joy,
so that we may share his wisdom
and become one with him
when he comes in glory,
for he lives and reigns with you and the Holy Spirit,
one God, for ever and ever.
℞. **Amen.** ↓

ALTERNATIVE OPENING PRAYER   [Christ's Wisdom]

Let us pray
   [in Advent time
   for the coming Savior to teach us wisdom]
Father in heaven,
the day draws near when the glory of your Son
will make radiant the night of the waiting world.
May the lure of greed not impede us from the joy
which moves the hearts of those who seek him.
May the darkness not blind us
to the vision of wisdom
which fills the minds of those who find him.
We ask this in the name of Jesus the Lord. ℟. **Amen.** ↓

FIRST READING Is 40:1-5, 9-11   [God Is Near]

> **Make ready the way for the Messiah. Make known the
> Good News, for God is near.**

A reading from the Book of the Prophet Isaiah

COMFORT, give comfort to my people,
    says your God.
Speak tenderly to Jerusalem, and proclaim to her
    that her service is at an end,
    her guilt is expiated;
indeed, she has received from the hand of the LORD
    double for all her sins.

    A voice cries out:
In the desert prepare the way of the LORD!
    Make straight in the wasteland a highway for our
       God!
Every valley shall be filled in,
    every mountain and hill shall be made low;
the rugged land shall be made a plain,
    the rough country, a broad valley.
Then the glory of the LORD shall be revealed,
    and all mankind shall see it together;
    for the mouth of the LORD has spoken.

Go up onto a high mountain,
　　Zion, herald of glad tidings;
cry out at the top of your voice,
　　Jerusalem, herald of good news!
Fear not to cry out
　　and say to the cities of Judah:
　　Here is your GOD!
Here comes with power
　　the Lord GOD,
　　who rules by his strong arm;
here is his reward with him,
　　his recompense before him.
Like a shepherd he feeds his flock;
　　in his arms he gathers the lambs,
carrying them in his bosom,
　　and leading the ewes with care.
The word of the Lord. ℟. **Thanks be to God.** ↓

RESPONSORIAL PSALM Ps 85　　　　　[God's Salvation]

℟. Lord, let us see your kind-ness, and grant us your salvation.

I will hear what God proclaims;
　　the LORD—for he proclaims peace to his people.
Near indeed is his salvation to those who fear him,
　　glory dwelling in our land.

℟. **Lord, let us see your kindness,**
　　and grant us your salvation.

Kindness and truth shall meet;
　　justice and peace shall kiss.
Truth shall spring out of the earth,
　　and justice shall look down from heaven.

℟. **Lord, let us see your kindness,**
　　and grant us your salvation.

The LORD himself will give his benefits;
　　our land shall yield its increase.

Justice shall walk before him,
    and prepare the way of his steps.

℟. **Lord, let us see your kindness,
    and grant us your salvation.** ↓

SECOND READING 2 Pt 3:8-14   [A New Earth]

There is no counting of time with God. He does not want anyone to perish. We await a new heaven and earth, relying on the justice of God.

A reading from the second Letter of Saint Peter

DO not ignore this one fact, beloved, that with the Lord one day is like a thousand years and a thousand years like one day. The Lord does not delay his promise, as some regard "delay," but he is patient with you, not wishing that any should perish but that all should come to repentance. But the day of the Lord will come like a thief, and then the heavens will pass away with a mighty roar and the elements will be dissolved by fire, and the earth and everything done on it will be found out.

Since everything is to be dissolved in this way, what sort of persons ought you to be, conducting yourselves in holiness and devotion, waiting for and hastening the coming of the day of God, because of which the heavens will be dissolved in flames and the elements melted by fire. But according to his promise we await new heavens and a new earth in which righteousness dwells. Therefore, beloved, since you await these things, be eager to be found without spot or blemish before him, at peace.—The word of the Lord. ℟. **Thanks be to God.** ↓

ALLELUIA Lk 3:4, 6   [Prepare the Way]

℟. **Alleluia, alleluia.**
Prepare the way for the Lord, make straight his paths:
all flesh shall see the salvation of God.
℟. **Alleluia, alleluia.** ↓

GOSPEL Mk 1:1-8   [Need for Repentance]

> John the Baptist announced the coming of Jesus. John called for repentance and promised that the Messiah would baptize in the Holy Spirit.

℣. The Lord be with you. ℟. **And also with you.**

✝ A reading from the holy Gospel according to Mark.
℟. **Glory to you, Lord.**

THE beginning of the gospel of Jesus Christ the Son of God.

As it is written in Isaiah the prophet:
Behold, I am sending my messenger ahead of you;
he will prepare your way.
A voice of one crying out in the desert:
"Prepare the way of the Lord,
make straight his paths."

John the Baptist appeared in the desert proclaiming a baptism of repentance for the forgiveness of sins. People of the whole Judean countryside and all the inhabitants of Jerusalem were going out to him and were being baptized by him in the Jordan River as they acknowledged their sins. John was clothed in camel's hair, with a leather belt around his waist. He fed on locusts and wild honey. And this is what he proclaimed: "One mightier than I is coming after me. I am not worthy to stoop and loosen the thongs of his sandals. I have baptized you with water; he will baptize you with the Holy Spirit."—The Gospel of the Lord. ℟. **Praise to you, Lord Jesus Christ.**

→ No. 14, p. 18

PRAYER OVER THE GIFTS   [Our Offering]

Lord,
we are nothing without you.
As you sustain us with your mercy,
receive our prayers and offerings.
We ask this through Christ our Lord.
℟. **Amen.**

→ No. 21, p. 22 (Pref. P 1)

COMMUNION ANT. Bar 5:5; 4:36   [Coming Joy]

Rise up, Jerusalem, stand on the heights, and see the joy that is coming to you from God. ↓

PRAYER AFTER COMMUNION   [Wise Judgment]

Father,
you give us food from heaven.
By our sharing in this mystery,
teach us to judge wisely the things of earth
and to love the things of heaven.
Grant this through Christ our Lord.
℟. **Amen.**   → No. 32, p. 70

Optional Solemn Blessings, p. 92, and Prayers Over the People, p. 99

"I baptize with water; but there is one among you whom you do not recognize."

DECEMBER 15

3rd SUNDAY OF ADVENT

ENTRANCE ANT. Phil 4:4, 5   [Mounting Joy]

Rejoice in the Lord always; again I say, rejoice! The Lord is near.   → No. 2, p. 10 (Omit Gloria)

OPENING PRAYER   [Joy of Salvation]

Let us pray
  [that God will fill us with joy
    at the coming of Christ]
Lord God,
may we, your people,
who look forward to the birthday of Christ
experience the joy of salvation
and celebrate that feast with love and thanksgiving.
We ask this through our Lord Jesus Christ, your Son,
who lives and reigns with you and the Holy Spirit,
one God, for ever and ever. ℟. **Amen.** ↓

ALTERNATIVE OPENING PRAYER   [Joy and Hope]

Let us pray
  [this Advent
    for joy and hope in the coming Lord]
Father of our Lord Jesus Christ,
ever faithful to your promises
and ever close to your Church:
the earth rejoices in hope of the Savior's coming
and looks forward with longing
to his return at the end of time.
Prepare our hearts and remove the sadness
that hinders us from feeling the joy and hope
which his presence will bestow,
for he is Lord for ever and ever. ℟. **Amen.** ↓

FIRST READING Is 61:1-2, 10-11   [God's Glad Tidings]

Isaiah has been sent to proclaim glad tidings to those in need. He rejoices in the Lord who will prove that he is the God of justice and peace.

A reading from the Book of the Prophet Isaiah

THE spirit of the Lord GOD is upon me,
  because the LORD has anointed me;
he has sent me to bring glad tidings to the poor,
  to heal the brokenhearted,

to proclaim liberty to the captives
    and release to the prisoners,
to announce a year of favor from the Lᴏʀᴅ
    and a day of vindication by our God.

I rejoice heartily in the Lᴏʀᴅ,
    in my God is the joy of my soul;
for he has clothed me with a robe of salvation,
    and wrapped me in a mantle of justice,
like a bridegroom adorned with a diadem,
    like a bride bedecked with her jewels.
As the earth brings forth its plants,
    and a garden makes its growth spring up,
so will the Lord Gᴏᴅ make justice and praise
    spring up before all the nations.
The word of the Lord. ℟. **Thanks be to God.** ↓

RESPONSORIAL PSALM Lk 1   [God's Mighty Works]

℟. **My soul   re - joic - es   in   my   God.**

My soul proclaims the greatness of the Lord;
    my spirit rejoices in God my Savior,
for he has looked upon his lowly servant.
    From this day all generations shall call me blessed:

℟. **My soul rejoices in my God.**

the Almighty has done great things for me,
    and holy is his Name.
He has mercy on those who fear him
    in every generation.

℟. **My soul rejoices in my God.**

He has filled the hungry with good things,
    and the rich he has sent away empty.
He has come to the help of his servant Israel
    for he has remembered his promise of mercy.

℟. **My soul rejoices in my God.** ↓

SECOND READING 1 Thes 5:16-24   [Christian Joy]

Paul admonishes that Christians should rejoice. He prays that the Christ-bearer will be free from any semblance of evil, but rather will grow in holiness.

A reading from the first Letter of Saint Paul
to the Thessalonians

BROTHERS and sisters: Rejoice always. Pray without ceasing. In all circumstances give thanks, for this is the will of God for you in Christ Jesus. Do not quench the Spirit. Do not despise prophetic utterances. Test everything; retain what is good. Refrain from every kind of evil.

May the God of peace make you perfectly holy and may you entirely, spirit, soul, and body, be preserved blameless for the coming of our Lord Jesus Christ. The one who calls you is faithful, and he will also accomplish it.—The word of the Lord. ℟. **Thanks be to God.** ↓

ALLELUIA Is 61:1 (cited in Lk 4:18)   [Witness]

℟. **Alleluia, alleluia.**
The Spirit of the Lord is upon me,
because he has anointed me
to bring glad tidings to the poor.
℟. **Alleluia, alleluia.** ↓

GOSPEL Jn 1:6-8, 19-28   [Witness to Christ]

John the Baptist is the forerunner of Jesus. He gives witness to Jesus by his preaching.

℣. The Lord be with you. ℟. **And also with you.**
✜ A reading from the holy Gospel according to John.
℟. **Glory to you, Lord.**

A MAN named John was sent from God. He came for testimony, to testify to the light, so that all might believe through him. He was not the light, but came to testify to the light.

And this is the testimony of John. When the Jews from Jerusalem sent priests and Levites to him to ask him, "Who are you?" he admitted and did not deny it, but admitted, "I am not the Christ."

So they asked him, "What are you then? Are you Elijah?" And he said, "I am not." "Are you the Prophet?" He answered, "No." So they said to him, "Who are you, so we can give an answer to those who sent us? What do you have to say for yourself?" He said:

"*I am the voice of one crying out in the desert,
make straight the way of the Lord,*

as Isaiah the prophet said." Some Pharisees were also sent. They asked him, "Why then do you baptize if you are not the Christ or Elijah or the Prophet?" John answered them, "I baptize with water; but there is one among you whom you do not recognize, the one who is coming after me, whose sandal strap I am not worthy to untie." This happened in Bethany across the Jordan, where John was baptizing.—The Gospel of the Lord. ℟. **Praise to you, Lord Jesus Christ.**   → No. 14, p. 18

PRAYER OVER THE GIFTS   [Continual Sacrifice]

Lord,
may the gift we offer in faith and love
be a continual sacrifice in your honor
and truly become our eucharist and our salvation.
Grant this through Christ our Lord.
℟. **Amen.**   → No. 21, p. 22 (Pref. P 1 or 2)

COMMUNION ANT. See Is 35:4   [Trust in God]

Say to the anxious: be strong and fear not, our God will come to save us. ↓

PRAYER AFTER COMMUNION   [Preparation for Christ]

God of mercy,
may this eucharist bring us your divine help,
free us from our sins,

and prepare us for the birthday of our Savior,
who is Lord for ever and ever.
℟. **Amen.**   ➔ No. 32, p. 70

Optional Solemn Blessings, p. 92, and Prayers Over the People, p. 99

"Do not be afraid, Mary, for you have found favor with God."

DECEMBER 22

4th SUNDAY OF ADVENT

ENTRANCE ANT. Is 45:8   [The Advent Plea]

**Let the clouds rain down the Just One, and the earth
bring forth a Savior.**   ➔ No. 2, p. 10 (Omit Gloria)

OPENING PRAYER   [From Suffering to Glory]

Let us pray
  [as Advent draws to a close,
    that Christ will truly come into our hearts]
Lord,
fill our hearts with your love,
and as you revealed to us by an angel
the coming of your Son as man,
so lead us through his suffering and death
to the glory of his resurrection,
for he lives and reigns with you and the Holy Spirit,
one God, for ever and ever. ℟. **Amen.** ↓

ALTERNATIVE OPENING PRAYER   [Operative Faith]

Let us pray
  [as Advent draws to a close
  for the faith that opens our lives
  to the Spirit of God]
Father, all-powerful God,
your eternal Word took flesh on our earth
when the Virgin Mary placed her life
at the service of your plan.
Lift our minds in watchful hope
to hear the voice which announces his glory
and open our minds to receive the Spirit
who prepares us for his coming.
We ask this through Christ our Lord. ℟. **Amen.** ↓

FIRST READING 2 Sm 7:1-5, 8b-12, 14a-16 [A King Forever]

   David wishes to build a temple to house the tables of the
Law, but God speaks to him, promising to exalt and secure
the House of David forever. The Lord will bring peace.

A reading from the second Book of Samuel

WHEN King David was settled in his palace, and
the LORD had given him rest from his enemies on
every side, he said to Nathan the prophet, "Here I am
living in a house of cedar, while the ark of God dwells
in a tent!" Nathan answered the king, "Go, do whatever you have in mind, for the LORD is with you." But
that night the LORD spoke to Nathan and said: "Go, tell
my servant David, 'Thus says the LORD: Should you
build me a house to dwell in?

  " 'It was I who took you from the pasture and from
the care of the flock to be commander of my people Israel. I have been with you wherever you went, and I
have destroyed all your enemies before you. And I
will make you famous like the great ones of the earth.
I will fix a place for my people Israel; I will plant them
so that they may dwell in their place without further

disturbance. Neither shall the wicked continue to afflict them as they did of old, since the time I first appointed judges over my people Israel. I will give you rest from all your enemies. The LORD also reveals to you that he will establish a house for you. And when your time comes and you rest with your ancestors, I will raise up your heir after you, sprung from your loins, and I will make his kingdom firm. I will be a father to him, and he shall be a son to me. Your house and your kingdom shall endure forever before me; your throne shall stand firm forever.' "—The word of the Lord. ℟. **Thanks be to God.** ↓

RESPONSORIAL PSALM Ps 89   [An Eternal Covenant]

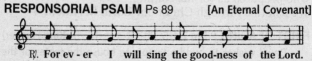

℟. For ev - er   I   will sing the good-ness of the Lord.

The promises of the LORD I will sing forever;
  through all generations my mouth shall proclaim
    your faithfulness.
For you have said, "My kindness is established forever";
    ever";
  in heaven you have confirmed your faithfulness.

℟. **For ever I will sing the goodness of the Lord.**

"I have made a covenant with my chosen one,
  I have sworn to David my servant:
forever will I confirm your posterity
  and establish your throne for all generations."

℟. **For ever I will sing the goodness of the Lord.**

"He shall say of me, 'You are my father,
  my God, the Rock, my savior.'
Forever I will maintain my kindness toward him,
  and my covenant with him stands firm."

℟. **For ever I will sing the goodness of the Lord.**↓

SECOND READING Rom 16:25-27   [Faith and Obedience]

God has revealed his plan of salvation through the coming of his Son, Jesus Christ. It is made known to all people that they may believe and obey.

A reading from the Letter of Saint Paul to the Romans

BROTHERS and sisters: To him who can strengthen you, according to my gospel and the proclamation of Jesus Christ, according to the revelation of the mystery kept secret for long ages but now manifested through the prophetic writings and, according to the command of the eternal God, made known to all nations to bring about the obedience of faith, to the only wise God, through Jesus Christ be glory forever and ever. Amen.—The word of the Lord. ℟. **Thanks be to God.** ↓

ALLELUIA Lk 1:38   [God's Handmaid]

℟. **Alleluia, alleluia.**
Behold, I am the handmaid of the Lord.
May it be done to me according to your word.
℟. **Alleluia, alleluia.** ↓

GOSPEL Lk 1:26-38   [Mary's Consent]

Gabriel speaks to Mary, announcing that she who is a virgin shall conceive through the Holy Spirit and give birth to a son. Mary agrees to God's request.

℣. The Lord be with you. ℟. **And also with you.**
✤ A reading from the holy Gospel according to Luke.
℟. **Glory to you, Lord.**

THE angel Gabriel was sent from God to a town of Galilee called Nazareth, to a virgin betrothed to a man named Joseph, of the house of David, and the virgin's name was Mary. And coming to her, he said, "Hail, full of grace! The Lord is with you." But she was greatly troubled at what was said and pondered what sort of greeting this might be. Then the angel said to her, "Do not be afraid, Mary, for you have found favor with God.

"Behold, you will conceive in your womb and bear a son, and you shall name him Jesus. He will be great and will be called Son of the Most High, and the Lord God will give him the throne of David his father, and he will rule over the house of Jacob forever, and of his kingdom there will be no end." But Mary said to the angel, "How can this be, since I have no relations with a man?" And the angel said to her in reply, "The Holy Spirit will come upon you, and the power of the Most High will overshadow you. Therefore the child to be born will be called holy, the Son of God. And behold, Elizabeth, your relative, has also conceived a son in her old age, and this is the sixth month for her who was called barren; for nothing will be impossible for God." Mary said, "Behold, I am the handmaid of the Lord. May it be done to me according to your word." Then the angel departed from her.—The Gospel of the Lord. ℟. **Praise to you, Lord Jesus Christ.**

➙ No. 14, p. 18

PRAYER OVER THE GIFTS   [Power of the Spirit]

Lord,
may the power of the Spirit,
which sanctified Mary the mother of your Son,
make holy the gifts we place upon this altar.
Grant this through Christ our Lord.
℟. **Amen.**   ➙ No. 21, p. 22 (Pref. P 2)

COMMUNION ANT. Is 7:14   [The Virgin-Mother]

The Virgin is with child and shall bear a son, and she will call him Emmanuel. ↓

PRAYER AFTER COMMUNION   [Growth in Holiness]

Lord,
in this sacrament

we receive the promise of salvation;
as Christmas draws near
make us grow in faith and love
to celebrate the coming of Christ our Savior,
who is Lord for ever and ever.
R̴. **Amen.**   ➜ No. 32, p. 70

Optional Solemn Blessings, p. 92, and Prayers Over the People, p. 99

The Word is made flesh.

DECEMBER 25

CHRISTMAS

MASS AT MIDNIGHT

ENTRANCE ANT. Ps 2:7   [Son of God]
**The Lord said to me: You are my Son; this day have I
begotten you.**

OR   [True Peace]
**Let us all rejoice in the Lord, for our Savior is born to
the world. True peace has descended from heaven.**
                                                 ➜ No. 2, p. 10

OPENING PRAYER   [Eternal Joy]
Let us pray
    [in the peace of Christmas midnight

that our joy in the birth of Christ
will last for ever]
Father,
you make this holy night radiant
with the splendor of Jesus Christ our light.
We welcome him as Lord, the true light of the world.
Bring us to eternal joy in the kingdom of heaven,
where he lives and reigns with you and the Holy
 Spirit,
one God, for ever and ever. ℟. **Amen.** ↓

ALTERNATIVE OPENING PRAYER   [Joy and Hope]

Let us pray
 [with joy and hope
 as we await the dawning of the Father's Word]
Lord our God,
with the birth of your Son
your glory breaks on the world.
Through the night hours of the darkened earth
we your people watch for the coming of your promised Son.
As we wait, give us a foretaste of the joy that you will
 grant us
when the fullness of his glory has filled the earth,
who lives and reigns with you for ever and ever.
℟. **Amen.** ↓

FIRST READING Is 9:1-6   [The Messiah's Kingdom]

**The Messiah is a promise of peace for the world. His reign
shall be vast and filled with justice. The power of God is
revealed through the weakness of humans.**

A reading from the Book of the Prophet Isaiah

THE people who walked in darkness
  have seen a great light;
upon those who dwelt in the land of gloom
 a light has shone.

You have brought them abundant joy
and great rejoicing,
as they rejoice before you as at the harvest,
as people make merry when dividing spoils.
For the yoke that burdened them,
the pole on their shoulder,
and the rod of their taskmaster
you have smashed, as on the day of Midian.
For every boot that tramped in battle,
every cloak rolled in blood,
will be burned as fuel for flames.
For a child is born to us, a son is given us;
upon his shoulder dominion rests.
They name him Wonder-Counselor, God-Hero,
Father-Forever, Prince of Peace.
His dominion is vast
and forever peaceful,
from David's throne, and over his kingdom,
which he confirms and sustains
by judgment and justice,
both now and forever.
The zeal of the LORD of hosts will do this!
The word of the Lord. ℟. **Thanks be to God.** ↓

RESPONSORIAL PSALM Ps 96 [Bless the Lord]

℟. Today is born our Sav - ior, Christ the Lord.

Sing to the LORD a new song;
sing to the LORD, all you lands.
Sing to the LORD; bless his name.

℟. **Today is born our Savior, Christ the Lord.**

Announce his salvation, day after day.
Tell his glory among the nations;
among all peoples, his wondrous deeds.

℟. **Today is born our Savior, Christ the Lord.**

Let the heavens be glad and the earth rejoice;
  let the sea and what fills it resound;
  let the plains be joyful and all that is in them!
Then shall all the trees of the forest exult.

℟. **Today is born our Savior, Christ the Lord.**

They shall exult before the LORD, for he comes,
  for he comes to rule the earth.
He shall rule the world with justice
  and the peoples with his constancy.

℟. **Today is born our Savior, Christ the Lord.** ↓

SECOND READING Ti 2:11-14   [Salvation for All]

God offers salvation to all people. His way asks us to reject
worldly desires—to live temperately and justly. He even
asked his only Son to sacrifice himself to redeem us.

A reading from the Letter of Saint Paul to Titus

BELOVED: The grace of God has appeared, saving
all and training us to reject godless ways and
worldly desires and to live temperately, justly, and devoutly in this age, as we await the blessed hope, the
appearance of the glory of our great God and savior
Jesus Christ, who gave himself for us to deliver us
from all lawlessness and to cleanse for himself a people as his own, eager to do what is good.—The word
of the Lord. ℟. **Thanks be to God.** ↓

ALLELUIA Lk 2:10-11   [Great Joy]

℟. **Alleluia, alleluia.**
I proclaim to you good news of great joy:
today a Savior is born for us,
Christ the Lord.
℟. **Alleluia, alleluia.** ↓

GOSPEL Lk 2:1-14   [Birth of Christ]

Caesar Augustus desired a world census. Joseph and Mary
go to Bethlehem where Jesus, the Lord of the universe, is
born in a stable. Glory to God and peace on earth!

℣. The Lord be with you. ℟. **And also with you.**

✚ A reading from the holy Gospel according to Luke.

℟. **Glory to you, Lord.**

IN those days a decree went out from Caesar Augustus that the whole world should be enrolled. This was the first enrollment, when Quirinius was governor of Syria. So all went to be enrolled, each to his own town. And Joseph too went up from Galilee from the town of Nazareth to Judea, to the city of David that is called Bethlehem, because he was of the house and family of David, to be enrolled with Mary, his betrothed, who was with child. While they were there, the time came for her to have her child, and she gave birth to her firstborn son. She wrapped him in swaddling clothes and laid him in a manger, because there was no room for them in the inn.

Now there were shepherds in that region living in the fields and keeping the night watch over their flock. The angel of the Lord appeared to them and the glory of the Lord shone around them, and they were struck with great fear. The angel said to them, "Do not be afraid; for behold, I proclaim to you good news of great joy that will be for all the people. For today in the city of David a savior has been born for you who is Christ and Lord. And this will be a sign for you: you will find an infant wrapped in swaddling clothes and lying in a manger." And suddenly there was a multitude of the heavenly host with the angel, praising God and saying:

"Glory to God in the highest
    and on earth peace to those on whom his favor
    rests."

The Gospel of the Lord. ℟. **Praise to you, Lord Jesus Christ.**   ➔ No. 14, p. 18

In the profession of faith, all genuflect at the words, and became man.

PRAYER OVER THE GIFTS   [Become Like Christ]

Lord,
accept our gifts on this joyful feast of our salvation.
By our communion with God made man
may we become more like him
who joins our lives to yours,
for he is Lord for ever and ever.
℟. **Amen.**   ➜ No. 21, p. 22 (Pref. P 3-5)

*When Eucharistic Prayer I is used, the special Christmas
form of* In union with the whole Church *is said.*

COMMUNION ANT. Jn 1:14   [Glory of Christ]

**The Word of God became man; we have seen his
glory.** ↓

PRAYER AFTER COMMUNION   [Following Christ]

God our Father,
we rejoice in the birth of our Savior.
May we share his life completely
by living as he has taught.
We ask this in the name of Jesus the Lord.
℟. **Amen.**   ➜ No. 32, p. 70

Optional Solemn Blessings, p. 92, and Prayers Over the People, p. 99

———————

MASS AT DAWN

ENTRANCE ANT. See Is 9:2, 6; Lk 1:33   [Prince of Peace]

**A light will shine on us this day, the Lord is born for
us: he shall be called Wonderful God, Prince of peace,
Father of the world to come; and his kingship will
never end.**   ➜ No. 2, p. 10

OPENING PRAYER　　　　　　　　[Light of Faith]

Let us pray
　[that the love of Christ
　will be a light to the world]
Father,
we are filled with the new light
by the coming of your Word among us.
May the light of faith
shine in our words and actions.
Grant this . . . for ever and ever. ℟. **Amen.** ↓

ALTERNATIVE OPENING PRAYER　　　　[Christ's Peace]

Let us pray
　[for the peace
　that comes from the Prince of Peace]
Almighty God and Father of light,
a child is born for us and a son is given to us.
Your eternal Word leaped down from heaven
in the silent watches of the night,
and now your Church is filled with wonder
at the nearness of her God.
Open our hearts to receive his life
and increase our vision with the rising of dawn,
that our lives may be filled with his glory and his
　peace,
who lives and reigns for ever and ever. ℟. **Amen.** ↓

FIRST READING Is 62:11-12　　　　[The Savior's Birth]

　　Isaiah foretells the birth of the Savior who will come to
　　Zion. These people will be called holy and they shall be re-
　　deemed.

　　A reading from the Book of the Prophet Isaiah

S EE, the LORD proclaims
　to the ends of the earth:
say to daughter Zion,
　your savior comes!

Here is his reward with him,
 his recompense before him.
They shall be called the holy people,
 the redeemed of the LORD,
and you shall be called "Frequented,"
 a city that is not forsaken.
The word of the Lord. ℟. **Thanks be to God.** ↓

RESPONSORIAL PSALM Ps 97   [Be Glad in the Lord]

 ℟. **A light will shine on us this day: the Lord is born for us.**

The LORD is king; let the earth rejoice;
 let the many isles be glad.
The heavens proclaim his justice,
 and all peoples see his glory.

℟. **A light will shine on us this day:
 the Lord is born for us.**

Light dawns for the just;
 and gladness, for the upright of heart.
Be glad in the LORD, you just,
 and give thanks to his holy name.

℟. **A light will shine on us this day:
 the Lord is born for us.** ↓

SECOND READING Ti 3:4-7 [Saved by God's Mercy]

**Christians are saved not because of their own merits but
because of the mercy of God. We are saved through baptism and renewal in the Holy Spirit.**

A reading from the Letter of Saint Paul to Titus

B ELOVED: When the kindness and generous love
of God our savior appeared, not because of any
righteous deeds we had done but because of his
mercy, he saved us through the bath of rebirth and renewal by the Holy Spirit, whom he richly poured out

on us through Jesus Christ our savior, so that we might be justified by his grace and become heirs in hope of eternal life.—The word of the Lord. ℟. **Thanks be to God.** ↓

ALLELUIA Lk 2:14   [Glory to God]

℟. **Alleluia, alleluia.**
Glory to God in the highest,
and on earth peace to those
on whom his favor rests.
℟. **Alleluia, alleluia.** ↓

GOSPEL Lk 2:15-20   [Jesus, the God-Man]

The shepherds, the poor of the people of God, come to pay homage to Jesus. Mary ponders and prays over the great event of God becoming one of us.

℣. The Lord be with you. ℟. **And also with you.**
✠ A reading from the holy Gospel according to Luke.
℟. **Glory to you, Lord.**

WHEN the angels went away from them to heaven, the shepherds said to one another, "Let us go, then, to Bethlehem to see this thing that has taken place, which the Lord has made known to us." So they went in haste and found Mary and Joseph, and the infant lying in the manger. When they saw this, they made known the message that had been told them about this child. All who heard it were amazed by what had been told them by the shepherds. And Mary kept all these things, reflecting on them in her heart. Then the shepherds returned, glorifying and praising God for all they had heard and seen, just as it had been told to them.—The Gospel of the Lord. ℟. **Praise to you, Lord Jesus Christ.**   → No. 14, p. 18

In the profession of faith, all genuflect at the words, and became man.

PRAYER OVER THE GIFTS   [Gift of Divine Life]

Father,
may we follow the example of your Son
who became man and lived among us.
May we receive the gift of divine life
through these offerings here on earth.
We ask this in the name of Jesus the Lord.
℟. **Amen.**   → No. 21, p. 22 (Pref. P 3-5)

*When Eucharistic Prayer I is used, the special Christmas
form of* In union with the whole Church *is said.*

COMMUNION ANT. See Zec 9:9   [The Holy One]

**Daughter of Zion, exult; shout aloud, daughter of
Jerusalem! Your King is coming, the Holy One, the
Savior of the world.** ↓

PRAYER AFTER COMMUNION   [Riches Revealed in Christ]

Lord,
with faith and joy
we celebrate the birthday of your Son.
Increase our understanding and our love
of the riches you have revealed in him,
who is Lord for ever and ever.
℟. **Amen.**   → No. 32, p. 70

Optional Solemn Blessings, p. 92, and Prayers Over the People, p. 99

MASS DURING THE DAY

ENTRANCE ANT. Is 9:6   [The Gift of God's Son]

**A child is born for us, a son given to us; dominion is
laid on his shoulder, and he shall be called Wonder-
ful-Counselor.**   → No. 2, p. 10

OPENING PRAYER   [Share in Christ's Glory]

Let us pray
   [for the glory promised by the birth of Christ]

Lord God,
we praise you for creating man,
and still more for restoring him in Christ.
Your Son shared our weakness:
may we share his glory,
for he lives and reigns with you and the Holy Spirit,
one God, for ever and ever. ℟. **Amen.** ↓

ALTERNATIVE OPENING PRAYER   [People of Light]

Let us pray
    [in the joy of Christmas
    because the Son of God lives among us]
God of love, Father of all,
the darkness that covered the earth
has given way to the bright dawn of your Word made
    flesh.
Make us a people of this light.
Make us faithful to your Word,
that we may bring your life to the waiting world.
Grant this through Christ our Lord. ℟. **Amen.** ↓

FIRST READING Is 52:7-10   [Your God Is King]

**God shows salvation to all people. He brings peace and
good news. He comforts his people and redeems them.**

A reading from the Book of the Prophet Isaiah

HOW beautiful upon the mountains
    are the feet of him who brings glad tidings,
announcing peace, bearing good news,
    announcing salvation, and saying to Zion,
    "Your God is King!"
Hark! Your sentinels raise a cry,
    together they shout for joy,
for they see directly, before their eyes,
    the LORD restoring Zion.
Break out together in song,
    O ruins of Jerusalem!

For the LORD comforts his people,
  he redeems Jerusalem.
The LORD has bared his holy arm
  in the sight of all the nations;
all the ends of the earth will behold
  the salvation of our God.
The word of the Lord. ℟. **Thanks be to God.** ↓

RESPONSORIAL PSALM Ps 98   [Sing a New Song]

℟. All the ends of the earth have seen the saving   power of God.

Sing to the LORD a new song,
  for he has done wondrous deeds;
his right hand has won victory for him,
  his holy arm.

℟. **All the ends of the earth have seen the saving
  power of God.**

The LORD has made his salvation known:
  in the sight of the nations he has revealed his jus-
    tice.
He has remembered his kindness and his faithfulness
  toward the house of Israel.

℟. **All the ends of the earth have seen the saving
  power of God.**

All the ends of the earth have seen
  the salvation by our God.
Sing joyfully to the LORD, all you lands;
  break into song; sing praise.

℟. **All the ends of the earth have seen the saving
  power of God.**

Sing praise to the LORD with the harp,
  with the harp and melodious song.

With trumpets and the sound of the horn
sing joyfully before the King, the LORD.

℟. **All the ends of the earth have seen the saving power of God.** ↓

SECOND READING Heb 1:1-6   [God Speaks through Jesus]

God now speaks through Jesus, his Son, who reflects his glory. The Son cleanses us from sin. Heaven and earth should worship him.

A reading from the Letter to the Hebrews

BROTHERS and sisters: In times past, God spoke in partial and various ways to our ancestors through the prophets; in these last days, he has spoken to us through the Son, whom he made heir of all things and through whom he created the universe,
who is the refulgence of his glory,
the very imprint of his being,
and who sustains all things by his mighty word.
When he had accomplished purification from sins,
he took his seat at the right hand of the Majesty on high,
as far superior to the angels
as the name he has inherited is more excellent than theirs.
For to which of the angels did God ever say:
You are my son; this day I have begotten you?
Or again:
I will be a father to him, and he shall be a son to me?
And again, when he leads the firstborn into the world,
he says:
Let all the angels of God worship him.
The word of the Lord. ℟. **Thanks be to God.** ↓

ALLELUIA   [Adore the Lord]

℟. **Alleluia, alleluia.**
A holy day has dawned upon us.
Come, you nations, and adore the Lord.

Today a great light has come upon the earth.
℟. **Alleluia, alleluia.** ↓

GOSPEL Jn 1:1-18 or 1:1-5, 9-14 [The True Light]
    John's opening words parallel the Book of Genesis. Jesus
    is the Word made flesh, the light of the world, who always
    was and will ever be.

*[If the "Shorter Form" is used, the indented text in brackets is
omitted.]*

℣. The Lord be with you. ℟. **And also with you.**
✛ A reading from the holy Gospel according to John.
℟. **Glory to you, Lord.**

IN the beginning was the Word,
    and the Word was with God,
        and the Word was God.
He was in the beginning with God.
All things came to be through him,
    and without him nothing came to be.
What came to be through him was life,
    and this life was the light of the human race;
the light shines in the darkness,
    and the darkness has not overcome it.
        [A man named John was sent from God. He
        came for testimony, to testify to the light, so
        that all might believe through him. He was
        not the light, but came to testify to the light.]
The true light, which enlightens everyone, was coming into the world.
    He was in the world,
        and the world came to be through him,
        but the world did not know him.
    He came to what was his own,
        but his own people did not accept him.

But to those who did accept him he gave power to become children of God, to those who believe in his
name, who were born not by natural generation nor
by human choice nor by a man's decision but of God.

And the Word became flesh
   and made his dwelling among us,
   and we saw his glory,
   the glory as of the Father's only Son,
   full of grace and truth.
      [John testified to him and cried out, saying,
"This was he of whom I said, 'The one who is
coming after me ranks ahead of me because
he existed before me.'" From his fullness we
have all received, grace in place of grace, because while the law was given through Moses,
grace and truth came through Jesus Christ. No
one has ever seen God. The only Son, God,
who is at the Father's side, has revealed him.]

The Gospel of the Lord. ℟. **Praise to you, Lord Jesus
Christ.**   ➜ No. 14, p. 18

*In the profession of faith, all genuflect at the words, and be-
came man.*

PRAYER OVER THE GIFTS   [Peace and Praise]

Almighty God,
the saving work of Christ
made our peace with you.
May our offering today
renew that peace within us
and give you perfect praise.
We ask this in the name of Jesus the Lord.
℟. **Amen.**   ➜ No. 21, p. 22 (Pref. P 3-5)

*When Eucharistic Prayer I is used, the special Christmas
form of* In union with the whole Church *is said.*

COMMUNION ANT. Ps 98:3   [God's Power]

**All the ends of the earth have seen the saving power
of God.** ↓

PRAYER AFTER COMMUNION   [Children of God]

Father,
the child born today is the Savior of the world.

He made us your children.
May he welcome us into your kingdom
where he lives and reigns with you for ever and ever.
℞. **Amen.**   → No. 32, p. 70

Optional Solemn Blessings, p. 92, and Prayers Over the People, p. 99

*Simeon said, "This child is destined to be the downfall
and the rise of many in Israel."*

DECEMBER 29

HOLY FAMILY

ENTRANCE ANT. Lk 2:16   [Jesus, Mary, and Joseph]
**The shepherds hastened to Bethlehem, where they
found Mary and Joseph, and the baby lying in a
manger.**   → No. 2, p. 10

OPENING PRAYER   [Peace in Families]
Let us pray
    [for peace in our families]
Father,
help us to live as the holy family,
united in respect and love.
Bring us to the joy and peace of your eternal home.
Grant this through our Lord Jesus Christ, your Son,

who lives and reigns with you and the Holy Spirit,
one God, for ever and ever. ℟. **Amen.** ↓

ALTERNATIVE OPENING PRAYER   [Value of Family Life]

Let us pray
   [as the family of God,
   who share in his life]
Father in heaven, creator of all,
you ordered the earth to bring forth life
and crowned its goodness by creating the family of man.
In history's moment when all was ready,
you sent your Son to dwell in time,
obedient to the laws of life in our world.
Teach us the sanctity of human love,
show us the value of family life,
and help us to live in peace with all men
that we may share in your life for ever.
We ask this through Christ our Lord. ℟. **Amen.** ↓

*The following readings (except the Gospel) are optional. In
their place, the readings for Year A, pp. 148-150, may be used.*

FIRST READING Gn 15:1-6; 21:1-3   [Abraham's Faith]

**Abraham believed in God. As a result, God gave him and his
wife a son in their old age. The family thus becomes the sign
of the faith of human beings and of the love of God.**

A reading from the Book of Genesis

THE word of the LORD came to Abram in a vision,
   saying: "Fear not, Abram! I am your shield; I will
make your reward very great." But Abram said, "O
Lord GOD, what good will your gifts be, if I keep on
being childless and have as my heir the steward of
my house, Eliezer?" Abram continued, "See, you have
given me no offspring, and so one of my servants will
be my heir." Then the word of the LORD came to him:
"No, that one shall not be your heir; your own issue
shall be your heir." The Lord took Abram outside and

said, "Look up at the sky and count the stars, if you can. Just so," he added, "shall your descendants be." Abram put his faith in the LORD, who credited it to him as an act of righteousness.

The LORD took note of Sarah as he had said he would; he did for her as he had promised. Sarah became pregnant and bore Abraham a son in his old age, at the set time that God had stated. Abraham gave the name Isaac to this son of his whom Sarah bore him.—The word of the Lord. ℟. **Thanks be to God.** ↓

RESPONSORIAL PSALM Ps 105   [God's Covenant]

℟. The Lord re - mem - bers his cov - e - nant for ev - er.

Give thanks to the LORD, invoke his name;
     make known among the nations his deeds.
Sing to him, sing his praise,
     proclaim all his wondrous deeds.

℟. **The Lord remembers his covenant for ever.**

Glory in his holy name;
     rejoice, O hearts that seek the LORD!
Look to the LORD in his strength;
     constantly seek his face.

℟. **The Lord remembers his covenant for ever.**

You descendants of Abraham, his servants,
     sons of Jacob, his chosen ones!
He, the LORD, is our God;
     throughout the earth his judgments prevail.

℟. **The Lord remembers his covenant for ever.**

He remembers forever his covenant
  which he made binding for a thousand generations
which he entered into with Abraham
  and by his oath to Isaac.

℟. **The Lord remembers his covenant for ever.** ↓

SECOND READING Heb 11:8, 11-12, 17-19   [Trust God]

Abraham believed God's promises and put his faith in him,
living that faith in every phase of his life. And since God is
faithful to his promises, faith becomes the source of hope
and happiness for his family. We should place our trust in
God's promises.

A reading from the Letter to the Hebrews

BROTHERS and sisters: By faith Abraham obeyed
when he was called to go out to a place that he
was to receive as an inheritance; he went out, not
knowing where he was to go. By faith he received
power to generate, even though he was past the normal age—and Sarah herself was sterile—for he
thought that the one who had made the promise was
trustworthy. So it was that there came forth from one
man, himself as good as dead, descendants as numer-
ous as the stars in the sky and as countless as the
sands on the seashore.

By faith Abraham, when put to the test, offered up
Isaac, and he who had received the promises was
ready to offer his only son, of whom it was said,
"Through Isaac descendants shall bear your name."
He reasoned that God was able to raise even from the
dead, and he received Isaac back as a symbol.—The
word of the Lord. ℟. **Thanks be to God.** ↓

ALLELUIA Heb 1:1-2   [God Speaks]

℟. **Alleluia, alleluia.**

In the past God spoke to our ancestors through the
  prophets;

in these last days, he has spoken to us through the Son.
℟. **Alleluia, alleluia.** ↓

GOSPEL Lk 2:22-40 or 2:22, 39-40   [God's Anointed One]

**Joseph and Mary take Jesus to the temple in Jerusalem to
be presented to the Lord. Simeon recognizes him as the
Anointed of the Lord and blesses him. The child returns to
Nazareth and grows to maturity.**

*[If the "Shorter Form" is used, the indented text in brackets is
omitted.]*

℣. The Lord be with you. ℟. **And also with you.**
✠ A reading from the holy Gospel according to Luke.
℟. **Glory to you, Lord.**

W HEN the days were completed for their purification according to the law of Moses, they took
him up to Jerusalem to present him to the Lord,
[just as it is written in the law of the Lord, *Every
male that opens the womb shall be consecrated to the Lord,* and to offer the sacrifice of
a pair of turtledoves or two young pigeons, in
accordance with the dictate in the law of the
Lord.

Now there was a man in Jerusalem whose
name was Simeon. This man was righteous and
devout, awaiting the consolation of Israel, and
the Holy Spirit was upon him. It had been revealed to him by the Holy Spirit that he should
not see death before he had seen the Christ of
the Lord. He came in the Spirit into the temple;
and when the parents brought in the child
Jesus to perform the custom of the law in regard to him, he took him into his arms and
blessed God, saying:

"Now, Master, you may let your servant go
    in peace, according to your word,
for my eyes have seen your salvation,

which you prepared in sight of all the
peoples,
a light for revelation to the Gentiles,
and glory for your people Israel."
The child's father and mother were amazed at
what was said about him; and Simeon blessed
them and said to Mary his mother, "Behold, this
child is destined for the fall and rise of many in
Israel, and to be a sign that will be contradicted—and you yourself a sword will pierce—
so that the thoughts of many hearts may be revealed." There was also a prophetess, Anna, the
daughter of Phanuel, of the tribe of Asher. She
was advanced in years, having lived seven
years with her husband after her marriage, and
then as a widow until she was eighty-four. She
never left the temple, but worshiped night and
day with fasting and prayer. And coming forward at that very time, she gave thanks to God
and spoke about the child to all who were
awaiting the redemption of Jerusalem.]
 When they had fulfilled all the prescriptions of the
law of the Lord, they returned to Galilee, to their
own town of Nazareth. The child grew and became
strong, filled with wisdom; and the favor of God
was upon him.—The Gospel of the Lord. ℟. **Praise to
you, Lord Jesus Christ.**   ➜ No. 14, p. 18

PRAYER OVER THE GIFTS   [Unite Our Families]
Lord,
accept this sacrifice
and through the prayers of Mary, the virgin Mother of
 God,
and of her husband, Joseph,
unite our families in peace and love.
We ask this in the name of Jesus the Lord.
℟. **Amen.**   ➜ No. 21, p. 22 (Pref. P 3-5)

When Eucharistic Prayer I is used, the special Christmas form of In union with the whole Church *is said.*

COMMUNION ANT. Bar 3:38   [God with Us]

Our God has appeared on earth, and lived among men. ↓

PRAYER AFTER COMMUNION   [Strength for Families]

Eternal Father,
we want to live as Jesus, Mary, and Joseph,
in peace with you and one another.
May this communion strengthen us
to face the troubles of life.
Grant this through Christ our Lord.
℟. **Amen.**   → No. 32, p. 70

Optional Solemn Blessings, p. 92, and Prayers Over the People, p. 99

The following readings (except the Gospel) from Year A may be used in place of the optional ones given on pp. 143-147.

FIRST READING Sir 3:2-7, 12-14   [Duties toward Parents]

Fidelity to Yahweh implies many particular virtues, and among them Sirach gives precedence to duties toward parents. He promises atonement for sin to those who honor their parents.

A reading from the Book of Sirach

GOD sets a father in honor over his children;
a mother's authority he confirms over her sons.
Whoever honors his father atones for sins,
and preserves himself from them.
When he prays, he is heard;
he stores up riches who reveres his mother.
Whoever honors his father is gladdened by children,
and when he prays, is heard.
Whoever reveres his father will live a long life;
he obeys his father who brings comfort to his mother.

My son, take care of your father when he is old;

grieve him not as long as he lives.
Even if his mind fail, be considerate of him;
  revile him not all the days of his life;
kindness to a father will not be forgotten,
  firmly planted against the debt of your sins
  —a house raised in justice to you.
The word of the Lord. ℟. **Thanks be to God.** ↓

RESPONSORIAL PSALM Ps 128   [Happiness in Families]

℟. **Bles-sed are those who fear the Lord and walk in his ways.**

Blessed is everyone who fears the LORD,
  who walks in his ways!
For you shall eat the fruit of your handiwork;
  blessed shall you be, and favored.—℟.

Your wife shall be like a fruitful vine
  in the recesses of your home;
your children like olive plants
  around your table.—℟.

Behold, thus is the man blessed
  who fears the LORD.
The LORD bless you from Zion:
  may you see the prosperity of Jerusalem
  all the days of your life.—℟. ↓

SECOND READING Col 3:12-21   [Plan for Family Life]
    **Paul describes the life a christian embraces through bap-
    tism.**

*[1f the "Shorter Form" is used, the indented text in brackets is
omitted.]*

A reading from the Letter of Saint Paul to the Colossians

BROTHERS and sisters: Put on, as God's chosen
ones, holy and beloved, heartfelt compassion,

kindness, humility, gentleness, and patience, bearing
with one another and forgiving one another, if one has
a grievance against another; as the Lord has forgiven
you, so must you also do. And over all these put on
love, that is, the bond of perfection. And let the peace
of Christ control your hearts, the peace into which
you were also called in one body. And be thankful. Let
the word of Christ dwell in you richly, as in all wisdom you teach and admonish one another, singing
psalms, hymns, and spiritual songs with gratitude in
your hearts to God. And whatever you do, in word or
in deed, do everything in the name of the Lord Jesus,
giving thanks to God the Father through him.

[Wives, be subordinate to your husbands, as is
proper in the Lord. Husbands, love your wives,
and avoid any bitterness toward them. Children,
obey your parents in everything, for this is pleasing to the Lord. Fathers, do not provoke your children, so they may not become discouraged.]

The word of the Lord. ℟. **Thanks be to God.** ↓

ALLELUIA Col 3:15a, 16a   **[Peace of Christ]**

℟. **Alleluia, alleluia.**
Let the peace of Christ control your hearts;
let the word of Christ dwell in you richly.
℟. **Alleluia, alleluia.**

"He was named Jesus . . ."

JANUARY 1, 2003

SOLEMNITY OF MARY, MOTHER OF GOD

ENTRANCE ANT. See Is 9:2, 6; Lk 1:33   [Wonderful God]

A light will shine on us this day, the Lord is born for us: he shall be called Wonderful God, Prince of peace, Father of the world to come; and his kingship will never end.

OR Sedulius   [Hail, Holy Mother]

Hail, holy Mother! The child to whom you gave birth is the King of heaven and earth for ever.

→ No. 2, p. 10

OPENING PRAYER   [Mary's Prayers]

Let us pray
   [that Mary, the mother of the Lord,
   will help us by her prayers]
God our Father,
may we always profit by the prayers
of the Virgin Mother Mary,
for you bring us life and salvation
through Jesus Christ her Son
who lives and reigns with you and the Holy Spirit,
one God, for ever and ever. ℟. **Amen.** ↓

151

ALTERNATIVE OPENING PRAYER [Gift of a Mother's Love]

Let us pray
  [in the name of Jesus,
   born of a virgin and Son of God]
Father,
source of light in every age,
the virgin conceived and bore your Son
who is called Wonderful God, Prince of Peace.
May her prayer, the gift of a mother's love,
be your people's joy through all ages.
May her response, born of a humble heart,
draw your Spirit to rest on your people.
Grant this through Christ our Lord. ℟. **Amen.** ↓

FIRST READING Nm 6:22-27   [The Aaronic Blessing]

God speaks to Moses instructing him to have Aaron and the Israelites pray that he may answer their prayers with blessings.

A reading from the Book of Numbers

T HE LORD said to Moses: "Speak to Aaron and his
  sons and tell them: This is how you shall bless the
Israelites. Say to them:

The LORD bless you and keep you!
The LORD let his face shine upon you, and be gracious
  to you!
The LORD look upon you kindly and give you peace!

So shall they invoke my name upon the Israelites and
I will bless them."—The word of the Lord. ℟. **Thanks be to God.** ↓

RESPONSORIAL PSALM Ps 67   [God Bless Us]

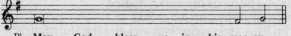

℟. May   God   bless   us   in   his mer -cy.

May God have pity on us and bless us;
  may he let his face shine upon us.

So may your way be known upon earth;
  among all nations, your salvation.

℟. **May God bless us in his mercy.**

May the nations be glad and exult
  because you rule the peoples in equity;
  the nations on the earth you guide.

℟. **May God bless us in his mercy.**

May the peoples praise you, O God;
  may all the peoples praise you!
May God bless us,
  and may all the ends of the earth fear him!

℟. **May God bless us in his mercy.** ↓

SECOND READING Gal 4:4-7   [Heirs by God's Design]

  **God sent Jesus, his Son, born of Mary, to deliver all from
  the bondage of sin and slavery of the law. By God's choice
  we are heirs of heaven.**

A reading from the Letter of Saint Paul to the Galatians

B‍ROTHERS and sisters: When the fullness of time
  had come, God sent his Son, born of a woman,
born under the law, to ransom those under the law, so
that we might receive adoption as sons. As proof that
you are sons, God sent the Spirit of his Son into our
hearts, crying out, "Abba, Father!" So you are no
longer a slave but a son, and if a son then also an heir,
through God.—The word of the Lord. ℟. **Thanks be to
God.** ↓

ALLELUIA Heb 1:1-2   [God Speaks]

℟. **Alleluia, alleluia.**
In the past God spoke to our ancestors through the
  prophets;
in these last days, he has spoken to us through the Son.
℟. **Alleluia, alleluia.** ↓

GOSPEL Lk 2:16-21   [The Name of Jesus]

When the shepherds came to Bethlehem, they began to understand the message of the angels. Mary prayed about this great event. Jesus received his name according to the Jewish ritual of circumcision.

℣. The Lord be with you. ℟. **And also with you.**
✛ A reading from the holy Gospel according to Luke.
℟. **Glory to you, Lord.**

THE shepherds went in haste to Bethlehem and found Mary and Joseph, and the infant lying in the manger. When they saw this, they made known the message that had been told them about this child. All who heard it were amazed by what had been told them by the shepherds. And Mary kept all these things, reflecting on them in her heart. Then the shepherds returned, glorifying and praising God for all they had heard and seen, just as it had been told to them. When eight days were completed for his circumcision, he was named Jesus, the name given him by the angel before he was conceived in the womb.— The Gospel of the Lord. ℟. **Praise to you, Lord Jesus Christ.**   → No. 14, p. 18

PRAYER OVER THE GIFTS   [Salvation Fulfilled]

God our Father,
we celebrate at this season
the beginning of our salvation.
On this feast of Mary, the Mother of God,
we ask that our salvation
will be brought to its fulfillment.
We ask this through Christ our Lord. ℟. **Amen.** ↓

PREFACE (P 56)   [Mary, Virgin and Mother]

℣. The Lord be with you. ℟. **And also with you.**
℣. Lift up your hearts. ℟. **We lift them up to the Lord.**
℣. Let us give thanks to the Lord our God. ℟. **It is right to give him thanks and praise.**

Father, all-powerful and ever-living God,
we do well always and everywhere to give you thanks
(as we celebrate . . . of the Blessed Virgin Mary).
Through the power of the Holy Spirit,
she became the virgin mother of your only Son,
our Lord Jesus Christ,
who is for ever the light of the world.
Through him the choirs of angels
and all the powers of heaven
praise and worship your glory.
May our voices blend with theirs
as we join in their unending hymn: ➜ No. 23, p. 23

When Eucharistic Prayer I is used, the special Christmas
form of In union with the whole Church *is said.*

COMMUNION ANT. Heb 13:18   [Jesus Forever]

Jesus Christ is the same yesterday, today, and for ever. ↓

PRAYER AFTER COMMUNION   [Mother of the Church]

Father,
as we proclaim the Virgin Mary
to be the mother of Christ and the mother of the
    Church,
may our communion with her Son
bring us to salvation.
We ask this through Christ our Lord.
℟. **Amen.**   ➜ No. 32, p. 70

Optional Solemn Blessings, p. 92, and Prayers Over the People, p. 99

"They prostrated themselves and did him homage."

JANUARY 5

EPIPHANY OF THE LORD

ENTRANCE ANT. See Mal 3:1; 1 Chr 29:12   **[Lord and Ruler]**

The Lord and ruler is coming; kingship is his, and government and power.   → No. 2, p. 10

OPENING PRAYER   **[Light of Faith]**

Let us pray
  [that we will be guided by the light of faith]
Father,
you revealed your Son to the nations
by the guidance of a star.
Lead us to your glory in heaven
by the light of faith.
We ask this through our Lord Jesus Christ, your Son,
who lives and reigns with you and the Holy Spirit,
one God, for ever and ever. ℟. **Amen.** ↓

ALTERNATIVE OPENING PRAYER   **[God's Love Is Near]**

Let us pray
  [grateful for the glory revealed today
   through God made man]
Father of light, unchanging God,
today you reveal to men of faith

the resplendent fact of the Word made flesh.
Your light is strong,
your love is near;
draw us beyond the limits which this world imposes,
to the life where your Spirit makes all life complete.
We ask this through Christ our Lord. ℟. **Amen.** ↓

FIRST READING Is 60:1-6   [Glory of God's Church]

> Jerusalem is favored by the Lord. Kings and peoples will
> come before you. The riches of the earth will be placed at
> the gates of Jerusalem.

A reading from the Book of the Prophet Isaiah

RISE up in splendor, Jerusalem! Your light has
come,
   the glory of the Lord shines upon you.
See, darkness covers the earth,
   and thick clouds cover the peoples;
but upon you the LORD shines,
   and over you appears his glory.
Nations shall walk by your light,
   and kings by your shining radiance.
Raise your eyes and look about;
   they all gather and come to you:
your sons come from afar,
   and your daughters in the arms of their nurses.

Then you shall be radiant at what you see,
   your heart shall throb and overflow,
for the riches of the sea shall be emptied out before
   you,
   the wealth of nations shall be brought to you.
Caravans of camels shall fill you,
   dromedaries from Midian and Ephah;
all from Sheba shall come
   bearing gold and frankincense,
   and proclaiming the praises of the LORD.
The word of the Lord. ℟. **Thanks be to God.** ↓

RESPONSORIAL PSALM Ps 72   [The Messiah-King]

℟. Lord,   every   nation   on   earth   will adore you.

O God, with your judgment endow the king,
   and with your justice, the king's son;
he shall govern your people with justice
   and your afflicted ones with judgment.

℟. **Lord, every nation on earth will adore you.**

Justice shall flower in his days,
   and profound peace, till the moon be no more.
May he rule from sea to sea,
   and from the River to the ends of the earth.

℟. **Lord, every nation on earth will adore you.**

The kings of Tarshish and the Isles shall offer gifts;
   the kings of Arabia and Seba shall bring tribute.
All kings shall pay him homage,
   all nations shall serve him.

℟. **Lord, every nation on earth will adore you.**

For he shall rescue the poor man when he cries out,
   and the afflicted when he has no one to help him.
He shall have pity for the lowly and the poor;
   the lives of the poor he shall save.

℟. **Lord, every nation on earth will adore you.** ↓

SECOND READING Eph 3:2-3a, 5-6   [Good News for All]

**Paul admits that God has revealed the divine plan of salva-
tion to him. Not only the Jews, but also the whole Gentile
world, will share in the Good News.**

A reading from the Letter of Saint Paul to the Ephesians

BROTHERS and sisters: You have heard of the
stewardship of God's grace that was given to me
for your benefit, namely, that the mystery was made

known to me by revelation. It was not made known to people in other generations as it has now been revealed to his holy apostles and prophets by the Spirit: that the Gentiles are coheirs, members of the same body, and copartners in the promise in Christ Jesus through the gospel.—The word of the Lord. ℟. **Thanks be to God.** ↓

ALLELUIA Mt 2:2   [Leading Star]

℟. **Alleluia, alleluia.**
We saw his star at its rising
and have come to do him homage.
℟. **Alleluia, alleluia.** ↓

GOSPEL Mt 2:1-12   [Magi with Gifts]

King Herod, being jealous of his earthly crown, was threatened by the coming of another king. The astrologers from the east followed the star to Bethlehem from which a ruler was to come.

℣. The Lord be with you. ℟. **And also with you.**
✠ A reading from the holy Gospel according to Matthew. ℟. **Glory to you, Lord.**

WHEN Jesus was born in Bethlehem of Judea, in the days of King Herod, behold, magi from the east arrived in Jerusalem, saying, "Where is the newborn king of the Jews? We saw his star at its rising and have come to do him homage." When King Herod heard this, he was greatly troubled, and all Jerusalem with him. Assembling all the chief priests and the scribes of the people, he inquired of them where the Christ was to be born. They said to him, "In Bethlehem of Judea, for thus it has been written through the prophet:

And you, Bethlehem, land of Judah,
    are by no means least among the rulers of Judah;
since from you shall come a ruler,

who is to shepherd my people Israel."
Then Herod called the magi secretly and ascertained
from them the time of the star's appearance. He sent
them to Bethlehem and said, "Go and search diligently
for the child. When you have found him, bring me
word, that I too may go and do him homage." After
their audience with the king they set out. And behold,
the star that they had seen at its rising preceded them,
until it came and stopped over the place where the
child was. They were overjoyed at seeing the star, and
on entering the house they saw the child with Mary
his mother. They prostrated themselves and did him
homage. Then they opened their treasures and offered
him gifts of gold, frankincense, and myrrh. And having been warned in a dream not to return to Herod,
they departed for their country by another way.—The
Gospel of the Lord. ℟. **Praise to you, Lord Jesus
Christ.**
→ No. 14, p. 18

PRAYER OVER THE GIFTS [Offering of Jesus]
Lord,
accept the offerings of your Church,
not gold, frankincense and myrrh,
but the sacrifice and food they symbolize:
Jesus Christ, who is Lord for ever and ever.
℟. **Amen.** ↓

PREFACE (P 6) [Jesus Revealed to All]
℣. The Lord be with you. ℟. **And also with you.**
℣. Lift up your hearts. ℟. **We lift them up to the Lord.**
℣. Let us give thanks to the Lord our God. ℟. **It is right
to give him thanks and praise.**

Father, all-powerful and ever-living God,
we do well always and everywhere to give you thanks.
Today you revealed in Christ your eternal plan of salvation
and showed him as the light of all peoples.

Now that his glory has shone among us
you have renewed humanity in his immortal image.
Now, with angels and archangels,
and the whole company of heaven,
we sing the unending hymn of your praise:

→ No. 23, p. 23

*When Eucharistic Prayer I is used, the special Epiphany
form of* In union with the whole Church *is said.*

COMMUNION ANT. See Mt 2:2   [Adore the Lord]

**We have seen his star in the east, and have come with
gifts to adore the Lord.** ↓

PRAYER AFTER COMMUNION   [Christ in the Eucharist]

Father,
guide us with your light.
Help us to recognize Christ in this eucharist
and welcome him with love,
for he is Lord for ever and ever.
℞. **Amen.**   → No. 32, p. 70

Optional Solemn Blessings, p. 92, and Prayers Over the People, p. 99

"You are my beloved Son; with you I am well pleased."

JANUARY 12

BAPTISM OF THE LORD

ENTRANCE ANT. See Mt 3:16-17   **[Beloved Son]**

When the Lord had been baptized, the heavens opened, and the Spirit came down like a dove to rest on him. Then the voice of the Father thundered: This is my beloved Son, with him I am well pleased.

→ No. 2, p. 10

OPENING PRAYER   **[Faithful to Our Baptism]**

Let us pray
   [that we will be faithful to our baptism]
Almighty, eternal God,
when the Spirit descended upon Jesus
at his baptism in the Jordan,
you revealed him as your own beloved Son.
Keep us, your children born of water and the Spirit,
faithful to our calling.
We ask this . . . for ever and ever. ℟. **Amen.** ↓

OR   **[God Became Man]**

Father,
your only Son revealed himself to us by becoming man.

162

May we who share his humanity
come to share his divinity,
for he lives and reigns with you and the Holy Spirit,
one God, for ever and ever. ℟. **Amen.** ↓

ALTERNATIVE OPENING PRAYER   [Radiating Christ]

Let us pray
    [as we listen to the voice of God's Spirit]
Father in heaven,
you revealed Christ as your Son
by the voice that spoke over the waters of the Jordan.
May all who share in the sonship of Christ
follow in his path of service to man,
and reflect the glory of his kingdom
even to the ends of the earth,
for he is Lord for ever and ever. ℟. **Amen.** ↓

*The following readings (except the Gospel) are optional. In
their place, the readings for Year A, pp. 168-170, may be used.*

FIRST READING Is 55:1-11   [Called through Baptism]

**The "water" stands for Baptism but also for the word of
God. Both will give us strength to keep moving, especially
if we make use of daily Bible readings.**

A reading from the Book of the Prophet Isaiah

THUS says the LORD:
    All you who are thirsty,
    come to the water!
You who have no money,
    come, receive grain and eat;
come, without paying and without cost,
    drink wine and milk!
Why spend your money for what is not bread,
    your wages for what fails to satisfy?
Heed me, and you shall eat well,
    you shall delight in rich fare.

Come to me heedfully,
  listen, that you may have life.
I will renew with you the everlasting covenant,
  the benefits assured to David.
As I made him a witness to the peoples,
  a leader and commander of nations,
so shall you summon a nation you knew not,
  and nations that knew you not shall run to you,
because of the LORD, your God,
  the Holy One of Israel, who has glorified you.

Seek the LORD while he may be found,
  call him while he is near.
Let the scoundrel forsake his way,
  and the wicked man his thoughts;
let him turn to the LORD for mercy;
  to our God, who is generous in forgiving.
For my thoughts are not your thoughts,
  nor are your ways my ways, says the LORD.
As high as the heavens are above the earth
  so high are my ways above your ways
  and my thoughts above your thoughts.

For just as from the heavens
  the rain and snow come down
and do not return there
  till they have watered the earth,
  making it fertile and fruitful,
giving seed to the one who sows
  and bread to the one who eats,
so shall my word be
  that goes forth from my mouth;
my word shall not return to me void,
  but shall do my will,
  achieving the end for which I sent it.
The word of the Lord. ℟. **Thanks be to God.** ↓

RESPONSORIAL PSALM Is 12   [Sing for Joy]

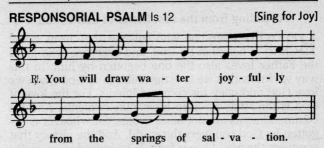

℟. You will draw water joyfully from the springs of salvation.

God indeed is my savior;
    I am confident and unafraid.
My strength and my courage is the LORD,
    and he has been my savior.
With joy you will draw water
    at the fountain of salvation.

℟. **You will draw water joyfully from the springs of salvation.**

Give thanks to the LORD, acclaim his name;
    among the nations make known his deeds,
    proclaim how exalted is his name.

℟. **You will draw water joyfully from the springs of salvation.**

Sing praise to the LORD for his glorious achievement;
    let this be known throughout all the earth.
Shout with exultation, O city of Zion,
    for great in your midst
    is the Holy One of Israel!

℟. **You will draw water joyfully from the springs of salvation.** ↓

SECOND READING 1 Jn 5:1-9   [Born of God]

At baptism, we had the love of God placed in us as in a seed, and it bore fruit both vertically and horizontally toward God and neighbor. If we practice our faith by keeping the commandments, we end up victors over the world.

A reading from the first Letter of Saint John

BELOVED: Everyone who believes that Jesus is the Christ is begotten by God, and everyone who loves the Father loves also the one begotten by him. In this way we know that we love the children of God when we love God and obey his commandments. For the love of God is this, that we keep his commandments. And his commandments are not burdensome, for whoever is begotten by God conquers the world. And the victory that conquers the world is our faith. Who indeed is the victor over the world but the one who believes that Jesus is the Son of God?

This is the one who came through water and blood, Jesus Christ, not by water alone, but by water and blood. The Spirit is the one who testifies, and the Spirit is truth. So there are three that testify, the Spirit, the water, and the blood, and the three are of one accord. If we accept human testimony, the testimony of God is surely greater. Now the testimony of God is this, that he has testified on behalf of his Son.—The word of the Lord. ℞. **Thanks be to God.** ↓

ALLELUIA Cf. Jn 1:29   [The Lamb of God]

℞. **Alleluia, alleluia.**

John saw Jesus approaching him, and said:

Behold the Lamb of God who takes away the sin of the world.

℞. **Alleluia, alleluia.** ↓

GOSPEL Mk 1:7-11   [Beloved Son]

The Spirit of God is seen coming upon Christ. The words of Isaiah are beginning to be fulfilled.

℣. The Lord be with you. ℞. **And also with you.**

✝ A reading from the holy Gospel according to Mark.

℞. **Glory to you, Lord.**

THIS is what John the Baptist proclaimed: "One mightier than I is coming after me. I am not worthy to stoop and loosen the thongs of his sandals. I have baptized you with water; he will baptize you with the Holy Spirit."

It happened in those days that Jesus came from Nazareth of Galilee and was baptized in the Jordan by John. On coming up out of the water he saw the heavens being torn open and the Spirit, like a dove, descending upon him. And a voice came from the heavens, "You are my beloved Son; with you I am well pleased."—The Gospel of the Lord. ℟. **Praise to you, Lord Jesus Christ.**

→ No. 14, p. 18

PRAYER OVER THE GIFTS   [Christ's Revelation]

Lord,
we celebrate the revelation of Christ your Son
who takes away the sins of the world.
Accept our gifts
and let them become one with his sacrifice,
for he is Lord for ever and ever. ℟. **Amen.** ↓

PREFACE (P 7)   [New Gift of Baptism]

℣. The Lord be with you. ℟. **And also with you.**
℣. Lift up your hearts. ℟. **We lift them up to the Lord.**
℣. Let us give thanks to the Lord our God. ℟. **It is right to give him thanks and praise.**

Father, all-powerful and ever-living God,
we do well always and everywhere to give you thanks.
You celebrated your new gift of baptism
by signs and wonders at the Jordan.
Your voice was heard from heaven
to awaken faith in the presence among us
of the Word made man.
Your Spirit was seen as a dove,
revealing Jesus as your servant,
and anointing him with joy as the Christ,
sent to bring to the poor

the good news of salvation.
In our unending joy we echo on earth
the song of the angels in heaven
as they praise your glory for ever: → No. 23, p. 23

COMMUNION ANT. Jn 1:32, 34   [Witness to God's Son]

**This is he of whom John said: I have seen and have
given witness that this is the Son of God.** ↓

PRAYER AFTER COMMUNION   [Children in Fact]

Lord,
you feed us with bread from heaven.
May we hear your Son with faith
and become your children in name and in fact.
We ask this in the name of Jesus the Lord.
℟. **Amen.**   → No. 32, p. 70

Optional Solemn Blessings, p. 92, and Prayers Over the People, p. 99

─────────────

*The following readings (except the Gospel) from Year A may
be used in place of the optional ones given on pp. 163-167.*

FIRST READING Is 42:1-4, 6-7   [Works of the Messiah]

The prophet Isaiah sees the spirit upon the Lord's servant
who will proclaim the "good news" to the poor, freedom
to prisoners and joy to those in sorrow.

A reading from the Book of the Prophet Isaiah

HERE is my servant whom I uphold,
my chosen one with whom I am pleased,
upon whom I have put my spirit;
he shall bring forth justice to the nations,
not crying out, not shouting,
not making his voice heard in the street.
A bruised reed he shall not break,
and a smoldering wick he shall not quench,
until he establishes justice on the earth;

the coastlands will wait for his teaching.

I, the LORD, have called you for the victory of justice,
    I have grasped you, by the hand;
I formed you, and set you
    as a covenant of the people,
    a light for the nations,
to open the eyes of the blind,
    to bring out prisoners from confinement,
    and from the dungeon, those who live in darkness.
The word of the Lord. ℟. **Thanks be to God.** ↓

RESPONSORIAL PSALM Ps 29   [Peace for God's People]

℟. The   Lord   will   bless   his   peo-ple with peace.

Give to the LORD, you sons of God,
    give to the LORD glory and praise,
give to the LORD the glory due his name;
    adore the LORD in holy attire.

℟. **The Lord will bless his people with peace.**

The voice of the LORD is over the waters,
    the LORD, over vast waters.
The voice of the LORD is mighty;
    the voice of the LORD is majestic.

℟. **The Lord will bless his people with peace.**

The God of glory thunders,
    and in his temple all say, "Glory!"
The LORD is enthroned above the flood;
    the LORD is enthroned as king forever.

℟. **The Lord will bless his people with peace.** ↓

SECOND READING Acts 10:34-38   [Anointed to Do Good]
    God anointed Jesus the Savior with the Holy Spirit and
    power. Jesus is the Lord of all, and he brought healing to
    all who were in the grip of the devil.

A reading from the Acts of the Apostles

PETER proceeded to speak to those gathered in the house of Cornelius, saying: "In truth, I see that God shows no partiality. Rather, in every nation whoever fears him and acts uprightly is acceptable to him. You know the word that he sent to the Israelites as he proclaimed peace through Jesus Christ, who is Lord of all, what has happened all over Judea, beginning in Galilee after the baptism that John preached, how God anointed Jesus of Nazareth with the Holy Spirit and power. He went about doing good and healing all those oppressed by the devil, for God was with him."—The word of the Lord. ℟. **Thanks be to God.** ↓

ALLELUIA Cf. Mk 9:7   [Hear Him]
℟. **Alleluia, alleluia.**
The heavens were opened and the voice of the Father thundered:
This is my beloved Son, listen to him.
℟. **Alleluia, alleluia.**

"Behold, the Lamb of God!"

JANUARY 19

2nd SUNDAY IN ORDINARY TIME

ENTRANCE ANT. Ps 66:4   [Proclaim His Glory]

May all the earth give you worship and praise, and
break into song to your name, O God, Most High.

→ No. 2, p. 10

OPENING PRAYER   [Peace in the World]

Let us pray
    [to our Father for the gift of peace]
Father of heaven and earth,
hear our prayers,
and show us the way to peace in the world.
Grant this through our Lord Jesus Christ, your Son,
who lives and reigns with you and the Holy Spirit,
one God, for ever and ever. ℟. **Amen.** ↓

ALTERNATIVE OPENING PRAYER
                              [Reflecting God's Peace]

Let us pray
    [for the gift of peace]

171

Almighty and ever-present Father,
your watchful care reaches from end to end
and orders all things in such power
that even the tensions and the tragedies of sin
cannot frustrate your loving plans.
Help us to embrace your will,
give us the strength to follow your call,
so that your truth may live in our hearts
and reflect peace to those who believe in your love.
We ask this through Christ our Lord. ℟. **Amen.** ↓

FIRST READING 1 Sm 3:3b-10, 19   [Answering God's Call]

**The Lord called Samuel, but he did not recognize him.
Samuel receives advice from Eli, who is already a prophet
for the Lord. Following instructions from Eli, Samuel listens
to the Lord.**

A reading from the first Book of Samuel

SAMUEL was sleeping in the temple of the LORD
where the ark of God was. The LORD called to
Samuel, who answered, "Here I am." Samuel ran to Eli
and said, "Here I am. You called me." "I did not call
you," Eli said. "Go back to sleep." So he went back to
sleep. Again the LORD called Samuel, who rose and
went to Eli. "Here I am," he said. "You called me." But
Eli answered, "I did not call you, my son. Go back to
sleep."

At that time Samuel was not familiar with the LORD,
because the LORD had not revealed anything to him as
yet. The LORD called Samuel again, for the third time.
Getting up and going to Eli, he said, "Here I am. You
called me." Then Eli understood that the LORD was
calling the youth. So he said to Samuel, "Go to sleep,
and if you are called, reply, 'Speak, LORD, for your servant is listening.'" When Samuel went to sleep in his
place, the LORD came and revealed his presence, calling out as before, "Samuel, Samuel!" Samuel answered, "Speak, for your servant is listening."

Samuel grew up, and the LORD was with him, not permitting any word of his to be without effect.—The word of the Lord. ℟. **Thanks be to God.** ↓

RESPONSORIAL PSALM Ps 40   [Doing God's Will]

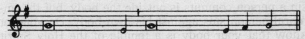

℟. **Here am I, Lord;   I   come   to do your will.**

I have waited, waited for the LORD,
    and he stooped toward me and heard my cry.
And he put a new song into my mouth,
    a hymn to our God.

℟. **Here am I, Lord; I come to do your will.**

Sacrifice or offering you wished not,
    but ears open to obedience you gave me.
Holocausts or sin-offerings you sought not;
    then said I, "Behold I come."

℟. **Here am I, Lord; I come to do your will.**

"In the written scroll it is prescribed for me,
to do your will, O my God, is my delight,
    and your law is within my heart!"

℟. **Here am I, Lord; I come to do your will.**

I announced your justice in the vast assembly;
    I did not restrain my lips, as you, O LORD, know.

℟. **Here am I, Lord; I come to do your will.** ↓

SECOND READING 1 Cor 6:13c-15a, 17-20 [The Spirit in Us]

> The body is made for the Lord. With the price of the Cross, Jesus redeemed all humanity. The Holy Spirit dwells within each person.

A reading from the first Letter of Saint Paul
to the Corinthians

BROTHERS and sisters: The body is not for immorality, but for the Lord, and the Lord is for the body; God raised the Lord and will also raise us by his power.

Do you not know that your bodies are members of Christ? But whoever is joined to the Lord becomes one Spirit with him. Avoid immorality. Every other sin a person commits is outside the body, but the immoral person sins against his own body. Do you not know that your body is a temple of the Holy Spirit within you, whom you have from God, and that you are not your own? For you have been purchased at a price. Therefore glorify God in your body.—The word of the Lord. ℟. **Thanks be to God.** ↓

ALLELUIA Jn 1:41, 17b   [The Messiah]

℟. **Alleluia, alleluia.**
We have found the Messiah:
Jesus Christ, who brings us truth and grace.
℟. **Alleluia, alleluia.** ↓

In place of the Alleluia given for each Sunday in Ordinary Time, another may be selected.

GOSPEL Jn 1:35-42   [Encountering Christ]

It was John the Baptist's purpose to point out Jesus, the Messiah. Andrew and his companion followed Jesus. Andrew summons Peter. Jesus identifies Peter and gives him a new name.

℣. The Lord be with you. ℟. **And also with you.**
✠ A reading from the holy Gospel according to John.
℟. **Glory to you, Lord.**

JOHN was standing with two of his disciples, and as he watched Jesus walk by, he said, "Behold, the Lamb of God." The two disciples heard what he said and followed Jesus. Jesus turned and saw them following him and said to them, "What are you looking for?" They said to him, "Rabbi"—which translated means Teacher—, "where are you staying?" He said to

them, "Come, and you will see." So they went and saw where Jesus was staying, and they stayed with him that day. It was about four in the afternoon. Andrew, the brother of Simon Peter, was one of the two who heard John and followed Jesus. He first found his own brother Simon and told him, "We have found the Messiah"—which is translated Christ. Then he brought him to Jesus. Jesus looked at him and said, "You are Simon the son of John; you will be called Cephas"—which is translated Peter.—The Gospel of the Lord. ℟.
Praise to you, Lord Jesus Christ.   ➜ No. 14, p. 18

PRAYER OVER THE GIFTS   [Work of Salvation]

Father,
may we celebrate the eucharist
with reverence and love,
for when we proclaim the death of the Lord
you continue the work of his redemption,
who is Lord for ever and ever.
℟. **Amen.**   ➜ No. 21, p. 22 (Pref. P 29-36)

COMMUNION ANT. Ps 23:5   [A Feast for Me]

The Lord has prepared a feast for me: given wine in plenty for me to drink. ↓

OR 1 Jn 4:16   [God's Love]

We know and believe in God's love for us. ↓

PRAYER AFTER COMMUNION   [One in Love]

Lord,
you have nourished us with bread from heaven.
Fill us with your Spirit,
and make us one in peace and love.
We ask this through Christ our Lord.
℟. **Amen.**   ➜ No. 32, p. 70

Optional Solemn Blessings, p. 92, and Prayers Over the People, p. 99

"Come after me, and I will make you fishers of men."

JANUARY 26

3rd SUNDAY IN ORDINARY TIME

ENTRANCE ANT. Ps 96:1, 6   **[Sing to the Lord]**

Sing a new song to the Lord! Sing to the Lord, all the earth. Truth and beauty surround him, he lives in holiness and glory.   → No. 2, p. 10

OPENING PRAYER   **[Working for Unity]**

Let us pray
    [for unity and peace]
All-powerful and ever-living God,
direct your love that is within us,
that our efforts in the name of your Son
may bring mankind to unity and peace.
We ask this through our Lord Jesus Christ, your Son,
who lives and reigns with you and the Holy Spirit,
one God, for ever and ever. ℟. **Amen.** ↓

ALTERNATIVE OPENING PRAYER   **[Vision of God]**

Let us pray
    [pleading that our vision
      may overcome our weakness]

Almighty Father,
the love you offer
always exceeds the furthest expression of our human
    longing,
for you are greater than the human heart.
Direct each thought, each effort of our life,
so that the limits of our faults and weaknesses
may not obscure the vision of your glory
or keep us from the peace you have promised.
We ask this through Christ our Lord. ℟. **Amen.** ↓

FIRST READING Jon 3:1-5, 10   [God's Mercy for All]

**The mercy of God is shown to the people of Nineveh. He
sends Jonah to Nineveh to preach penance for sin. The
king proclaims a universal fast to appease the Lord.**

A reading from the Book of the Prophet Jonah

THE word of the LORD came to Jonah, saying: "Set
out for the great city of Nineveh, and announce to
it the message that I will tell you." So Jonah made
ready and went to Nineveh, according to the LORD's
bidding. Now Nineveh was an enormously large city;
it took three days to go through it. Jonah began his
journey through the city, and had gone but a single
day's walk announcing, "Forty days more and Nineveh shall be destroyed," when the people of Nineveh
believed God; they proclaimed a fast and all of them,
great and small, put on sackcloth.

    When God saw by their actions how they turned
from their evil way, he repented of the evil that he had
threatened to do to them; he did not carry it out.—The
word of the Lord. ℟. **Thanks be to God.** ↓

RESPONSORIAL PSALM Ps 25   [God's Ways]

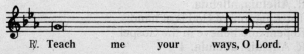

℟. **Teach   me   your   ways, O Lord.**

Your ways, O LORD, make known to me;
  teach me your paths,
guide me in your truth and teach me,
  for you are God my savior.

℟. **Teach me your ways, O Lord.**

Remember that your compassion, O LORD,
  and your love are from of old.
In your kindness remember me,
  because of your goodness, O LORD.

℟. **Teach me your ways, O Lord.**

Good and upright is the LORD;
  thus he shows sinners the way.
He guides the humble to justice,
  he teaches the humble his way.

℟. **Teach me your ways, O Lord.** ↓

SECOND READING 1 Cor 7:29-31   [Shortness of Time]

Paul warns the Corinthians of the shortness of time in this
world. All must conduct themselves worthily in the eyes of
God and be detached from this world's pleasure.

A reading from the first Letter of Saint Paul
to the Corinthians

I TELL you, brothers and sisters, the time is running
out. From now on, let those having wives act as not
having them, those weeping as not weeping, those rejoicing as not rejoicing, those buying as not owning,
those using the world as not using it fully. For the
world in its present form is passing away.—The word
of the Lord. ℟. **Thanks be to God.** ↓

ALLELUIA Mk 1:15   [Repent and Believe]

℟. **Alleluia, alleluia.**
The kingdom of God is at hand.
Repent and believe in the Gospel.
℟. **Alleluia, alleluia.** ↓

GOSPEL Mk 1:14-20   [Come After Me]

Jesus began to preach the "good news" of salvation. He
called Simon and Andrew, James and John, to follow him.
At once, they accepted the call to become "fishers of men."

℣. The Lord be with you. ℟. **And also with you.**
✠ A reading from the holy Gospel according to Mark.
℟. **Glory to you, Lord.**

A FTER John had been arrested, Jesus came to
 Galilee proclaiming the gospel of God: "This is the
time of fulfillment. The kingdom of God is at hand.
Repent, and believe in the gospel."

As he passed by the Sea of Galilee, he saw Simon
and his brother Andrew casting their nets into the sea;
they were fishermen. Jesus said to them, "Come after
me, and I will make you fishers of men." Then they
abandoned their nets and followed him. He walked
along a little farther and saw James, the son of
Zebedee, and his brother John. They too were in a
boat mending their nets. Then he called them. So they
left their father Zebedee in the boat along with the
hired men and followed him.—The Gospel of the Lord.
℟. **Praise to you, Lord Jesus Christ.**   ➔ No. 14, p. 18

PRAYER OVER THE GIFTS   [Offerings of Salvation]

Lord,
receive our gifts.
Let our offerings make us holy
and bring us salvation.
Grant this through Christ our Lord.
℟. **Amen.**   ➔ No. 21, p. 22 (Pref. P 29-36)

COMMUNION ANT. Ps 34:6   [Gladness]
**Look up at the Lord with gladness and smile; your
face will never be ashamed.** ↓

OR Jn 8:12   [Light of Life]

**I am the light of the world, says the Lord; the man
who follows me will have the light of life.** ↓

PRAYER AFTER COMMUNION   [New Life]

God, all-powerful Father,
may the new life you give us increase our love
and keep us in the joy of your kingdom.
We ask this in the name of Jesus the Lord.
℟. **Amen.**   → No. 32, p. 70

Optional Solemn Blessings, p. 92, and Prayers Over the People, p. 99

"This child is destined for the fall and rise of many in Israel."

FEBRUARY 2

PRESENTATION OF THE LORD
(4th SUNDAY IN ORDINARY TIME)

BLESSING OF CANDLES AND PROCESSION
First Form: Procession

*The people gather in a chapel or other suitable place outside
the church where the Mass will be celebrated. They carry unlighted candles.*

*While the candles are being lighted, this canticle or another
hymn is sung:*

[The Lord's Light]

The Lord will come with mighty power, and give light to the eyes of all who serve him, alleluia.

The priest greets the people as usual, and briefly invites the people to take an active part in this celebration. He may use these or similar words:

[Welcoming Christ]

Forty days ago we celebrated the joyful feast of the birth of our Lord Jesus Christ. Today we recall the holy day on which he was presented in the temple, fulfilling the law of Moses and at the same time going to meet his faithful people. Led by the Spirit, Simeon and Anna came to the temple, recognized Christ as their Lord, and proclaimed him with joy.

United by the Spirit, may we now go to the house of God to welcome Christ the Lord. There we shall recognize him in the breaking of bread until he comes again in glory.

Then the priest joins his hands and blesses the candles:

[Light to the Nations]

Let us pray.
God our Father, source of all light,
today you revealed to Simeon
your Light of revelation to the nations.
Bless ✜ these candles and make them holy.
May we who carry them to praise your glory
walk in the path of goodness
and come to the light that shines for ever.
Grant this through Christ our Lord. ℟. **Amen.** ↓

OR   [Light of Glory]

Let us pray.
God our Father, source of eternal light,
fill the hearts of all believers
with the light of faith.
May we who carry these candles in your church

come with joy to the light of glory.
We ask this through Christ our Lord. ℟. **Amen.** ↓

He sprinkles the candles in silence.

The priest then takes the candle prepared for him, and the procession begins with the acclamation:

Let us go in peace to meet the Lord.

During the procession, the following canticle or another hymn is sung:

ANTIPHON   [The Glory of Israel]
Christ is the light of the nations
and the glory of Israel his people.

CANTICLE   [God's Salvation]
Now, Lord, you have kept your word:
let your servant go in peace.

The Antiphon is repeated: "Christ is the light, etc."

With my own eyes I have seen the salvation
which you have prepared in the sight of every people.

The Antiphon is repeated: "Christ is the light, etc."

A light to reveal you to the nations
and the glory of your people Israel.

The Antiphon is repeated: "Christ is the light, etc."

As the procession enters the church, the Entrance Song of the Mass is sung. When the priest reaches the altar, he venerates it, and may incense it. Then he goes to the chair (and replaces the cope with the chasuble). After the Gloria, he sings or says the Opening Prayer. The Mass continues as usual.

Second Form: Solemn Entrance

The people, carrying unlighted candles, assemble in the church. The priest, vested in white, is accompanied by his ministers and by a representative group of the faithful. They go to a suitable place (either in front of the door or in the church itself) where most of the congregation can easily take part.

Then the candles are lighted while the antiphon, The Lord will come, *or another hymn is sung.*

After the greeting and introduction, he blesses the candles, as above, and goes in procession to the altar, while all are singing. The Mass is as described above.

THE MASS

ENTRANCE ANT. Ps 48:10-11   [God's Loving Kindness]

Within your temple we ponder your loving kindness, O God. As your praise reaches to the ends of the earth, your right hand is filled with justice.

➜ No. 2, p. 10

OPENING PRAYER   [Led into God's Presence]

All-powerful Father,
Christ your Son became man for us
and was presented in the temple.
May he free our hearts from sin
and bring us into your presence.
We ask this through our Lord Jesus Christ, your Son,
who lives and reigns with you and the Holy Spirit,
one God, for ever and ever. ℟. **Amen.** ↓

FIRST READING Mal 3:1-4   [With Purified Hearts]

Malachi speaks of God's great intervention in sacred history—God's speaking to the patriarch (Gn 16, 7ff), and to Moses (Ex 3, 2), and God's leading the way through the Red Sea (Ex 23, 20). These wondrous ways in which God is manifested will be applied to messianic messengers.

A reading from the Book of the Prophet Malachi

THUS says the Lord God:
Lo, I am sending my messenger
to prepare the way before me;
and suddenly there will come to the temple
the LORD whom you seek,
and the messenger of the covenant whom you desire.
Yes, he is coming, says the LORD of hosts.

But who will endure the day of his coming?
And who can stand when he appears?
For he is like the refiner's fire,
or like the fuller's lye.
He will sit refining and purifying silver,
and he will purify the sons of Levi,
refining them like gold or like silver
that they may offer due sacrifice to the LORD.
Then the sacrifice of Judah and Jerusalem
will please the LORD,
as in the days of old, as in years gone by.
The word of the Lord. ℟. **Thanks be to God.** ↓

RESPONSORIAL PSALM Ps 24   [The King of Glory]

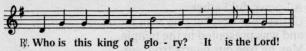

℟. **Who is this king of glo - ry?   It   is the Lord!**

Lift up, O gates, your lintels;
reach up, you ancient portals,
that the king of glory may come in!

℟. **Who is this king of glory?
It is the Lord!**

Who is this king of glory?
The LORD, strong and mighty,
the LORD, mighty in battle.

℟. **Who is this king of glory?
It is the Lord!**

Lift up, O gates, your lintels;
reach up, you ancient portals,
that the king of glory may come in!

℟. **Who is this king of glory?
It is the Lord!**

Who is this king of glory?
The LORD of hosts; he is the king of glory.

℞. **Who is this king of glory?**
   It is the Lord! ↓

SECOND READING Heb 2:14-18   [Christ Our Brother]

In the biblical sense, "flesh" means human nature considered in its weakness. It is contrasted with "spirit" and God. Because of the connection between sin and death, Christ overcame the power of death through his priestly work.

A reading from the Letter to the Hebrews

SINCE the children share in blood and flesh, Jesus likewise shared in them, that through death he might destroy the one who has the power of death, that is, the devil, and free those who through fear of death had been subject to slavery all their life. Surely he did not help angels but rather the descendants of Abraham; therefore, he had to become like his brothers and sisters in every way, that he might be a merciful and faithful high priest before God to expiate the sins of the people. Because he himself was tested through what he suffered, he is able to help those who are being tested.—The word of the Lord. ℞. **Thanks be to God.** ↓

ALLELUIA Lk 2:32   [Christ the Light]

℞. **Alleluia, alleluia.**
A light of revelation to the Gentiles
and glory for your people Israel.
℞. **Alleluia, alleluia.** ↓

GOSPEL Lk 2:22-40 or 2:22-32   [The Lord's Salvation]

Mary is seen here, united with Jesus and Joseph in the Temple ceremony. Jesus is formally recognized as a member of God's chosen people through whom world salvation was to be achieved.

[If the "Shorter Form" is used, the indented text in brackets is omitted.]

℣. The Lord be with you. ℟. **And also with you.**

✛ A reading from the holy Gospel according to Luke.
℟. **Glory to you, Lord.**

WHEN the days were completed for their purification according to the law of Moses, Mary and
Joseph took Jesus up to Jerusalem to present him to
the Lord, just as it is written in the law of the Lord,
*Every male that opens the womb shall be consecrated
to the Lord,* and to offer the sacrifice of *a pair of turtledoves or two young pigeons,* in accordance with the
dictate in the law of the Lord.

Now there was a man in Jerusalem whose name
was Simeon. This man was righteous and devout,
awaiting the consolation of Israel, and the Holy Spirit
was upon him. It had been revealed to him by the
Holy Spirit that he should not see death before he had
seen the Christ of the Lord. He came in the Spirit into
the temple; and when the parents brought in the child
Jesus to perform the custom of the law in regard to
him, he took him into his arms and blessed God, saying:

"Now, Master, you may let your servant go
    in peace, according to your word,
for my eyes have seen your salvation,
    which you prepared in sight of all the peoples,
a light for revelation to the Gentiles,
    and glory for your people Israel."

[The child's father and mother were amazed at
what was said about him; and Simeon blessed
them and said to Mary his mother, "Behold, this
child is destined for the fall and rise of many in
Israel, and to be a sign that will be contradicted—
and you yourself a sword will pierce—so that the
thoughts of many hearts may be revealed." There
was also a prophetess, Anna, the daughter of
Phanuel, of the tribe of Asher. She was advanced

in years, having lived seven years with her husband after her marriage, and then as a widow until she was eighty-four. She never left the temple, but worshiped night and day with fasting and prayer. And coming forward at that very time, she gave thanks to God and spoke about the child to all who were awaiting the redemption of Jerusalem.

When they had fulfilled all the prescriptions of the law of the Lord, they returned to Galilee, to their own town of Nazareth. The child grew and became strong, filled with wisdom; and the favor of God was upon him.]

The Gospel of the Lord. ℟. **Praise to you, Lord Jesus Christ.**   ➜ No. 14, p. 18

PRAYER OVER THE GIFTS   [Lamb without Blemish]

Lord,
accept the gifts your Church offers you with joy,
since in fulfillment of your will
your Son offered himself as a lamb without blemish
for the life of the world.
We ask this through Christ our Lord. ℟. **Amen.** ↓

PREFACE (P 49)   [Manifestation of Christ the Light]

℣. The Lord be with you. ℟. **And also with you.**
℣. Lift up your hearts. ℟. **We lift them up to the Lord.**
℣. Let us give thanks to the Lord our God. ℟. **It is right to give him thanks and praise.**

Father, all-powerful and ever-living God,
we do well always and everywhere to give you thanks
through Jesus Christ our Lord.
Today your Son,
who shares your eternal splendor,
was presented in the temple,
and revealed by the Spirit
as the glory of Israel

and the light of all peoples.
Our hearts are joyful,
for we have seen your salvation,
and now with the angels and saints
we praise you for ever: → No. 23, p. 23

COMMUNION ANT. Lk 2:30-31   [Sight of Salvation]
**With my own eyes I have seen the salvation which
you have prepared in the sight of all the nations.** ↓

PRAYER AFTER COMMUNION   [Preparing To Meet Christ]
Lord,
you fulfilled the hope of Simeon,
who did not die
until he had been privileged to welcome the Messiah.
May this communion perfect your grace in us
and prepare us to meet Christ
when he comes to bring us into everlasting life,
for he is Lord for ever and ever.
℞. **Amen.**   → No. 32, p. 70

Optional Solemn Blessings, p. 92, and Prayers Over the People, p. 99

"[Jesus] helped her . . . [and] the fever left her."

FEBRUARY 9

5th SUNDAY IN ORDINARY TIME

ENTRANCE ANT. Ps 95:6-7   **[Adoration]**

**Come, let us worship the Lord. Let us bow down in
the presence of our maker, for he is the Lord our God.**

→ No. 2, p. 10

OPENING PRAYER   **[God's Care]**

Let us pray

   [that God will watch over us and protect us]

Father,

watch over your family

and keep us safe in your care,

for all our hope is in you.

Grant this through our Lord Jesus Christ, your Son,

who lives and reigns with you and the Holy Spirit,

one God, for ever and ever. ℞. **Amen.** ↓

ALTERNATIVE OPENING PRAYER   **[God's Presence]**

Let us pray

   [with reverence in the presence of the living God]

In faith and love we ask you, Father,

to watch over your family gathered here.

189

In your mercy and loving kindness
no thought of ours is left unguarded,
no tear unheeded, no joy unnoticed.
Through the prayer of Jesus
may the blessings promised to the poor in spirit
lead us to the treasures of your heavenly kingdom.
We ask this in the name of Jesus the Lord. ℟. **Amen.** ↓

FIRST READING Jb 7:1-4, 6-7   [Life Is Fleeting]

Job describes our life on earth. The days of our life come to a swift end. However, we are heartened by the fuller revelation of an eternal life hereafter, which Christ brought to us and about which Job did not have a clear idea.

A reading from the Book of Job

JOB spoke, saying:
Is not man's life on earth a drudgery?
Are not his days those of a hireling?
He is a slave who longs for the shade,
    a hireling who waits for his wages.
So I have been assigned months of misery,
    and troubled nights have been allotted to me.
If in bed I say, "When shall I arise?"
    then the night drags on;
I am filled with restlessness until the dawn.
My days are swifter than a weaver's shuttle;
    they come to an end without hope.
Remember that my life is like the wind;
    I shall not see happiness again.
The word of the Lord. ℟. **Thanks be to God.** ↓

RESPONSORIAL PSALM Ps 147 [Healer of Brokenhearted]

℟. **Praise the Lord, who heals the brokenhearted.**
℟. Or: **Alleluia.**

Praise the LORD, for he is good;
  sing praise to our God, for he is gracious;
  it is fitting to praise him.
The LORD rebuilds Jerusalem;
  the dispersed of Israel he gathers.

℟. **Praise the Lord, who heals the brokenhearted.**

℟. Or: **Alleluia.**

He heals the brokenhearted
  and binds up their wounds.
He tells the number of the stars;
  he calls each by name.

℟. **Praise the Lord, who heals the brokenhearted.**

℟. Or: **Alleluia.**

Great is our LORD and mighty in power;
  to his wisdom there is no limit.
The LORD sustains the lowly;
  the wicked he casts to the ground.

℟. **Praise the Lord, who heals the brokenhearted.** ↓

℟. Or: **Alleluia.** ↓

SECOND READING 1 Cor 9:16-19, 22-23   [All Things to All]

> Paul writes that he must preach the gospel. Although he has no obligation to any person, he has tried to become one with his hearers to convince them of the saving message of the gospel.

A reading from the first Letter of Saint Paul
to the Corinthians

BROTHERS and sisters: If I preach the gospel, this is no reason for me to boast, for an obligation has been imposed on me, and woe to me if I do not preach it! If I do so willingly, I have a recompense, but if unwillingly, then I have been entrusted with a stewardship. What then is my recompense? That, when I preach, I offer the gospel free of charge so as not to make full use of my right in the gospel.

FEB. 9   5th Sunday in Ordinary Time   **192**

Although I am free in regard to all, I have made myself a slave to all so as to win over as many as possible. To the weak I became weak, to win over the weak. I have become all things to all, to save at least some. All this I do for the sake of the gospel, so that I too may have a share in it.—The word of the Lord. ℟. **Thanks be to God.** ↓

ALLELUIA Mt 8:17   [Look to Christ]

℟. **Alleluia, alleluia.**
Christ took away our infirmities
and bore our diseases.
℟. **Alleluia, alleluia.** ↓

GOSPEL Mk 1:29-39   [Jesus the Healer]

Jesus visits the home of Simon and Andrew. He cures Simon's mother-in-law. Jesus also expels many demons and then goes off to pray alone. When found by Simon, Jesus goes in the villages to preach the good news.

℣. The Lord be with you. ℟. **And also with you.**
✝ A reading from the holy Gospel according to Mark.
℟. **Glory to you, Lord.**

ON leaving the synagogue Jesus entered the house of Simon and Andrew with James and John. Simon's mother-in-law lay sick with a fever. They immediately told him about her. He approached, grasped her hand, and helped her up. Then the fever left her and she waited on them.

When it was evening, after sunset, they brought to him all who were ill or possessed by demons. The whole town was gathered at the door. He cured many who were sick with various diseases, and he drove out many demons, not permitting them to speak because they knew him. Rising very early before dawn, he left and went off to a deserted place, where he prayed. Simon and those who were with him pursued him and

on finding him said, "Everyone is looking for you." He told them, "Let us go on to the nearby villages that I may preach there also. For this purpose have I come." So he went into their synagogues, preaching and driving out demons throughout the whole of Galilee.—The Gospel of the Lord. ℟. **Praise to you, Lord Jesus Christ.**
                                                → No. 14, p. 18

PRAYER OVER THE GIFTS   [Eternal Life]

Lord our God,
may the bread and wine
you give us for our nourishment on earth
become the sacrament of our eternal life.
We ask this through Christ our Lord.
℟. **Amen.**   → No. 21, p. 22 (Pref. P 29-36)

COMMUNION ANT. Ps 107:8-9   [The Lord's Kindness]

Give praise to the Lord for his kindness, for his wonderful deeds toward men. He has filled the hungry with good things, he has satisfied the thirsty. ↓

OR Mt 5:5-6   [The Sorrowing]

Happy are the sorrowing; they shall be consoled. Happy those who hunger and thirst for what is right; they shall be satisfied. ↓

PRAYER AFTER COMMUNION   [Salvation and Joy]

God our Father,
you give us a share in the one bread and the one cup
and make us one in Christ.
Help us to bring your salvation and joy
to all the world.
We ask this through Christ our Lord.
℟. **Amen.**   → No. 32, p. 70

Optional Solemn Blessings, p. 92, and Prayers Over the People, p. 99

"*[Jesus] stretched out his hand, touched him, and said, . . . 'Be made clean.'*"

FEBRUARY 16

6th SUNDAY IN ORDINARY TIME

ENTRANCE ANT. Ps 31:3-4   [Rock of Safety]

Lord, be my rock of safety, the stronghold that saves me. For the honor of your name, lead me and guide me. ➜ No. 2, p. 10

OPENING PRAYER   [Living in God's Presence]

Let us pray
   [that everything we do
   will be guided by God's law of love]
God our Father,
you have promised to remain for ever
with those who do what is just and right.
Help us to live in your presence.
We ask this through our Lord Jesus Christ, your Son,
who lives and reigns with you and the Holy Spirit,
one God, for ever and ever. ℟. **Amen.** ↓

ALTERNATIVE OPENING PRAYER   [God's Wisdom]

Let us pray
   [for the wisdom that is greater than human words]

Father in heaven,
the loving plan of your wisdom took flesh in Jesus
    Christ,
and changed mankind's history
by his command of perfect love.
May our fulfillment of his command reflect your wis-
    dom
and bring your salvation to the ends of the earth.
We ask this through Christ our Lord. ℟. **Amen.** ↓

FIRST READING Lv 13:1-2, 44-46   [Law of Leprosy]

**The Lord instructs Moses and Aaron on the legal prescrip-
tions that are to be followed by those who have leprosy.**

A reading from the Book of Leviticus

THE LORD said to Moses and Aaron, "If someone
has on his skin a scab or pustule or blotch which
appears to be the sore of leprosy, he shall be brought
to Aaron, the priest, or to one of the priests among his
descendants. If the man is leprous and unclean, the
priest shall declare him unclean by reason of the sore
on his head.

    "The one who bears the sore of leprosy shall keep
his garments rent and his head bare, and shall muffle
his beard; he shall cry out, 'Unclean, unclean!' As long
as the sore is on him he shall declare himself unclean,
since he is in fact unclean. He shall dwell apart, making his abode outside the camp."—The word of the
Lord. ℟. **Thanks be to God.** ↓

RESPONSORIAL PSALM Ps 32   [Turning to God]

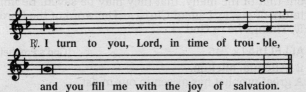

℟. I turn to you, Lord, in time of trou-ble,
and you fill me with the joy of salvation.

Blessed is he whose fault is taken away,
  whose sin is covered.
Blessed the man to whom the LORD imputes not guilt,
  in whose spirit there is no guile.

℞. **I turn to you, Lord, in time of trouble,**
    and you fill me with the joy of salvation.

Then I acknowledged my sin to you,
  my guilt I covered not.
I said, "I confess my faults to the LORD,"
  and you took away the guilt of my sin.

℞. **I turn to you, Lord, in time of trouble,**
    and you fill me with the joy of salvation.

Be glad in the LORD and rejoice, you just;
  exult, all you upright of heart.

℞. **I turn to you, Lord, in time of trouble,**
    and you fill me with the joy of salvation. ↓

SECOND READING 1 Cor 10:31—11:1   [All for God's Glory]

  Paul directs that whatever is done should be for the glory
  of God. Since he is acting in imitation of Christ, the people
  should follow his example.

A reading from the first Letter of Saint Paul
to the Corinthians

BROTHERS and sisters: Whether you eat or drink,
or whatever you do, do everything for the glory of
God. Avoid giving offense, whether to the Jews or
Greeks or the church of God, just as I try to please
everyone in every way, not seeking my own benefit
but that of the many, that they may be saved. Be imitators of me, as I am of Christ.—The word of the Lord.
℞. **Thanks be to God.** ↓

ALLELUIA Lk 7:16   [God's Prophet]
℞. **Alleluia, alleluia.**
A great prophet has arisen in our midst,

God has visited his people.

℟. **Alleluia, alleluia.** ↓

GOSPEL Mk 1:40-45   [Gratitude]

> Upon request, Jesus cured a leper, reminding him to follow the directions of the Mosaic law and to tell no one. Since the cured leper spread the news of his cure, Jesus could no longer openly enter a town.

℣. The Lord be with you. ℟. **And also with you.**

✝ A reading from the holy Gospel according to Mark. ℟. **Glory to you, Lord.**

A LEPER came to Jesus and kneeling down begged him and said, "If you wish, you can make me clean." Moved with pity, he stretched out his hand, touched him, and said to him, "I do will it. Be made clean." The leprosy left him immediately, and he was made clean. Then, warning him sternly, he dismissed him at once.

He said to him, "See that you tell no one anything, but go, show yourself to the priest and offer for your cleansing what Moses prescribed; that will be proof for them."

The man went away and began to publicize the whole matter. He spread the report abroad so that it was impossible for Jesus to enter a town openly. He remained outside in deserted places, and people kept coming to him from everywhere.—The Gospel of the Lord. ℟. **Praise to you, Lord Jesus Christ.**

→ No. 14, p. 18

PRAYER OVER THE GIFTS   [Obedience]

Lord,
we make this offering in obedience to your word.
May it cleanse and renew us,
and lead us to our eternal reward.
We ask this in the name of Jesus the Lord.
℟. **Amen.**   → No. 21, p. 22 (Pref. P 29-36)

COMMUNION ANT. Ps 78:29-30   [God's Food]

They ate and were filled; the Lord gave them what they wanted: they were not deprived of their desire. ↓

OR Jn 3:16   [God's Love]

God loved the world so much, he gave his only Son, that all who believe in him might not perish, but might have eternal life. ↓

PRAYER AFTER COMMUNION   [Bread of Life]

Lord,
you give us food from heaven.
May we always hunger
for the bread of life.
Grant this through Christ our Lord.
℟. **Amen.**   → No. 32, p. 70

Optional Solemn Blessings, p. 92, and Prayers Over the People, p. 99

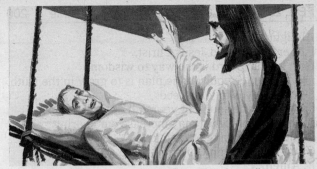

"Rise, pick up your mat, and go home."

FEBRUARY 23

7th SUNDAY IN ORDINARY TIME

ENTRANCE ANT. Ps 13:6   [God's Mercy]

**Lord, your mercy is my hope, my heart rejoices in
your saving power. I will sing to the Lord for his
goodness to me.**   → No. 2, p. 10

OPENING PRAYER   [Imitating Christ]

Let us pray
   [that God will make us more like Christ, his Son]
Father,
keep before us the wisdom and love
you have revealed in your Son.
Help us to be like him
in word and deed,
for he lives and reigns with you and the Holy Spirit,
one God, for ever and ever. ℞. **Amen.** ↓

ALTERNATIVE OPENING PRAYER   [God's Life]

Let us pray
   [to the God of power and might,
   for his mercy is our hope]

199

Almighty God,
Father of our Lord Jesus Christ,
faith in your word is the way to wisdom,
and to ponder your divine plan is to grow in the truth.
Open our eyes to your deeds,
our ears to the sound of your call,
so that our every act may increase our sharing
in the life you have offered us.
Grant this through Christ our Lord.
℟. **Amen.** ↓

FIRST READING Is 43:18-19, 21-22, 24b-25   [God's Pardon]

> **The prophet tells the Jews who are about to return from
> exile in Babylon that in their worship services they should
> not only remember/celebrate the events of the past (the
> traditional exodus from bondage in Egypt), but also the
> new exodus—from bondage in Babylon.**

A reading from the Book of the Prophet Isaiah

THUS says the LORD:
Remember not the events of the past,
   the things of long ago consider not;
see, I am doing something new!
   Now it springs forth, do you not perceive it?
In the desert I make a way,
   in the wasteland, rivers.
The people whom I formed for myself,
   that they might announce my praise.
Yet you did not call upon me, O Jacob,
   for you grew weary of me, O Israel.
You burdened me with your sins,
   and wearied me with your crimes.
It is I, I, who wipe out,
   for my own sake, your offenses;
   your sins I remember no more.
The word of the Lord. ℟. **Thanks be to God.** ↓

RESPONSORIAL PSALM Ps 41   [Plea for Pardon]

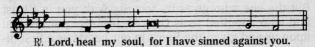

℟. **Lord, heal my soul, for I have sinned against you.**

Blessed is the one who has regard for the lowly and
   the poor;
   in the day of misfortune the LORD will deliver him.
The LORD will keep and preserve him;
   and make him blessed on the earth,
   and not give him over to the will of his enemies.

℟. **Lord, heal my soul, for I have sinned against you.**

The LORD will help him on his sickbed,
   he will take away all his ailment when he is ill.
Once I said, "O LORD, have pity on me;
   heal me, though I have sinned against you."

℟. **Lord, heal my soul, for I have sinned against you.**

But because of my integrity you sustain me
   and let me stand before you forever.
Blessed be the LORD, the God of Israel,
   from all eternity. Amen. Amen.

℟. **Lord, heal my soul, for I have sinned against you.** ↓

SECOND READING 2 Cor 1:18-22   [God's Promise]

**Accused of being unstable, Paul goes back to the basics of
the Christian message. He refers to God's promises which
are stable and to which all of us attach our "Amen."**

A reading from the second Letter of Saint Paul
to the Corinthians

BROTHERS and sisters: As God is faithful, our
   word to you is not "yes" and "no." For the Son of
God, Jesus Christ, who was proclaimed to you by us,
Silvanus and Timothy and me, was not "yes" and "no,"
but "yes" has been in him. For however many are the
promises of God, their Yes is in him; therefore, the

Amen from us also goes through him to God for glory.
But the one who gives us security with you in Christ
and who anointed us is God; he has also put his seal
upon us and given the Spirit in our hearts as a first installment.—The word of the Lord. ℟. **Thanks be to
God.** ↓

ALLELUIA Cf. Lk 4:18   [Glad Tidings and Liberty]

℟. **Alleluia, alleluia.**
The Lord sent me to bring glad tidings to the poor,
and to proclaim liberty to captives.
℟. **Alleluia, alleluia.** ↓

GOSPEL Mk 2:1-12   [Healing of Body and Soul]

**The story of the paralytic stresses not just that Jesus is a
wonderworker, but that the Church has authority to forgive
sins in God's name.**

℟. The Lord be with you. ℟. **And also with you.**
✠ A reading from the holy Gospel according to Mark.
℟. **Glory to you, Lord.**

W HEN Jesus returned to Capernaum after some
days, it became known that he was at home.
Many gathered together so that there was no longer
room for them, not even around the door, and he
preached the word to them. They came bringing to
him a paralytic carried by four men. Unable to get
near Jesus because of the crowd, they opened up the
roof above him. After they had broken through, they
let down the mat on which the paralytic was lying.
When Jesus saw their faith, he said to the paralytic,
"Child, your sins are forgiven." Now some of the
scribes were sitting there asking themselves, "Why
does this man speak that way? He is blaspheming.
Who but God alone can forgive sins?" Jesus immediately knew in his mind what they were thinking to
themselves, so he said, "Why are you thinking such

things in your hearts? Which is easier, to say to the paralytic, 'Your sins are forgiven,' or to say, 'Rise, pick up your mat and walk'? But that you may know that the Son of Man has authority to forgive sins on earth"—he said to the paralytic, "I say to you, rise, pick up your mat, and go home." He rose, picked up his mat at once, and went away in the sight of everyone. They were all astounded and glorified God, saying, "We have never seen anything like this."—The Gospel of the Lord. ℟. **Praise to you, Lord Jesus Christ.**   → No. 14, p. 18

PRAYER OVER THE GIFTS   [Spirit and Truth]

Lord,
as we make this offering,
may our worship in Spirit and truth
bring us salvation.
We ask this in the name of Jesus the Lord.
℟. **Amen.**   → No. 21, p. 22 (Pref. P 29-36)

COMMUNION ANT. Ps 9:2-3   [Joy in God]

I will tell all your marvelous works. I will rejoice and be glad in you, and sing to your name, Most High. ↓

OR Jn 11:27   [Belief in Christ]

Lord, I believe that you are the Christ, the Son of God, who was to come into this world. ↓

PRAYER AFTER COMMUNION   [Example of Love]

Almighty God,
help us to live the example of love
we celebrate in this eucharist,
that we may come to its fulfillment in your presence.
We ask this through Christ our Lord.
℟. **Amen.**   → No. 32, p. 70

Optional Solemn Blessings, p. 92, and Prayers Over the People, p. 99

"No one pours new wine into old wineskins."

MARCH 2

8th SUNDAY IN ORDINARY TIME

ENTRANCE ANT. Ps 18:19-20   [God Our Strength]

The Lord has been my strength; he has led me into freedom. He saved me because he loves me.

→ No. 2, p. 10

OPENING PRAYER   [Freedom]

Let us pray

  [that God will bring peace to the world

   and freedom to his Church]

Lord,

guide the course of world events

and give your Church the joy and peace

of serving you in freedom.

We ask this through our Lord Jesus Christ, your Son,

who lives and reigns with you and the Holy Spirit,

one God, for ever and ever. ℟. **Amen.** ↓

ALTERNATIVE OPENING PRAYER   [Peace]

Let us pray

  [that the peace of Christ

   may find welcome in the world]

Father in heaven,
form in us the likeness of your Son
and deepen his life within us.
Send us as witnesses of gospel joy
into a world of fragile peace and broken promises.
Touch the hearts of all men with your love
that they in turn may love one another.
We ask this through Christ our Lord. ℟. **Amen.** ↓

FIRST READING Hos 2:16b, 17b, 21-22   [God's Love]

The Bible sees human beings as related to God in a sacred partnership, called a covenant. Hosea is the first prophet to attribute marital characteristics to this sacred partnership.

A reading from the Book of the Prophet Hosea

THUS says the LORD:
I will lead her into the desert
and speak to her heart.
She shall respond there as in the days of her youth,
when she came up from the land of Egypt.
I will espouse you to me forever:
I will espouse you in right and in justice,
in love and in mercy;
I will espouse you in fidelity,
and you shall know the LORD.
The word of the Lord. ℟. **Thanks be to God.** ↓

RESPONSORIAL PSALM Ps 103   [Pardon and Redemption]

℟. The Lord   is   kind   and   mer - ci - ful.

Bless the LORD, O my soul,
and all my being, bless his holy name.
Bless the LORD, O my soul,
and forget not all his benefits.

℟. **The Lord is kind and merciful.**

He pardons all your iniquities,
  heals all your ills.
He redeems your life from destruction,
  crowns you with kindness and compassion.

℟. **The Lord is kind and merciful.**

Merciful and gracious is the LORD,
  slow to anger and abounding in kindness.
Not according to our sins does he deal with us,
  nor does he requite us according to our crimes.

℟. **The Lord is kind and merciful.**

As far as the east is from the west,
  so far has he put our transgressions from us.
As a father has compassion on his children,
  so the LORD has compassion on those who fear him.

℟. **The Lord is kind and merciful.** ↓

SECOND READING 2 Cor 3:1-6   [The Spirit Gives Life]
  You are a letter of Christ written in the Spirit.

A reading from the second Letter of Saint Paul
                to the Corinthians

BROTHERS and sisters: Do we need, as some do, letters of recommendation to you or from you? You are our letter, written on our hearts, known and read by all, shown to be a letter of Christ ministered by us, written not in ink but by the Spirit of the living God, not on tablets of stone but on tablets that are hearts of flesh.

  Such confidence we have through Christ toward God. Not that of ourselves we are qualified to take credit for anything as coming from us; rather, our qualification comes from God, who has indeed qualified us as ministers of a new covenant, not of letter but of spirit; for the letter brings death, but the Spirit gives life.—The word of the Lord. ℟. **Thanks be to God.** ↓

ALLELUIA Jas 1:18   [New Birth]

℟. **Alleluia, alleluia.**
The Father willed to give us birth by the word of truth
that we may be a kind of firstfruits of his creation.
℟. **Alleluia, alleluia.** ↓

GOSPEL Mk 2:18-22   [A Time for Fasting]

The bridegroom is still with the disciples.

℣. The Lord be with you. ℟. **And also with you.**
✝ A reading from the holy Gospel according to Mark.
℟. **Glory to you, Lord.**

THE disciples of John and of the Pharisees were accustomed to fast. People came to him and objected,
"Why do the disciples of John and the disciples of the
Pharisees fast, but your disciples do not fast?" Jesus
answered them, "Can the wedding guests fast while
the bridegroom is with them? As long as they have the
bridegroom with them they cannot fast. But the days
will come when the bridegroom is taken away from
them, and then they will fast on that day. No one sews
a piece of unshrunken cloth on an old cloak. If he
does, its fullness pulls away, the new from the old,
and the tear gets worse. Likewise, no one pours new
wine into old wineskins. Otherwise, the wine will
burst the skins, and both the wine and the skins are
ruined. Rather, new wine is poured into fresh wineskins."—The Gospel of the Lord. ℟. **Praise to you,
Lord Jesus Christ.**   → No. 14, p. 18

PRAYER OVER THE GIFTS   [Sign of Worship]

God our Creator,
may this bread and wine we offer
as a sign of our love and worship
lead us to salvation.
Grant this through Christ our Lord.
℟. **Amen.**   → No. 21, p. 22 (Pref. P 29-36)

COMMUNION ANT. Ps 13:6   [God's Goodness]

I will sing to the Lord for his goodness to me, I will sing the name of the Lord, Most High. ↓

OR Mt 28:20   [Christ's Presence]

I, the Lord, am with you always, until the end of the world. ↓

PRAYER AFTER COMMUNION   [Strength and Life]

God of salvation,
may this sacrament which strengthens us here on
    earth
bring us to eternal life.
We ask this in the name of Jesus the Lord.
℟. **Amen.**   → No. 32, p. 70

Optional Solemn Blessings, p. 92, and Prayers Over the People, p. 99

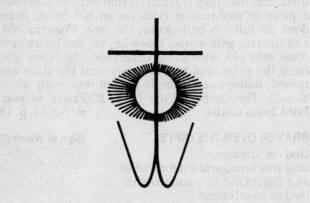

Jesus was "tempted by Satan."

MARCH 9

1st SUNDAY OF LENT

ENTRANCE ANT. Ps 91:15-16   [Long Life]

**When he calls to me, I will answer; I will rescue him
and give him honor. Long life and contentment will
be his.**   → No. 2, p. 10 (Omit Gloria)

OPENING PRAYER   [Christ's Saving Love]

Let us pray
  [that this Lent will help us reproduce in our lives
  the self-sacrificing love of Christ]
Father,
through our observance of Lent,
help us to understand the meaning
of your Son's death and resurrection,
and teach us to reflect it in our lives.
Grant this through our Lord Jesus Christ, your Son,
who lives and reigns with you and the Holy Spirit,
one God, for ever and ever. ℟. **Amen.** ↓

ALTERNATIVE OPENING PRAYER   [Spirit of Repentance]

Let us pray

209

[at the beginning of Lent
for the spirit of repentance]
Lord our God,
you formed man from the clay of the earth
and breathed into him the spirit of life,
but he turned from your face and sinned.
In this time of repentance
we call out for your mercy.
Bring us back to you
and to the life your Son won for us
by his death on the cross,
for he lives and reigns for ever and ever. ℟. **Amen.** ↓

FIRST READING Gn 9:8-15   [Sign of the Covenant]

God promises Noah that the world will never again be destroyed by a flood. God gives a sign of his covenant—his rainbow among the clouds.

A reading from the Book of Genesis

GOD said to Noah and to his sons with him: "See, I am now establishing my covenant with you and your descendants after you and with every living creature that was with you: all the birds, and the various tame and wild animals that were with you and came out of the ark. I will establish my covenant with you, that never again shall all bodily creatures be destroyed by the waters of a flood; there shall not be another flood to devastate the earth." God added: "This is the sign that I am giving for all ages to come, of the covenant between me and you and every living creature with you: I set my bow in the clouds to serve as a sign of the covenant between me and the earth. When I bring clouds over the earth, and the bow appears in the clouds, I will recall the covenant I have made between me and you and all living beings, so that the waters shall never again become a flood to destroy all mortal beings."—The word of the Lord. ℟. **Thanks be to God.** ↓

RESPONSORIAL PSALM Ps 25   [Keeping God's Covenant]

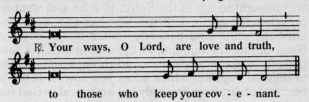

℟. Your ways, O Lord, are love and truth, to those who keep your cov - e - nant.

Your ways, O LORD, make known to me;
  teach me your paths.
Guide me in your truth and teach me,
  for you are God my savior.

℟. **Your ways, O Lord, are love and truth,**
  to those who keep your covenant.

Remember that your compassion, O LORD,
  and your love are from of old.
In your kindness remember me,
  because of your goodness, O LORD.

℟. **Your ways, O Lord, are love and truth,**
  to those who keep your covenant.

Good and upright is the LORD;
  thus he shows sinners the way.
He guides the humble to justice,
  and he teaches the humble his way.

℟. **Your ways, O Lord, are love and truth,**
  to those who keep your covenant. ↓

SECOND READING 1 Pt 3:18-22 [Power of the Resurrection]

Christ died once for sin. Because of sin, God destroyed the
earth by water. Now Christians are saved by the water of
baptism. It becomes the pledge of resurrection.

A reading from the first Letter of Saint Peter

BELOVED: Christ suffered for sins once, the righteous for the sake of the unrighteous, that he

might lead you to God. Put to death in the flesh, he was brought to life in the Spirit. In it he also went to preach to the spirits in prison, who had once been dis-obedient while God patiently waited in the days of Noah during the building of the ark, in which a few persons, eight in all, were saved through water. This prefigured baptism, which saves you now. It is not a removal of dirt from the body but an appeal to God for a clear conscience, through the resurrection of Jesus Christ, who has gone into heaven and is at the right hand of God, with angels, authorities, and powers subject to him.—The word of the Lord. ℟. **Thanks be to God.** ↓

VERSE BEFORE THE GOSPEL Mt 4:4b [God's Living Word]

℟. **Praise to you, Lord Jesus Christ, king of endless glory!**

Man does not live on bread alone,
but on every word that comes forth from the mouth of God.

℟. **Praise to you, Lord Jesus Christ, king of endless glory!** ↓

GOSPEL Mk 1:12-15   [Time of Fulfillment]

Jesus prayed in the desert for forty days. After John's ar-rest, Jesus came forth, announcing the time of fulfillment. It is the time to believe and reform.

℣. The Lord be with you. ℟. **And also with you.**
✢ A reading from the holy Gospel according to Mark.
℟. **Glory to you, Lord.**

T HE Spirit drove Jesus out into the desert, and he remained in the desert for forty days, tempted by Satan. He was among wild beasts, and the angels ministered to him.

After John had been arrested, Jesus came to Galilee proclaiming the gospel of God: "This is the time of ful-

fillment. The kingdom of God is at hand. Repent, and believe in the gospel."—The Gospel of the Lord. ℟.
Praise to you, Lord Jesus Christ.   → No. 14, p. 18

PRAYER OVER THE GIFTS   [Better Lives]
Lord,
make us worthy to bring you these gifts.
May this sacrifice
help to change our lives.
We ask this in the name of Jesus the Lord. ℟. **Amen.** ↓

PREFACE (P 12)   [Christ's Self-Denial]
℣. The Lord be with you. ℟. **And also with you.**
℣. Lift up your hearts. ℟. **We lift them up to the Lord.**
℣. Let us give thanks to the Lord our God. ℟. **It is right to give him thanks and praise.**

Father, all-powerful and ever-living God,
we do well always and everywhere to give you thanks
through Jesus Christ our Lord.
His fast of forty days
makes this a holy season of self-denial.
By rejecting the devil's temptations
he has taught us
to rid ourselves of the hidden corruption of evil,
and so to share his paschal meal in purity of heart,
until we come to its fulfillment
in the promised land of heaven.
Now we join the angels and the saints
as they sing their unending hymn of praise:
                                  → No. 23, p. 23

COMMUNION ANT. Mt 4:4   [Life-Giving Word]
Man does not live on bread alone, but on every word that comes from the mouth of God. ↓

OR Ps 91:4   [Refuge in God]
The Lord will overshadow you, and you will find refuge under his wings. ↓

PRAYER AFTER COMMUNION   [Words and Bread of Life]

Father,
you increase our faith and hope,
you deepen our love in this communion.
Help us to live by your words
and to seek Christ, our bread of life,
who is Lord for ever and ever.
℟. **Amen.**   ➡ No. 32, p. 70

Optional Solemn Blessings, p. 92, and Prayers Over the People, p. 99

*"Elijah appeared to them along with Moses,
and they were conversing with Jesus."*

MARCH 16
2nd SUNDAY OF LENT

ENTRANCE ANT. Ps 25:6, 3, 22   [God's Mercies]

**Remember your mercies, Lord, your tenderness from
ages past. Do not let our enemies triumph over us; O
God, deliver Israel from all her distress.**

OR Ps 27:8-9   [God's Face]

**My heart has prompted me to seek your face; I seek
it, Lord; do not hide from me.**
                      ➡ No. 2, p. 10 (Omit Gloria)

OPENING PRAYER   [Our Response]

Let us pray
    [for the grace to respond
    to the Word of God]
God our Father,
help us to hear your Son.
Enlighten us with your word,
that we may find the way to your glory.
We ask this through our Lord Jesus Christ, your Son,
who lives and reigns with you and the Holy Spirit,
one God, for ever and ever. ℟. **Amen.** ↓

ALTERNATIVE OPENING PRAYER   [Gift of Integrity]

Let us pray
    [in this season of Lent
    for the gift of integrity]
Father of light,
in you is found no shadow of change
but only the fullness of life and limitless truth.
Open our hearts to the voice of your Word
and free us from the original darkness that shadows
    our vision.
Restore our sight that we may look upon your Son
who calls us to repentance and a change of heart,
for he lives and reigns with you for ever and ever.
℟. **Amen.** ↓

FIRST READING Gn 22:1-2, 9a, 10-13, 15-18

[Testing of Abraham]

Abraham and his son, Isaac, prefigure God, the Father, and
Jesus, his divine Son. God tests Abraham's faith and because of it, God promises abundant blessings on the family
of Abraham and all his descendants.

A reading from the Book of Genesis

GOD put Abraham to the test. He called to him,
"Abraham!" "Here I am!" he replied. Then God
said: "Take your son Isaac, your only one, whom you

love, and go to the land of Moriah. There you shall offer him up as a holocaust on a height that I will point out to you."

When they came to the place of which God had told him, Abraham built an altar there and arranged the wood on it. Then he reached out and took the knife to slaughter his son. But the LORD's messenger called to him from heaven, "Abraham, Abraham!" "Here I am!" he answered. "Do not lay your hand on the boy," said the messenger. "Do not do the least thing to him. I know now how devoted you are to God, since you did not withhold from me your own beloved son." As Abraham looked about, he spied a ram caught by its horns in the thicket. So he went and took the ram and offered it up as a holocaust in place of his son.

Again the LORD's messenger called to Abraham from heaven and said: "I swear by myself, declares the LORD, that because you acted as you did in not with-holding from me your beloved son, I will bless you abundantly and make your descendants as countless as the stars of the sky and the sands of the seashore; your descendants shall take possession of the gates of their enemies, and in your descendants all the nations of the earth shall find blessing—all this because you obeyed my command."—The word of the Lord. ℟. **Thanks be to God.** ↓

RESPONSORIAL PSALM Ps 116   [Walking with God]

℟. I will walk before the Lord, in the land of the liv- ing.

I believed, even when I said,
  "I am greatly afflicted."

Precious in the eyes of the LORD
  is the death of his faithful ones.

℟. **I will walk before the Lord, in the land of the living.**

O LORD, I am your servant;
  I am your servant, the son of your handmaid;
  you have loosed my bonds.
To you will I offer sacrifice of thanksgiving,
  and I will call upon the name of the LORD.

℟. **I will walk before the Lord, in the land of the living.**

My vows to the LORD I will pay
  in the presence of all his people,
in the courts of the house of the LORD,
  in your midst, O Jerusalem.

℟. **I will walk before the Lord, in the land of the living.** ↓

SECOND READING Rom 8:31b-34   [God Is for Us]

  God sent his Son into the world to die for us. Who is then
going to judge God's chosen ones? Is this not the right of
Jesus, who loves those for whom he gave his life?

A reading from the Letter of Saint Paul to the Romans

BROTHERS and sisters: If God is for us, who can be
against us? He who did not spare his own Son but
handed him over for us all, how will he not also give
us everything else along with him?
  Who will bring a charge against God's chosen ones?
It is God who acquits us. Who will condemn? Christ
Jesus it is who died—or, rather, was raised—who also
is at the right hand of God, who indeed intercedes for
us.—The word of the Lord. ℟. **Thanks be to God.** ↓

VERSE BEFORE THE GOSPEL Cf. Mt 17:5   [Beloved Son]

℟. **Praise and honor to you, Lord Jesus Christ!**
From the shining cloud the Father's voice is heard:
This is my beloved Son, listen to him.
℟. **Praise and honor to you, Lord Jesus Christ!** ↓

GOSPEL Mk 9:2-10   [Jesus Transfigured]

Jesus becomes transfigured before Peter, James and John. God spoke, "This is my Son, my beloved. Listen to him." Jesus asked his disciples to keep this a strict secret until he would be raised from the dead.

℣. The Lord be with you. ℟. **And also with you.**

✛ A reading from the holy Gospel according to Mark.
℟. Glory to you, Lord.

JESUS took Peter, James, and John and led them up a high mountain apart by themselves. And he was transfigured before them, and his clothes became dazzling white, such as no fuller on earth could bleach them. Then Elijah appeared to them along with Moses, and they were conversing with Jesus. Then Peter said to Jesus in reply, "Rabbi, it is good that we are here! Let us make three tents: one for you, one for Moses, and one for Elijah." He hardly knew what to say, they were so terrified. Then a cloud came, casting a shadow over them; from the cloud came a voice, "This is my beloved Son. Listen to him." Suddenly, looking around, they no longer saw anyone but Jesus alone with them.

As they were coming down from the mountain, he charged them not to relate what they had seen to anyone, except when the Son of Man had risen from the dead. So they kept the matter to themselves, questioning what rising from the dead meant.—The Gospel of the Lord. ℟. **Praise to you, Lord Jesus Christ.**

→ No. 14, p. 18

PRAYER OVER THE GIFTS   [Holiness]

Lord,
make us holy.
May this eucharist take away our sins
that we may be prepared
to celebrate the resurrection.
We ask this in the name of Jesus the Lord. ℟. **Amen.** ↓

PREFACE (P 13)   [Jesus in Glory]

℣. The Lord be with you. ℟. **And also with you.**
℣. Lift up your hearts. ℟. **We lift them up to the Lord.**
℣. Let us give thanks to the Lord our God. ℟. **It is right to give him thanks and praise.**

Father, all-powerful and ever-living God,
we do well always and everywhere to give you thanks
through Jesus Christ our Lord.
On your holy mountain he revealed himself in glory
in the presence of his disciples.
He had already prepared them for his approaching
    death.
He wanted to teach them through the Law and the
    Prophets
that the promised Christ had first to suffer
and so come to the glory of his resurrection.
In our unending joy we echo on earth
the song of the angels in heaven
as they praise your glory for ever: → No. 23, p. 23

COMMUNION ANT. Mt 17:5   [Son of God]

This is my Son, my beloved, in whom is all my delight: listen to him. ↓

PRAYER AFTER COMMUNION   [Life To Come]

Lord,
we give thanks for these holy mysteries
which bring to us here on earth
a share in the life to come, through Christ our Lord.
℟. **Amen.**   → No. 32, p. 70

Optional Solemn Blessings, p. 92, and Prayers Over the People, p. 99

"Stop making my Father's house a marketplace."

MARCH 23

3rd SUNDAY OF LENT

The Ritual Mass for the First Scrutiny assigned to this Sunday in the Rite of Christian Initiation of Adults is found on p. 226.

ENTRANCE ANT. Ps 25:15-16 [Eyes on God]
My eyes are ever fixed on the Lord, for he releases my feet from the snare. O look at me and be merciful, for I am wretched and alone.

OR Ez 36:23-26 [A New Spirit]
I will prove my holiness through you. I will gather you from the ends of the earth; I will pour clean water on you and wash away all your sins. I will give you a new spirit within you, says the Lord.

→ No. 2, p. 10 (Omit Gloria)

OPENING PRAYER [Prayer, Fasting, Works]
Let us pray
  [for confidence in the love of God
  and the strength to overcome all our weakness]
Father,
you have taught us to overcome our sins
by prayer, fasting and works of mercy.
When we are discouraged by our weakness,
give us confidence in your love.

We ask this through our Lord Jesus Christ, your Son,
who lives and reigns with you and the Holy Spirit,
one God, for ever and ever. ℟. **Amen.** ↓

ALTERNATIVE OPENING PRAYER   [A New Heart]

Let us pray
  [to the Father and ask him
  to form a new heart within us]
God of all compassion, Father of all goodness,
to heal the wounds our sins and selfishness bring
  upon us
you bid us turn to fasting, prayer, and sharing with
  our brothers.
We acknowledge our sinfulness, our guilt is ever before us:
when our weakness causes discouragement,
let your compassion fill us with hope
and lead us through a Lent of repentance to the
  beauty of Easter joy.
Grant this through Christ our Lord. ℟. **Amen.** ↓

FIRST READING Ex 20:1-17 or 20:1-3, 7-8, 12-17
                              [Ten Commandments]

**God speaks to his people and gives them a code of life to
follow—the Commandments. The first three describe how
he is to be worshiped and the remaining rules outline how
the people are to respect and live with one another.**

*[If the "Shorter Form" is used, the indented text in brackets is
omitted.]*

A reading from the Book of Exodus

IN those days, God delivered all these commandments: "I, the LORD, am your God, who brought you
out of the land of Egypt, that place of slavery. You
shall not have other gods besides me.

  [You shall not carve idols for yourselves in the
  shape of anything in the sky above or on the

earth below or in the waters beneath the earth; you shall not bow down before them or worship them. For I, the LORD, your God, am a jealous God, inflicting punishment for their fathers' wickedness on the children of those who hate me, down to the third and fourth generation; but bestowing mercy down to the thousandth generation, on the children of those who love me and keep my commandments.]

"You shall not take the name of the LORD, your God, in vain. For the LORD will not leave unpunished him who takes his name in vain.

"Remember to keep holy the sabbath day.

[Six days you may labor and do all your work, but the seventh day is the sabbath of the LORD, your God. No work may be done then either by you, or your son or daughter, or your male or female slave, or your beast, or by the alien who lives with you. In six days the LORD made the heavens and the earth, the sea and all that is in them; but on the seventh day he rested. That is why the LORD has blessed the sabbath day and made it holy.]

"Honor your father and your mother, that you may have a long life in the land which the LORD, your God, is giving you.

"You shall not kill.

"You shall not commit adultery.

"You shall not steal.

"You shall not bear false witness against your neighbor.

"You shall not covet your neighbor's house. You shall not covet your neighbor's wife, nor his male or female slave, nor his ox or ass, nor anything else that belongs to him."—The word of the Lord. ℞. **Thanks be to God.** ↓

RESPONSORIAL PSALM Ps 19   [Words of Life]

℟. Lord, you have the words of ever-last-ing life.

The law of the LORD is perfect,
  refreshing the soul;
the decree of the LORD is trustworthy,
  giving wisdom to the simple.—℟.

The precepts of the LORD are right,
  rejoicing the heart;
the command of the LORD is clear,
  enlightening the eye.—℟.

The fear of the LORD is pure,
  enduring forever;
the ordinances of the LORD are true,
  all of them just.—℟.

They are more precious than gold,
  than a heap of purest gold;
sweeter also than syrup
  or honey from the comb.—℟. ↓

SECOND READING 1 Cor 1:22-25 [Christ, the Power of God]

Paul admits that the preaching of Christ crucified is regarded as absurd by some. Still, for those who have faith, Christ is the power and wisdom of God.

A reading from the first Letter of Saint Paul
to the Corinthians

BROTHERS and sisters: Jews demand signs and Greeks look for wisdom, but we proclaim Christ crucified, a stumbling block to Jews and foolishness to Gentiles, but to those who are called, Jews and Greeks alike, Christ the power of God and the wisdom of God. For the foolishness of God is wiser than human wisdom, and the weakness of God is stronger than human strength.—The word of the Lord. ℟. **Thanks be to God.** ↓

VERSE BEFORE THE GOSPEL Jn 3:16   [God's Love]

℟. **Glory and praise to you, Lord Jesus Christ!**

God so loved the world that he gave his only Son,
so that everyone who believes in him might have
   eternal life.

℟. **Glory and praise to you, Lord Jesus Christ!** ↓

GOSPEL Jn 2:13-25   [Prediction of the Resurrection]

Jesus becomes angry when the temple, which is to be a
house of prayer, is turned into a place of business. He
drives the merchants out.

℣. The Lord be with you. ℟. **And also with you.**

✝ A reading from the holy Gospel according to John.

℟. **Glory to you, Lord.**

SINCE the Passover of the Jews was near, Jesus
went up to Jerusalem. He found in the temple area
those who sold oxen, sheep, and doves, as well as the
money changers seated there. He made a whip out of
cords and drove them all out of the temple area, with
the sheep and oxen, and spilled the coins of the
money changers and overturned their tables, and to
those who sold doves he said, "Take these out of here,
and stop making my Father's house a marketplace."
His disciples recalled the words of Scripture, *Zeal for
your house will consume me.* At this the Jews answered and said to him, "What sign can you show us
for doing this?" Jesus answered and said to them, "Destroy this temple and in three days I will raise it up."
The Jews said, "This temple has been under construction for forty-six years, and you will raise it up in
three days?" But he was speaking about the temple of
his body. Therefore, when he was raised from the
dead, his disciples remembered that he had said this,
and they came to believe the Scripture and the word
Jesus had spoken.

While he was in Jerusalem for the feast of Passover,
many began to believe in his name when they saw the

signs he was doing. But Jesus would not trust himself to them because he knew them all, and did not need anyone to testify about human nature. He himself understood it well.—The Gospel of the Lord. ℞. **Praise to you, Lord Jesus Christ.**   → No. 14, p. 18

Or the Gospel (Jn 4:5-42) from Year A may be said, p. 228.

PRAYER OVER THE GIFTS   [Forgiveness]

Lord,
by the grace of this sacrifice
may we who ask forgiveness
be ready to forgive one another.
We ask this through Christ our Lord.
℞. **Amen.**   → No. 21, p. 22 (Pref. P 8-9)

When the Gospel of the Samaritan Woman is read, see p. 231 for Preface (P 14).

COMMUNION ANT. Ps 84:4-5   [God's House]

The sparrow even finds a home, the swallow finds a nest wherein to place her young, near to your altars, Lord of hosts, my King, my God! How happy they who dwell in your house! For ever they are praising you. ↓

When the Gospel of the Samaritan Woman is read:

COMMUNION ANT. Jn 4:13-14   [Water of Eternal Life]

Whoever drinks the water that I shall give him, says the Lord, will have a spring inside him, welling up for eternal life. ↓

PRAYER AFTER COMMUNION   [Unity and Peace]

Lord,
in sharing this sacrament
may we receive your forgiveness
and be brought together in unity and peace.
We ask this through Christ our Lord.
℞. **Amen.**   → No. 32, p. 70

Optional Solemn Blessings, p. 92, and Prayers Over the People, p. 99

MASS FOR THE FIRST SCRUTINY

This Mass is celebrated when the First Scrutiny takes place during the Rite of Christian Initiation of Adults, usually on the 3rd Sunday of Lent.

ENTRANCE ANT. Ez 36:23-26   [A New Spirit]
I will prove my holiness through you. I will gather you from the ends of the earth; I will pour clean water on you and wash away all your sins. I will give you a new spirit within you, says the Lord.

→ No. 2, p. 10 (Omit Gloria)

OPENING PRAYER   [Growth in Wisdom and Love]
Lord,
you call these chosen ones
to the glory of a new birth in Christ, the second Adam.
Help them grow in wisdom and love
as they prepare to profess their faith in you.
Grant this . . . for ever and ever. ℟. **Amen.** ↓

FIRST READING Ex 17:3-7   [Water from Rock]
The Israelites murmured against God in their thirst. God directs Moses to strike a rock with his staff, and water issues forth.

A reading from the Book of Exodus

IN those days, in their thirst for water, the people grumbled against Moses, saying, "Why did you ever make us leave Egypt? Was it just to have us die here of thirst with our children and our livestock?" So Moses cried out to the LORD, "What shall I do with this people? A little more and they will stone me!" The LORD answered Moses, "Go over there in front of the people, along with some of the elders of Israel, holding in your hand, as you go, the staff with which you struck the river. I will be standing there in front of you on the rock in Horeb. Strike the rock, and the water will flow from it for the people to drink." This Moses did, in the presence of the elders of Israel. The place was called Massah and Meribah, because the Israelites quarreled there and tested the LORD, saying, "Is the LORD in our midst or not?"— The word of the Lord. ℟. **Thanks be to God.** ↓

RESPONSORIAL PSALM Ps 95   [The Lord Our Rock]

℟. **If today you hear his voice, harden not your hearts.**

Come, let us sing joyfully to the LORD;
   let us acclaim the Rock of our salvation.
Let us come into his presence with thanksgiving;
   let us joyfully sing psalms to him.—℟.

Come, let us bow down in worship;
   let us kneel before the LORD who made us.
For he is our God,
   and we are the people he shepherds, the flock he
      guides.—℟.

Oh, that today you would hear his voice:
   "Harden not your hearts as at Meribah,
   as in the day of Massah in the desert,
where your fathers tempted me;
   they tested me though they had seen my works."—℟. ↓

SECOND READING Rom 5:1-2, 5-8   [God's Love for Us]

Through Jesus we have received the grace of faith. The love of God has been poured upon us. Jesus laid down his life for us while we were still sinners.

A reading from the Letter of Saint Paul to the Romans

BROTHERS and sisters: Since we have been justified by faith, we have peace with God through our Lord Jesus Christ, through whom we have gained access by faith to this grace in which we stand, and we boast in hope of the glory of God.

   And hope does not disappoint, because the love of God has been poured out into our hearts through the Holy

Spirit who has been given to us. For Christ, while we were still helpless, died at the appointed time for the ungodly. Indeed, only with difficulty does one die for a just person, though perhaps for a good person one might even find courage to die. But God proves his love for us in that while we were still sinners Christ died for us.—The word of the Lord. ℟. **Thanks be to God.** ↓

VERSE BEFORE THE GOSPEL Cf. Jn 4: 42, 15 [Living Water]

℟. **Glory and praise to you, Lord Jesus Christ!**
Lord, you are truly the Savior of the world;
give me living water, that I may never thirst again.
℟. **Glory and praise to you, Lord Jesus Christ!** ↓

GOSPEL Jn 4:5-42 or 4:5-15, 19b-26, 39, 40-42   [Samaritan Woman]

> **Jesus speaks to the Samaritan woman at the well. He searches her soul, and she recognizes him as a prophet. Jesus speaks of the water of eternal life. He also notes the fields are ready for harvest.**

[If the "Shorter Form" is used, the indented text in brackets is omitted.]

℣. The Lord be with you. ℟. **And also with you.**
✠ A reading from the holy Gospel according to John. ℟. **Glory to you, Lord.**

JESUS came to a town of Samaria called Sychar, near the plot of land that Jacob had given to his son Joseph. Jacob's well was there. Jesus, tired from his journey, sat down there at the well. It was about noon.

A woman of Samaria came to draw water. Jesus said to her, "Give me a drink." His disciples had gone into the town to buy food. The Samaritan woman said to him, "How can you, a Jew, ask me, a Samaritan woman, for a drink?"—For Jews use nothing in common with Samaritans.—Jesus answered and said to her, "If you knew the gift of God and who is saying to you, 'Give me a drink,' you would have asked him and he would have given you living water." The woman said to him, "Sir, you do not even have a bucket and the cistern is deep; where then can you get this living water? Are you greater than our father Jacob, who gave us this cistern and drank from it himself with his children and his flocks?" Jesus answered and said to her, "Everyone who drinks this water will be thirsty again; but whoever drinks the water I shall give will never thirst; the water I shall give will become in him a spring of water welling up to eternal life." The woman said to him, "Sir, give me this water, so that I may not be thirsty or have to keep coming here to draw water."

[Jesus said to her, "Go call your husband and come back." The woman answered and said to him, "I do not have a husband." Jesus answered her, "You are right in saying, 'I do not have a husband.' For you have had five husbands, and the one you have now is not your husband. What you have said is true."]

[The woman said to him, "Sir,] I can see that you are a prophet. Our ancestors worshiped on this mountain; but you people say that the place to worship is in Jerusalem." Jesus said to her, "Believe me, woman, the hour is coming when you will worship the Father neither on this mountain nor in Jerusalem. You people worship what you do not understand; we worship what we understand, because salvation is from the Jews. But the hour is coming, and is now here, when true worshippers will worship the Father in Spirit and truth; and indeed the Father seeks such people to worship him. God is Spirit, and those who worship him must worship in Spirit and truth." The woman said to him, "I know that the Messiah is coming, the one called the Christ; when he comes, he will tell us everything." Jesus said to her, "I am he, the one speaking with you."

[At that moment his disciples returned, and were amazed that he was talking with a woman, but still no one said, "What are you looking for?" or

"Why are you talking with her?" The woman left her water jar and went into the town and said to the people, "Come see a man who told me everything I have done. Could he possibly be the Christ?" They went out of the town and came to him. Meanwhile, the disciples urged him, "Rabbi, eat." But he said to them, "I have food to eat of which you do not know." So the disciples said to one another, "Could someone have brought him something to eat?" Jesus said to them, "My food is to do the will of the one who sent me and to finish his work. Do you not say, 'In four months the harvest will be here'? I tell you, look up and see the fields ripe for the harvest. The reaper is already receiving payment and gathering crops for eternal life, so that the sower and reaper can rejoice together. For here the saying is verified that 'One sows and another reaps.' I sent you to reap what you have not worked for; others have done the work, and you are sharing the fruits of their work."]

Many of the Samaritans of that town began to believe in him because of the word of the woman who testified, "He told me everything I have done." When the Samaritans came to him, they invited him to stay with them; and he stayed there two days. Many more began to believe in him because of his word, and they said to the woman, "We no longer believe because of your word; for we have heard for ourselves, and we know that this is truly the savior of the world."—The Gospel of the Lord. ℟. **Praise to you, Lord Jesus Christ.**   → No. 14, p. 18

PRAYER OVER THE GIFTS   [Faith and Love]

Lord God,
give faith and love to your children
and lead them safely to the banquet
you have prepared for them.
We ask this in the name of Jesus the Lord.
℟. **Amen.** ↓

PREFACE (P 14)   [Gift of Faith]

℣. The Lord be with you. ℟. **And also with you.**
℣. Lift up your hearts. ℟. **We lift them up to the Lord.**
℣. Let us give thanks to the Lord our God. ℟. **It is right to give him thanks and praise.**

Father, all-powerful and ever-living God,
we do well always and everywhere to give you thanks
through Jesus Christ our Lord.
When he asked the woman of Samaria for water to drink,
Christ had already prepared for her the gift of faith.
In his thirst to receive her faith
he awakened in her heart the fire of your love.
With thankful praise,
in company with the angels
we glorify the wonders of your power: → No. 23, p. 23

When Eucharistic Prayer I is used, the special Christian Initiation forms of Remember, Lord, your people *and* Father, accept this offering *are said.*

Remember, Lord, these godparents
who will present your chosen men and women for
    baptism.

(the names of the godparents are mentioned).

Lord, remember all of us . . . (p. 24).

Father,
accept this offering
from your whole family.
We offer it especially for the men and women
you call to share your life
through the living waters of baptism.

[Through Christ our Lord. Amen.]

The rest follows the Roman Canon, pp. 25-28.

COMMUNION ANT. Jn 4:13-14   [Water of Eternal Life]

Whoever drinks the water that I shall give him, says the Lord, will have a spring inside him, welling up for eternal life. ↓

PRAYER AFTER COMMUNION   [God's Protection]

Lord,
be present in our lives
with your gifts of salvation.
Prepare these men and women for your sacraments
and protect them in your love.
We ask this in the name of Jesus the Lord.
℟. **Amen.**   → No. 32, p. 70

Optional Solemn Blessings, p. 92, and Prayers Over the People, p. 99

"The light came into the world, but people preferred darkness to light."

MARCH 30

4th SUNDAY OF LENT

The Ritual Mass for the Second Scrutiny assigned to this Sunday in the Rite of Christian Initiation of Adults is found on p. 238.

ENTRANCE ANT. See Is 66:10-11   [Rejoice]

Rejoice, Jerusalem! Be glad for her, you who love her; rejoice with her, you who mourned for her, and you will find contentment at her consoling breasts.

→ No. 2, p. 10 (Omit Gloria)

OPENING PRAYER   [Faith and Love]

Let us pray
  [for a greater faith and love]
Father of peace,
we are joyful in your Word,
your Son Jesus Christ,
who reconciles us to you.
Let us hasten toward Easter
with the eagerness of faith and love.
We ask this through our Lord Jesus Christ, your Son,
who lives and reigns with you and the Holy Spirit,
one God, for ever and ever. ℟. **Amen.** ↓

ALTERNATIVE OPENING PRAYER   [Bringing Peace]

Let us pray
  [that by growing in love this lenten season
  we may bring the peace of Christ to our world]
God our Father,
your Word, Jesus Christ, spoke peace to a sinful world
and brought mankind the gift of reconciliation
by the suffering and death he endured.
Teach us, the people who bear his name,
to follow the example he gave us:
may our faith, hope, and charity
turn hatred to love, conflict to peace, death to eternal life.
We ask this through Christ our Lord. ℟. **Amen.** ↓

FIRST READING 2 Chr 36:14-16, 19-23
                                        [Punishment for Infidelity]

The Israelites were repeatedly unfaithful to God. They ig-
nored the prophets sent to them. God allowed them to fall
to the Chaldeans. Jeremiah had foretold this punishment.

A reading from the second Book of Chronicles

IN those days, all the princes of Judah, the priests, and the people added infidelity to infidelity, practicing all the abominations of the nations and polluting the LORD's temple which he had consecrated in Jerusalem.

Early and often did the LORD, the God of their fathers, send his messengers to them, for he had compassion on his people and his dwelling place. But they mocked the messengers of God, despised his warnings, and scoffed at his prophets, until the anger of the LORD against his people was so inflamed that there was no remedy. Their enemies burnt the house of God, tore down the walls of Jerusalem, set all its palaces afire, and destroyed all its precious objects. Those who escaped the sword were carried captive to Babylon, where they became servants of the king of the Chaldeans and his sons until the kingdom of the Persians came to power. All this was to fulfill the word of the LORD spoken by Jeremiah: "Until the land has retrieved its lost sabbaths, during all the time it lies waste it shall have rest while seventy years are fulfilled."

In the first year of Cyrus, king of Persia, in order to fulfill the word of the LORD spoken by Jeremiah, the LORD inspired King Cyrus of Persia to issue this proclamation throughout his kingdom, both by word of mouth and in writing: "Thus says Cyrus, king of Persia: All the kingdoms of the earth the LORD, the God of heaven, has given to me, and he has also charged me to build him a house in Jerusalem, which is in Judah. Whoever, therefore, among you belongs to any part of his people, let him go up, and may his God be with him!"—The word of the Lord. ℞. **Thanks be to God.** ↓

RESPONSORIAL PSALM Ps 137   [Remembrance of Zion]

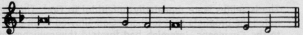

℞. **Let my tongue be silenced, if I ever for - get you!**

By the streams of Babylon
  we sat and wept
  when we remembered Zion.
On the aspens of that land
  we hung up our harps.—℟.

Though there our captors asked of us
  the lyrics of our songs,
and our despoilers urged us to be joyous:
  "Sing for us the songs of Zion!"—℟.

How could we sing a song of the LORD
  in a foreign land?
If I forget you, Jerusalem,
  may my right hand be forgotten!—℟.

May my tongue cleave to my palate
  if I remember you not,
if I place not Jerusalem
  ahead of my joy.—℟. ↓

SECOND READING Eph 2:4-10   [God's Gift: Salvation]

> God's mercy and love brought Jesus into the world. Salvation is God's gift, it is not the work of human beings. Jesus leads all to perform good works.

A reading from the Letter of Saint Paul
to the Ephesians

B ROTHERS and sisters: God, who is rich in mercy, because of the great love he had for us, even when we were dead in our transgressions, brought us to life with Christ—by grace you have been saved—, raised us up with him, and seated us with him in the heavens in Christ Jesus, that in the ages to come he might show the immeasurable riches of his grace in his kindness to us in Christ Jesus. For by grace you have been saved through faith, and this is not from you; it is the gift of God; it is not from works, so no one may boast. For we are his handiwork, created in Christ Jesus for the good works that God has prepared in advance, that we should live in them.—The word of the Lord. ℟. **Thanks be to God.** ↓

VERSE BEFORE THE GOSPEL Jn 3:16   [God's Love]

℟. **Glory to you, Word of God, Lord Jesus Christ!**
God so loved the world that he gave his only Son,
so everyone who believes in him might have eternal
  life.
℟. **Glory to you, Word of God, Lord Jesus Christ!** ↓

GOSPEL Jn 3:14-21   [Salvation in Christ]

Jesus is to die on the cross—the proof of God's unlimited love for his people. God sent Jesus that we might believe. Through belief in him human beings will be saved.

℣. The Lord be with you. ℟. **And also with you.**
✠ A reading from the holy Gospel according to John.
℟. **Glory to you, Lord.**

JESUS said to Nicodemus: "Just as Moses lifted up the serpent in the desert, so must the Son of Man be lifted up, so that everyone who believes in him may have eternal life."

For God so loved the world that he gave his only Son, so that everyone who believes in him might not perish but might have eternal life. For God did not send his Son into the world to condemn the world, but that the world might be saved through him. Whoever believes in him will not be condemned, but whoever does not believe has already been condemned, because he has not believed in the name of the only Son of God. And this is the verdict, that the light came into the world, but people preferred darkness to light, because their works were evil. For everyone who does wicked things hates the light and does not come toward the light, so that his works might not be exposed. But whoever lives the truth comes to the light, so that his works may be clearly seen as done in God.

—The Gospel of the Lord. ℟. **Praise to you, Lord Jesus Christ.**   → No. 14, p. 18

Or the Gospel (Jn 9:1-41) from Year A may be said, p. 240.

PRAYER OVER THE GIFTS   [Increased Reverence]

Lord,
we offer you these gifts
which bring us peace and joy.
Increase our reverence by this eucharist,
and bring salvation to the world.
We ask this through Christ our Lord.
℟. **Amen.**   → No. 21, p. 22 (Pref. P 29-36)

When the Gospel of the man born blind is read, see p. 243 for Preface (P 15).

COMMUNION ANT. Ps 122:3-4   [Praise]

To Jerusalem, that binds them together in unity, the tribes of the Lord go up to give him praise. ↓

When the Gospel of the man born blind is read:

COMMUNION ANT. See Jn 9:11   [Spiritual Sight]

The Lord rubbed my eyes: I went away and washed; then I could see, and I believed in God. ↓

PRAYER AFTER COMMUNION   [Light of the Gospel]

Father,
you enlighten all who come into the world.
Fill our hearts with the light of your gospel,
that our thoughts may please you,
and our love be sincere.
Grant this through Christ our Lord.
℟. **Amen.**   → No. 32, p. 70

Optional Solemn Blessings, p. 92, and Prayers Over the People, p. 99

MASS FOR THE SECOND SCRUTINY

This Mass is celebrated when the Second Scrutiny takes place during the Rite of Christian Initiation of Adults, usually on the 4th Sunday of Lent.

ENTRANCE ANT. Ez 36:23-26   **[A New Spirit]**

I will prove my holiness through you. I will gather you from the ends of the earth; I will pour clean water on you and wash away all your sins. I will give you a new spirit within you, says the Lord.

→ No. 2, p. 10 (Omit Gloria)

OPENING PRAYER   **[Rebirth into the Kingdom]**

Almighty and eternal God,
may your Church increase in true joy.
May these candidates for baptism,
and all the family of man,
be reborn into the life of your kingdom.
We ask this . . . for ever and ever. ℟. **Amen.** ↓

FIRST READING 1 Sm 16:1b, 6-7, 10-13a

[The Lord's Anointed]

God directs Samuel to anoint David king. God looks into the heart of each person.

A reading from the first Book of Samuel

THE LORD said to Samuel: "Fill your horn with oil, and be on your way. I am sending you to Jesse of Bethlehem, for I have chosen my king from among his sons."

As Jesse and his sons came to the sacrifice, Samuel looked at Eliab and thought, "Surely the LORD's anointed is here before him." But the LORD said to Samuel: "Do not judge from his appearance or from his lofty stature, because I have rejected him. Not as man sees does God see, because man sees the appearance but the LORD looks into the heart." In the same way Jesse presented seven sons before Samuel, but Samuel said to Jesse, "The LORD has not chosen any one of these." Then Samuel asked Jesse, "Are these all the sons you have?" Jesse replied, "There is still the youngest, who is tending the sheep." Samuel said to Jesse, "Send for him; we will not begin the sacrificial banquet until he arrives here." Jesse sent and had the young man brought to them. He was ruddy, a youth handsome to behold and making a splendid appearance. The LORD said, "There—anoint him, for this is the one!" Then Samuel, with the horn of oil in hand, anointed him in the presence of his brothers; and from that day on, the spirit of the LORD rushed upon David.—The word of the Lord. ℟. **Thanks be to God.** ↓

RESPONSORIAL PSALM Ps 23   [The Lord's Protection]

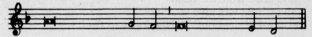

℟.   **The Lord is my shep-herd, there is noth-ing I shall want.**

The LORD is my shepherd, I shall not want.
    In verdant pastures he gives me repose;
beside restful waters he leads me;
    he refreshes my soul.—℟.

He guides me in right paths
    for his name's sake.
Even though I walk in the dark valley
    I fear no evil; for you are at my side
with your rod and your staff
    that give me courage.—℟.

You spread the table before me
    in the sight of my foes;
you anoint my head with oil;
    my cup overflows.—℟.

Only goodness and kindness follow me
    all the days of my life;
and I shall dwell in the house of the LORD
    for years to come.—℟. ↓

SECOND READING Eph 5:8-14   [Children of Light]

We are to walk in the light which shows goodness, justice, and truth. Christ gives this light whereby we live.

A reading from the Letter of Saint Paul to the Ephesians

BROTHERS and sisters: You were once darkness, but now you are light in the Lord. Live as children of light, for light produces every kind of goodness and righteousness and truth. Try to learn what is pleasing to the Lord. Take no part in the fruitless works of darkness; rather expose them, for it is shameful even to mention the things done by them in secret; but everything exposed by the light becomes visible, for everything that becomes visible is light. Therefore, it says:

"Awake, O sleeper,
   and arise from the dead,
   and Christ will give you light."

The word of the Lord. ℟. **Thanks be to God.** ↓

VERSE BEFORE THE GOSPEL Jn 8:12   [Light of Life]

℟. **Glory to you, Word of God, Lord Jesus Christ!**
I am the light of the world, says the Lord;
whoever follows me will have the light of life.
℟. **Glory to you, Word of God, Lord Jesus Christ!** ↓

GOSPEL Jn 9:1-41 or 9:1, 6-9, 13-17, 34-38   [Cure of Blind Man]
   Jesus is the light. He cures a man born blind by bringing him
   to see. Jesus identifies himself as the Son of Man.

[If the "Shorter Form" is used, the indented text in brackets is omitted.]

℣. The Lord be with you. ℟. **And also with you.**
✝ A reading from the holy Gospel according to John.
℟. **Glory to you, Lord.**

AS Jesus passed by he saw a man blind from birth. [His disciples asked him, "Rabbi, who sinned, this man or his parents, that he was born blind?" Jesus answered, "Neither he nor his parents sinned; it is so that the works of God might be made visible through him. We have to do the works of the one who sent me while it is day. Night is coming when no one can work. While I am in the world, I am the light of the world." When he had said this,] he spat on the ground and made clay with the saliva, and smeared the clay on his eyes, and said to him, "Go wash in the Pool of Siloam"—which means Sent—. So he went and washed, and came back able to see.

His neighbors and those who had seen him earlier as a beggar said, "Isn't this the one who used to sit and beg?" Some said, "It is, " but others said, "No, he just looks like him." He said, "I am."

[So they said to him, "How were your eyes opened?" He replied, "The man called Jesus made clay and anointed my eyes and told me, 'Go to Siloam and wash.' So I went there and washed and was able to see." And they said to him, "Where is he?" He said, "I don't know."]

They brought the one who was once blind to the Pharisees. Now Jesus had made clay and opened his eyes on a sabbath. So then the Pharisees also asked him how he was able to see. He said to them, "He put clay on my eyes, and I washed, and now I can see." So some of the Pharisees said, "This man is not from God, because he does not keep the sabbath." But others said, "How can a sinful man do such signs?" And there was a division among them. So they said to the blind man again, "What do you have to say about him, since he opened your eyes?" He said, "He is a prophet."

[Now the Jews did not believe that he had been blind and gained his sight until they summoned the parents of the one who had gained his sight. They asked them, "Is this your son, who you say was born blind? How does he now see?" His parents answered and said, "We know that this is our son and that he was born blind. We do not know how he sees now, nor do we know who opened his eyes. Ask him, he is of age; he can speak for himself." His parents said this because they were afraid of the Jews, for the Jews had already agreed that if anyone acknowledged him as the Christ, he would be expelled from the synagogue. For this reason his parents said, "He is of age; question him."

So a second time they called the man who had been blind and said to him, "Give God the praise! We know that this man is a sinner." He replied, "If he is a sinner, I do not know. One thing I do know is that I was blind and now I see." So they said to him, "What did he do to you? How did he open your eyes?" He answered them, "I told you already and you did not listen. Why do you want to hear it again? Do you want to become his disciples, too?" They ridiculed him and said, "You are that man's disciple; we are disciples of Moses! We know that God spoke to Moses, but we do not know where this one is from." The man answered and said to them, "This is what is so amazing, that you do not know where he is from, yet he opened my eyes. We know that God does not listen to sinners, but if one is devout and does his will, he listens to him. It is unheard of that anyone ever opened the eyes of a person born blind. If this man were not from God, he would not be able to do anything."]

They answered and said to him, "You were born totally in sin, and are you trying to teach us?" Then they threw him out.

When Jesus heard that they had thrown him out, he found him and said, "Do you believe in the Son of Man?" He answered and said, "Who is he, sir, that I may believe in him?" Jesus said to him, "You have seen him, and the one speaking with you is he." He said, "I do believe, Lord," and he worshiped him.

[Then Jesus said, "I came into this world for judgment, so that those who do not see might see, and those who do see might become blind."

Some of the Pharisees who were with him heard this and said to him, "Surely we are not also blind, are we?" Jesus said to them, "If you were blind, you would have no sin; but now you are saying, 'We see,' so your sin remains."]

The Gospel of the Lord. ℟. **Praise to you, Lord Jesus Christ.**   → No. 14, p. 18

PRAYER OVER THE GIFTS   [Faith and Love]

Lord,
we offer these gifts
in joy and thanksgiving for our salvation.
May the example of our faith and love
help your chosen ones on their way to salvation.
Grant this through Christ our Lord. ℟. **Amen.** ↓

PREFACE (P 15)   [From Darkness to Light]

℣. The Lord be with you. ℟. **And also with you.**
℣. Lift up your hearts. ℟. **We lift them up to the Lord.**
℣. Let us give thanks to the Lord our God. ℟. **It is right to give him thanks and praise.**

Father, all-powerful and ever-living God,
we do well always and everywhere to give you thanks,
through Jesus Christ our Lord.
He came among us as a man,
to lead mankind from darkness
into the light of faith.
Through Adam's fall we were born as slaves of sin,
but now through baptism in Christ
we are reborn as your adopted children.
Earth unites with heaven
to sing the new song of creation,
as we adore and praise you for ever: → No. 23, p. 23

When Eucharistic Prayer I is used, the special Christian Initiation forms of Remember, Lord, your people *and* Father, accept this offering *are said.*

Remember, Lord, these godparents
who will present your chosen men and women for baptism.

(the names of the godparents are mentioned).

Lord, remember all of us . . . (p. 24).

Father,
accept this offering
from your whole family.
We offer it especially for the men and women

you call to share your life
through the living waters of baptism.

[Through Christ our Lord. Amen.]

The rest follows the Roman Canon, pp. 25-28.

COMMUNION ANT. See Jn 9:11   [Spiritual Sight]
**The Lord rubbed my eyes: I went away and washed; then I
could see, and I believed in God.** ↓

PRAYER AFTER COMMUNION   [Joy of Salvation]
Lord,
be close to your family.
Rule and guide us on our way to your kingdom
and bring us to the joy of salvation.
Grant this through Christ our Lord.
℟. **Amen.**   → No. 32, p. 70

Optional Solemn Blessings, p. 92, and Prayers Over the People, p. 99

Some bystanders heard a voice from heaven and maintained,
"An angel has spoken to him."

APRIL 6

5th SUNDAY OF LENT

The Ritual Mass for the Third Scrutiny assigned to this Sunday in the Rite of Christian Initiation of Adults is found on p. 250.

ENTRANCE ANT. Ps 43:1-2   [Rescue Me]
Give me justice, O God, and defend my cause against the wicked; rescue me from deceitful and unjust men. You, O God, are my refuge.

→ No. 2, p. 10 (Omit Gloria)

OPENING PRAYER   [Courage To Follow Christ]
Let us pray
   [for the courage to follow Christ]
Father,
help us to be like Christ your Son,
who loved the world and died for our salvation.
Inspire us by his love,
guide us by his example,
who lives and reigns with you and the Holy Spirit,
one God, for ever and ever. ℟. **Amen.** ↓

245

ALTERNATIVE OPENING PRAYER

[Transforming the World]

Let us pray
  [for the courage to embrace the world
  in the name of Christ]
Father in heaven,
the love of your Son led him to accept the suffering of
  the cross
that his brothers might glory in new life.
Change our selfishness into self-giving.
Help us to embrace the world you have given us,
that we may transform the darkness of its pain
into the life and joy of Easter.
Grant this through Christ our Lord. ℟. **Amen.** ↓

FIRST READING Jer 31:31-34

[A New Covenant]

**The Lord promises a new covenant wherein his law will be
written in the hearts of his people. They will recognize God
as their Lord and he will forgive their sins.**

A reading from the Book of the Prophet Jeremiah

THE days are coming, says the LORD, when I will
make a new covenant with the house of Israel and
the house of Judah. It will not be like the covenant I
made with their fathers the day I took them by the
hand to lead them forth from the land of Egypt; for
they broke my covenant, and I had to show myself
their master, says the LORD. But this is the covenant
that I will make with the house of Israel after those
days, says the LORD. I will place my law within them,
and write it upon their hearts; I will be their God, and
they shall be my people. No longer will they have
need to teach their friends and relatives how to know
the LORD. All, from least to greatest, shall know me,
says the LORD, for I will forgive their evildoing and remember their sin no more.—The word of the Lord. ℟.
Thanks be to God. ↓

RESPONSORIAL PSALM Ps 51   [A Clean Heart]

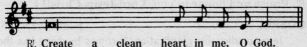

℟. **Create   a   clean   heart in me, O God.**

Have mercy on me, O God, in your goodness;
  in the greatness of your compassion wipe out my of-
    fense.
Thoroughly wash me from my guilt
  and of my sin cleanse me.—℟.
A clean heart create for me, O God,
  and a steadfast spirit renew within me.
Cast me not out from your presence,
  and your Holy Spirit take not from me.—℟.
Give me back the joy of your salvation,
  and a willing spirit sustain in me.
I will teach transgressors your ways,
  and sinners shall return to you.—℟. ↓

SECOND READING Heb 5:7-9   [Christ's Obedience]

**We recall how Jesus prayed to his Father. Through obedi-
ence to suffering, Jesus became perfect and is the source of
salvation for all who obey him.**

A reading from the Letter to the Hebrews

IN the days when Christ Jesus was in the flesh, he offered prayers and supplications with loud cries and
tears to the one who was able to save him from death,
and he was heard because of his reverence. Son
though he was, he learned obedience from what he
suffered; and when he was made perfect, he became
the source of eternal salvation for all who obey him.—
The word of the Lord. ℟. **Thanks be to God.** ↓

VERSE BEFORE THE GOSPEL Jn 12:26   [Follow Me]
℟. **Praise and honor to you, Lord Jesus Christ!**
Whoever serves me must follow me, says the Lord;

and where I am, there also will my servant be.
℟. **Praise and honor to you, Lord Jesus Christ!** ↓

GOSPEL Jn 12:20-33   [Christ Draws All]

> Jesus predicts his glorification. It comes by dying like the grain of wheat. Those who love their life inordinately will lose it. The Father from heaven answers Jesus.

℣. The Lord be with you. ℟. **And also with you.**
✛ A reading from the holy Gospel according to John.
℟. **Glory to you, Lord.**

SOME Greeks who had come to worship at the Passover Feast came to Philip, who was from Bethsaida in Galilee, and asked him, "Sir, we would like to see Jesus." Philip went and told Andrew; then Andrew and Philip went and told Jesus. Jesus answered them, "The hour has come for the Son of Man to be glorified. Amen, amen, I say to you, unless a grain of wheat falls to the ground and dies, it remains just a grain of wheat; but if it dies, it produces much fruit. Whoever loves his life loses it, and whoever hates his life in this world will preserve it for eternal life. Whoever serves me must follow me, and where I am, there also will my servant be. The Father will honor whoever serves me.

"I am troubled now. Yet what should I say? 'Father, save me from this hour'? But it was for this purpose that I came to this hour. Father, glorify your name." Then a voice came from heaven, "I have glorified it and will glorify it again." The crowd there heard it and said it was thunder; but others said, "An angel has spoken to him." Jesus answered and said, "This voice did not come for my sake but for yours. Now is the time of judgment on this world; now the ruler of this world will be driven out. And when I am lifted up from the earth, I will draw everyone to myself." He said this indicating the kind of death he would die.—The Gospel of the Lord. ℟. **Praise to you, Lord Jesus Christ.**   → No. 14, p. 18

Or the Gospel (Jn 11:1-45) from Year A may be said, p. 252.

PRAYER OVER THE GIFTS   [Take Away Sins]
Almighty God,
may the sacrifice we offer
take away the sins of those
whom you enlighten with the Christian faith.
We ask this in the name of Jesus the Lord.
℟. **Amen.**   → No. 21, p. 22 (Pref. P 8-9)

When the Gospel of Lazarus is read, see p. 254 for Preface (P 16).

COMMUNION ANT. Jn 12:24-25   [Life Through Death]
**I tell you solemnly: Unless a grain of wheat falls on
the ground and dies, it remains a single grain; but if it
dies, it yields a rich harvest.** ↓

When the Gospel of Lazarus is read:

COMMUNION ANT. Jn 11:26   [Eternal Life]
**He who lives and believes in me will not die for ever,
said the Lord.** ↓

PRAYER AFTER COMMUNION   [Union with Jesus]
Almighty Father,
by this sacrifice
may we always remain one with your Son, Jesus
    Christ,
whose body and blood we share,
for he is Lord for ever and ever.
℟. **Amen.**   → No. 32, p. 70

Optional Solemn Blessings, p. 92, and Prayers Over the People, p. 99

MASS FOR THE THIRD SCRUTINY

This Mass is celebrated when the Third Scrutiny takes place during the Rite of Christian Initiation of Adults, usually on the 5th Sunday of Lent.

ENTRANCE ANT. Ez 36:23-26   [A New Spirit]
I will prove my holiness through you. I will gather you from the ends of the earth; I will pour clean water on you and wash away all your sins. I will give you a new spirit within you, says the Lord.   → No. 2, p. 10 (Omit Gloria)

OPENING PRAYER   [Members of the Church]
Lord,
enlighten your chosen ones with the word of life.
Give them a new birth
in the waters of baptism
and make them living members of the Church.
Grant this . . . for ever and ever. ℟. **Amen.** ↓

FIRST READING Ez 37:12-14   [The Lord's Promise]
The Lord promises to bring his people back to their home-
land. He will be with them and they will know him.

A reading from the Book of the Prophet Ezekiel

THUS says the LORD God: O my people, I will open your graves and have you rise from them, and bring you back to the land of Israel. Then you shall know that I am the LORD, when I open your graves and have you rise from them, O my people! I will put my spirit in you that you may live, and I will settle you upon your land; thus you shall know that I am the LORD. I have promised, and I will do it, says the LORD.—The word of the Lord. ℟.
Thanks be to God. ↓

RESPONSORIAL PSALM Ps 130   [Mercy and Redemption]

℟. With the Lord there is mer-cy and fullness of redemption.

Out of the depths I cry to you, O LORD;
  LORD, hear my voice!
Let your ears be attentive
  to my voice in supplication.—℟.

If you, O LORD, mark iniquities,
  LORD, who can stand?
But with you is forgiveness,
  that you may be revered.—℟.

I trust in the LORD;
  my soul trusts in his word.
More than sentinels wait for the dawn,
  let Israel wait for the LORD.—℟.

For with the LORD is kindness
  and with him is plenteous redemption;
and he will redeem Israel
  from all their iniquities.—℟. ↓

SECOND READING Rom 8:8-11 [Indwelling of Christ's Spirit]

> The followers of Jesus live in the Spirit of God. The same
> Spirit who brought Jesus back to life will bring mortal bod-
> ies to life since God's Spirit dwells in them.

A reading from the Letter of Saint Paul to the Romans

BROTHERS and sisters: Those who are in the flesh cannot please God. But you are not in the flesh; on the
contrary, you are in the spirit, if only the Spirit of God
dwells in you. Whoever does not have the Spirit of Christ
does not belong to him. But if Christ is in you, although
the body is dead because of sin, the spirit is alive because
of righteousness. If the Spirit of the one who raised Jesus
from the dead dwells in you, the one who raised Christ
from the dead will give life to your mortal bodies also,
through his Spirit dwelling in you.—The word of the
Lord. ℟. **Thanks be to God.** ↓

VERSE BEFORE THE GOSPEL Jn 11:25a, 26 [Resurrection]

℟. **Praise and honor to you, Lord Jesus Christ!**
I am the resurrection and the life, says the Lord;

whoever believes in me will never die.
℟. **Praise and honor to you, Lord Jesus Christ!** ↓

GOSPEL Jn 11:1-45 or 11:3-7, 17, 20-27, 33b-45   **[Lazarus]**

Lazarus, the brother of Martha and Mary, died and was buried. When Jesus came, he assured them that he was the resurrection and the life. Jesus gave life back to Lazarus.

[If the "Shorter Form" is used, the indented text in brackets is omitted.]

℣. The Lord be with you. ℟. **And also with you.**
✛ A reading from the holy Gospel according to John. ℟.
Glory to you, Lord.

[N]OW a man was ill, Lazarus from Bethany, the village of Mary and her sister Martha. Mary was the one who had anointed the Lord with perfumed oil and dried his feet with her hair; it was her brother Lazarus who was ill.]
[So] the sisters sent word to Jesus saying, "Master, the one you love is ill." When Jesus heard this he said, "This illness is not to end in death, but is for the glory of God, that the Son of God may be glorified through it." Now Jesus loved Martha and her sister and Lazarus. So when he heard that he was ill, he remained for two days in the place where he was. Then after this he said to his disciples, "Let us go back to Judea."

[The disciples said to him, "Rabbi, the Jews were just trying to stone you, and you want to go back there?" Jesus answered, "Are there not twelve hours in a day? If one walks during the day, he does not stumble, because he sees the light of this world. But if one walks at night, he stumbles, because the light is not in him." He said this, and then told them, "Our friend Lazarus is asleep, but I am going to awaken him." So the disciples said to him, "Master, if he is asleep, he will be saved." But Jesus was talking about his death, while they thought that he meant ordinary sleep. So then Jesus said to them clearly, "Lazarus has died.

And I am glad for you that I was not there, that you may believe. Let us go to him." So Thomas, called Didymus, said to his fellow disciples, "Let us also go to die with him."]

When Jesus arrived, he found that Lazarus had already been in the tomb for four days.

[Now Bethany was near Jerusalem, only about two miles away. And many of the Jews had come to Martha and Mary to comfort them about their brother.] When Martha heard that Jesus was coming, she went to meet him; but Mary sat at home. Martha said to Jesus, "Lord, if you had been here, my brother would not have died. But even now I know that whatever you ask of God, God will give you." Jesus said to her, "Your brother will rise." Martha said to him, "I know he will rise, in the resurrection on the last day." Jesus told her, "I am the resurrection and the life; whoever believes in me, even if he dies, will live, and everyone who lives and believes in me will never die. Do you believe this?" She said to him, "Yes, Lord. I have come to believe that you are the Christ, the Son of God, the one who is coming into the world."

[When she had said this, she went and called her sister Mary secretly, saying, "The teacher is here and is asking for you." As soon as she heard this, she rose quickly and went to him. For Jesus had not yet come into the village, but was still where Martha had met him. So when the Jews who were with her in the house comforting her saw Mary get up quickly and go out, they followed her, presuming that she was going to the tomb to weep there. When Mary came to where Jesus was and saw him, she fell at his feet and said to him, "Lord, if you had been here, my brother would not have died." When Jesus saw her weeping and the Jews who had come with her weeping,]

he became perturbed and deeply troubled, and said, "Where have you laid him?" They said to him, "Sir, come and see." And Jesus wept. So the Jews said, "See how he loved him." But some of them said, "Could not the one who opened the eyes of the blind man have done something so that this man would not have died?"

So Jesus, perturbed again, came to the tomb. It was a cave, and a stone lay across it. Jesus said, "Take away the stone." Martha, the dead man's sister, said to him, "Lord, by now there will be a stench; he has been dead for four days." Jesus said to her, "Did I not tell you that if you believe you will see the glory of God?" So they took away the stone. And Jesus raised his eyes and said, "Father, I thank you for hearing me. I know that you always hear me; but because of the crowd here I have said this, that they may believe that you sent me." And when he had said this, he cried out in a loud voice, "Lazarus, come out!" The dead man came out, tied hand and foot with burial bands, and his face was wrapped in a cloth. So Jesus said to them, "Untie him and let him go."

Now many of the Jews who had come to Mary and seen what he had done began to believe in him.—The Gospel of the Lord. ℟. **Praise to you, Lord Jesus Christ.**

→ No. 14, p. 18

PRAYER OVER THE GIFTS   [Preparing for Baptism]

Almighty God,
hear our prayer for these men and women
who have begun to learn the Christian faith,
and by this sacrifice prepare them for baptism.
We ask this through Christ our Lord. ℟. **Amen.**

PREFACE (P 16)   [Christ Raised Lazarus]

℣. The Lord be with you. ℟. **And also with you.**
℣. Lift up your hearts. ℟. **We lift them up to the Lord.**
℣. Let us give thanks to the Lord our God. ℟. **It is right to give him thanks and praise.**

Father, all-powerful and ever-living God,
we do well always and everywhere to give you thanks
through Jesus Christ our Lord.
As a man like us, Jesus wept for Lazarus his friend.

As the eternal God, he raised Lazarus from the dead.
In his love for us all,
Christ gives us the sacraments
to lift us up to everlasting life.
Through him the angels of heaven offer their prayer of
    adoration
as they rejoice in your presence for ever.
May our voices be one with theirs
in their triumphant hymn of praise: ➜ No. 23, p. 23

*When Eucharistic Prayer I is used, the special Christian Ini-
tiation forms of* Remember, Lord, your people *and* Father,
accept this offering *are said.*

Remember, Lord, these godparents
who will present your chosen men and women for
    baptism.

(the names of the godparents are mentioned).

Lord, remember all of us . . . (p. 24).

Father,
accept this offering
from your whole family.
We offer it especially for the men and women
you call to share your life
through the living waters of baptism.

[Through Christ our Lord. Amen.]

The rest follows the Roman Canon, pp. 25-28.

COMMUNION ANT. Jn 11:26   [Eternal Life]

**He who lives and believes in me will not die for ever, said
the Lord.** ↓

PRAYER AFTER COMMUNION   [God's Children]

Lord,
may your people be one in spirit
and serve you with all their heart.
Free them from all fear.

Give them joy in your gifts
and love for those
who are to be reborn as your children.
We ask this through Christ our Lord.
℟. **Amen.**   → No. 32, p. 70

Optional Solemn Blessings, p. 92, and Prayers Over the People, p. 99

*"Blessed are you who have come to us
so rich in love and mercy."*

APRIL 13

PALM SUNDAY OF THE LORD'S PASSION

*On this day the Church celebrates Christ's entrance into
Jerusalem to accomplish his paschal mystery. Accordingly,
the memorial of this event is included in every Mass, with the
procession or the solemn entrance before the principal Mass,
with the simple entrance before the other Masses. The solemn
entrance (but not the procession) may be repeated before
other Masses that are usually well attended.*

Commemoration of the Lord's Entrance
into Jerusalem

FIRST FORM: THE PROCESSION

*At the scheduled time, the congregation assembles in a sec-
ondary church or chapel or in some other suitable place distinct from the church to which the procession will move. The
faithful carry palm branches.*

*The following antiphon or any other appropriate song is
sung.*

ANTIPHON Mt 21:9   [Hosanna]

**Hosanna to the Son of David,
the King of Israel.**

**Blessed is he who comes
in the name of the Lord.
Hosanna in the highest.**

*The priest then greets the people in the usual way and gives a
brief introduction, inviting them to take a full part in the celebration, using these or similar words:*

Dear friends in Christ, for five weeks of Lent we have
been preparing, by works of charity and self-sacrifice,
for the celebration of our Lord's paschal mystery.
Today we come together to begin this solemn celebration in union with the whole Church throughout the
world. Christ entered in triumph into his own city, to
complete his work as our Messiah: to suffer, to die,
and to rise again. Let us remember with devotion this
entry which began his saving work and follow him
with a lively faith. United with him in his suffering on
the cross, may we share his resurrection and new life.

*Afterwards the priest, with hands joined, says one of the fol-
lowing prayers:*

PRAYER   **[Following Christ]**
Let us pray.
Almighty God,
we pray you
bless ✚ these branches
and make them holy.
Today we joyfully acclaim Jesus our Messiah and
    King.
May we reach one day the happiness of the new and
    everlasting Jerusalem
by faithfully following him
who lives and reigns for ever and ever. ℟. **Amen.** ↓

OR   **[Christ Our King]**
Let us pray.
Lord,
increase the faith of your people

and listen to our prayers.
Today we honor Christ our triumphant King
by carrying these branches.
May we honor you every day
by living always in him,
for he is Lord for ever and ever. ℟. **Amen.** ↓

The priest sprinkles the branches with holy water in silence.

Then the account of the Lord's entrance is proclaimed from one of the four gospels. This is done in the usual way or, if there is no deacon, by the priest.

GOSPEL Mk 11:1-10   [Jesus' Triumphal Entry]

In triumphant glory Jesus comes into Jerusalem. The people spread their cloaks on the ground for him, wave olive branches and sing in his honor.

℣. The Lord be with you. ℟. **And also with you.**
✛ A reading from the holy Gospel according to Mark.
℟. **Glory to you, Lord.**

WHEN Jesus and his disciples drew near to Jerusalem, to Bethphage and Bethany at the Mount of Olives, he sent two of his disciples and said to them, "Go into the village opposite you, and immediately on entering it, you will find a colt tethered on which no one has ever sat. Untie it and bring it here. If anyone should say to you, 'Why are you doing this?' reply, 'The Master has need of it and will send it back here at once.'" So they went off and found a colt tethered at a gate outside on the street, and they untied it. Some of the bystanders said to them, "What are you doing, untying the colt?" They answered them just as Jesus had told them to, and they permitted them to do it. So they brought the colt to Jesus and put their cloaks over it. And he sat on it. Many people spread their cloaks on the road, and others spread leafy branches that they had cut from the fields. Those preceding him as well as those following kept crying out:

"Hosanna!
Blessed is he who comes in the name of the Lord!
Blessed is the kingdom of our father David that is
    to come!
Hosanna in the highest!"

The Gospel of the Lord. ℟. **Praise to you, Lord Jesus Christ.**

OR

GOSPEL Jn 12:12-16   [Blessed Is Israel's King]

(See commentary in preceding Gospel.)

℣. The Lord be with you. ℟. **And also with you.**
✣ A reading from the holy Gospel according to John.
℟. **Glory to you, Lord.**

WHEN the great crowd that had come to the feast
heard that Jesus was coming to Jerusalem, they
took palm branches and went out to meet him, and
cried out:
"Hosanna!
"Blessed is he who comes in the name of the Lord,
    the king of Israel."
Jesus found an ass and sat upon it, as is written:
Fear no more, O daughter Zion;
see, your king comes, seated upon an ass's colt.
His disciples did not understand this at first, but when
Jesus had been glorified they remembered that these
things were written about him and that they had done
this for him.—The Gospel of the Lord. ℟. **Praise to
you, Lord Jesus Christ.**

*After the gospel, a brief homily may be given. Before the pro-
cession begins, the celebrant or other suitable minister may
address the people in these or similar words:*

Let us go forth in peace
praising Jesus our Messiah,
as did the crowds who welcomed him to Jerusalem.

The procession to the church where Mass will be celebrated then begins.

If incense is used, the thurifer goes first with a lighted censer, followed by the cross-bearer (with the cross suitably decorated) between two ministers with lighted candles, then the priest with the ministers, and finally the congregation carrying branches.

During the procession, the choir and people sing the following or other appropriate songs:

ANTIPHON 1   [Hosanna]

**The children of Jerusalem
welcomed Christ the King.
They carried olive branches
and loudly praised the Lord:
Hosanna in the highest.**

The above antiphon may be repeated between verses of Psalm 24.

PSALM 24   [The King of Glory]

**The LORD's are the earth and its fullness;
    the world and those who dwell in it.
For he founded it upon the seas
    and established it upon the rivers.**

Repeat antiphon 1

**Who can ascend the mountain of the LORD?
    or who may stand in his holy place?
He whose hands are sinless, whose heart is clean,
    who desires not what is vain,
    nor swears deceitfully to his neighbor.**

Repeat antiphon 1

**He shall receive a blessing from the LORD,
    a reward from God his savior.
Such is the race that seeks for him,
    that seeks the face of the God of Jacob.**

Repeat antiphon 1

Lift up, O gates, your lintels;
   reach up, you ancient portals,
   that the king of glory may come in!
Who is this king of glory?
   The LORD, strong and mighty,
   the LORD, mighty in battle.

Repeat antiphon 1

Lift up, O gates, your lintels;
   reach up, you ancient portals,
   that the king of glory may come in!
Who is this king of glory?
   The LORD of hosts; he is the king of glory.

Repeat antiphon 1

ANTIPHON 2   **[Hosanna]**

The children of Jerusalem
welcomed Christ the King.
They spread their cloaks before him
and loudly praised the Lord:
Hosanna to the Son of David!
Blessed is he who comes
in the name of the Lord!

The above antiphon may be repeated between the verses of Psalm 47.

PSALM 47   **[The Great King]**

All you peoples, clap your hands,
   shout to God with cries of gladness.
For the LORD, the Most High, the awesome,
   is the great king over all the earth.

Repeat antiphon 2

He brings peoples under us;
   nations under our feet.
He chooses for us our inheritance,
   the glory of Jacob, whom he loves.

Repeat antiphon 2

God mounts his throne amid shouts of joy;
   the LORD, amid trumpet blasts.

Sing praise to God, sing praise;
  sing praise to our king, sing praise.

Repeat antiphon 2

For king of all the earth is God;
  sing hymns of praise.
God reigns over the nations,
  God sits upon his holy throne.

Repeat antiphon 2

The princes of the peoples are gathered together
  with the people of the God of Abraham.
For God's are the guardians of the earth;
  he is supreme.

Repeat antiphon 2

A hymn in honor of Christ the King, such as All Glory, Laud
and Honor, *is sung during the procession. See p. 614 for text.*

*As the procession enters the church, the following responsory
or another song which refers to the Lord's entrance is sung.*

RESPONSORY   [Hosanna]

R̹. The children of Jerusalem
welcomed Christ the King.
They proclaimed the resurrection of life,
and, waving olive branches,
they loudly praised the Lord:
Hosanna in the highest.

V̹. When the people heard that Jesus
was entering Jerusalem,
they went to meet him
and, waving olive branches,
they loudly praised the Lord:
Hosanna in the highest.

*When the priest comes to the altar he venerates it and may
also incense it. Then he goes to his chair (removes the cope
and puts on the chasuble) and begins immediately the open-*

ing prayer of Mass, which concludes the procession. Mass then continues in the usual way.

SECOND FORM: THE SOLEMN ENTRANCE

If the procession cannot be held outside the church, the commemoration of the Lord's entrance may be celebrated before the principal Mass with the solemn entrance, which takes place within the church.

The faithful, holding the branches, assemble either in front of the church door or inside the church. The priest and ministers, with a representative group of the faithful, go to a suitable place in the church outside the sanctuary, so that most of the people will be able to see the rite.

While the priest goes to the appointed place, the antiphon Hosanna *or other suitable song is sung. Then the blessing of branches and proclamation of the gospel about the Lord's entrance into Jerusalem take place, as above. After the gospel the priest, with the ministers and the group of the faithful, moves solemnly through the church to the sanctuary, while the responsory* The children of Jerusalem *or other appropriate song is sung.*

When the priest comes to the altar he venerates it, goes to his chair, and immediately begins the opening prayer of Mass, which then continues in the usual way.

THIRD FORM: THE SIMPLE ENTRANCE

At all other Masses on this Sunday, if the solemn entrance is not held, the Lord's entrance is commemorated with the following simple entrance.

While the priest goes to the altar, the entrance antiphon with its psalm or another song with the same theme is sung.

ENTRANCE ANT.   [Praise the Lord]

Six days before the solemn passover the Lord came to Jerusalem, and children waving palm branches ran out to welcome him. They loudly praised the Lord: Blessed are you who have come to us so rich in love and mercy.

PSALM 24:9-10   [The King of Glory]
Open wide the doors and gates.
Lift high the ancient portals.
The King of glory enters.
Who is this King of glory?
He is God the mighty Lord.
Hosanna in the highest.
Blessed are you who have come to us
so rich in love and mercy.
Hosanna in the highest.

Where neither the procession nor the solemn entrance can be
celebrated, there should be a Bible service on the theme of the
Lord's messianic entrance and passion, either on Saturday
evening or on Sunday at a convenient time.

MASS

After the procession or solemn entrance the priest begins the
Mass with the opening prayer.

OPENING PRAYER   [Union with Christ]
Let us pray
    [for a closer union with Christ
    during this holy season]
Almighty, ever-living God,
you have given the human race Jesus Christ our Savior
as a model of humility.
He fulfilled your will
by becoming man and giving his life on the cross.
Help us to bear witness to you
by following his example of suffering
and make us worthy to share in his resurrection.
We ask this through our Lord Jesus Christ, your Son,
who lives and reigns with you and the Holy Spirit,
one God, for ever and ever. ℟. **Amen.** ↓

ALTERNATIVE OPENING PRAYER

[Guided by Christ's Truth]

Let us pray
   [as we accompany our King to Jerusalem]
Almighty Father of our Lord Jesus Christ,
you sent your Son
to be born of woman and to die on a cross,
so that through the obedience of one man,
estrangement might be dissolved for all men.
Guide our minds by his truth
and strengthen our lives by the example of his death,
that we may live in union with you
in the kingdom of your promise.
Grant this through Christ our Lord. ℟. **Amen.** ↓

FIRST READING Is 50:4-7 [Christ's Suffering]

**Isaiah was persecuted and struck by his own people; he
was spit upon and beaten. He proclaims the true faith and
suffers to atone for the sins of his people. Here we see a
foreshadowing of the true servant of God.**

A reading from the Book of the Prophet Isaiah

THE Lord GOD has given me
  a well-trained tongue,
that I might know how to speak to the weary
  a word that will rouse them.
Morning after morning
  he opens my ear that I may hear;
and I have not rebelled,
  have not turned back.
I gave my back to those who beat me,
  my cheeks to those who plucked my beard;
my face I did not shield
  from buffets and spitting.
The Lord GOD is my help,
  therefore I am not disgraced;
I have set my face like flint,
  knowing that I shall not be put to shame.
The word of the Lord. ℟. **Thanks be to God.** ↓

RESPONSORIAL PSALM Ps 22   [Christ's Abandonment]

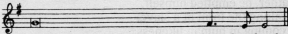

℟. My God, my God, why have you a - ban - doned me?

All who see me scoff at me;
  they mock me with parted lips, they wag their heads:
"He relied on the Lord; let him deliver him,
  let him rescue him, if he loves him."

℟. **My God, my God, why have you abandoned me?**

Indeed, many dogs surround me,
  a pack of evildoers closes in upon me;
they have pierced my hands and my feet;
  I can count all my bones.

℟. **My God, my God, why have you abandoned me?**

They divide my garments among them,
  and for my vesture they cast lots.
But you, O Lord, be not far from me;
  O my help, hasten to aid me.

℟. **My God, my God, why have you abandoned me?**

I will proclaim your name to my brethren;
  in the midst of the assembly I will praise you:
"You who fear the Lord, praise him;
  all you descendants of Jacob, give glory to him;
  revere him, all you descendants of Israel!"

℟. **My God, my God, why have you abandoned me?** ↓

SECOND READING Phil 2:6-11   [Humility]

**Paul urges us to humility by which we are made like to
Christ, our Lord, who, putting off the majesty of his divinity, became man and humbled himself in obedience to the
ignominious death of the cross.**

A reading from the Letter of Saint Paul
to the Philippians

CHRIST Jesus, though he was in the form of God,
did not regard equality with God

something to be grasped.
Rather, he emptied himself,
taking the form of a slave,
coming in human likeness;
and found human in appearance,
he humbled himself,
becoming obedient to the point of death,
even death on a cross.
Because of this, God greatly exalted him
and bestowed on him the name
which is above every name,
that at the name of Jesus
every knee should bend,
of those in heaven and on the earth and under the earth,
and every tongue confess that
Jesus Christ is Lord,
to the glory of God the Father.
The word of the Lord. ℟. **Thanks be to God.** ↓

VERSE BEFORE THE GOSPEL Phil 2:8-9 [Obedient to Death]
℟. **Praise to you, Lord Jesus Christ, king of endless glory!**
Christ became obedient to the point of death,
even death on a cross.
Because of this, God greatly exalted him
and bestowed on him a name which is above every name.
℟. **Praise to you, Lord Jesus Christ, king of endless glory!** ↓

GOSPEL Mk 14:1—15:47 or 15:1-39   [Christ's Passion]
Mark recounts the events that led up to the betrayal of Jesus and his final condemnation—his death on the cross. At the Last Supper, Jesus institutes the Holy Eucharist.

When the Shorter Form is read, the Passion begins at no. 8 below and ends after no. 13, pp. 274-276.

The fourteen subheadings introduced into the reading enable those who so desire to meditate on this text while making the Stations of the Cross.

The Passion may be read by lay readers, with the part of Christ, if possible, read by a priest. The Narrator is noted by N, the words of Jesus by a ✠ and the words of others by V (Voice) and C (Crowd). The part of the Crowd (C) printed in boldface type may be recited by the people.

We participate in the passion narrative in several ways: by reading it and reflecting on it during the week ahead; by listening with faith as it is proclaimed; by respectful posture during the narrative; by reverent silence after the passage about Christ's death. We do not hold the palms during the reading on Passion Sunday.

The message of the liturgy in proclaiming the passion narratives in full is to enable the assembly to see vividly the love of Christ for each person, despite their sins, a love that even death could not vanquish. The crimes during the Passion of Christ cannot be attributed indiscriminately to all Jews of that time, nor to Jews today. The Jewish people should not be referred to as though rejected or cursed, as if this view followed Scripture. The Church ever keeps in mind that Jesus, his mother Mary, and the Apostles were Jewish. As the Church has always held, Christ freely suffered his passion and death because of the sins of all, that all might be saved.

N. THE Passion of our Lord Jesus Christ according to Mark.

1. PLOT AGAINST JESUS AND SUPPER AT BETHANY

N. THE Passover and the Feast of Unleavened Bread were to take place in two days' time. So the chief priests and the scribes were seeking a way to arrest him by treachery and put him to death. They said, **C. "Not during the festival, for fear that there may be a riot among the people."**

N. When he was in Bethany reclining at table in the house of Simon the leper, a woman came with an alabaster jar of perfumed oil, costly genuine spikenard.

She broke the alabaster jar and poured it on his head.
There were some who were indignant. **C. "Why has
there been this waste of perfumed oil? It could have
been sold for more than three hundred days' wages
and the money given to the poor." N.** They were infu-
riated with her. Jesus said, ✣ *"Let her alone. Why do
you make trouble for her? She has done a good thing
for me. The poor you will always have with you, and
whenever you wish you can do good to them, but you
will not always have me. She has done what she
could. She has anticipated anointing my body for
burial. Amen, I say to you, wherever the gospel is proclaimed to the whole world, what she has done will be
told in memory of her."*

2. THE TREASON OF JUDAS

N. THEN Judas Iscariot, one of the Twelve, went
off to the chief priests to hand him over to
them. When they heard him they were pleased and
promised to pay him money. Then he looked for an
opportunity to hand him over.

3. THE LAST SUPPER

N. ON the first day of the Feast of Unleavened
Bread, when they sacrificed the Passover
lamb, his disciples said to him, **C. "Where do you
want us to go and prepare for you to eat the
Passover?" N.** He sent two of his disciples and said to
them, ✣ *"Go into the city and a man will meet you,
carrying a jar of water. Follow him. Wherever he enters, say to the master of the house, 'The Teacher
says, "Where is my guest room where I may eat the
Passover with my disciples?" ' Then he will show you
a large upper room furnished and ready. Make the
preparations for us there." N.* The disciples then went
off, entered the city, and found it just as he had told
them; and they prepared the Passover.

When it was evening, he came with the Twelve. And as they reclined at table and were eating, Jesus said, ✠ *"Amen, I say to you, one of you will betray me, one who is eating with me."* **N.** They began to be distressed and to say to him, one by one, **V.** "Surely it is not I?" **N.** He said to them, ✠ *"One of the Twelve, the one who dips with me into the dish. For the Son of Man indeed goes, as it is written of him, but woe to that man by whom the Son of Man is betrayed. It would be better for that man if he had never been born."*

N. While they were eating, he took bread, said the blessing, broke it, and gave it to them, and said, ✠ *"Take it; this is my body."* **N.** Then he took a cup, gave thanks, and gave it to them, and they all drank from it. He said to them, ✠ *"This is my blood of the covenant, which will be shed for many. Amen, I say to you, I shall not drink again the fruit of the vine until the day when I drink it new in the kingdom of God."* **N.** Then, after singing a hymn, they went out to the Mount of Olives.

N. Then Jesus said to them, ✠ *"All of you will have your faith shaken, for it is written:*

I will strike the shepherd,
  and the sheep will be dispersed.
But after I have been raised up, I shall go before you to Galilee." **N.** Peter said to him, **V.** "Even though all should have their faith shaken, mine will not be." **N.** Then Jesus said to him, ✠ *"Amen, I say to you, this very night before the cock crows twice you will deny me three times."* **N.** But he vehemently replied, **V.** "Even though I should have to die with you, I will not deny you." **N.** And they all spoke similarly.

4. THE PRAYER IN GETHSEMANE

N. **T**HEN they came to a place named Gethsemane, and he said to his disciples, ✠ *"Sit here while I* *pray.*" **N.** He took with him Peter, James, and John, and began to be troubled and distressed. Then he said to them, ✚ *"My soul is sorrowful even to death. Remain here and keep watch."* **N.** He advanced a little and fell to the ground and prayed that if it were possible the hour might pass by him; he said, ✚ *"Abba, Father, all things are possible to you. Take this cup away from me, but not what I will but what you will."* **N.** When he returned he found them asleep. He said to Peter, ✚ *"Simon, are you asleep? Could you not keep watch for one hour? Watch and pray that you may not undergo the test. The spirit is willing but the flesh is weak."* **N.** Withdrawing again, he prayed, saying the same thing. Then he returned once more and found them asleep, for they could not keep their eyes open and did not know what to answer him. He returned a third time and said to them, ✚ *"Are you still sleeping and taking your rest? It is enough. The hour has come. Behold, the Son of Man is to be handed over to sinners. Get up, let us go. See, my betrayer is at hand."*

5. THE ARREST OF JESUS

N. **T**HEN, while he was still speaking, Judas, one of the Twelve, arrived, accompanied by a crowd with swords and clubs who had come from the chief priests, the scribes, and the elders. His betrayer had arranged a signal with them, saying, **V.** "The man I shall kiss is the one; arrest him and lead him away securely." **N.** He came and immediately went over to him and said, **V.** "Rabbi." **N.** And he kissed him. At this they laid hands on him and arrested him. One of the bystanders drew his sword, struck the high priest's servant, and cut off his ear. Jesus said to them in reply, ✚ *"Have you come out as against a robber, with swords and clubs, to seize me? Day after day I was with you teaching in the temple area, yet you did not arrest me; but that the Scriptures may be ful-*

filled." **N.** And they all left him and fled. Now a young man followed him wearing nothing but a linen cloth about his body. They seized him, but he left the cloth behind and ran off naked.

6. JESUS BEFORE CAIAPHAS

N. **T**HEY led Jesus away to the high priest, and all the chief priests and the elders and the scribes came together. Peter followed him at a distance into the high priest's courtyard and was seated with the guards, warming himself at the fire. The chief priests and the entire Sanhedrin kept trying to obtain testimony against Jesus in order to put him to death, but they found none. Many gave false witness against him, but their testimony did not agree. Some took the stand and testified falsely against him, alleging, **C.** **"We heard him say, 'I will destroy this temple made with hands and within three days I will build another not made with hands.' "** **N.** Even so their testimony did not agree. The high priest rose before the assembly and questioned Jesus, saying, **V.** "Have you no answer? What are these men testifying against you?" **N.** But he was silent and answered nothing. Again the high priest asked him and said to him, **V.** "Are you the Christ, the son of the Blessed One?" **N.** Then Jesus answered, ✝ *"I am;*

and 'you will see the Son of Man
seated at the right hand of the Power
and coming with the clouds of heaven.' "

N. At that the high priest tore his garments and said, **V.** "What further need have we of witnesses? You have heard the blasphemy. What do you think?" **N.** They all condemned him as deserving to die. Some began to spit on him. They blindfolded him and struck him and said to him, **C.** **"Prophesy!"** **N.** And the guards greeted him with blows.

7. PETER'S DENIAL

N. WHILE Peter was below in the courtyard, one of the high priest's maids came along. Seeing Peter warming himself, she looked intently at him and said, **C. "You too were with the Nazarene, Jesus." N.** But he denied it saying, **V.** "I neither know nor understand what you are talking about." **N.** So he went out into the outer court. Then the cock crowed. The maid saw him and began again to say to the bystanders, **C. "This man is one of them." N.** Once again he denied it. A little later the bystanders said to Peter once more, **C. "Surely you are one of them; for you too are a Galilean." N.** He began to curse and to swear, **V.** "I do not know this man about whom you are talking." **N.** And immediately a cock crowed a second time. Then Peter remembered the word that Jesus had said to him, "Before the cock crows twice you will deny me three times." He broke down and wept.

[Beginning of Shorter Form]

8. JESUS BEFORE PILATE

N. AS soon as morning came, the chief priests with the elders and the scribes, that is, the whole Sanhedrin, held a council. They bound Jesus, led him away, and handed him over to Pilate. Pilate questioned him, **V.** "Are you the king of the Jews?" **N.** He said to him in reply, ✝ *"You say so." ***N.** The chief priests accused him of many things. Again Pilate questioned him, **V.** "Have you no answer? See how many things they accuse you of." **N.** Jesus gave him no further answer, so that Pilate was amazed.

9. BARABBAS

N. NOW on the occasion of the feast he used to release to them one prisoner whom they requested. A man called Barabbas was then in prison along with the rebels who had committed murder in a rebellion. The crowd came forward and began to ask him to do for them as he was accustomed. Pilate answered, **V.** "Do you want me to release to you the king of the Jews?" **N.** For he knew that it was out of envy that the chief priests had handed him over. But the chief priests stirred up the crowd to have him release Barabbas for them instead. Pilate again said to them in reply, **V.** "Then what do you want me to do with the man you call the king of the Jews?" **N.** They shouted again, **C.** "**Crucify him.**" **N.** Pilate said to them, **V.** "Why? What evil has he done?" **N.** They only shouted the louder, **C.** "**Crucify him.**" **N.** So Pilate, wishing to satisfy the crowd, released Barabbas to them and, after he had Jesus scourged, handed him over to be crucified.

10. THE CROWNING WITH THORNS

N. THE soldiers led him away inside the palace, that is, the praetorium, and assembled the whole cohort. They clothed him in purple and, weaving a crown of thorns, placed it on him. They began to salute him with, **C.** "**Hail, King of the Jews!**" **N.** and kept striking his head with a reed and spitting upon him. They knelt before him in homage. And when they had mocked him, they stripped him of the purple cloak, dressed him in his own clothes, and led him out to crucify him.

11. THE CRUCIFIXION

N. THEY pressed into service a passer-by, Simon, a Cyrenian, who was coming in from the country, the father of Alexander and Rufus, to carry his cross.

They brought him to the place of Golgotha—which is translated Place of the Skull—.They gave him wine drugged with myrrh, but he did not take it. Then they crucified him and divided his garments by casting lots for them to see what each should take. It was nine o'clock in the morning when they crucified him. The inscription of the charge against him read, "The King of the Jews." With him they crucified two revolutionaries, one on his right and one on his left.

12. ON CALVARY

N. **T**HOSE passing by reviled him, shaking their heads and saying, **C.** **"Aha! You who would destroy the temple and rebuild it in three days, save yourself by coming down from the cross."** **N.** Likewise the chief priests, with the scribes, mocked him among themselves and said, **C.** **"He saved others; he cannot save himself. Let the Christ, the King of Israel, come down now from the cross that we may see and believe."** **N.** Those who were crucified with him also kept abusing him.

13. THE DEATH OF JESUS

N. **A**T noon darkness came over the whole land until three in the afternoon. And at three o'clock Jesus cried out in a loud voice, ✠ *"Eloi, Eloi, lema sabachthani?"* **N.** which is translated, ✠ *"My God, my God, why have you forsaken me?"* **N.** Some of the bystanders who heard it said, **C.** **"Look, he is calling Elijah."** **N.** One of them ran, soaked a sponge with wine, put it on a reed and gave it to him to drink, saying, **V.** "Wait, let us see if Elijah comes to take him down." **N.** Jesus gave a loud cry and breathed his last.

Here all kneel and pause for a short time.

The veil of the sanctuary was torn in two from top to bottom. When the centurion who stood facing him saw how he breathed his last he said, **V.** "Truly this man was the Son of God!"

[End of Shorter Form]

14. THE BURIAL

N. **T**HERE were also women looking on from a distance. Among them were Mary Magdalene, Mary the mother of the younger James and of Joses, and Salome. These women had followed him when he was in Galilee and ministered to him. There were also many other women who had come up with him to Jerusalem.

When it was already evening, since it was the day of preparation, the day before the sabbath, Joseph of Arimathea, a distinguished member of the council, who was himself awaiting the kingdom of God, came and courageously went to Pilate and asked for the body of Jesus. Pilate was amazed that he was already dead. He summoned the centurion and asked him if Jesus had already died. And when he learned of it from the centurion, he gave the body to Joseph. Having bought a linen cloth, he took him down, wrapped him in the linen cloth, and laid him in a tomb that had been hewn out of the rock. Then he rolled a stone against the entrance to the tomb. Mary Magdalene and Mary the mother of Joses watched where he was laid.—The Gospel of the Lord. ℟. **Praise to you, Lord Jesus Christ.**

→ No. 14, p. 18

PRAYER OVER THE GIFTS   [Pleasing to God]

Lord,
may the suffering and death of Jesus, your only Son,
make us pleasing to you.
Alone we can do nothing,
but may this perfect sacrifice
win us your mercy and love.
We ask this in the name of Jesus the Lord. ℟. **Amen.** ↓

PREFACE (P 19)   [Raised to Holiness of Life]

℣. The Lord be with you. ℟. **And also with you.**
℣. Lift up your hearts. ℟. **We lift them up to the Lord.**

℣. Let us give thanks to the Lord our God. ℟. **It is right to give him thanks and praise.**

Father, all-powerful and ever-living God,
we do well always and everywhere to give you thanks
through Jesus Christ our Lord.
Though he was sinless, he suffered willingly for sin-
     ners.
Though innocent, he accepted death to save the guilty.
By his dying he has destroyed our sins.
By his rising he has raised us up to holiness of life.
We praise you, Lord, with all the angels
in their song of joy: ➔ No. 23, p. 23

COMMUNION ANT. Mt 26:42   [God's Will]
**Father, if this cup may not pass, but I must drink it,
then your will be done. ↓**

PRAYER AFTER COMMUNION   [Perseverance]
Lord,
you have satisfied our hunger with this eucharistic
     food.
The death of your Son gives us hope and strengthens
     our faith.
May his resurrection give us perseverance
and lead us to salvation.
We ask this through Christ our Lord.
℟. **Amen.**   ➔ No. 32, p. 70

Optional Solemn Blessings, p. 92, and Prayers Over the People, p. 99

"The Spirit of the Lord is upon me."

APRIL 17

HOLY THURSDAY

CHRISM MASS

This Mass, which the bishop concelebrates with his presbyterium and at which the oils are blessed, manifests the communion of the priests with their bishop. It is thus desirable that, if possible, all the priests take part in it, together with parish representatives, and receive communion under both kinds. This day also is dedicated to the renewal of priestly ministry.

ENTRANCE ANT. Rv 1:6   [Kingdom of Priests]

Jesus Christ has made us a kingdom of priests to serve his God and Father: glory and kingship be his for ever and ever. Amen.   → No. 2, p. 10

The Gloria is sung or said.

OPENING PRAYER   [Faithful Witnesses]

Father,
by the power of the Holy Spirit
you anointed your only Son Messiah and Lord of creation;
you have given us a share in his consecration
to priestly service in your Church.

Help us to be faithful witnesses in the world
to the salvation Christ won for all mankind.
We ask this . . . for ever and ever. ℟. **Amen.** ↓

FIRST READING Is 61:1-3ab, 6a, 8b-9   [The Lord's Anointed]

**Isaiah the prophet, anointed by God to bring the Good
News to the poor, proclaims a message filled with hope. It
is one that replaces mourning with gladness.**

A reading from the Book of the Prophet Isaiah

THE spirit of the Lord GOD is upon me,
  because the LORD has anointed me;
he has sent me to bring glad tidings to the poor,
  to heal the brokenhearted,
to proclaim liberty to the captives
  and release to the prisoners,
to announce a year of favor from the LORD
  and a day of vindication by our God,
  to comfort all who mourn;
to place on those who mourn in Zion
  a diadem instead of ashes,
to give them oil of gladness in place of mourning,
  a glorious mantle instead of a listless spirit.
You yourselves shall be named priests of the LORD,
  ministers of our God you shall be called.
I will give them their recompense faithfully,
  a lasting covenant I will make with them.
Their descendants shall be renowned among the nations,
  and their offspring among the peoples;
all who see them shall acknowledge them
  as a race the LORD has blessed.
The word of the Lord. ℟. **Thanks be to God.** ↓

RESPONSORIAL PSALM Ps 89   [God the Savior]

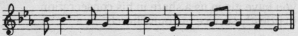

℟. **For ev - er I will sing the good-ness of the Lord.**

I have found David, my servant;
   with my holy oil I have anointed him,
that my hand may be always with him,
   and that my arm may make him strong.—℟.

My faithfulness and my kindness shall be with him,
   and through my name shall his horn be exalted.
"He shall say of me, 'You are my father,
   my God, the Rock my savior.' "—℟. ↓

SECOND READING Rv 1:5-8   [The Alpha and the Omega]

God says, "I am the Alpha and the Omega, the one who is
and who was and who is to come, the almighty!" All shall
see God as he comes amid the clouds.

A reading from the Book of Revelation

JESUS Christ is the faithful witness, the firstborn of
the dead and ruler of the kings of earth. To him
who loves us and has freed us from our sins by his
blood, who has made us into a kingdom, priests for
his God and Father, to him be glory and power forever
and ever! Amen.
   Behold, he is coming amid the clouds,
      and every eye will see him,
      even of those who pierced him.
   All the peoples of the earth will lament him.
      Yes. Amen.
"I am the Alpha and the Omega," says the Lord God,
"the one who is and who was and who is to come, the
almighty!"—The word of the Lord. ℟. **Thanks be to
God.** ↓

VERSE BEFORE THE GOSPEL Is 61:1(cited in Lk 4:18)
[Glad Tidings]

℟. **Glory to you, Word of God, Lord Jesus Christ!**
The Spirit of the Lord is upon me
for he sent me to bring glad tidings to the poor.
℟. **Glory to you, Word of God, Lord Jesus Christ!** ↓

GOSPEL Lk 4:16-21   [Christ the Messiah]

Jesus reads in the synagogue at Nazareth the words of Isaiah quoted in the first reading. Jesus is the Anointed One. He tells the people that today Isaiah's prophecy is fulfilled.

℣. The Lord be with you. ℟. **And also with you.**
✠ A reading from the holy Gospel according to Luke.
℟. **Glory to you, Lord.**

JESUS came to Nazareth, where he had grown up, and went according to his custom into the synagogue on the sabbath day. He stood up to read and was handed a scroll of the prophet Isaiah. He unrolled the scroll and found the passage where it was written:

The Spirit of the Lord is upon me,
because he has anointed me
    to bring glad tidings to the poor.
He has sent me to proclaim liberty to captives
    and recovery of sight to the blind,
    to let the oppressed go free,
and to proclaim a year acceptable to the Lord.

Rolling up the scroll, he handed it back to the attendant and sat down, and the eyes of all in the synagogue looked intently at him. He said to them, "Today this Scripture passage is fulfilled in your hearing."— The Gospel of the Lord. ℟. **Praise to you, Lord Jesus Christ.** ↓

Renewal of Commitment to Priestly Service

After the homily the bishop speaks to the priests:

My brothers,
today we celebrate the memory of the first eucharist,
at which our Lord Jesus Christ
shared with his apostles and with us
his call to the priestly service of his Church.
Now, in the presence of your bishop and God's holy
    people,

are you ready to renew your own dedication to Christ
as priests of his new covenant?

Priests: I am.

Bishop: At your ordination
you accepted the responsibilities of the priesthood
out of love for the Lord Jesus and his Church.
Are you resolved to unite yourselves more closely to
    Christ
and to try to become more like him
by joyfully sacrificing your own pleasure and ambi-
    tion
to bring his peace and love to your brothers and sis-
    ters?

Priests: I am.

Bishop: Are you resolved
to be faithful ministers of the mysteries of God,
to celebrate the eucharist and the other liturgical ser-
    vices
with sincere devotion?
Are you resolved to imitate Jesus Christ,
the head and shepherd of the Church,
by teaching the Christian faith
without thinking of your own profit,
solely for the well-being of the people
you were sent to serve?

Priests: I am.

Then the bishop addresses the people:

My brothers and sisters,
pray for your priests.
Ask the Lord to bless them with the fullness of his love,
to help them be faithful ministers of Christ the High
    Priest,
so that they will be able to lead you to him,
the fountain of your salvation.

**People: Lord Jesus Christ, hear us and answer our
    prayer.**

Bishop: Pray also for me
that despite my own unworthiness
I may faithfully fulfill the office of apostle
which Jesus Christ, has entrusted to me.
Pray that I may become more like
our High Priest and Good Shepherd,
the teacher and servant of all,
and so be a genuine sign
of Christ's loving presence among you.

People: Lord Jesus Christ, hear us and answer our prayer.

Bishop: May the Lord in his love
keep you close to him always,
and may he bring all of us,
his priests and people,
to eternal life.
All: **Amen.**

The Profession of Faith and General Intercessions are omitted.   ➔ **No. 17, p. 20**

PRAYER OVER THE GIFTS   [New Life]

Lord God,
may the power of this sacrifice
cleanse the old weakness of our human nature.
Give us a newness of life
and bring us to salvation.
Grant this through Christ our Lord. ℟. **Amen.** ↓

PREFACE (P 20)   [Continuation of Christ's Priesthood]

℣. The Lord be with you. ℟. **And also with you.**
℣. Lift up your hearts. ℟. **We lift them up to the Lord.**
℣. Let us give thanks to the Lord our God. ℟. **It is right to give him thanks and praise.**

Father, all-powerful and ever-living God,
we do well always and everywhere to give you thanks.
By your Holy Spirit

you anointed your only Son
High Priest of the new and eternal covenant.
With wisdom and love you have planned
that this one priesthood should continue in the Church.
Christ gives the dignity of a royal priesthood
to the people he has made his own.
From these, with a brother's love,
he chooses men to share his sacred ministry
by the laying on of hands.
He appoints them to renew in his name
the sacrifice of our redemption
as they set before your family his paschal meal.
He calls them to lead your holy people in love,
nourish them by your word,
and strengthen them through the sacraments.
Father, they are to give their lives in your service
and for the salvation of your people
as they strive to grow in the likeness of Christ
and honor you by their courageous witness of faith
    and love.
We praise you Lord, with all the angels and saints
in their song of joy: ➜ No. 23, p. 23

COMMUNION ANT. Ps 89:2   [The Lord's Faithfulness]

**For ever I will sing the goodness of the Lord; I will
proclaim your faithfulness to all generations.** ↓

PRAYER AFTER COMMUNION   [Renewed in Christ]

Lord God almighty,
you have given us fresh strength
in these sacramental gifts.
Renew in us the image of Christ's goodness.
We ask this in the name of Jesus the Lord.
℟. **Amen.**   ➜ No. 32, p. 70

Optional Solemn Blessings, p. 92, and Prayers Over the People, p. 99

"Do this in remembrance of me."

APRIL 17

HOLY THURSDAY

EVENING MASS OF THE LORD'S SUPPER

The Evening Mass of the Lord's Supper commemorates the institution of the Holy Eucharist and the sacrament of Holy Orders. It was at this Mass that Jesus changed bread and wine into his Body and Blood. He then directed his disciples to carry out this same ritual: "Do this in remembrance of me."

Introductory Rites and Liturgy of the Word

ENTRANCE ANT. See Gal 6:14   [Glory in the Cross]

We should glory in the cross of our Lord Jesus Christ, for he is our salvation, our life and our resurrection; through him we are saved and made free.

→ No. 2, p. 10

During the singing of the Gloria, *the church bells are rung and then remain silent until the Easter Vigil, unless the conference of bishops or the Ordinary decrees otherwise.*

OPENING PRAYER   [Fullness of Love]

God our Father,
we are gathered here to share in the supper
which your only Son left to his Church to reveal his
  love.

He gave it to us when he was about to die
and commanded us to celebrate it as the new and eter-
　nal sacrifice.
We pray that in this eucharist
we may find the fullness of love and life.
Grant this through our Lord Jesus Christ, your Son,
who lives and reigns with you and the Holy Spirit,
one God, for ever and ever. ℟. **Amen.** ↓

FIRST READING Ex 12:1-8, 11-14   [The First Passover]

**For the protection of the Jewish people, strict religious and
dietary instructions are given to Moses by God. The law of
the Passover meal requires that the doorposts and lintels of
each house be marked with the blood of the sacrificial ani-
mal so that the LORD can "go through Egypt striking down
every firstborn of the land, both man and beast."**

A reading from the Book of Exodus

THE LORD said to Moses and Aaron in the land of
　Egypt, "This month shall stand at the head of your
calendar; you shall reckon it the first month of the
year. Tell the whole community of Israel: On the tenth
of this month every one of your families must procure
for itself a lamb, one apiece for each household. If a
family is too small for a whole lamb, it shall join the
nearest household in procuring one and shall share in
the lamb in proportion to the number of persons who
partake of it. The lamb must be a year-old male and
without blemish. You may take it from either the
sheep or the goats. You shall keep it until the four-
teenth day of this month, and then, with the whole assembly of Israel present, it shall be slaughtered during
the evening twilight. They shall take some of its blood
and apply it to the two doorposts and the lintel of
every house in which they partake of the lamb. That
same night they shall eat its roasted flesh with unleavened bread and bitter herbs.

"This is how you are to eat it: with your loins girt, sandals on your feet and your staff in hand, you shall eat like those who are in flight. It is the Passover of the LORD. For on this same night I will go through Egypt, striking down every firstborn of the land, both man and beast, and executing judgment on all the gods of Egypt—I, the LORD! But the blood will mark the houses where you are. Seeing the blood, I will pass over you; thus, when I strike the land of Egypt, no destructive blow will come upon you.

"This day shall be a memorial feast for you, which all your generations shall celebrate with pilgrimage to the LORD, as a perpetual institution."—The word of the Lord. ℟. **Thanks be to God.** ↓

RESPONSORIAL PSALM Ps 116   [Thanksgiving]

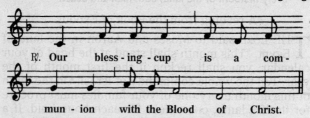

℟. Our bless-ing-cup is a com-mun-ion with the Blood of Christ.

How shall I make a return to the LORD
 for all the good he has done for me?
The cup of salvation I will take up,
 and I will call upon the name of the LORD.—℟.

Precious in the eyes of the LORD
 is the death of his faithful ones.
I am your servant, the son of your handmaid;
 you have loosed my bonds.—℟.

To you will I offer sacrifice of thanksgiving,
 and I will call upon the name of the LORD.
My vows to the LORD I will pay
 in the presence of all his people.—℟. ↓

SECOND READING 1 Cor 11:23-26   [The Lord's Supper]

Paul recounts the events of the Last Supper which were handed down to him. The changing of bread and wine into the Body and Blood of the Lord proclaimed again his death. It was to be a sacrificial meal.

A reading from the first Letter of Saint Paul
to the Corinthians

BROTHERS and sisters: I received from the Lord what I also handed on to you, that the Lord Jesus, on the night he was handed over, took bread, and, after he had given thanks, broke it and said, "This is my body that is for you. Do this in remembrance of me." In the same way also the cup, after supper, saying, "This cup is the new covenant in my blood. Do this, as often as you drink it, in remembrance of me." For as often as you eat this bread and drink the cup, you proclaim the death of the Lord until he comes.— The word of the Lord. ℟. **Thanks be to God.** ↓

VERSE BEFORE THE GOSPEL Jn 13:34 [Love One Another]

℟. **Praise to you, Lord Jesus Christ, king of endless glory!**

I give you a new commandment, says the Lord:
love one another as I have loved you.

℟. **Praise to you, Lord Jesus Christ, king of endless glory!** ↓

GOSPEL Jn 13:1-15   [Love and Service]

Jesus washes the feet of his disciples to prove to them his sincere love and great humility which they should imitate. He teaches them that, although free from sin and not unworthy to receive his most holy body and blood, they should be purified of all evil inclinations.

℣. The Lord be with you. ℟. **And also with you.**
✢ A reading from the holy Gospel according to John.
℟. **Glory to you, Lord.**

Before the feast of Passover, Jesus knew that his hour had come to pass from this world to the Father. He loved his own in the world and he loved them to the end. The devil had already induced Judas, son of Simon the Iscariot, to hand him over. So, during supper, fully aware that the Father had put everything into his power and that he had come from God and was returning to God, he rose from supper and took off his outer garments. He took a towel and tied it around his waist. Then he poured water into a basin and began to wash the disciples' feet and dry them with the towel around his waist. He came to Simon Peter, who said to him, "Master, are you going to wash my feet?" Jesus answered and said to him, "What I am doing, you do not understand now, but you will understand later." Peter said to him, "You will never wash my feet." Jesus answered him, "Unless I wash you, you will have no inheritance with me." Simon Peter said to him, "Master, then not only my feet, but my hands and head as well." Jesus said to him, "Whoever has bathed has no need except to have his feet washed, for he is clean all over; so you are clean, but not all." For he knew who would betray him; for this reason, he said, "Not all of you are clean."

So when he had washed their feet and put his garments back on and reclined at table again, he said to them, "Do you realize what I have done for you? You call me 'teacher' and 'master,' and rightly so, for indeed I am. If I, therefore, the master and teacher, have washed your feet, you ought to wash one another's feet. I have given you a model to follow, so that as I have done for you, you should also do."—The Gospel of the Lord. ℟. **Praise to you, Lord Jesus Christ.** ↓

The homily should explain the principal mysteries which are commemorated in this Mass: the institution of the eucharist, the institution of the priesthood, and Christ's commandment of brotherly love.

Washing of Feet

Depending on pastoral circumstances, the washing of feet follows the homily.

The men who have been chosen are led by the ministers to chairs prepared in a suitable place. Then the priest (removing his chasuble if necessary) goes to each man. With the help of the ministers, he pours water over each one's feet and dries them.

Meanwhile some of the following antiphons or other appropriate songs are sung.

ANTIPHON 1 See Jn 13:4, 5,15   [Jesus' Example]

**The Lord Jesus,
when he had eaten with his disciples,
poured water into a basin
and began to wash their feet, saying:
This example I leave you.**

ANTIPHON 2 Jn 13:6, 7, 8   [Peter's Understanding]

**Lord, do you wash my feet?
Jesus said to him:
If I do not wash your feet,
you can have no part with me.**

℣. **So he came to Simon Peter,
who said to him:
Lord, do you wash my feet?**

℣. **Now you do not know what I am doing,
but later you will understand.
Lord, do you wash my feet?**

ANTIPHON 3 See Jn 13:14   [Service]

**If I, your Lord and Teacher, have washed your feet,
then surely you must wash one another's feet.**

ANTIPHON 4 Jn 13:35   [Identified by Love]

If there is this love among you,
all will know that you are my disciples.

℣. Jesus said to his disciples:
If there is this love among you,
all will know that you are my disciples.

ANTIPHON 5 Jn 13:34   [New Commandment]

I give you a new commandment:
love one another as I have loved you, says the Lord.

ANTIPHON 6 1 Cor 13:13   [Greatest Is Love]

Faith, hope, and love,
let these endure among you;
and the greatest of these is love.

*The general intercessions follow the washing of feet, or, if
this does not take place, they follow the homily. The profession of faith is not said in this Mass.*

The Liturgy of the Eucharist

*At the beginning of the liturgy of the eucharist, there may be
a procession of the faithful with gifts for the poor. During the
procession the following may be sung, or another appropriate
song.*

[Christ's Love]

Ant. ℣.   Where charity and love are found, there is
God.

℣. The love of Christ has gathered us together into
one.

℣. Let us rejoice and be glad in him.

℣. Let us fear and love the living God,

℣. and love each other from the depths of our heart.

Ant. Where charity and love are found, there is God.

℣. Therefore when we are together,

℣. let us take heed not to be divided in mind.

℣. Let there be an end to bitterness and quarrels, an
end to strife,

℣. **and in our midst be Christ our God.**
Ant. **Where charity and love are found, there is God.**
℣. **And, in company with the blessed, may we see**
℣. **your face in glory, Christ our God,**
℣. **pure and unbounded joy**
℣. **for ever and ever.**
Ant. **Where charity and love are found, there is God.**

→ No. 17, p. 20

PRAYER OVER THE GIFTS   [Work of Redemption]

Lord,
make us worthy to celebrate these mysteries.
Each time we offer this memorial sacrifice
the work of our redemption is accomplished.
We ask this in the name of Jesus the Lord.
℟. **Amen.**   → No. 21, p. 22 (Pref. P 47)

When Eucharistic Prayer I is used, the special Holy Thurs-
day forms of In union with the whole Church, Father, accept this offering, *and* The day before he suffered *are said:*

In union with the whole Church
we celebrate that day
when Jesus Christ, our Lord,
was betrayed for us.
We honor Mary,
the ever-virgin mother of Jesus Christ our Lord and
    God.
We honor Joseph, her husband,
the apostles and martyrs
Peter and Paul, Andrew,
(James, John, Thomas,
James, Philip,
Bartholomew, Matthew, Simon and Jude;
we honor Linus, Cletus, Clement, Sixtus,
Cornelius, Cyprian, Lawrence, Chrysogonus,
John and Paul, Cosmas and Damian)
and all the saints.
May their merits and prayers

gain us your constant help and protection.
(Through Christ our Lord. Amen.)

Father, accept this offering
from your whole family
in memory of the day when Jesus Christ, our Lord,
gave the mysteries of his body and blood
for his disciples to celebrate.
Grant us your peace in this life,
save us from final damnation,
and count us among those you have chosen.
(Through Christ our Lord. Amen.)

Bless and approve our offering;
make it acceptable to you,
an offering in spirit and in truth.
Let it become for us
the body and blood of Jesus Christ,
your only Son, our Lord.

The day before he suffered
to save us and all men,
that is, today,
he took bread in his sacred hands
and looking up to heaven,
to you, his almighty Father,
he gave you thanks and praise.
He broke the bread,
gave it to his disciples, and said:

Take this, all of you, and eat it:
this is my body which will be given up for you.

The rest follows the Roman canon, pp. 26-28.

COMMUNION ANT. 1 Cor 11:24-25 [In Remembrance of Christ]
**This body will be given for you. This is the cup of the
new covenant in my blood; whenever you receive
them, do so in remembrance of me.** ↓

After the distribution of communion, the ciborium with hosts for Good Friday is left on the altar.

A period of silence may be observed after communion, or a psalm or song of praise may be sung.

PRAYER AFTER COMMUNION [New Life]

Almighty God,
we receive new life
from the supper your Son gave us in this world.
May we find full contentment
in the meal we hope to share
in your eternal kingdom.
We ask this through Christ our Lord. ℟. **Amen.**

The Mass concludes with this prayer.

Transfer of the Holy Eucharist

After the prayer the priest stands before the altar and puts incense in the thurible. Kneeling, he incenses the Blessed Sacrament three times. Then he receives the humeral veil, takes the ciborium, and covers it with the ends of the veil.

The Blessed Sacrament is carried through the church in procession, led by a cross-bearer and accompanied by candles and incense, to the place of reposition prepared in a chapel suitably decorated for the occasion. During the procession the hymn Pange, lingua *(exclusive of the last two stanzas) or some other eucharistic song is sung.*

PANGE LINGUA [Adoring the Lord]

Sing my tongue, the Savior's glory,
Of his flesh the mystery sing;
Of his blood all price exceeding,
Shed by our immortal king,
Destined for the world's redemption,
From a noble womb to spring.

Of a pure and spotless Virgin
Born for us on earth below,
He, as man with man conversing,
Stayed the seeds of truth to sow;
Then he closed in solemn order
Wondrously his life of woe.

On the night of that Last Supper,

Seated with his chosen band,

He, the paschal victim eating,

First fulfills the law's command;

Then as food to all his brethren

Gives himself with his own hand.

Word made Flesh, the bread of nature,

By his word to flesh he turns;

Wine into his blood he changes:

What though sense no change discerns,

Only be the heart in earnest,

Faith her lesson quickly learns.

When the procession reaches the place of reposition, the priest sets the ciborium down. Then he puts incense in the thurible and, kneeling, incenses the Blessed Sacrament, while Tantum ergo Sacramentum *is sung. The tabernacle of reposition is then closed.*

Down in adoration falling,

Lo! the sacred host we hail,

Lo! o'er ancient forms departing

Newer rites of grace prevail;

Faith for all defects supplying,

Where the feeble senses fail.

To the everlasting Father,

And the Son who reigns on high

With the Holy Spirit proceeding

Forth from each eternally,

Be salvation, honor, blessing,

Might and endless majesty. Amen.

After a period of silent adoration, the priest and ministers genuflect and return to the sacristy.

Then the altar is stripped and, if possible, the crosses are removed from the church. It is desirable to cover any crosses which remain in the church.

The faithful should be encouraged to continue adoration before the Blessed Sacrament for a suitable period of time during the night.

"And bowing his head, [Jesus] handed over the spirit."

APRIL 18

GOOD FRIDAY

CELEBRATION OF THE LORD'S PASSION

The liturgy of Good Friday recalls graphically the passion and death of Jesus. The reading of the passion describes the suffering and death of Jesus. Today we show great reverence for the crucifix, the sign of our redemption.

According to the Church's ancient tradition, the sacraments, except for Penance and the Anointing of the Sick, are not celebrated today or tomorrow. The celebration of the Lord's passion takes place in the afternoon, about three o'clock, unless pastoral reasons suggest a later hour.

The priest and deacon, wearing red Mass vestments, go to the altar. There they make a reverence and prostrate themselves, or they may kneel. All pray silently for a while. Then the priest goes to the chair with the ministers. He faces the people and, with hands joined, sings or says one of the following prayers.

PRAYER [Make Us Holy]

Lord,
by shedding his blood for us,
your Son, Jesus Christ,
established the paschal mystery.

In your goodness, make us holy
and watch over us always.
We ask this through Christ our Lord. ℟. **Amen.** ↓

OR   [Likeness of Christ]

Lord,
by the suffering of Christ your Son
you have saved us all from the death
we inherited from sinful Adam.
By the law of nature
we have borne the likeness of his manhood.
May the sanctifying power of grace
help us to put on the likeness of our Lord in heaven,
who lives and reigns for ever and ever. ℟. **Amen.** ↓

PART ONE: LITURGY OF THE WORD

FIRST READING Is 52:13—53:12   [Suffering and Glory]

The suffering Servant shall be raised up and exalted. The Servant remains one with all people in sorrow and yet distinct from each of them in innocence of life and total service to God. The doctrine of expiatory suffering finds supreme expression in these words.

A reading from the Book of the Prophet Isaiah

SEE, my servant shall prosper,
he shall be raised high and greatly exalted.
Even as many were amazed at him—
    so marred was his look beyond human semblance
    and his appearance beyond that of the sons of man—
so shall he startle many nations,
    because of him kings shall stand speechless;
for those who have not been told shall see,
    those who have not heard shall ponder it.

Who would believe what we have heard?
    To whom has the arm of the LORD been revealed?
He grew up like a sapling before him,
    like a shoot from the parched earth;

there was in him no stately bearing to make us look at
   him,
   nor appearance that would attract us to him.
He was spurned and avoided by people,
   a man of suffering, accustomed to infirmity,
one of those from whom people hide their faces,
   spurned, and we held him in no esteem.

Yet it was our infirmities that he bore,
   our sufferings that he endured,
while we thought of him as stricken,
   as one smitten by God and afflicted.
But he was pierced for our offenses,
   crushed for our sins;
upon him was the chastisement that makes us whole,
   by his stripes we were healed.
We had all gone astray like sheep,
   each following his own way;
but the LORD laid upon him
   the guilt of us all.

Though he was harshly treated, he submitted
   and opened not his mouth;
like a lamb led to the slaughter
   or a sheep before the shearers,
   he was silent and opened not his mouth.
Oppressed and condemned, he was taken away,
      and who would have thought any more of his des-
         tiny?
When he was cut off from the land of the living,
   and smitten for the sin of his people,
a grave was assigned him among the wicked
   and a burial place with evildoers,
though he had done no wrong
   nor spoken any falsehood.
But the LORD was pleased
   to crush him in infirmity.

If he gives his life as an offering for sin,
   he shall see his descendants in a long life,

and the will of the LORD shall be accomplished
through him.
Because of his affliction
he shall see the light in fullness of days;
through his suffering, my servant shall justify many,
and their guilt he shall bear.
Therefore I will give him his portion among the great,
and he shall divide the spoils with the mighty,
because he surrendered himself to death
and was counted among the wicked;
and he shall take away the sins of many,
and win pardon for their offenses.
The word of the Lord. ℟. **Thanks be to God.** ↓

RESPONSORIAL PSALM Ps 31   [Trust in God]

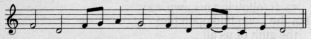

℟. Fa - ther, in -to your hands I com - mend my spir - it.

In you, O LORD, I take refuge;
let me never be put to shame.
In your justice rescue me.
Into your hands I commend my spirit;
you will redeem me, O LORD, O faithful God.

℟. **Father, into your hands I commend my spirit.**

For all my foes I am an object of reproach,
a laughingstock to my neighbors, and a dread to my
friends;
they who see me abroad flee from me.
I am forgotten like the unremembered dead;
I am like a dish that is broken.

℟. **Father, into your hands I commend my spirit.**

But my trust is in you, O LORD;
I say, "You are my God."

In your hands is my destiny; rescue me
   from the clutches of my enemies and my persecutors.

℟. **Father, into your hands I commend my spirit.**

Let your face shine upon your servant;
   save me in your kindness.
Take courage and be stouthearted,
   all you who hope in the LORD.

℟. **Father, into your hands I commend my spirit.** ↓

SECOND READING Heb 4:14-16; 5:7-9   [Access to Christ]

The theme of the compassionate high priest appears again in this passage. In him the Christian can approach God confidently and without fear. Christ learned obedience from his sufferings whereby he became the source of eternal life for all.

A reading from the Letter to the Hebrews

Brothers and sisters: Since we have a great high priest who has passed through the heavens, Jesus, the Son of God, let us hold fast to our confession. For we do not have a high priest who is unable to sympathize with our weaknesses, but one who has similarly been tested in every way, yet without sin. So let us confidently approach the throne of grace to receive mercy and to find grace for timely help.

In the days when Christ was in the flesh, he offered prayers and supplications with loud cries and tears to the one who was able to save him from death, and he was heard because of his reverence. Son though he was, he learned obedience from what he suffered; and when he was made perfect, he became the source of eternal salvation for all who obey him.—The word of the Lord. ℟. **Thanks be to God.** ↓

VERSE BEFORE THE GOSPEL Phil 2:8-9   [Obedient for Us]

℟. **Praise and honor to you, Lord Jesus Christ!**
Christ became obedient to the point of death,
even death on a cross.
Because of this, God greatly exalted him
and bestowed on him the name which is above every
     other name.
℟. **Praise and honor to you, Lord Jesus Christ!**

GOSPEL Jn 18:1—19:42   [Christ's Passion]

Finally the passion is read in the same way as on the preceding Sunday. The narrator is noted by N, the words of Jesus by a ✠ and the words of others by V (Voice) and C (Crowd). The parts of the Crowd (C) printed in boldface type may be recited by the people.

It is important for us to understand the meaning of Christ's sufferings today. See the note on p. 269.

> The beginning scene is Christ's agony in the garden. Our Lord knows what is to happen. The Scriptures recount the betrayal, the trial, the condemnation, and the crucifixion of Jesus.

N. **T**HE Passion of our Lord Jesus Christ according to John

1. JESUS IS ARRESTED

N. **J**ESUS went out with his disciples across the Kidron valley to where there was a garden, into which he and his disciples entered. Judas his betrayer also knew the place, because Jesus had often met there with his disciples. So Judas got a band of soldiers and guards from the chief priests and the Pharisees and went there with lanterns, torches, and weapons. Jesus, knowing everything that was going to happen to him, went out and said to them, ✠ *"Whom are you looking for?"* **N.** They answered him, **C. "Jesus the Nazarene."** **N.** He said to them, ✠ *"I AM."* **N.** Judas his betrayer was also with them. When he said to them, "I AM, " they turned away and fell to the ground. So he again asked them, ✠ *"Whom are you looking for?"* **N.** They said, **C. "Jesus the Nazarene."** **N.** Jesus answered, ✠ *"I told you that I AM. So if you are looking for me, let these men go."* **N.** This was to fulfill what he had said, "I have not lost any of those you gave me." Then Simon Peter, who had a sword, drew it, struck the high priest's slave, and cut off his right ear. The slave's name was Malchus. Jesus said to Peter, ✠ *"Put your sword into its scabbard. Shall I not drink the cup that the Father gave me?"*

N. So the band of soldiers, the tribune, and the Jewish guards seized Jesus, bound him, and brought him to Annas first. He was the father-in-law of Caiaphas, who was high priest that year. It was Caiaphas who had counseled the Jews that it was better that one man should die rather than the people.

2. PETER'S FIRST DENIAL

N. SIMON Peter and another disciple followed Jesus. Now the other disciple was known to the high priest, and he entered the courtyard of the high priest with Jesus. But Peter stood at the gate outside. So the other disciple, the acquaintance of the high priest, went out and spoke to the gatekeeper and brought Peter in. Then the maid who was the gatekeeper said to Peter, **C. "You are not one of this man's disciples, are you?"** **N.** He said, **V.** "I am not." **N.** Now the slaves and the guards were standing around a charcoal fire that they had made, because it was cold, and were warming themselves. Peter was also standing there keeping warm.

3. THE INQUIRY BEFORE ANNAS

N. THE high priest questioned Jesus about his disciples and about his doctrine. Jesus answered him, ✠ *"I have spoken publicly to the world. I have always taught in a synagogue or in the temple area* *where all the Jews gather, and in secret I have said nothing. Why ask me? Ask those who heard me what I said to them. They know what I said."* **N.** When he had said this, one of the temple guards standing there struck Jesus and said, **V.** "Is this the way you answer the high priest?" **N.** Jesus answered him, ✚ *"If I have spoken wrongly, testify to the wrong; but if I have spoken rightly, why do you strike me?"* **N.** Then Annas sent him bound to Caiaphas the high priest.

4. THE FURTHER DENIALS

N. **N**OW Simon Peter was standing there keeping warm. And they said to him, **C.** **"You are not one of his disciples, are you?"** **N.** He denied it and said, **V.** "I am not." **N.** One of the slaves of the high priest, a relative of the one whose ear Peter had cut off, said, **C.** **"Didn't I see you in the garden with him?"** **N.** Again Peter denied it. And immediately the cock crowed.

5. JESUS BROUGHT BEFORE PILATE

N. **T**HEN they brought Jesus from Caiaphas to the praetorium. It was morning. And they themselves did not enter the praetorium, in order not to be defiled so that they could eat the Passover. So Pilate came out to them and said, **V.** "What charge do you bring against this man?" **N.** They answered and said to him, **C.** **"If he were not a criminal, we would not have handed him over to you."** **N.** At this, Pilate said to them, **V.** "Take him yourselves, and judge him according to your law." **N.** The Jews answered him, **C.** **"We do not have the right to execute anyone,"** **N.** in order that the word of Jesus might be fulfilled that he said indicating the kind of death he would die.

6. JESUS QUESTIONED BY PILATE

N. **S**O Pilate went back into the praetorium and summoned Jesus and said to him, **V.** "Are you the King of the Jews?" **N.** Jesus answered, ✠ *"Do you say this on your own or have others told you about me?"* **N.** Pilate answered, **V.** "I am not a Jew, am I? Your own nation and the chief priests handed you over to me. What have you done?" **N.** Jesus answered, ✠ *"My kingdom does not belong to this world. If my kingdom did belong to this world, my attendants would be fighting to keep me from being handed over to the Jews. But as it is, my kingdom is not here."* **N.** So Pilate said to him, **V.** "Then you are a king?" **N.** Jesus answered, ✠ *"You say I am a king. For this I was born and for this I came into the world, to testify to the truth. Everyone who belongs to the truth listens to my voice."* **N.** Pilate said to him, **V.** "What is truth?"

7. BARABBAS CHOSEN OVER JESUS

N. WHEN he had said this, he again went out to the Jews and said to them, **V.** "I find no guilt in him. But you have a custom that I release one prisoner to you at Passover. Do you want me to release to you the King of the Jews?" **N.** They cried out again, **C.** **"Not this one but Barabbas!"** **N.** Now Barabbas was a revolutionary.

8. JESUS IS SCOURGED

N. THEN Pilate took Jesus and had him scourged. And the soldiers wove a crown out of thorns and placed it on his head, and clothed him in a purple cloak, and they came to him and said, **C.** **"Hail, King of the Jews!"** **N.** And they struck him repeatedly.

9. JESUS IS PRESENTED TO THE CROWD

N. ONCE more Pilate went out and said to them, **V.** "Look, I am bringing him out to you, so that you may know that I find no guilt in him." **N.** So Jesus came out, wearing the crown of thorns and the purple cloak. And Pilate said to them, **V.** "Behold, the man!" **N.** When the chief priests and the guards saw him they cried out, **C.** **"Crucify him, crucify him!"** **N.** Pilate said to them, **V.** "Take him yourselves and crucify him. I find no guilt in him." **N.** The Jews answered, **C.** **"We have a law, and according to that law he ought to die, because he made himself the Son of God."**

10. JESUS AGAIN QUESTIONED BY PILATE

N. NOW when Pilate heard this statement, he became even more afraid, and went back into the praetorium and said to Jesus, **V.** "Where are you from?" **N.** Jesus did not answer him. So Pilate said to him, **V.** "Do you not speak to me? Do you not know that I have power to release you and I have power to crucify you?" [**N.** Jesus answered him,] ✢ *"You would have no power over me if it had not been given to you from above. For this reason the one who handed me over to you has the greater sin."*

11. JESUS SENTENCED TO BE CRUCIFIED

N. CONSEQUENTLY, Pilate tried to release him; but the Jews cried out, **C.** **"If you release him, you are not a Friend of Caesar. Everyone who makes himself a king opposes Caesar."** **N.** When Pilate heard these words he brought Jesus out and seated him on the judge's bench in the place called Stone Pavement, in Hebrew, Gabbatha. It was preparation day for Passover, and it was about noon. And he said to the Jews, **V.** "Behold, your king!" **N.** They cried out, **C.** **"Take him away, take him away! Crucify him!"** **N.** Pilate said to them, **V.** "Shall I crucify your king?" **N.** The chief priests answered, **C.** **"We have no king but Caesar."** **N.** Then he handed him over to them to be crucified.

12. CRUCIFIXION AND DEATH

N. SO they took Jesus, and, carrying the cross himself, he went out to what is called the Place of the Skull, in Hebrew, Golgotha. There they crucified him, and with him two others, one on either side, with Jesus in the middle. Pilate also had an inscription written and put on the cross. It read, "Jesus the Nazarene, the King of the Jews." Now many of the Jews read this inscription, because the place where Jesus was crucified was near the city; and it was written in Hebrew, Latin, and Greek. So the chief priests of the Jews said to Pilate, **C.** **"Do not write 'The King of the Jews,' but that he said, 'I am the King of the Jews.' "** **N.** Pilate answered, **V.** "What I have written, I have written."

N. When the soldiers had crucified Jesus, they took his clothes and divided them into four shares, a share for each soldier. They also took his tunic, but the tunic was seamless, woven in one piece from the top down. So they said to one another, **C.** **"Let's not tear it, but cast lots for it to see whose it will be, "** **N.** in order that the passage of Scripture might be fulfilled that says:

> They divided my garments among them,
> and for my vesture they cast lots.

This is what the soldiers did. Standing by the cross of Jesus were his mother and his mother's sister, Mary the wife of Clopas, and Mary of Magdala. When Jesus saw his mother and the disciple there whom he loved he said to his mother, ✠ *"Woman, behold, your son."* **N.** Then he said to the disciple, ✠ *"Behold, your mother."* **N.** And from that hour the disciple took her into his home.

After this, aware that everything was now finished, in order that the Scripture might be fulfilled, Jesus said, ✠ *"I thirst."* **N.** There was a vessel filled with common wine. So they put a sponge soaked in wine on a sprig of hyssop and put it up to his mouth. When Jesus had taken the wine, he said, ✠ *"It is finished."* And bowing his head, he handed over the spirit.

Here all kneel and pause for a short time.

13. THE BLOOD AND WATER

N. **N**OW since it was preparation day, in order that the bodies might not remain on the cross on the sabbath, for the sabbath day of that week was a solemn one, the Jews asked Pilate that their legs be broken and that they be taken down. So the soldiers came and broke the legs of the first and then of the other one who was crucified with Jesus. But when they came to Jesus and saw that he was already dead, they did not break his legs, but one soldier thrust his lance into his side, and immediately blood and water flowed out. An eyewitness has testified, and his testimony is true; he knows that he is speaking the truth, so that you also may come to believe. For this happened so that the Scripture passage might be fulfilled:

Not a bone of it will be broken.

And again another passage says:

They will look upon him whom they have pierced.

14. BURIAL OF JESUS

N. **A**FTER this, Joseph of Arimathea, secretly a disciple of Jesus for fear of the Jews, asked Pilate if he could remove the body of Jesus. And Pilate permitted it. So he came and took his body. Nicodemus, the one who had first come to him at night, also came bringing a mixture of myrrh and aloes weighing about one hundred pounds. They took the body of Jesus and bound it with burial cloths along with the spices, according to the Jewish burial custom. Now in the place where he had been crucified there was a garden, and in the garden a new tomb, in which no one had yet been buried. So they laid Jesus there because of the Jewish preparation day; for the tomb was close by.— The Gospel of the Lord. ℟. **Praise to you, Lord Jesus Christ.**   → No. 14, p. 18

GENERAL INTERCESSIONS

The general intercessions conclude the liturgy of the word.
The deacon, standing at the ambo, sings or says the introduc-
tion in which each intention is stated. All kneel and pray
silently for some period of time, and then the priest, with
hands outstretched, standing either at the chair or at the
altar, sings or says the prayer. The people may either kneel
or stand throughout the entire period of the general interces-
sions.

I. For the Church

Let us pray, dear friends,
for the holy Church of God throughout the world,
that God the almighty Father
guide it and gather it together
so that we may worship him
in peace and tranquility.

Silent prayer. Then the priest sings or says:

Almighty and eternal God,
you have shown your glory to all nations
in Christ, your Son.
Guide the work of your Church.
Help it to persevere in faith,
proclaim your name,
and bring your salvation to people everywhere.
We ask this through Christ our Lord. ℟. **Amen.** ↓

II. For the Pope

Let us pray
for our Holy Father, Pope N.,
that God who chose him to be bishop
may give him health and strength
to guide and govern God's holy people.

Silent prayer. Then the priest sings or says:

Almighty and eternal God,
you guide all things by your word,
you govern all Christian people.

In your love protect the Pope you have chosen for us.
Under his leadership deepen our faith
and make us better Christians.
We ask this through Christ our Lord. ℞. **Amen.** ↓

III. For the clergy and laity of the Church

Let us pray
for N., our bishop,
for all bishops, priests and deacons,
for all who have a special ministry in the Church
and for all God's people.

Silent prayer. Then the priest sings or says:

Almighty and eternal God,
your Spirit guides the Church
and makes it holy.
Listen to our prayers
and help each of us
in his own vocation
to do your work more faithfully.
We ask this through Christ our Lord. ℞. **Amen.** ↓

IV. For those preparing for baptism

Let us pray
for those [among us] preparing for baptism,
that God in his mercy
make them responsive to his love,
forgive their sins through the waters of new birth,
and give them life in Jesus Christ our Lord.

Silent prayer. Then the priest sings or says:

Almighty and eternal God,
you continually bless your Church with new members.
Increase the faith and understanding
of those [among us] preparing for baptism.
Give them a new birth in these living waters
and make them members of your chosen family.
We ask this through Christ our Lord. ℞. **Amen.** ↓

V. For the unity of Christians

Let us pray
for all our brothers and sisters
who share our faith in Jesus Christ,
that God may gather and keep together in one Church
all those who seek the truth with sincerity.

Silent prayer. Then the priest sings or says:

Almighty and eternal God,
you keep together those you have united.
Look kindly on all who follow Jesus your Son.
We are all consecrated to you by our common baptism.
Make us one in the fullness of faith,
and keep us one in the fellowship of love.
We ask this through Christ our Lord. ℟. **Amen.** ↓

VI. For the Jewish people

Let us pray
for the Jewish people,
the first to hear the word of God,
that they may continue to grow in the love of his name
and in faithfulness to his covenant.

Silent prayer. Then the priest sings or says:

Almighty and eternal God,
long ago you gave your promise to Abraham and his
    posterity.
Listen to your Church as we pray
that the people you first made your own
may arrive at the fullness of redemption.
We ask this through Christ our Lord. ℟. **Amen.** ↓

VII. For those who do not believe in Christ

Let us pray
for those who do not believe in Christ,
that the light of the Holy Spirit
may show them the way to salvation.

Silent prayer. Then the priest sings or says:

Almighty and eternal God,
enable those who do not acknowledge Christ
to find the truth
as they walk before you in sincerity of heart.
Help us to grow in love for one another,
to grasp more fully the mystery of your godhead,
and to become more perfect witnesses of your love
in the sight of men.
We ask this through Christ our Lord. ℟. **Amen.** ↓

VIII. For those who do not believe in God

Let us pray
for those who do not believe in God,
that they may find him
by sincerely following all that is right.

Silent prayer. Then the priest sings or says:

Almighty and eternal God,
you created mankind
so that all might long to find you
and have peace when you are found.
Grant that, in spite of the hurtful things
that stand in their way,
they may all recognize in the lives of Christians
the tokens of your love and mercy,
and gladly acknowledge you
as the one true God and Father of us all.
We ask this through Christ our Lord. ℟. **Amen.** ↓

IX. For all in public office

Let us pray
for those who serve us in public office,
that God may guide their minds and hearts,
so that all men may live in true peace and freedom.

Silent prayer. Then the priest sings or says:

Almighty and eternal God,
you know the longings of men's hearts

and you protect their rights.
In your goodness
watch over those in authority,
so that people everywhere may enjoy
religious freedom, security, and peace.
We ask this through Christ our Lord. ℟. **Amen.** ↓

X. For those in special need

Let us pray, dear friends,
that God the almighty Father
may heal the sick,
comfort the dying,
give safety to travelers,
free those unjustly deprived of liberty,
and rid the world of falsehood,
hunger, and disease.

Silent prayer. Then the priest sings or says:

Almighty, ever-living God,
you give strength to the weary
and new courage to those who have lost heart.
Hear the prayers of all who call on you in any trouble
that they may have the joy of receiving your help in
  their need.
We ask this through Christ our Lord. ℟. **Amen.** ↓

PART TWO: VENERATION OF THE CROSS

*After the general intercessions, the veneration of the cross
takes place. Pastoral demands will determine which of the
two forms is more effective and should be chosen.*

First Form of Showing the Cross

*The veiled cross is carried to the altar, accompanied by two
ministers with lighted candles. Standing at the altar, the
priest takes the cross, uncovers the upper part of it, then ele-
vates it and begins the invitation* This is the wood of the
cross. *He is assisted in the singing by the deacon or, if convenient, by the choir. All respond:* Come, let us worship. *At the
end of the singing all kneel and venerate the cross briefly in
silence; the priest remains standing and holds the cross high.*

Then the priest uncovers the right arm of the cross, lifts it up, and again begins the invitation This is the wood of the cross, *and the rite is repeated as before.*

Finally he uncovers the entire cross, lifts it up, and begins the invitation This is the wood of the cross *a third time, and the rite is repeated as before.*

Accompanied by two ministers with lighted candles, the priest then carries the cross to the entrance of the sanctuary or to another suitable place. There he lays the cross down or hands it to the ministers to hold. Candles are placed on either side of the cross, and the veneration follows as below.

Second Form of Showing the Cross

The priest or deacon, accompanied by the ministers or by another suitable minister, goes to the church door. There he takes the (uncovered) cross, and the ministers take lighted candles. They go in procession through the church to the sanctuary. Near the entrance of the church, in the middle of the church, and at the entrance to the sanctuary, the one carrying the cross stops, lifts it up and sings the invitation This is the wood of the cross. *All respond:* Come, let us worship. *After each response all kneel and venerate the cross briefly in silence as above.*

Then the cross and candles are placed at the entrance to the sanctuary.

INVITATION

℣. This is the wood of the cross, on which hung the Savior of the world.

℞. **Come, let us worship.**

Veneration of the Cross

The priest, clergy, and faithful approach to venerate the cross in a kind of procession. They make a simple genuflection or perform some other appropriate sign of reverence according to local custom, for example, kissing the cross.

During the veneration the antiphon We worship you, Lord, *the reproaches or other suitable songs are sung. All who have venerated the cross return to their places and sit.*

Only one cross should be used for the veneration. If the number of people makes it impossible for everyone to venerate the cross individually, the priest may take the cross, after some of the faithful have venerated it, and stand in the center in front of the altar. In a few words he invites the people to venerate the cross and then holds it up briefly for them to worship in silence.

In the United States, if pastoral reasons suggest that there be individual veneration even though the number of people is very large, a second or third cross may be used.

After the veneration, the cross is carried to its place at the altar, and the lighted candles are placed around the altar or near the cross.

Songs at the Veneration of the Cross

Individual parts are indicated by no. 1 (first choir) and no. 2 (second choir); parts sung by both choirs together are indicated by nos. 1 and 2.

ANTIPHON   [Holy Cross]

1 and 2: Antiphon
**We worship you, Lord,
we venerate your cross,
we praise your resurrection.
Through the cross you brought joy to the world.**

1: Psalm 67:2
**May God be gracious and bless us;
and let his face shed its light upon us.**

1 and 2: Antiphon
**We worship you, Lord,
we venerate your cross,
we praise your resurrection.
Through the cross you brought joy to the world.**

I

REPROACHES

1 and 2: **My people, what have I done to you?
How have I offended you? Answer me!**

1: **I led you out of Egypt, from slavery to freedom,
but you led your Savior to the cross.**

2: My people, what have I done to you?
How have I offended you? Answer me!

1: Holy is God!

2: Holy and strong!

1: Holy immortal One,
have mercy on us!

1 and 2: For forty years I led you safely through the desert.
I fed you with manna from heaven,
and brought you to a land of plenty;
but you led your Savior to the cross.

1: Holy is God!

2: Holy and strong!

1: Holy immortal One,
have mercy on us!

1 and 2: What more could I have done for you?
I planted you as my fairest vine,
but you yielded only bitterness:
when I was thirsty you gave me vinegar to drink,
and you pierced your Savior with a lance.

1: Holy is God!

2: Holy and strong!

1: Holy immortal One,
have mercy on us!

II

1: For your sake I scourged your captors and their firstborn sons,
but you brought your scourges down on me.

2: My people, what have I done to you?
How have I offended you? Answer me!

1: I led you from slavery to freedom
and drowned your captors in the sea,
but you handed me over to your high priests.

2: My people, what have I done to you?
How have I offended you? Answer me!

1: I opened the sea before you,
but you opened my side with a spear.

2: My people, what have I done to you?
How have I offended you? Answer me!

1: I led you on your way in a pillar of cloud,
but you led me to Pilate's court.

2: My people, what have I done to you?
How have I offended you? Answer me!

1: I bore you up with manna in the desert,
but you struck me down and scourged me.

2: My people, what have I done to you?
How have I offended you? Answer me!

1: I gave you saving water from the rock,
but you gave me gall and vinegar to drink.

2: My people, what have I done to you?
How have I offended you? Answer me!

1: For you I struck down the kings of Canaan,
but you struck my head with a reed.

2: My people, what have I done to you?
How have I offended you? Answer me!

1: I gave you a royal scepter,
but you gave me a crown of thorns.

2: My people, what have I done to you?
How have I offended you? Answer me!

1: I raised you to the height of majesty,
but you have raised me high on a cross.

2: My people, what have I done to you?
How have I offended you? Answer me!

HYMN: PANGE LINGUA   [Sing to the Lord]

Sing, my tongue, the Savior's
glory;
    tell his triumph far and
    wide;
Tell aloud the famous story
    of his body crucified;
How upon the cross a victim,
    vanquishing in death, he
    died.

Eating of the tree forbidden,
    man had sunk in Satan's
    snare,
When our pitying Creator did
    this second tree prepare;
Destined, many ages later,
    that first evil to repair.
Such the order God ap-
    pointed

when for sin he would
atone;
To the serpent thus opposing
schemes yet deeper than
his own;
Thence the remedy procur-
ing,
when the fatal wound had
come.

So when now at length the
fullness
of the sacred time drew
nigh,
Then the Son, the world's
Creator,
left his Father's throne on
high;
From a virgin's womb ap-
pearing,
clothed in our mortality.

All within a lowly manger,
lo, a tender babe he lies!
See his gentle Virgin Mother
lull to sleep his infant
cries!
While the limbs of God incarnate
round with swathing
bands she ties.

Thus did Christ to perfect
manhood
in our mortal flesh attain:
Then of his free choice he
goeth
to a death of bitter pain;
And as a lamb, upon the
altar of the cross,
for us is slain.

Lo, with gall his thirst he
quenches!

See the thorns upon his
brow!
Nails his tender flesh are
rending!
See, his side is opened
now!
Whence, to cleanse the
whole creation,
streams of blood and
water flow.

Lofty tree, bend down thy
branches,
to embrace thy sacred
load;
Oh, relax the native tension
of that all too rigid wood;
Gently, gently bear the members
of thy dying King and
God.

Tree, which solely wast
found worthy
the world's great Victim to
sustain.
Harbor from the raging tem-
pest!
Ark, that saved the world
again!
Tree, with sacred blood
anointed
of the Lamb for sinners
slain.

Blessing, honor everlasting,
to the immortal Deity;
To the Father, Son, and
Spirit,
equal praises ever be;
Glory through the earth and
heaven
to Trinity in Unity. Amen.

PART THREE: HOLY COMMUNION

The altar is covered with a cloth and the corporal and book are placed on it. Then the deacon or, if there is no deacon, the priest brings the ciborium with the Blessed Sacrament from the place of reposition to the altar without any procession, while all stand in silence.

The priest comes from his chair, genuflects, and goes up to the altar. With hands joined, he says aloud:

Let us pray with confidence to the Father
in the words our Savior gave us:

He extends his hands and continues, with all present:

Our Father . . .

With hands extended, the priest continues alone:

Deliver us, Lord, from every evil,
and grant us peace in our day.
In your mercy keep us free from sin
and protect us from all anxiety
as we wait in joyful hope
for the coming of our Savior, Jesus Christ.

The people end the prayer with the acclamation:

For the kingdom, the power, and the glory are yours, now and for ever.

Then the priest says quietly:

Lord Jesus Christ, with faith in your love and mercy
   I eat your body and drink your blood.
Let it not bring me condemnation, but health in mind
   and body.

Taking the host, the priest says aloud:

This is the Lamb of God
who takes away the sins of the world.
Happy are those who are called to his supper.

He adds, once only, with the people:

**Lord, I am not worthy to receive you,
but only say the word and I shall be healed.**

Facing the altar, he reverently consumes the body of Christ.

Then communion is distributed to the faithful. Any appropriate song may be sung during communion.

When the communion has been completed, a suitable minister may take the ciborium to a place prepared outside the church or, if circumstances require, may place it in the tabernacle.

A period of silence may now be observed. The priest then says the following prayer:

Let us pray.   **[Serving God]**
Almighty and eternal God,
you have restored us to life
by the triumphant death and resurrection of Christ.
Continue this healing work within us.
May we who participate in this mystery
never cease to serve you.
We ask this through Christ our Lord. ℟. **Amen.** ↓

For the dismissal the priest faces the people, extends his hands toward them, and says the following prayer:

PRAYER OVER THE PEOPLE   **[Salvation Assured]**
Lord,
send down your abundant blessing
upon your people who have devoutly recalled the
    death of your Son
in the sure hope of the resurrection.
Grant them pardon; bring them comfort.
May their faith grow stronger
and their eternal salvation be assured.
We ask this through Christ our Lord. ℟. **Amen.** ↓

All depart in silence. The altar is stripped at a convenient time.

APRIL 19

HOLY SATURDAY

On Holy Saturday the Church waits at the Lord's tomb, meditating on his suffering and death. The altar is left bare, and the sacrifice of the Mass is not celebrated. Only after the solemn vigil during the night, held in anticipation of the resurrection, does the Easter celebration begin, with a spirit of joy that overflows into the following period of fifty days.

"He is not here, for he has been raised."

APRIL 19

EASTER VIGIL

In accord with ancient tradition, this night is one of vigil for the Lord (Ex 12:42). The Gospel of Luke (12:35ff) is a reminder to the faithful to have their lamps burning ready, to be like men awaiting their master's return so that when he arrives he will find them wide awake and will seat them at his table.

The night vigil is arranged in four parts: (a) a brief service of light; (b) the liturgy of the word, when the Church meditates on all the wonderful things God has done for his people from the beginning; (c) the liturgy of baptism, when new members of the Church are reborn as the day of resurrection approaches; and (d) the liturgy of the eucharist, when the whole Church is called to the table which the Lord has prepared for his people through his death and resurrection.

PART ONE
SOLEMN BEGINNING OF THE VIGIL:
THE SERVICE OF LIGHT
Blessing of the Fire and Lighting the Candle

All the lights in the church are put out.

A large fire is prepared in a suitable place outside the church. When the people have assembled, the priest goes there with the ministers, one of whom carries the Easter candle.

321

If it is not possible to light the fire outside the church, the rite is carried out as below, p. 323.

The priest greets the congregation in the usual manner and briefly instructs them about the vigil in these or similar words:

Dear friends in Christ,   **[Honoring Christ's Memory]**
on this most holy night,
when our Lord Jesus Christ passed from death to life,
the Church invites her children throughout the world
to come together in vigil and prayer.
This is the passover of the Lord:
if we honor the memory of his death and resurrection
by hearing his word and celebrating his mysteries,
then we may be confident
that we shall share his victory over death
and live with him for ever in God.

Then the fire is blessed.

[Light of the World]

Let us pray.
Father,
we share in the light of your glory
through your Son, the light of the world.
Make this new fire ✚ holy, and inflame us with new
    hope.
Purify our minds by this Easter celebration
and bring us one day to the feast of eternal light.
We ask this through Christ our Lord. ℟. **Amen.** ↓

The Easter candle is lighted from the new fire.

Preparation of the Candle

Depending on the nature of the congregation, it may seem appropriate to stress the dignity and significance of the Easter candle with other symbolic rites. This may be done as follows:

After the blessing of the new fire, an acolyte or one of the ministers brings the Easter candle to the celebrant, who cuts a cross in the wax with a stylus. Then he traces the Greek let-

ter alpha above the cross, the letter omega below, and the numerals of the current year between the arms of the cross. Meanwhile he says:

1. Christ yesterday and today *(as he traces the vertical arm of the cross),*
2. the beginning and the end *(the horizontal arm),*
3. Alpha *(alpha, above the cross),*
4. and Omega *(omega, below the cross);*
5. all time belongs to him *(the first numeral, in the upper left corner of the cross),*
6. and all the ages *(the second numeral in the upper right corner);*
7. to him be glory and power *(the third numeral in the lower left corner),*
8. through every age for ever. Amen. *(the last numeral in the lower right corner).*

```
        A
     2  |  0
    ─────┼─────
        |
     0  |
        Ω
```

When the cross and other marks have been made, the priest may insert five grains of incense in the candle. He does this in the form of a cross, saying:

1. By his holy
2. and glorious wounds
3. may Christ our Lord
4. guard us
5. and keep us. Amen.

```
       1
   4   2   5
       3
```

The priest lights the candle from the new fire, saying:

May the light of Christ, rising in glory,
dispel the darkness of our hearts and minds.

Any or all of the preceding rites may be used, depending on local pastoral circumstances. The conferences of bishops may also determine other rites better adapted to the culture of the people.

Where it may be difficult to have a large fire, the blessing of the fire is adapted to the circumstances. When the people have assembled in the church as on other occasions, the priest goes with the ministers (carrying the Easter candle) to the church door. If possible, the people turn to face the priest.

The greeting and brief instruction take place as above, p. 322. Then the fire is blessed and, if desired, the candle is prepared and lighted as above.

Procession

Then the deacon or, if there is no deacon, the priest takes the Easter candle, lifts it high, and sings alone:

Christ our light.

All answer:

Thanks be to God.

The conferences of bishops may determine a richer acclamation.

Then all enter the church, led by the deacon with the Easter candle. If incense is used, the thurifer goes before the deacon.

At the church door the deacon lifts the candle high and sings a second time:

Christ our light.

All answer:

Thanks be to God.

All light their candles from the Easter candle and continue in the procession.

When the deacon arrives before the altar, he faces the people and sings a third time:

Christ our light.

All answer:

Thanks be to God.

Then the lights in the church are put on.

Easter Proclamation (Exsultet)

When he comes to the altar, the priest goes to his chair. The deacon places the Easter candle on a stand in the middle of the sanctuary or near the lectern. If incense is used, the

*priest puts some in the censer, as at the gospel of Mass. Then
the deacon asks the blessing of the priest, who says in a low
voice:*

The Lord be in your heart and on your lips,
that you may worthily proclaim his Easter praise.
In the name of the Father, and of the Son ✠ and of the
Holy Spirit. ℟. **Amen.** ↓

*The book and candle may be incensed. Then the deacon or, if
there is no deacon, the priest sings the Easter proclamation
at the lectern or pulpit. All stand and hold lighted candles.*

*If necessary, the Easter proclamation may be sung by one
who is not a deacon. In this case the bracketed words are
omitted.*

[When the shorter form is used, omit the italicized parts.]

Rejoice, heavenly powers! Sing, choirs of angels!
   Exult, all creation around God's throne!
   Jesus Christ, our King, is risen!
   Sound the trumpet of salvation!

Rejoice, O earth, in shining splendor,
   radiant in the brightness of your King!
   Christ has conquered! Glory fills you!
   Darkness vanishes for ever!

Rejoice, O Mother Church! Exult in glory!
   The risen Savior shines upon you!
   Let this place resound with joy,
   echoing the mighty song of all God's people!

*[My dearest friends, standing with me in this holy
      light,
   join me in asking God for mercy,
   that he may give his unworthy minister
   grace to sing his Easter praises.]*

[℣. The Lord be with you. ℟. **And also with you.**]
℣. Lift up your hearts. ℟. **We lift them up to the Lord.**
℣. Let us give thanks to the Lord our God. ℟. **It is
right to give him thanks and praise.**

It is truly right
that with full hearts and minds and voices
we should praise the unseen God, the all-powerful
     Father,
and his only Son, our Lord Jesus Christ.
For Christ has ransomed us with his blood,
     and paid for us the price of Adam's sin
     to our eternal Father!
This is our passover feast,
     when Christ, the true Lamb, is slain,
     whose blood consecrates the homes of all believers.
This is the night when first you saved our fathers:
     you freed the people of Israel from their slavery
     and led them dry-shod through the sea.
This is the night when the pillar of fire
     destroyed the darkness of sin!
This is the night when Christians everywhere,
     washed clean of sin
     and freed from all defilement,
     are restored to grace and grow together in holiness.
This is the night when Jesus Christ
     broke the chains of death
     and rose triumphant from the grave.
What good would life have been to us,
     had Christ not come as our Redeemer?
Father, how wonderful your care for us!
     How boundless your merciful love!
     To ransom a slave
     you gave away your Son.
O happy fault, O necessary sin of Adam,
     which gained for us so great a Redeemer!
Most blessed of all nights, chosen by God
     to see Christ rising from the dead!
Of this night scripture says:
     "The night will be as clear as day:
     it will become my light, my joy."

The power of this holy night
dispels all evil, washes guilt away,
restores lost innocence, brings mourners joy;
*it casts out hatred, brings us peace, and humbles
earthly pride.*
Night truly blessed when heaven is wedded to earth
and man is reconciled with God!
Therefore, heavenly Father, in the joy of this night,
receive our evening sacrifice of praise,
your Church's solemn offering.
Accept this Easter candle,
a flame divided but undimmed,
a pillar of fire that glows to the honor of God.

Shorter form only:
May it always dispel the darkness of this night!

Let it mingle with the lights of heaven
and continue bravely burning
to dispel the darkness of this night!
May the Morning Star which never sets find this flame
still burning:
Christ, that Morning Star, who came back from the
dead,
and shed his peaceful light on all mankind,
your Son who lives and reigns for ever and ever.
℟. **Amen.** ↓

PART TWO

LITURGY OF THE WORD

In this vigil, the mother of all vigils, nine readings are pro-
vided, seven from the Old Testament and two from the New
Testament (the epistle and gospel).

The number of readings from the Old Testament may be re-
duced for pastoral reasons, but it must always be borne in
mind that the reading of the word of God is the fundamental

element of the Easter Vigil. At least three readings from the Old Testament should be read, although for more serious reasons the number may be reduced to two. The reading of Exodus 14 (reading 3), however, is never to be omitted.

After the Easter proclamation, the candles are put aside and all sit down. Before the readings begin, the priest speaks to the people in these or similar words:

Dear friends in Christ,   **[Attentive Listening]**
we have begun our solemn vigil.
Let us now listen attentively to the word of God,
recalling how he saved his people throughout history
and, in the fullness of time,
sent his own Son to be our Redeemer.
Through this Easter celebration,
may God bring to perfection
the saving work he has begun in us.

The readings follow. A reader goes to the lectern and proclaims the first reading. Then the cantor leads the psalm and the people respond. All rise and the priest sings or says Let us pray. *When all have prayed silently for a while, he sings or says the prayer.*

Instead of the responsorial psalm a period of silence may be observed. In this case the pause after Let us pray *is omitted.*

FIRST READING Gn 1:1—2:2 or 1:1, 26-31a **[God Our Creator]**

God created the world and all that is in it. He saw that it was good. This reading from the first book of the Bible shows that God loved all that he made.

[If the "Shorter Form" is used, the indented text in brackets is omitted.]

A reading from the Book of Genesis

IN the beginning, when God created the heavens and
the earth,
[the earth was a formless wasteland, and darkness covered the abyss, while a mighty wind swept over the waters.

Then God said, "Let there be light," and there was light. God saw how good the light was. God then separated the light from the darkness. God called the light "day," and the darkness he called "night." Thus evening came, and morning followed—the first day.

Then God said, "Let there be a dome in the middle of the waters, to separate one body of water from the other." And so it happened: God made the dome, and it separated the water above the dome from the water below it. God called the dome "the sky." Evening came, and morning followed—the second day.

Then God said, "Let the water under the sky be gathered into a single basin, so that the dry land may appear." And so it happened: the water under the sky was gathered into its basin, and the dry land appeared. God called the dry land "the earth," and the basin of the water he called "the sea." God saw how good it was. Then God said, "Let the earth bring forth vegetation: every kind of plant that bears seed and every kind of fruit tree on earth that bears fruit with its seed in it." And so it happened: the earth brought forth every kind of plant that bears seed and every kind of fruit tree on earth that bears fruit with its seed in it. God saw how good it was. Evening came, and morning followed—the third day.

Then God said: "Let there be lights in the dome of the sky, to separate day from night. Let them mark the fixed times, the days and the years, and serve as luminaries in the dome of the sky, to shed light upon the earth." And so it happened: God made the two great lights, the greater one to govern the day, and the lesser one to govern the night; and he made the stars. God set them in the dome of the sky, to shed light upon the earth, to govern the day and the night, and to separate the light from the darkness. God saw how good it was. Evening came, and morning followed—the fourth day.

Then God said, "Let the water teem with an abundance of living creatures, and on the earth let birds fly beneath the dome of the sky." And so it happened: God created the great sea monsters and all kinds of swimming creatures with which the water teems, and all kinds of winged birds. God saw how good it was, and God blessed them, saying, "Be fertile, multiply, and fill the water of the seas; and let the birds multiply on the earth." Evening came, and morning followed—the fifth day.

Then God said, "Let the earth bring forth all kinds of living creatures: cattle, creeping things, and wild animals of all kinds." And so it happened: God made all kinds of wild animals, all kinds of cattle, and all kinds of creeping things of the earth. God saw how good it was. Then]
God said: "Let us make man in our image, after our likeness. Let them have dominion over the fish of the sea, the birds of the air, and the cattle, and over all the wild animals and all the creatures that crawl on the ground."

God created man in his image;
in the divine image he created him;
male and female he created them.

God blessed them, saying: "Be fertile and multiply; fill the earth and subdue it. Have dominion over the fish of the sea, the birds of the air, and all the living things that move on the earth." God also said: "See, I give you every seed-bearing plant all over the earth and every tree that has seed-bearing fruit on it to be your food; and to all the animals of the land, all the birds of the air, and all the living creatures that crawl on the ground, I give all the green plants for food." And so it happened. God looked at everything he had made, and he found it very good.

[Evening came, and morning followed—the sixth day.

Thus the heavens and the earth and all their array were completed. Since on the seventh day God was finished with the work he had been doing, he rested on the seventh day from all the work he had undertaken.]

The word of the Lord. ℟. **Thanks be to God.** ↓

RESPONSORIAL PSALM Ps 104   [Come, Holy Spirit]

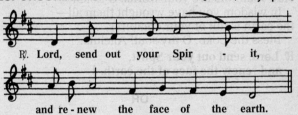

℟. Lord, send out your Spir - it,

and re - new the face of the earth.

Bless the LORD, O my soul!
O LORD, my God, you are great indeed!
You are clothed with majesty and glory,
    robed in light as with a cloak.

℟. **Lord, send out your Spirit,**
    and renew the face of the earth.

You fixed the earth upon its foundation,
    not to be moved forever;
with the ocean, as with a garment, you covered it;
    above the mountains the waters stood.

℟. **Lord, send out your Spirit,**
    and renew the face of the earth.

You send forth springs into the watercourses
    that wind among the mountains.

Beside them the birds of heaven dwell;
   from among the branches they send forth their
   song.

℞. **Lord, send out your Spirit,**
   and renew the face of the earth.

You water the mountains from your palace;
   the earth is replete with the fruit of your works.
You raise grass for the cattle,
   and vegetation for men's use,
producing bread from the earth.

℞. **Lord, send out your Spirit,**
   and renew the face of the earth.

How manifold are your works, O LORD!
   In wisdom you have wrought them all—
the earth is full of your creatures.
   Bless the LORD, O my soul! Alleluia.

℞. **Lord, send out your Spirit,**
   and renew the face of the earth. ↓

OR

RESPONSORIAL PSALM Ps 33   [The Lord's Goodness]

℞. The earth is full of the
good - ness of the Lord.

Upright is the word of the LORD,
   and all his works are trustworthy.
He loves justice and right;
   of the kindness of the LORD the earth is full.

℞. **The earth is full of the goodness of the Lord.**

By the word of the LORD the heavens were made;
  by the breath of his mouth all their host.
He gathers the waters of the sea as in a flask;
  in cellars he confines the deep.

℟. **The earth is full of the goodness of the Lord.**

Blessed the nation whose God is the LORD,
  the people he has chosen for his own inheritance.
From heaven the LORD looks down;
  he sees all mankind.

℟. **The earth is full of the goodness of the Lord.**

Our soul waits for the LORD,
  who is our help and our shield.
May your kindness, O LORD, be upon us
  who have put our hope in you.

℟. **The earth is full of the goodness of the Lord.** ↓

PRAYER   [New Creation]

Let us pray.
Almighty and eternal God,
you created all things in wonderful beauty and order.
Help us now to perceive
how still more wonderful is the new creation
by which in the fullness of time
you redeemed your people
through the sacrifice of our passover, Jesus Christ,
who lives and reigns for ever and ever. ℟. **Amen.** ↓

OR

PRAYER (on the creation of man)   [Our Redemption]

Let us pray.
Lord God,
the creation of man was a wonderful work,
his redemption still more wonderful.
May we persevere in right reason
against all that entices to sin

and so attain to everlasting joy.
We ask this through Christ our Lord. ℟. **Amen.** ↓

SECOND READING Gn 22:1-18 or 22:1-2, 9a, 10-13, 15-18

[Obedience to God]

Abraham is obedient to the will of God. Because God asks him, without hesitation he prepares to sacrifice his son Isaac. In the new order, God sends his Son to redeem man by his death on the cross.

[If the "Shorter Form" is used, the indented text in brackets is omitted.]

A reading from the Book of Genesis

GOD put Abraham to the test. He called to him, "Abraham!" "Here I am," he replied. Then God said: "Take your son Isaac, your only one, whom you love, and go to the land of Moriah. There you shall offer him up as a holocaust on a height that I will point out to you."

[Early the next morning Abraham saddled his donkey, took with him his son Isaac, and two of his servants as well, and with the wood that he had cut for the holocaust, set out for the place of which God had told him.

On the third day Abraham got sight of the place from afar. Then he said to his servants: "Both of you stay here with the donkey, while the boy and I go on over yonder. We will worship and then come back to you." Thereupon Abraham took the wood for the holocaust and laid it on his son Isaac's shoulders, while he himself carried the fire and the knife. As the two walked on together, Isaac spoke to his father Abraham. "Father!" Isaac said. "Yes, son," he replied. Isaac continued, "Here are the fire and the wood, but where is the sheep for the holocaust?" "Son," Abraham answered, "God himself will provide the sheep for the holocaust." Then the two continued going forward.]

When they came to the place of which God had told him, Abraham built an altar there and arranged the wood on it.

[Next he tied up his son Isaac, and put him on top of the wood on the altar.]

Then he reached out and took the knife to slaughter his son. But the LORD's messenger called to him from heaven, "Abraham, Abraham!" "Here I am," he answered. "Do not lay your hand on the boy," said the messenger. "Do not do the least thing to him. I know now how devoted you are to God, since you did not withhold from me your own beloved son." As Abraham looked about, he spied a ram caught by its horns in the thicket. So he went and took the ram and offered it up as a holocaust in place of his son.

[Abraham named the site Yahweh-yireh; hence people now say, "On the mountain the LORD will see."]

Again the LORD's messenger called to Abraham from heaven and said: "I swear by myself, declares the LORD, that because you acted as you did in not withholding from me your beloved son, I will bless you abundantly and make your descendants as countless as the stars of the sky and the sands of the seashore; your descendants shall take possession of the gates of their enemies, and in your descendants all the nations of the earth shall find blessing—all this because you obeyed my command."—The word of the Lord. ℟. **Thanks be to God.** ↓

RESPONSORIAL PSALM Ps 16   [God Our Hope]

℟. You   are   my   in-   her-i-tance, O   Lord.

O LORD, my allotted portion and my cup,
  you it is who hold fast my lot.
I set the LORD ever before me;
  with him at my right I shall not be disturbed.

℟. **You are my inheritance, O Lord.**

Therefore my heart is glad and my soul rejoices,
  my body, too, abides in confidence;
because you will not abandon my soul to the nether-
    world,
    nor will you suffer your faithful one to undergo cor-
      ruption.

℟. **You are my inheritance, O Lord.**

You will show me the path to life,
  fullness of joys in your presence,
  the delights at your right hand forever.

℟. **You are my inheritance, O Lord.** ↓

PRAYER   [Response to God's Call]

Let us pray.
God and Father of all who believe in you,
you promised Abraham that he would become the
  father of all nations,
and through the death and resurrection of Christ
you fulfill that promise:
everywhere throughout the world you increase your
  chosen people.
May we respond to your call
by joyfully accepting your invitation to the new life of
  grace.
We ask this through Christ our Lord. ℟. **Amen.** ↓

THIRD READING Ex 14:15—15:1   [Exodus]

  Moses leads the Israelites out of Egypt. He opens a path of
  escape through the Red Sea. God protects his people.
  Through the waters of baptism, human beings are freed
  from sin.

A reading from the Book of Exodus

THE LORD said to Moses, "Why are you crying out to me? Tell the Israelites to go forward. And you, lift up your staff and, with hand outstretched over the sea, split the sea in two, that the Israelites may pass through it on dry land. But I will make the Egyptians so obstinate that they will go in after them. Then I will receive glory through Pharaoh and all his army, his chariots and charioteers. The Egyptians shall know that I am the LORD, when I receive glory through Pharaoh and his chariots and charioteers."

The angel of God, who had been leading Israel's camp, now moved and went around behind them. The column of cloud also, leaving the front, took up its place behind them, so that it came between the camp of the Egyptians and that of Israel. But the cloud now became dark, and thus the night passed without the rival camps coming any closer together all night long. Then Moses stretched out his hand over the sea, and the LORD swept the sea with a strong east wind throughout the night and so turned it into dry land. When the water was thus divided, the Israelites marched into the midst of the sea on dry land, with the water like a wall to their right and to their left.

The Egyptians followed in pursuit; all Pharaoh's horses and chariots and charioteers went after them right into the midst of the sea. In the night watch just before dawn the LORD cast through the column of the fiery cloud upon the Egyptian force a glance that threw it into a panic; and he so clogged their chariot wheels that they could hardly drive. With that the Egyptians sounded the retreat before Israel, because the LORD was fighting for them against the Egyptians.

Then the LORD told Moses, "Stretch out your hand over the sea, that the water may flow back upon the Egyptians, upon their chariots and their charioteers." So Moses stretched out his hand over the sea, and at dawn the sea flowed back to its normal depth. The Egyptians were fleeing head on toward the sea, when the Lord hurled them into its midst. As the water flowed back, it covered the chariots and the charioteers of Pharaoh's whole army which had followed the Israelites into the sea. Not a single one of them escaped. But the Israelites had marched on dry land through the midst of the sea, with the water like a wall to their right and to their left. Thus the Lord saved Israel on that day from the power of the Egyptians. When Israel saw the Egyptians lying dead on the seashore and beheld the great power that the Lord had shown against the Egyptians, they feared the Lord and believed in him and in his servant Moses.

Then Moses and the Israelites sang this song to the Lord:

I will sing to the Lord, for he is gloriously triumphant;
    horse and chariot he has cast into the sea.
The word of the Lord. ℟. **Thanks be to God.** ↓

RESPONSORIAL PSALM Ex 15   [God the Savior]

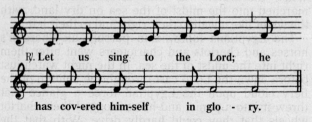

℟. Let us sing to the Lord; he has cov-ered him-self in glo-ry.

I will sing to the Lord, for he is gloriously triumphant;
    horse and chariot he has cast into the sea.
My strength and my courage is the Lord,
    and he has been my savior.
He is my God, I praise him;
    the God of my father, I extol him.

℟. **Let us sing to the Lord;**
   he has covered himself in glory.

The LORD is a warrior,
   LORD is his name!
Pharaoh's chariots and army he hurled into the sea;
   the elite of his officers were submerged into the Red
      Sea.

℟. **Let us sing to the Lord;**
   he has covered himself in glory.

The flood waters covered them,
   they sank into the depths like a stone.
Your right hand, O LORD, magnificent in power,
   your right hand, O LORD, has shattered the enemy.

℟. **Let us sing to the Lord;**
   he has covered himself in glory.

You brought in the people you redeemed
   and planted them on the mountain of your inheri-
      tance—
the place where you made your seat, O LORD,
   the sanctuary, O LORD, which your hands estab-
      lished.
The LORD shall reign forever and ever.

℟. **Let us sing to the Lord;**
   he has covered himself in glory. ↓

PRAYER   [Children of Abraham]

Let us pray.
Father,
even today we see the wonders
of the miracles you worked long ago.
You once saved a single nation from slavery,
and now you offer that salvation to all through baptism.
May the peoples of the world become true sons of
   Abraham
and prove worthy of the heritage of Israel.
We ask this through Christ our Lord. ℟. **Amen.** ↓

OR

PRAYER   [New Birth]

Let us pray.
Lord God,
in the new covenant
you shed light on the miracles you worked in ancient
    times:
the Red Sea is a symbol of our baptism,
and the nation you freed from slavery
is a sign of your Christian people.
May every nation
share the faith and privilege of Israel
and come to new birth in the Holy Spirit.
We ask this through Christ our Lord. ℟. **Amen.** ↓

FOURTH READING Is 54:5-14   [God's Love]

> For a time, God hid from his people, but his love for them
> is everlasting. He takes pity on them and promises them
> prosperity.

A reading from the Book of the Prophet Isaiah

THE One who has become your husband is your
    Maker; his name is the LORD of hosts;
your redeemer is the Holy One of Israel,
    called God of all the earth.
The LORD calls you back,
    like a wife forsaken and grieved in spirit,
a wife married in youth and then cast off,
    says your God.
For a brief moment I abandoned you,
    but with great tenderness I will take you back.
In an outburst of wrath, for a moment
    I hid my face from you;
but with enduring love I take pity on you,
    says the LORD, your redeemer.
This is for me like the days of Noah,
    when I swore that the waters of Noah
    should never again deluge the earth;

so I have sworn not to be angry with you,
  or to rebuke you.
Though the mountains leave their place
  and the hills be shaken,
my love shall never leave you
  nor my covenant of peace be shaken,
  says the LORD, who has mercy on you.
O afflicted one, storm-battered and unconsoled,
  I lay your pavements in carnelians,
  and your foundations in sapphires;
I will make your battlements of rubies,
  your gates of carbuncles,
  and all your walls of precious stones.
All your sons shall be taught by the LORD,
  and great shall be the peace of your children.
In justice shall you be established,
  far from the fear of oppression,
  where destruction cannot come near you.
The word of the Lord. ℟. **Thanks be to God.** ↓

RESPONSORIAL PSALM Ps 30   [God Our Help]

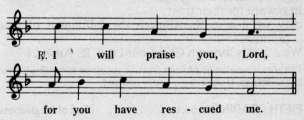

℟. I will praise you, Lord, for you have res-cued me.

I will extol you, O LORD, for you drew me clear
  and did not let my enemies rejoice over me.
O LORD, you brought me up from the netherworld;
  you preserved me from among those going down
    into the pit.

℟. **I will praise you, Lord,**
  for you have rescued me.

Sing praise to the LORD, you his faithful ones,
  and give thanks to his holy name.
For his anger lasts but a moment;
  a lifetime, his good will.
At nightfall, weeping enters in,
  but with the dawn, rejoicing.

℟. **I will praise you, Lord,**
  for you have rescued me.

Hear, O LORD, and have pity on me;
  O LORD, be my helper.
You changed my mourning into dancing;
  O LORD, my God, forever will I give you thanks.

℟. **I will praise you, Lord,**
  for you have rescued me. ↓

PRAYER   [Fulfillment of God's Promise]

Let us pray.
Almighty and eternal God,
glorify your name by increasing your chosen people
as you promised long ago.
In reward for their trust,
may we see in the Church the fulfillment of your
  promise.
We ask this through Christ our Lord. ℟. **Amen.** ↓

Prayers may also be chosen from those given after the follow-
ing readings, if the readings are omitted.

FIFTH READING Is 55:1-11   [God of Forgiveness]

  God is a loving Father and he calls his people back. He
  promises an everlasting covenant with them. God is merciful, generous, and forgiving.

  A reading from the Book of the Prophet Isaiah

T HUS says the LORD:
  All you who are thirsty,
  come to the water!

You who have no money,
come, receive grain and eat;
come, without paying and without cost,
drink wine and milk!
Why spend your money for what is not bread;
your wages for what fails to satisfy?
Heed me, and you shall eat well,
you shall delight in rich fare.
Come to me heedfully,
listen, that you may have life.
I will renew with you the everlasting covenant,
the benefits assured to David.
As I made him a witness to the peoples,
a leader and commander of nations,
so shall you summon a nation you knew not,
and nations that knew you not shall run to you,
because of the LORD, your God,
the Holy One of Israel, who has glorified you.

Seek the LORD while he may be found,
call him while he is near.
Let the scoundrel forsake his way,
and the wicked man his thoughts;
let him turn to the LORD for mercy;
to our God, who is generous in forgiving.
For my thoughts are not your thoughts,
nor are your ways my ways, says the LORD.
As high as the heavens are above the earth,
so high are my ways above your ways,
and my thoughts above your thoughts.

For just as from the heavens
the rain and snow come down
and do not return there
till they have watered the earth,
making it fertile and fruitful,
giving seed to the one who sows
and bread to the one who eats,

so shall my word be
  that goes forth from my mouth;
my word shall not return to me void,
  but shall do my will,
    achieving the end for which I sent it.
The word of the Lord. ℟. **Thanks be to God.** ↓

RESPONSORIAL PSALM Is 12 [Make Known God's Deeds]

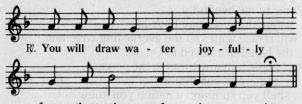

℟. You will draw wa-ter joy-ful-ly from the springs of sal-va-tion.

God indeed is my savior;
  I am confident and unafraid.
My strength and my courage is the LORD,
  and he has been my savior.
With joy you will draw water
  at the fountain of salvation.

℟. **You will draw water joyfully from the springs of salvation.**

Give thanks to the LORD, acclaim his name;
  among the nations make known his deeds,
  proclaim how exalted is his name.

℟. **You will draw water joyfully from the springs of salvation.**

Sing praise to the LORD for his glorious achievement;
  let this be known throughout all the earth.
Shout with exultation, O city of Zion,
  for great in your midst
  is the Holy One of Israel!

℟. **You will draw water joyfully from the springs of salvation.** ↓

PRAYER   [Growth in Goodness]
Let us pray.
Almighty, ever-living God,
only hope of the world,
by the preaching of the prophets
you proclaimed the mysteries we are celebrating
    tonight.
Help us to be your faithful people,
for it is by your inspiration alone
that we can grow in goodness.
We ask this through Christ our Lord. ℟. **Amen.** ↓

SIXTH READING Bar 3:9-15, 32—4:4   [Walk in God's Ways]

Baruch tells the people of Israel to walk in the ways of
God. They have to learn prudence, wisdom, understanding.
Then they will have peace forever.

A reading from the Book of the Prophet Baruch

HEAR, O Israel, the commandments of life:
    listen, and know prudence!
How is it, Israel,
    that you are in the land of your foes,
    grown old in a foreign land,
defiled with the dead,
    accounted with those destined for the netherworld?
You have forsaken the fountain of wisdom!
    Had you walked in the way of God,
    you would have dwelt in enduring peace.
Learn where prudence is,
    where strength, where understanding;
that you may know also
    where are length of days, and life,
    where light of the eyes, and peace.
Who has found the place of wisdom,
    who has entered into her treasuries?

The One who knows all things knows her;
    he has probed her by his knowledge—

the One who established the earth for all time,
    and filled it with four-footed beasts;
he who dismisses the light, and it departs,
    calls it, and it obeys him trembling;
before whom the stars at their posts
    shine and rejoice;
when he calls them, they answer, "Here we are!"
    shining with joy for their Maker.
Such is our God;
    no other is to be compared to him:
he has traced out all the way of understanding,
    and has given her to Jacob, his servant,
    to Israel, his beloved son.

Since then she has appeared on earth,
    and moved among people.
She is the book of the precepts of God,
    the law that endures forever;
all who cling to her will live,
    but those will die who forsake her.
Turn, O Jacob, and receive her:
    walk by her light toward splendor.
Give not your glory to another,
    your privileges to an alien race.
Blessed are we, O Israel;
    for what pleases God is known to us!
The word of the Lord. ℞. **Thanks be to God.** ↓

RESPONSORIAL PSALM Ps 19   [Words of Eternal Life]

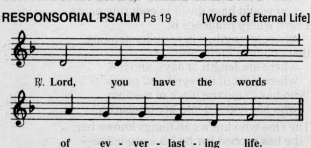

℞. Lord,   you   have   the   words
of   ev - ver - last - ing   life.

The law of the LORD is perfect,
    refreshing the soul;
the decree of the LORD is trustworthy,
    giving wisdom to the simple.

R̰/. **Lord, you have the words of everlasting life.**

The precepts of the LORD are right,
    rejoicing the heart;
the command of the LORD is clear,
    enlightening the eye.

R̰/. **Lord, you have the words of everlasting life.**

The fear of the LORD is pure,
    enduring forever;
the ordinances of the LORD are true,
    all of them just.

R̰/. **Lord, you have the words of everlasting life.**

They are more precious than gold,
    than a heap of purest gold;
sweeter also than syrup
    or honey from the comb.

R̰/. **Lord, you have the words of everlasting life.** ↓

PRAYER   [Hear Our Prayer]

Let us pray.
Father,
you increase your Church
by continuing to call all people to salvation.
Listen to our prayers
and always watch over those you cleanse in baptism.
We ask this through Christ our Lord. R̰/. **Amen.** ↓

SEVENTH READING Ez 36:16-28   [God's People]

Ezekiel, as God's prophet, speaks for God who is to keep
his name holy among his people. All shall know the holiness of God. He will cleanse his people from idol worship
and make them his own again. This promise is again fulfilled in baptism in the restored order of redemption.

A reading from the Book of the Prophet Ezekiel

THE word of the LORD came to me, saying: Son of man, when the house of Israel lived in their land, they defiled it by their conduct and deeds. Therefore I poured out my fury upon them because of the blood that they poured out on the ground, and because they defiled it with idols. I scattered them among the nations, dispersing them over foreign lands; according to their conduct and deeds I judged them. But when they came among the nations wherever they came, they served to profane my holy name, because it was said of them: "These are the people of the LORD, yet they had to leave their land." So I have relented because of my holy name which the house of Israel profaned among the nations where they came. Therefore say to the house of Israel: Thus says the Lord GOD: Not for your sakes do I act, house of Israel, but for the sake of my holy name, which you profaned among the nations to which you came. I will prove the holiness of my great name, profaned among the nations, in whose midst you have profaned it. Thus the nations shall know that I am the LORD, says the Lord GOD, when in their sight I prove my holiness through you. For I will take you away from among the nations, gather you from all the foreign lands, and bring you back to your own land. I will sprinkle clean water upon you to cleanse you from all your impurities, and from all your idols I will cleanse you. I will give you a new heart and place a new spirit within you, taking from your bodies your stony hearts and giving you natural hearts. I will put my spirit within you and make you live by my statutes, careful to observe my decrees. You shall live in the land I gave your fathers; you shall be my people, and I will be your God.—The word of the Lord. ℞. Thanks be to God. ↓

When baptism is celebrated, Responsorial Psalm 42 is used; when baptism is not celebrated, Is 12 or Ps 51 is used.

RESPONSORIAL PSALM Ps 42   **[Longing for God]**

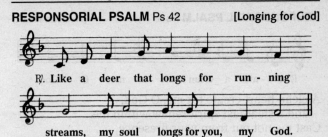

℟. Like a deer that longs for run - ning
streams, my soul longs for you, my God.

Athirst is my soul for God, the living God.
  When shall I go and behold the face of God?

℟. **Like a deer that longs for running streams,
  my soul longs for you, my God.**

I went with the throng
  and led them in procession to the house of God,
amid loud cries of joy and thanksgiving,
  with the multitude keeping festival.

℟. **Like a deer that longs for running streams,
  my soul longs for you, my God.**

Send forth your light and your fidelity;
  they shall lead me on
and bring me to your holy mountain,
  to your dwelling-place.

℟. **Like a deer that longs for running streams,
  my soul longs for you, my God.**

Then will I go into the altar of God,
  the God of my gladness and joy;
then will I give you thanks upon the harp,
  O God, my God!

℟. **Like a deer that longs for running streams,
  my soul longs for you, my God.** ↓

OR

*When baptism is not celebrated, the Responsorial Psalm after
the Fifth Reading (Is 12:2-3, 4bcd, 5-6) as above, p. 344, may
be used; or the following:*

RESPONSORIAL PSALM Ps 51   [A Clean Heart]

℟. Cre - ate   a   clean heart   in   me,   O   God.

A clean heart create for me, O God,
   and a steadfast spirit renew within me.
Cast me not out from your presence,
   and your Holy Spirit take not from me.

℟. **Create a clean heart in me, O God.**

Give me back the joy of your salvation,
   and a willing spirit sustain in me.
I will teach transgressors your ways,
   and sinners shall return to you.

℟. **Create a clean heart in me, O God.**

For you are not pleased with sacrifices;
   should I offer a holocaust, you would not accept it.
My sacrifice, O God, is a contrite spirit;
   a heart contrite and humbled, O God, you will not
      spurn.

℟. **Create a clean heart in me, O God.** ↓

PRAYER   [Lasting Salvation]
Let us pray.
God of unchanging power and light,
look with mercy and favor on your entire Church.
Bring lasting salvation to mankind,
so that the world may see
the fallen lifted up,
the old made new,
and all things brought to perfection,
through him who is their origin,
our Lord Jesus Christ,
who lives and reigns for ever and ever. ℟. **Amen.** ↓

OR

PRAYER   [Confirm Our Hope]

Let us pray.
Father,
you teach us in both the Old and the New Testament
to celebrate this passover mystery.
Help us to understand your great love for us.
May the goodness you now show us
confirm our hope in your future mercy.
We ask this through Christ our Lord. ℟. **Amen.** ↓

After the last reading from the Old Testament with its responsory and prayer, the altar candles are lighted, and the priest intones the Gloria, *which is taken up by all present. The church bells are rung, according to local custom.*

At the end of the hymn, the priest sings or says the opening prayer in the usual way.

OPENING PRAYER   [Renewed in Mind and Body]

Let us pray.
Lord God,
you have brightened this night
with the radiance of the risen Christ.
Quicken the spirit of sonship in your Church;
renew us in mind and body
to give you whole-hearted service.
Grant this through our Lord Jesus Christ, your Son,
who lives and reigns with you and the Holy Spirit,
one God, for ever and ever. ℟. **Amen.** ↓

Then a reader proclaims the reading from the Apostle Paul.

EPISTLE Rom 6:3-11   [Alive in Christ]

By Baptism the Christian is not merely identified with the
dying Christ, who has won a victory over sin, but is introduced into the very act by which Christ died to sin.

A reading from the Letter of Saint Paul to the Romans

BROTHERS and sisters: Are you unaware that we who were baptized into Christ Jesus were baptized into his death? We were indeed buried with him through baptism into death, so that, just as Christ was raised from the dead by the glory of the Father, we too might live in newness of life.

For if we have grown into union with him through a death like his, we shall also be united with him in the resurrection. We know that our old self was crucified with him, so that our sinful body might be done away with, that we might no longer be in slavery to sin. For a dead person has been absolved from sin. If, then, we have died with Christ, we believe that we shall also live with him. We know that Christ, raised from the dead, dies no more; death no longer has power over him. As to his death, he died to sin once and for all; as to his life, he lives for God. Consequently, you too must think of yourselves as being dead to sin and living for God in Christ Jesus.—The word of the Lord. ℟. **Thanks be to God.** ↓

After the Epistle all rise, and the priest solemnly intones the alleluia, *which is repeated by all present.*

RESPONSORIAL PSALM Ps 118   [God's Mercy]

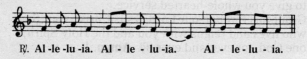

℟. **Al-le-lu-ia. Al-le-lu-ia.   Al-le-lu-ia.**

Give thanks to the LORD, for he is good,
  for his mercy endures forever.
Let the house of Israel say,
  "His mercy endures forever."

℟. **Alleluia. Alleluia. Alleluia.**

The right hand of the L<small>ORD</small> has struck with power;
  the right hand of the L<small>ORD</small> is exalted.
I shall not die, but live,
  and declare the works of the L<small>ORD</small>.

℞. **Alleluia. Alleluia. Alleluia.**

The stone which the builders rejected
  has become the cornerstone.
By the L<small>ORD</small> has this been done;
  it is wonderful in our eyes.

℞. **Alleluia. Alleluia. Alleluia.**

Incense may be used at the Gospel, but candles are not carried.

GOSPEL Mk 16:1-7   [The Resurrection]

Jesus has risen; he is not here. The cross has yielded to the empty tomb. Although Peter is singled out, the Easter message is first announced to the faithful, devoted women who followed Jesus.

℣. The Lord be with you. ℞. **And also with you.**
✠ A reading from the holy Gospel according to Mark.
℞. **Glory to you, Lord.**

W<small>HEN</small> the Sabbath was over, Mary Magdalene, Mary, the mother of James, and Salome brought spices so that they might go and anoint him. Very early when the sun had risen, on the first day of the week, they came to the tomb. They were saying to one another, "Who will roll back the stone for us from the entrance of the tomb?" When they looked up, they saw that the stone had been rolled back; it was very large. On entering the tomb they saw a young man sitting on the right side, clothed in a white robe, and they were utterly amazed. He said to them, "Do not be amazed! You seek Jesus of Nazareth, the crucified. He has been raised; he is not here. Behold the place where they laid him. But go and tell his disciples and Peter, 'He is going before you to Galilee; there you will see him, as he told you.' "—The Gospel of the Lord. ℟. **Praise to you, Lord Jesus Christ.**

PART THREE

LITURGY OF SACRAMENTS OF INITIATION

The following is taken from the Rite of Christian Initiation of Adults.

Celebration of Baptism

PRESENTATION OF THE CANDIDATES

An assisting deacon or other minister calls the candidates for baptism forward and their godparents present them. The invitation to prayer and the Litany of the Saints follow.

INVITATION TO PRAYER   [Supportive Prayer]

The celebrant addresses the following or a similar invitation for the assembly to join in prayer for the candidates for baptism.

Dear friends, let us pray to almighty God for our brothers and sisters, N. and N., who are asking for baptism. He has called them and brought them to this moment; may he grant them light and strength to follow Christ with resolute hearts and to profess the faith of the Church. May he give them the new life of the Holy Spirit, whom we are about to call down on this water.

LITANY OF THE SAINTS   [Petitioning the Saints]

The singing of the Litany of the Saints is led by cantors and may include, at the proper place, names of other saints (for example, the titular of the church, the patron saints of the place or of those to be baptized) or petitions suitable to the occasion.

Lord, have mercy.
Lord, have mercy.

Christ, have mercy.
Christ, have mercy.

Lord, have mercy.
Lord, have mercy.

Holy Mary, Mother of God, **pray for us.**

Saint Michael, **pray for us.**

Holy angels of God, **pray for us.**

Saint John the Baptist, **pray for us.**

Saint Joseph, **pray for us.**

Saint Peter and Saint Paul, **pray for us.**

Saint Andrew, **pray for us.**

Saint John, **pray for us.**

Saint Mary Magdalene, **pray for us.**

Saint Stephen, **pray for us.**

Saint Ignatius, **pray for us.**

Saint Lawrence, **pray for us.**

Saint Perpetua and Saint Felicity, **pray for us.**

Saint Agnes, **pray for us.**

Saint Gregory, **pray for us.**

Saint Augustine, **pray for us.**

Saint Athanasius, **pray for us.**

Saint Basil, **pray for us.**

Saint Martin, **pray for us.**

Saint Benedict, **pray for us.**

Saint Francis and Saint Dominic, **pray for us.**

Saint Francis Xavier, **pray for us.**

Saint John Vianney, **pray for us.**

Saint Catherine, **pray for us.**

Saint Teresa, **pray for us.**

All holy men and women, **pray for us.**

Lord, be merciful, **Lord, save your people.**

From all evil, **Lord, save your people.**

From every sin, **Lord, save your people.**

From everlasting death, **Lord, save your people.**

By your coming as man, **Lord, save your people.**

By your death and rising to new life, **Lord, save your people.**

By your gift of the Holy Spirit, **Lord, save your people.**

Be merciful to us sinners, **Lord, hear our prayer.**

Give new life to these chosen ones by the grace of baptism, **Lord, hear our prayer.**

Jesus, Son of the living God, **Lord, hear our prayer.**

Christ, hear us.
Christ, hear us.

Lord Jesus, hear our prayer.
Lord Jesus, hear our prayer.

BLESSING OF THE WATER   [Grace-Filled Water]

Facing the font (or vessel) containing the water, the celebrant sings or says the following:

Father,
you give us grace through sacramental signs,
which tell us the wonders of your unseen power.
In baptism we use your gift of water,
which you have made a rich symbol of the grace
you give us in this sacrament.
At the very dawn of creation
your Spirit breathed on the waters,
making them the wellspring of all holiness.
The waters of the great flood
you made a sign of the waters of baptism,
that make an end of sin
and a new beginning of goodness.
Through the waters of the Red Sea
you led Israel out of slavery,
to be an image of God's holy people,
set free from sin by baptism.
In the waters of the Jordan
your Son was baptized by John
and anointed with the Spirit.
Your Son willed that water and blood should flow
from his side
as he hung upon the cross.
After his resurrection he told his disciples:
"Go out and teach all nations,

baptizing them in the name of the Father and of the Son and of the Holy Spirit."

Father,
look now with love upon your Church,
and unseal for it the fountain of baptism.
By the power of the Spirit
give to this water the grace of your Son,
so that in the sacrament of baptism
all those whom you have created in your likeness may be cleansed from sin
and rise to a new birth of innocence
by water and the Holy Spirit.

Here, if this can be done conveniently, the celebrant before continuing lowers the Easter candle into the water once or three times, then holds it there until the acclamation at the end of the blessing.

We ask you, Father, with your Son
to send the Holy Spirit upon the waters of this font.
May all who are buried with Christ in the death of baptism
rise also with him to newness of life.
We ask this through Christ our Lord.
All: **Amen.**

The celebrant then raises it and the people sing the following or another suitable acclamation:

**Springs of water, bless the Lord.
Give him glory and praise for ever.**

PROFESSION OF FAITH   [Witnessing to Our Faith]

After the blessing of the water, the celebrant continues with the profession of faith, which includes the renunciation of sin and the profession itself.

RENUNCIATION OF SIN   [Reject Evil]

Using one of the following formularies, the celebrant questions all the elect together; or, after being informed of each candidate's name by the godparents, he may use the same formularies to question the candidates individually.

A

Do you reject sin so as to live in the freedom of God's children? **I do.**

Do you reject the glamor of evil, and refuse to be mastered by sin? **I do.**

Do you reject Satan, father of sin and prince of darkness? **I do.**

B

Do you reject Satan, and all his works, and all his empty promises? **I do.**

C

Do you reject Satan? **I do.**
And all his works? **I do.**
And all his empty promises? **I do.**

PROFESSION OF FAITH   [We Do Believe]

Then the celebrant, informed again of each candidate's name by the godparents, questions each candidate individually. Each candidate is baptized immediately after his or her profession of faith.

Celebrant: N., do you believe in God, the Father almighty,
    creator of heaven and earth?
Candidate: **I do.**
Celebrant: Do you believe in Jesus Christ, his only Son, our Lord,
    who was born of the Virgin Mary,
    was crucified, died and was buried,
    rose from the dead,
    and is now seated at the right hand of the Father?
Candidate: **I do.**
Celebrant: Do you believe in the Holy Spirit,
    the holy Catholic Church, the communion of saints,
    the forgiveness of sins, the resurrection of the body,
    and the life everlasting?
Candidate: **I do.**

BAPTISM [Children of God]

The celebrant baptizes each candidate either by immersion or by the pouring of water.

N., I baptize you in the name of the Father, and of the Son, and of the Holy Spirit.

EXPLANATORY RITES

The celebration of baptism continues with the explanatory rites, after which the celebration of confirmation normally follows.

ANOINTING AFTER BAPTISM   [Chrism of Salvation]

If the confirmation of those baptized is separated from their baptism, the celebrant anoints them with chrism immediately after baptism.

The God of power and Father of our Lord Jesus Christ has freed you from sin
and brought you to new life
through water and the Holy Spirit.

He now anoints you with the chrism of salvation,
so that, united with his people,
you may remain for ever a member of Christ
who is Priest, Prophet, and King.

Newly baptized: **Amen.**

In silence each of the newly baptized is anointed with chrism on the crown of the head.

CLOTHING WITH A BAPTISMAL GARMENT
[Clothed in Christ]

The garment used in this rite may be white or of a color that conforms to local custom. If circumstances suggest, this rite may be omitted.

N. and N., you have become a new creation
and have clothed yourselves in Christ.

Receive this baptismal garment
and bring it unstained to the judgment seat of our
  Lord Jesus Christ,
so that you may have everlasting life.

Newly baptized: **Amen.**

PRESENTATION OF A LIGHTED CANDLE [Light of Christ]

The celebrant takes the Easter candle in his hands or touches it, saying:

Godparents, please come forward to give to the newly
baptized the light of Christ.

*A godparent of each of the newly baptized goes to the cele-
brant, lights a candle from the Easter candle, then presents it
to the newly baptized.*

You have been enlightened by Christ.
Walk always as children of the light
and keep the flame of faith alive in your hearts.
When the Lord comes, may you go out to meet him
with all the saints in the heavenly kingdom.

Newly baptized: **Amen.**

Renewal of Baptismal Promises

INVITATION   [Call to Renewal]

*After the celebration of baptism, the celebrant addresses the
community, in order to invite those present to the renewal of
their baptismal promises; the candidates for reception into
full communion join the rest of the community in this renunciation of sin and profession of faith. All stand and hold
lighted candles. The celebrant may use the following or similar words.*

Dear friends, through the paschal mystery we have
been buried with Christ in baptism, so that we may
rise with him to newness of life. Now that we have
completed our Lenten observance, let us renew the
promises we made in baptism when we rejected Satan

and his works, and promised to serve God faithfully in his holy Catholic Church.

RENEWAL OF BAPTISMAL PROMISES

RENUNCIATION OF SIN   [Reject Evil]

A

Celebrant: Do you reject sin so as to live in the freedom of God's children?

All: **I do.**

Celebrant: Do you reject the glamor of evil, and refuse to be mastered by sin?

All: **I do.**

Celebrant: Do you reject Satan, father of sin and prince of darkness?

All: **I do.**

B

Celebrant: Do you reject Satan?

All: **I do.**

Celebrant: And all his works?

All: **I do.**

Celebrant: And all his empty promises?

All: **I do.**

PROFESSION OF FAITH   [We Do Believe

Then the celebrant continues:

Celebrant: Do you believe in God, the Father almighty, creator of heaven and earth?

All: **I do.**

Celebrant: Do you believe in Jesus Christ, his only Son, our Lord,
who was born of the Virgin Mary,
was crucified, died and was buried,
rose from the dead,
and is now seated at the right hand of the Father?

All: **I do.**

Celebrant: Do you believe in the Holy Spirit,
the holy Catholic Church, the communion of saints,
the forgiveness of sins, the resurrection of the body,
and the life everlasting?
All: **I do.**

SPRINKLING WITH BAPTISMAL WATER [Water of Life]

The celebrant sprinkles all the people with the blessed baptismal water, while all sing the following song or any other that is baptismal in character.

Antiphon See Ez 47:1-2, 9

**I saw water flowing
from the right side of the temple, alleluia.
It brought God's life and his salvation,
and the people sang in joyful praise:
alleluia, alleluia.**

The celebrant then concludes with the following prayer.

God, the all-powerful Father of our Lord Jesus Christ,
has given us a new birth by water and the Holy Spirit
and forgiven all our sins.
May he also keep us faithful to our Lord Jesus Christ
for ever and ever.
All: **Amen.**

Celebration of Reception

INVITATION [Call To Come Forward]

If baptism has been celebrated at the font, the celebrant, the assisting ministers, and the newly baptized with their godparents proceed to the sanctuary. As they do so the assembly may sing a suitable song.

Then in the following or similar words the celebrant invites the candidates for reception, along with their sponsors, to come into the sanctuary and before the community to make a profession of faith.

N. and N., of your own free will you have asked to be received into the full communion of the Catholic

Church. You have made your decision after careful thought under the guidance of the Holy Spirit. I now invite you to come forward with your sponsors and in the presence of this community to profess the Catholic faith. In this faith you will be one with us for the first time at the eucharistic table of the Lord Jesus, the sign of the Church's unity.

PROFESSION BY THE CANDIDATES   [Belief in Church]

When the candidates for reception and their sponsors have taken their places in the sanctuary, the celebrant asks the candidates to make the following profession of faith. The candidates say:

I believe and profess all that the holy Catholic Church believes, teaches, and proclaims to be revealed by God.

ACT OF RECEPTION   [Full Communion]

Then the candidates with their sponsors go individually to the celebrant, who says to each candidate (laying his right hand on the head of any candidate who is not to receive confirmation):

N., the Lord receives you into the Catholic Church.
His loving kindness has led you here,
so that in the unity of the Holy Spirit
you may have full communion with us
in the faith that you have professed in the presence of
    his family.

Celebration of Confirmation

INVITATION   [Strength in the Spirit]

The newly baptized with their godparents and, if they have not received the sacrament of confirmation, the newly received with their sponsors, stand before the celebrant. He first speaks briefly to the newly baptized and the newly received in these or similar words.

My dear candidates for confirmation, by your baptism you have been born again in Christ and you have become members of Christ and of his priestly people. Now you are to share in the outpouring of the Holy Spirit among us, the Spirit sent by the Lord upon his apostles at Pentecost and given by them and their successors to the baptized.

The promised strength of the Holy Spirit, which you are to receive, will make you more like Christ and help you to be witnesses to his suffering, death, and resurrection. It will strengthen you to be active members of the Church and to build up the Body of Christ in faith and love.

My dear friends, let us pray to God our Father, that he will pour out the Holy Spirit on these candidates for confirmation to strengthen them with his gifts and anoint them to be more like Christ, the Son of God.

All pray briefly in silence.

LAYING ON OF HANDS   [Gifts of the Spirit]

The celebrant holds his hands outstretched over the entire group of those to be confirmed and says the following prayer.

All-powerful God, Father of our Lord Jesus Christ,
by water and the Holy Spirit
you freed your sons and daughters from sin
and gave them new life.
Send your Holy Spirit upon them
to be their helper and guide.
Give them the spirit of wisdom and understanding,
the spirit of right judgment and courage,
the spirit of knowledge and reverence.
Fill them with the spirit of wonder and awe in your
    presence.
We ask this through Christ our Lord.
℞. **Amen.**

ANOINTING WITH CHRISM   [Sealed in the Spirit]

Either or both godparents and sponsors place the right hand on the shoulder of the candidate; and a godparent or a sponsor of the candidate gives the candidate's name to the minister of the sacrament. During the conferral of the sacrament an appropriate song may be sung.

The minister of the sacrament dips his right thumb in the chrism and makes the sign of the cross on the forehead of the one to be confirmed as he says:

N., be sealed with the Gift of the Holy Spirit.
Newly confirmed: **Amen.**
Minister: Peace be with you.
Newly confirmed: **And also with you.**

After all have received the sacrament, the newly confirmed as well as the godparents and sponsors are led to their places in the assembly.

[Since the profession of faith is not said, the general intercessions (no. 15, p. 19) begin immediately and for the first time the neophytes take part in them.]

PART FOUR

LITURGY OF THE EUCHARIST

The priest goes to the altar and begins the liturgy of the eucharist in the usual way.

It is fitting that the bread and wine be brought forward by the newly baptized.

PRAYER OVER THE GIFTS   [God's Saving Work]

Lord,
accept the prayers and offerings of your people.
With your help
may this Easter mystery of our redemption
bring to perfection the saving work you have begun in
   us.
We ask this through Christ our Lord. R̸. **Amen.** ↓

Preface of Easter I (P 21: on this Easter day), p. 81.

When Eucharistic Prayer I is used, the special Easter forms of In union with the whole Church, *and* Father, accept this offering *are said.*

COMMUNION ANT. 1 Cor 5:7-8   [Sincerity and Truth]
Christ has become our paschal sacrifice; let us feast with the unleavened bread of sincerity and truth, alleluia. ↓

PRAYER AFTER COMMUNION   [Peace and Love]
Lord,
you have nourished us with your Easter sacraments.
Fill us with your Spirit,
and make us one in peace and love.
We ask this through Christ our Lord. ℟. **Amen.**

The deacon (or the priest) sings or says the dismissal as follows:

Go in the peace of Christ, alleluia, alleluia.

OR

The Mass is ended, go in peace, alleluia, alleluia.

OR

Go in peace to love and serve the Lord, alleluia, alleluia.

℟. **Thanks be to God, alleluia, alleluia.**

"I have risen: I am with you once more."

APRIL 20

EASTER SUNDAY

ENTRANCE ANT. Ps 139:18, 5-6   [Christ's Resurrection]

I have risen: I am with you once more; you placed your hand on me to keep me safe. How great is the depth of your wisdom, alleluia!

OR Lk 24:34; see Rv 1:6   [King and Lord]

The Lord has indeed risen, alleluia. Glory and kingship be his for ever and ever.   → No. 2, p. 10

OPENING PRAYER   [Renewal]

Let us pray
  [that the risen Christ will raise us up
    and renew our lives]
God our Father,
by raising Christ your Son
you conquered the power of death
and opened for us the way to eternal life.
Let our celebration today
raise us up and renew our lives
by the Spirit that is within us.
Grant this . . . for ever and ever. ℟. **Amen.** ↓

ALTERNATIVE OPENING PRAYER   [God's Life]

Let us pray
  [on this Easter morning for the life
  that never again shall see darkness]
God our Father, creator of all,
today is the day of Easter joy.
This is the morning on which the Lord appeared to
  men
who had begun to lose hope
and opened their eyes to what the scriptures foretold:
that first he must die, and then he would rise
and ascend into his Father's glorious presence.
May the risen Lord
breathe on our minds and open our eyes
that we may know him in the breaking of bread,
and follow him in his risen life.
Grant this through Christ our Lord. ℟. **Amen.** ↓

FIRST READING Acts 10:34a, 37-43   [Salvation in Christ]

**In his sermon Peter sums up the "good news," the Gospel.
Salvation comes through Christ, the beloved Son of the
Father, the anointed of the Holy Spirit.**

A reading from the Acts of the Apostles

PETER proceeded to speak and said: "You know
what has happened all over Judea, beginning in
Galilee after the baptism that John preached, how
God anointed Jesus of Nazareth with the Holy Spirit
and power. He went about doing good and healing all
those oppressed by the devil, for God was with him.
We are witnesses of all that he did both in the country
of the Jews and in Jerusalem. They put him to death
by hanging him on a tree. This man God raised on the
third day and granted that he be visible, not to all the
people, but to us, the witnesses chosen by God in advance, who ate and drank with him after he rose from
the dead. He commissioned us to preach to the people

and testify that he is the one appointed by God as judge of the living and the dead. To him all the prophets bear witness, that everyone who believes in him will receive forgiveness of sins through his name.—The word of the Lord. ℟. **Thanks be to God.** ↓

RESPONSORIAL PSALM Ps 118   [The Day of the Lord]

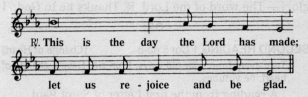

℟. This is the day the Lord has made;
let us re-joice and be glad.

℟. Or: **Alleluia.**

Give thanks to the LORD, for he is good,
  for his mercy endures forever.
Let the house of Israel say,
  "His mercy endures forever."—℟.

The right hand of the LORD has struck with power;
  the right hand of the LORD is exalted.
I shall not die, but live,
  and declare the works of the LORD.—℟.

The stone which the builders rejected
  has become the cornerstone.
By the LORD has this been done;
  it is wonderful in our eyes.—℟. ↓

One of the following texts may be chosen as the Second Reading.

SECOND READING Col 3:1-4   [Seek Heavenly Things]

Look to the glory of Christ in which we share because our lives are hidden in him (through baptism) and we are destined to share in the glory.

A reading from the Letter of Saint Paul to the Colossians

BROTHERS and sisters: If then you were raised with Christ, seek what is above, where Christ is seated at the right hand of God. Think of what is above, not of what is on earth. For you have died, and your life is hidden with Christ in God. When Christ your life appears, then you too will appear with him in glory.—The word of the Lord. ℞. **Thanks be to God.** ↓

OR

SECOND READING 1 Cor 5:6b-8   [Change of Heart]

Turn away from your old ways, from sin. Have a change of heart; be virtuous.

A reading from the first Letter of Saint Paul
to the Corinthians

BROTHERS and sisters: Do you not know that a little yeast leavens all the dough? Clear out the old yeast, so that you may become a fresh batch of dough, inasmuch as you are unleavened. For our paschal lamb, Christ, has been sacrificed. Therefore, let us celebrate the feast, not with the old yeast, the yeast of malice and wickedness, but with the unleavened bread of sincerity and truth.—The word of the Lord. ℞. **Thanks be to God.** ↓

SEQUENCE *(Victimae paschali laudes)*   [Hymn to the Victor]

Christians, to the Paschal Victim
    Offer your thankful praises!
A Lamb the sheep redeems;
    Christ, Who only is sinless,
    Reconciles sinners to the Father.
Death and life have contended in that combat stupendous:
    The Prince of life, who died, reigns immortal.
Speak, Mary, declaring
    What you saw, wayfaring.

"The tomb of Christ, who is living,
    The glory of Jesus' resurrection;
Bright angels attesting,
    The shroud and napkin resting.
Yes, Christ my hope is arisen;
    To Galilee he goes before you."
Christ indeed from death is risen, our new life obtaining.
    Have mercy, victor King, ever reigning!
    Amen. Alleluia. ↓

ALLELUIA Cf. 1 Cor 5:7b-8a   [Joy in the Lord]

℟. **Alleluia, alleluia.**
Christ, our paschal lamb, has been sacrificed;
let us then feast with joy in the Lord.
℟. **Alleluia, alleluia.** ↓

(For Morning Mass)

GOSPEL Jn 20:1-9   [Renewed Faith]
    Let us discover the empty tomb and ponder this mystery,
    and like Christ's first followers be strengthened in our
    faith.

℣. The Lord be with you. ℟. **And also with you.**
✝ A reading from the holy Gospel according to John.
℟. **Glory to you, Lord.**

ON the first day of the week, Mary of Magdala
    came to the tomb early in the morning, while it
was still dark, and saw the stone removed from the
tomb. So she ran and went to Simon Peter and to the
other disciple whom Jesus loved, and told them, "They
have taken the Lord from the tomb, and we don't know
where they put him." So Peter and the other disciple
went out and came to the tomb. They both ran, but the
other disciple ran faster than Peter and arrived at the
tomb first; he bent down and saw the burial cloths

there, but did not go in. When Simon Peter arrived after him, he went into the tomb and saw the burial cloths there, and the cloth that had covered his head, not with the burial cloths but rolled up in a separate place. Then the other disciple also went in, the one who had arrived at the tomb first, and he saw and believed. For they did not yet understand the Scripture that he had to rise from the dead.—The Gospel of the Lord. ℟. **Praise to you, Lord Jesus Christ.** → No. 14, p. 18

OR

GOSPEL Mk 16:1-7   [The Resurrection]
See p. 353.

(For an Afternoon or Evening Mass)

GOSPEL Lk 24:13-35   [The Messiah's Need To Suffer]
Let us accept the testimony of these two witnesses that our hearts may burn with the fire of faith.

℣. The Lord be with you. ℟. **And also with you.**
✝ A reading from the holy Gospel according to Luke.
℟. **Glory to you, Lord.**

THAT very day, the first day of the week, two of Jesus' disciples were going to a village seven miles from Jerusalem called Emmaus, and they were conversing about all the things that had occurred. And it happened that while they were conversing and debating, Jesus himself drew near and walked with them, but their eyes were prevented from recognizing him. He asked them, "What are you discussing as you walk along?" They stopped, looking downcast. One of them, named Cleopas, said to him in reply, "Are you the only visitor to Jerusalem who does not know of the things that have taken place there in these days?" And he replied to them, "What sort of things?" They said to him, "The things that happed to Jesus the Nazarene, who was a prophet mighty in deed and word before God and all the people, how our chief priests and rulers both handed him over to a sentence of death and crucified him. But we were hoping that he would be the one to redeem Israel; and besides all this, it is now the third day since this took place. Some women from our group, however. have astounded us: they were at the tomb early in the morning and did not find his body; they came back and reported that they had indeed seen a vision of angels who announced that he was alive. Then some of those with us went to the tomb and found things just as the women had described, but him they did not see."

And he said to them, "Oh, how foolish you are! How slow of heart to believe all that the prophets spoke! Was is not necessary that the Christ should suffer these things and enter into his glory?" Then beginning with Moses and all the prophets, he interpreted to them what referred to him in all the Scriptures. As they approached the village to which they were going, he gave the impression that he was going on farther. But they urged him, "Stay with us, for it is nearly evening and the day is almost over." So he went in to stay with them.

And it happened that, while he was with them at table, he took bread, said the blessing, broke it, and gave it to them. With that their eyes were opened and they recognized him, but he vanished from their sight. They said to each other, "Were not our hearts burning within us while he spoke to us on the way and opened the Scriptures to us?" So they set out at once and returned to Jerusalem where they found gathered together the eleven and those with them who were saying, "The Lord has truly been raised and has appeared to Simon!" Then the two recounted what had taken place on the way and how he was made known to

them in the breaking of bread.—The Gospel of the
Lord. ℟. **Praise to you, Lord Jesus Christ.**

➜ No. 14, p. 18

Renewal of Baptismal Promises, p. 360 (omit Creed).

PRAYER OVER THE GIFTS   [Renewing Sacrifice]

Lord,
with Easter joy we offer you the sacrifice
by which your Church is reborn and nourished
through Christ our Lord. ℟. **Amen.**

➜ No. 21, p. 22 (Pref. P 21: on this Easter Day)

*When Eucharistic Prayer I is used, the special Easter forms
of* In union with the whole Church *and* Father, accept
this offering *are said.*

COMMUNION ANT. 1 Cor 5:7-8   [Sincerity and Truth]

**Christ has become our paschal sacrifice; let us feast
with the unleavened bread of sincerity and truth, alleluia.** ↓

PRAYER AFTER COMMUNION   [Glory of Resurrection]

Father of love,
watch over your Church
and bring us to the glory of the resurrection
promised by this Easter sacrament.
We ask this in the name of Jesus the Lord.
℟. **Amen.**

➜ No. 32, p. 70

Optional Solemn Blessings, p. 92, and Prayers Over the People, p. 99

"Thomas answered . . . , 'My Lord and my God!' "

APRIL 27

2nd SUNDAY OF EASTER

ENTRANCE ANT. 1 Pt 2:2   **[Thirst for Spiritual Milk]**
Like newborn children you should thirst for milk, on which your spirit can grow to strength, alleluia.

OR 4 Ezr 2:36-37   **[Give Thanks]**
Rejoice to the full in the glory that is yours, and give thanks to God who called you to his kingdom, alleluia. ➔ No. 2, p. 10

OPENING PRAYER   **[Renewed Gift of Life]**
Let us pray
   [for a deeper awareness of our Christian baptism]
God of mercy,
you wash away our sins in water,
you give us new birth in the Spirit,
and redeem us in the blood of Christ.
As we celebrate Christ's resurrection
increase our awareness of these blessings,
and renew your gift of life within us.

375

We ask this through our Lord Jesus Christ, your Son,
who lives and reigns with you and the Holy Spirit,
one God, for ever and ever. ℟. **Amen.** ↓

ALTERNATIVE OPENING PRAYER

[Growth as God's People]

Let us pray
　[as Christians thirsting for the risen life]
Heavenly Father and God of mercy,
we no longer look for Jesus among the dead,
for he is alive and has become the Lord of life.
From the waters of death you raise us with him
and renew your gift of life within us.
Increase in our minds and hearts
the risen life we share with Christ
and help us to grow as your people
toward the fullness of eternal life with you.
We ask this through Christ our Lord. ℟. **Amen.** ↓

FIRST READING Acts 4:32-35　　[True Christian Fellowship]

**The faithful lived a common life, sharing all their goods.
The apostles worked many miracles. They prayed together
and broke bread. Daily their numbers increased.**

A reading from the Acts of the Apostles

THE community of believers was of one heart and
mind, and no one claimed that any of his possessions was his own, but they had everything in common. With great power the apostles bore witness to
the resurrection of the Lord Jesus, and great favor
was accorded them all. There was no needy person
among them, for those who owned property or houses
would sell them, bring the proceeds of the sale, and
put them at the feet of the apostles, and they were distributed to each according to need.—The word of the
Lord. ℟. **Thanks be to God.** ↓

RESPONSORIAL PSALM Ps 118   [The Lord's Goodness]

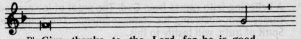

R̹. Give thanks to the Lord for he is good,

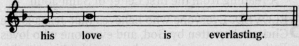

his love is everlasting.

R̹. Or: **Alleluia.**

Let the house of Israel say,
  "His mercy endures forever."
Let the house of Aaron say,
  "His mercy endures forever."
Let those who fear the LORD say,
  "His mercy endures forever."

R̹. **Give thanks to the Lord for he is good,**
  his love is everlasting.

R̹. Or: **Alleluia.**

I was hard pressed and was falling,
  but the LORD helped me.
My strength and my courage is the LORD,
  and he has been my savior.
The joyful shout of victory
  in the tents of the just:

R̹. **Give thanks to the Lord for he is good,**
  his love is everlasting.

R̹. Or: **Alleluia.**

The stone which the builders rejected
  has become the cornerstone.
By the LORD has this been done;
  it is wonderful in our eyes.
This is the day the LORD has made;
  let us be glad and rejoice in it.

R̹. **Give thanks to the Lord for he is good,**
  his love is everlasting. ↓

R̹. Or: **Alleluia.** ↓

SECOND READING 1 Jn 5:1-6 [The Power of Faith]

A believing faith comes from God. The proof of loving God comes from observing his commandments. The Spirit, the Spirit of truth, will testify to this.

A reading from the first Letter of Saint John

BELOVED: Everyone who believes that Jesus is the Christ is begotten by God, and everyone who loves the Father loves also the one begotten by him. In this way we know that we love the children of God when we love God and obey his commandments. For the love of God is this, that we keep his commandments. And his commandments are not burdensome, for whoever is begotten by God conquers the world. And the victory that conquers the world is our faith. Who indeed is the victor over the world but the one who believes that Jesus is the Son of God?

This is the one who came through water and blood, Jesus Christ, not by water alone, but by water and blood. The Spirit is the one that testifies, and the Spirit is truth.—The word of the Lord. ℟. **Thanks be to God.** ↓

ALLELUIA Jn 20:29 [Blind Faith]

℟. **Alleluia, alleluia.**
You believe in me, Thomas, because you have seen me, says the Lord;
blessed are those who have not seen me, but still believe!
℟. **Alleluia, alleluia.** ↓

GOSPEL Jn 20:19-31 [Living Faith]

Jesus appears to the disciples, coming through locked doors. He shows them his hands and side. He greets them in peace and gives them the power to forgive sin. A week later Jesus appears again and speaks directly to Thomas who now professes his belief.

℣. The Lord be with you. ℟. **And also with you.**
✠ A reading from the holy Gospel according to John.
℟. **Glory to you, Lord.**

ON the evening of that first day of the week, when the doors were locked, where the disciples were, for fear of the Jews, Jesus came and stood in their midst and said to them, "Peace be with you." When he had said this, he showed them his hands and his side. The disciples rejoiced when they saw the Lord. Jesus said to them again, "Peace be with you. As the Father has sent me, so I send you." And when he had said this, he breathed on them and said to them, "Receive the Holy Spirit. Whose sins you forgive are forgiven them, and whose sins you retain are retained."

Thomas, called Didymus, one of the Twelve, was not with them when Jesus came. So the other disciples said to him, "We have seen the Lord." But he said to them, "Unless I see the mark of the nails in his hands and put my finger into the nailmarks and put my hand into his side, I will not believe."

Now a week later his disciples were again inside and Thomas was with them. Jesus came, although the doors were locked, and stood in their midst and said, "Peace be with you." Then he said to Thomas, "Put your finger here and see my hands, and bring your hand and put it into my side, and do not be unbelieving, but believe." Thomas answered and said to him, "My Lord and my God!" Jesus said to him, "Have you come to believe because you have seen me? Blessed are those who have not seen and have believed."

Now Jesus did many other signs in the presence of his disciples that are not written in this book. But these are written that you may come to believe that Jesus is the Christ, the Son of God, and that through

this belief you may have life in his name.—The Gospel
of the Lord. ℟. **Praise to you, Lord Jesus Christ.**

→ No. 14, p. 18

PRAYER OVER THE GIFTS   [Offerings Leading to Bliss]

Lord,
through faith and baptism
we have become a new creation.
Accept the offerings of your people
(and of those born again in baptism)
and bring us to eternal happiness.
Grant this through Christ our Lord.
℟. **Amen.**   → No. 21, p. 22 (Pref. P 21)

*When Eucharistic Prayer I is used, the special Easter forms
of* In union with the whole Church *and* Father, accept
this offering *are said.*

COMMUNION ANT. See Jn 20:27   [Believe]

**Jesus spoke to Thomas: Put your hand here, and see
the place of the nails. Doubt no longer, but believe, alleluia.** ↓

PRAYER AFTER COMMUNION   [Devout Reception]

Almighty God,
may the Easter sacraments we have received
live for ever in our minds and hearts.
We ask this through Christ our Lord.
℟. **Amen.**   → No. 32, p. 70

Optional Solemn Blessings, p. 92, and Prayers Over the People, p. 99

"It is written that the Christ would suffer and rise from the dead. . . ."

MAY 4

3rd SUNDAY OF EASTER

ENTRANCE ANT. Ps 33:5-6   **[Praise the Lord]**

Let all the earth cry out to God with joy; praise the glory of his name; proclaim his glorious praise, alleluia.   → No. 2, p. 10

OPENING PRAYER   **[Hope of Resurrection]**

Let us pray
  [that Christ will give us
  a share in the glory of his unending life]
God our Father,
may we look forward with hope to our resurrection,
for you have made us your sons and daughters,
and restored the joy of our youth.
We ask this through our Lord Jesus Christ, your Son,
who lives and reigns with you and the Holy Spirit,
one God, for ever and ever. ℟. **Amen.** ↓

ALTERNATIVE OPENING PRAYER   **[Eternal Light]**

Let us pray
  [in confident peace and Easter hope]

381

Father in heaven, author of all truth,
a people once in darkness has listened to your Word
and followed your Son as he rose from the tomb.
Hear the prayer of this newborn people
and strengthen your Church to answer your call.
May we rise and come forth into the light of day
to stand in your presence until eternity dawns.
We ask this through Christ our Lord. ℟. **Amen.** ↓

FIRST READING Acts 3:13-15, 17-19　　[Culpable Ignorance]

**Peter teaches how God glorified his Son, but the people
were guilty of crucifying Jesus. They acted out of ignorance, however. Now they are to reform and ask God for
forgiveness.**

A reading from the Acts of the Apostles

PETER said to the people: "The God of Abraham,
the God of Isaac, and the God of Jacob, the God of
our fathers, has glorified his servant Jesus, whom you
handed over and denied in Pilate's presence when he
had decided to release him. You denied the Holy and
Righteous One and asked that a murderer be released
to you. The author of life you put to death, but God
raised him from the dead; of this we are witnesses.
Now I know, brothers, that you acted out of ignorance, just as your leaders did; but God has thus
brought to fulfillment what he had announced beforehand through the mouth of all the prophets, that his
Christ would suffer. Repent, therefore, and be con-
verted, that your sins may be wiped away."—The
word of the Lord. ℟. **Thanks be to God.** ↓

RESPONSORIAL PSALM Ps 4　　[Divine Security]

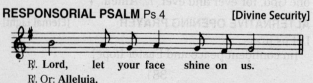

℟. Lord,　let your face　shine on　us.
℟. Or: **Alleluia.**

When I call, answer me, O my just God,
  you who relieve me when I am in distress;
  have pity on me, and hear my prayer!

℟. **Lord, let your face shine on us.**

℟. Or: **Alleluia.**

Know that the LORD does wonders for his faithful one;
  the LORD will hear me when I call upon him.

℟. **Lord, let your face shine on us.**

℟. Or: **Alleluia.**

O LORD, let the light of your countenance shine upon us!
  You put gladness into my heart.

℟. **Lord, let your face shine on us.**

℟. Or: **Alleluia.**

As soon as I lie down, I fall peacefully asleep,
  for you alone, O LORD,
  bring security to my dwelling.

℟. **Lord, let your face shine on us.** ↓

℟. Or: **Alleluia.** ↓

SECOND READING 1 Jn 2:1-5a   [Fruitful Knowledge]

If anyone should sin, Jesus is an offering for sin—for the sins of the whole world. Anyone who claims to know Jesus but disobeys the commandments is a liar.

A reading from the first Letter of Saint John

MY children, I am writing this to you so that you may not commit sin. But if anyone does sin, we have an Advocate with the Father, Jesus Christ the righteous one. He is expiation for our sins, and not for our sins only but for those of the whole world. The way we may be sure that we know him is to keep his commandments. Those who say, "I know him," but do not keep his commandments are liars, and the truth is not in them. But whoever keeps his word, the love of God is truly perfected in him.—The word of the Lord.
℟. **Thanks be to God.** ↓

ALLELUIA Cf. Lk 24:32   [With Hearts Burning]

℟. **Alleluia, alleluia.**
Lord Jesus, open the Scriptures to us;
make our hearts burn while you speak to us.
℟. **Alleluia, alleluia.** ↓

GOSPEL Lk 24:35-48   [Understanding the Scriptures]

Again Jesus appears in the midst of the disciples. He proves he is not a ghost. He eats with them and reassures them that all that happened was to fulfill the words of the Scriptures.

℣. The Lord be with you. ℟. **And also with you.**
✚ A reading from the holy Gospel according to Luke.
℟. **Glory to you, Lord.**

THE two disciples recounted what had taken place
on the way, and how Jesus was made known to
them in the breaking of bread.

While they were still speaking about this, he stood
in their midst and said to them, "Peace be with you."
But they were startled and terrified and thought that
they were seeing a ghost. Then he said to them, "Why
are you troubled? And why do questions arise in your
hearts? Look at my hands and my feet, that it is I myself. Touch me and see, because a ghost does not have
flesh and bones as you can see I have." And as he said
this, he showed them his hands and his feet. While
they were still incredulous for joy and were amazed,
he asked them, "Have you anything here to eat?" They
gave him a piece of baked fish; he took it and ate it in
front of them.

He said to them, "These are my words that I spoke
to you while I was still with you, that everything written about me in the law of Moses and in the prophets
and psalms must be fulfilled." Then he opened their
minds to understand the Scriptures. And he said to
them, "Thus it is written that the Christ would suffer

and rise from the dead on the third day and that repentance, for the forgiveness of sins, would be
preached in his name to all the nations, beginning
from Jerusalem. You are witnesses of these things."—
The Gospel of the Lord. ℟. **Praise to you, Lord Jesus
Christ.**   ➙ No. 14, p. 18

PRAYER OVER THE GIFTS   [Perfect Joy]

Lord,
receive these gifts from your Church.
May the great joy you give us
come to perfection in heaven.
Grant this through Christ our Lord.
℟. **Amen.**   ➙ No. 21, p. 22 (Pref. P 21-25)

COMMUNION ANT. Lk 24:46-47   [Penance]

**Christ had to suffer and to rise from the dead on the
third day. In his name penance for the remission of
sins is to be preached to all nations, alleluia.** ↓

PRAYER AFTER COMMUNION   [The Lord's Kindness]

Lord,
look on your people with kindness
and by these Easter mysteries
bring us to the glory of the resurrection.
We ask this in the name of Jesus the Lord.
℟. **Amen.**   ➙ No. 32, p. 70

Optional Solemn Blessings, p. 92, and Prayers Over the People, p. 99

"I am the good shepherd."

MAY 11

4th SUNDAY OF EASTER

ENTRANCE ANT. Ps 33:5-6   [God the Creator]

The earth is full of the goodness of the Lord; by the word of the Lord the heavens were made, alleluia.

→ No. 2, p. 10

OPENING PRAYER   [Strengthened in Christ]

Let us pray
  [that Christ our shepherd
  will lead us through the difficulties of this life]
Almighty and ever-living God,
give us new strength
from the courage of Christ our shepherd,
and lead us to join the saints in heaven,
where he lives and reigns with you and the Holy
  Spirit,
one God for ever and ever. ℟. **Amen.** ↓

ALTERNATIVE OPENING PRAYER   [God Our Helper]

Let us pray
  [to God our helper in time of distress]
God and Father of our Lord Jesus Christ,
though your people walk in the valley of darkness,

no evil should they fear;
for they follow in faith the call of the shepherd
whom you have sent for their hope and strength.
Attune our minds to the sound of his voice,
lead our steps in the path he has shown,
that we may know the strength of his outstretched arm
and enjoy the light of your presence for ever.
We ask this through Christ our Lord. ℟. **Amen.** ↓

FIRST READING Acts 4:8-12   [Salvation in Jesus]

Peter explains the cure of the cripple. It was a miracle performed in the name of Jesus, whom the people had rejected and crucified. There is no salvation except in Jesus.

A reading from the Acts of the Apostles

PETER, filled with the Holy Spirit, said: "Leaders of
the people and elders: If we are being examined
today about a good deed done to a cripple, namely, by
what means he was saved, then all of you and all the
people of Israel should know that it was in the name
of Jesus Christ the Nazarene whom you crucified,
whom God raised from the dead; in his name this man
stands before you healed. He is *the stone rejected by
you, the builders, which has become the cornerstone.*
There is no salvation through anyone else, nor is there
any other name under heaven given to the human
race by which we are to be saved."—The word of the
Lord. ℟. **Thanks be to God.** ↓

RESPONSORIAL PSALM Ps 118   [Refuge in God]

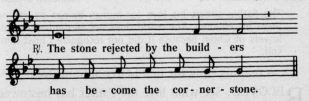

℟. The stone rejected by the build - ers
has be - come the cor - ner - stone.

℟. Or: **Alleluia.**

Give thanks to the LORD, for he is good,
    for his mercy endures forever.
It is better to take refuge in the LORD
    than to trust in man.
It is better to take refuge in the LORD
    than to trust in princes.

℟. **The stone rejected by the builders has become the
    cornerstone.**

℟. Or: **Alleluia.**

I will give thanks to you, for you have answered me
    and have been my savior.
The stone which the builders rejected
    has become the cornerstone.
By the LORD has this been done;
    it is wonderful in our eyes.

℟. **The stone rejected by the builders has become the
    cornerstone.**

℟. Or: **Alleluia.**

Blessed is he who comes in the name of the LORD;
    we bless you from the house of the LORD.
I will give thanks to you, for you have answered me
    and have been my savior.
Give thanks to the LORD, for he is good;
    for his kindness endures forever.

℟. **The stone rejected by the builders has become the
    cornerstone.** ↓

℟. Or: **Alleluia.** ↓

SECOND READING 1 Jn 3:1-2 [Children of God]

The Father shows his love for human beings by calling
them his children. The world does not recognize the followers of Christ because it did not recognize Christ himself.

A reading from the first Letter of Saint John

BELOVED: See what love the Father has bestowed
on us that we may be called the children of God.

Yet so we are. The reason the world does not know us is that it did not know him. Beloved, we are God's children now; what we shall be has not yet been revealed. We do know that when it is revealed we shall be like him, for we shall see him as he is.—The word of the Lord. ℟. **Thanks be to God.** ↓

ALLELUIA Jn 10:14   [God's Sheep]

℟. **Alleluia, alleluia.**
I am the good shepherd, says the Lord;
I know my sheep, and mine know me.
℟. **Alleluia, alleluia.** ↓

GOSPEL Jn 10:11-18   [The Good Shepherd]

   Jesus compares himself to "the good Shepherd." A shepherd cares for his sheep, lives and dies for them if necessary. There is to be one flock and one shepherd.

℣. The Lord be with you. ℟. **And also with you.**
✛ A reading from the holy Gospel according to John.
℟. **Glory to you, Lord.**

JESUS said: "I am the good shepherd. A good shepherd lays down his life for the sheep. A hired man, who is not a shepherd and whose sheep are not his own, sees a wolf coming and leaves the sheep and runs away, and the wolf catches and scatters them. This is because he works for pay and has no concern for the sheep. I am the good shepherd, and I know mine and mine know me, just as the Father knows me and I know the Father; and I will lay down my life for the sheep. I have other sheep that do not belong to this fold. These also I must lead, and they will hear my voice, and there will be one flock, one shepherd. This is why the Father loves me, because I lay down my life in order to take it up again. No one takes it from me, but I lay it down on my own. I have power to lay it down, and power to take it up again. This command I

have received from my Father."—The Gospel of the
Lord. ℟. **Praise to you, Lord Jesus Christ.**

→ No. 14, p. 18

PRAYER OVER THE GIFTS   [Eternal Joy]

Lord,
restore us by these Easter mysteries.
May the continuing work of our redeemer
bring us eternal joy.
We ask this through Christ our Lord.
℟. **Amen.**

→ No. 21, p. 22 (Pref. P 21-25)

COMMUNION ANT.   [The Risen Shepherd]

**The Good Shepherd is risen! He who laid down his
life for his sheep, who died for his flock, he is risen,
alleluia.** ↓

PRAYER AFTER COMMUNION   [Eternal Shepherd]

Father, eternal shepherd,
watch over the flock redeemed by the blood of Christ
and lead us to the promised land.
Grant this through Christ our Lord.
℟. **Amen.**

→ No. 32, p. 70

Optional Solemn Blessings, p. 92, and Prayers Over the People, p. 99

"I am the true vine, and my Father is the vine grower."

MAY 18

5th SUNDAY OF EASTER

ENTRANCE ANT. Ps 98:1, 2   [Marvelous Deeds]

Sing to the Lord a new song, for he has done marvelous deeds; he has revealed to the nations his saving power, alleluia.   → No. 2, p. 10

OPENING PRAYER   [True Freedom]

Let us pray
   [that we may enjoy true freedom]
God our Father,
look upon us with love.
You redeem us and make us your children in Christ.
Give us true freedom
and bring us to the inheritance you promised.
We ask this through our Lord Jesus Christ, your Son,
who lives and reigns with you and the Holy Spirit,
one God, for ever and ever. ℟. **Amen.** ↓

ALTERNATIVE OPENING PRAYER   [God's Praise]

Let us pray
   [in the freedom of the sons of God]

Father of our Lord Jesus Christ,
you have revealed to the nations your saving power
and filled all ages with the words of a new song.
Hear the echo of this hymn.
Give us voice to sing your praise
throughout this season of joy.
We ask this through Christ our Lord. ℟. **Amen.** ↓

FIRST READING Acts 9:26-31   [Paul's Conversion]

**Because of Paul's earlier reputation, the Christians were
fearful of him. He was then accepted and began to spread
the message of the gospel.**

A reading from the Acts of the Apostles

WHEN Saul arrived in Jerusalem he tried to join
the disciples, but they were all afraid of him, not
believing that he was a disciple. Then Barnabas took
charge of him and brought him to the apostles, and he
reported to them how he had seen the Lord, and that
he had spoken to him, and how in Damascus he had
spoken out boldly in the name of Jesus. He moved
about freely with them in Jerusalem, and spoke out
boldly in the name of the Lord. He also spoke and de-
bated with the Hellenists, but they tried to kill him.
And when the brothers learned of this, they took him
down to Caesarea and sent him on his way to Tarsus.

The church throughout all Judea, Galilee, and
Samaria was at peace. It was being built up and
walked in the fear of the Lord, and with the consolation of the Holy Spirit it grew in numbers.—The word
of the Lord. ℟. **Thanks be to God.** ↓

RESPONSORIAL PSALM Ps 22   [Praise God]

℟. **I will praise you, Lord, in the assembly of your people.**

℟. Or: **Alleluia.**

I will fulfill my vows before those who fear the LORD.
  The lowly shall eat their fill;
they who seek the LORD shall praise him:
  "May your hearts live forever!"

℟. **I will praise you, Lord, in the assembly of your people.**

℟. Or: **Alleluia.**

All the ends of the earth
  shall remember and turn to the LORD;
all the families of the nations
  shall bow down before him.

℟. **I will praise you, Lord, in the assembly of your people.**

℟. Or: **Alleluia.**

To him alone shall bow down
  all who sleep in the earth;
before him shall bend
  all who go down into the dust.

℟. **I will praise you, Lord, in the assembly of your people.**

℟. Or: **Alleluia.**

And to him my soul shall live;
  my descendants shall serve him.
Let the coming generation be told of the LORD
  that they may proclaim to a people yet to be born
  the justice he has shown.

℟. **I will praise you, Lord, in the assembly of your people.** ↓

℟. Or: **Alleluia.** ↓

SECOND READING 1 Jn 3:18-24   [Love in Action]

**Christians are to love in deed and in truth. A clear con-
science is proof of God's favor. To keep the commandments is to please God.**

A reading from the first letter of Saint John

CHILDREN, let us love not in word or speech but in deed and truth.

Now this is how we shall know that we belong to the truth and reassure our hearts before him in whatever our hearts condemn, for God is greater than our hearts and knows everything. Beloved, if our hearts do not condemn us, we have confidence in God and receive from him whatever we ask, because we keep his commandments and do what pleases him. And his commandment is this: we should believe in the name of his Son, Jesus Christ, and love one another just as he commanded us. Those who keep his commandments remain in him, and he in them, and the way we know that he remains in us is from the Spirit he gave us.—The word of the Lord. ℟. **Thanks be to God.** ↓

ALLELUIA Jn 15:4a, 5b   [Indwelling]

℟. **Alleluia, alleluia.**
Remain in me as I remain in you, says the Lord.
Whoever remains in me will bear much fruit.
℟. **Alleluia, alleluia.** ↓

GOSPEL Jn 15:1-8   [Vine and the Branches]

Jesus compared himself to the vine and the branches. Whoever is united to Jesus will do good and be rewarded. But anyone who does not live in Jesus will wither like a cut-off vine.

℣. The Lord be with you. ℟. **And also with you.**
✝ A reading from the holy Gospel according to John.
℟. **Glory to you, Lord.**

JESUS said to his disciples: "I am the true vine, and my Father is the vine grower. He takes away every branch in me that does not bear fruit, and every one that does he prunes so that it bears more fruit. You are already pruned because of the word that I spoke to you. Remain in me, as I remain in you. Just as a branch cannot bear fruit on its own unless it remains on the vine, so neither can you unless you remain in me. I am the vine, you are the branches. Whoever remains in me and I in him will bear much fruit, because without me you can do nothing. Anyone who does not remain in me will be thrown out like a branch and wither; people will gather them and throw them into a fire and they will be burned. If you remain in me and my words remain in you, ask for whatever you want and it will be done for you. By this is my Father glorified, that you bear much fruit and become my disciples."—The Gospel of the Lord. ℟. **Praise to you, Lord Jesus Christ.**

→ No. 14, p. 18

PRAYER OVER THE GIFTS   [Guided by God's Truth]

Lord God,
by this holy exchange of gifts
you share with us your divine life.
Grant that everything we do
may be directed by the knowledge of your truth.
We ask this in the name of Jesus the Lord.
℟. **Amen.**   → No. 21, p. 22 (Pref. P 21-25)

COMMUNION ANT. Jn 15: 5   [Union with Christ]

I am the vine and you are the branches, says the Lord; he who lives in me, and I in him, will bear much fruit, alleluia. ↓

PRAYER AFTER COMMUNION   [New Life]

Merciful Father,
may these mysteries give us new purpose
and bring us to a new life in you.
Grant this through Christ our Lord.
℟. **Amen.**   → No. 32, p. 70

Optional Solemn Blessings, p. 92, and Prayers Over the People, p. 99

"This I command you: love one another."

MAY 25
6th SUNDAY OF EASTER

ENTRANCE ANT. Is 48:20   **[Spiritual Freedom]**

Speak out with a voice of joy; let it be heard to the ends of the earth: The Lord has set his people free, alleluia.   ➔ No. 2, p. 10

OPENING PRAYER   **[Operative Faith]**

Let us pray
   [that we may practice in our lives
   the faith we profess]
Ever-living God,
help us to celebrate our joy
in the resurrection of the Lord
and to express in our lives
the love we celebrate.
Grant this . . . for ever and ever. ℟. **Amen.** ↓

ALTERNATIVE OPENING PRAYER   **[Resurrection]**

Let us pray
   [in silence, reflecting on the joy of Easter]
God our Father, maker of all,
the crown of your creation was the Son of Man,
born of a woman, but without beginning;
he suffered for us but lives for ever.

396

May our mortal lives be crowned with the ultimate joy
of rising with him,
who is Lord for ever and ever. ℟. **Amen.** ↓

FIRST READING Acts 10:25-26, 34-35, 44-48 [God Loves All]

**Peter visits Cornelius and his family. God will favor anyone
who acts uprightly, Jews, and Gentiles alike. He gave
orders that all who believe should be baptized.**

A reading from the Acts of the Apostles

WHEN Peter entered, Cornelius met him and,
falling at his feet, paid him homage. Peter, however, raised him up, saying, "Get up. I myself am also
a human being."

Then Peter proceeded to speak and said, "In truth, I
see that God shows no partiality. Rather, in every nation whoever fears him and acts uprightly is acceptable to him."

While Peter was still speaking these things, the Holy
Spirit fell upon all who were listening to the word. The
circumcised believers who had accompanied Peter
were astounded that the gift of the Holy Spirit should
have been poured out on the Gentiles also, for they
could hear them speaking in tongues and glorifying
God. Then Peter responded, "Can anyone withhold the
water for baptizing these people, who have received
the Holy Spirit even as we have?" He ordered them to
be baptized in the name of Jesus Christ.—The word of
the Lord. ℟. **Thanks be to God.** ↓

RESPONSORIAL PSALM Ps 98   [Revelation to the Nations]

℟. **The Lord has revealed to the nations his saving power.**

℟. Or: **Alleluia.**

Sing to the LORD a new song,
    for he has done wondrous deeds;

his right hand has won victory for him,
   his holy arm.—℟.

The LORD has made his salvation known:
   in the sight of the nations he has revealed his jus-
     tice.

He has remembered his kindness and his faithfulness
   toward the house of Israel.—℟.

All the ends of the earth have seen
   the salvation by our God.

Sing joyfully to the LORD, all you lands;
   break into song; sing praise.—℟. ↓

SECOND READING 1 Jn 4:7-10   [God Is Love]

**Christians should love one another as God himself is love.
A person without love does not know God. Love is that
God has sent his Son as an offering for sin.**

A reading from the first Letter of Saint John

BELOVED, let us love one another, because love is
of God; everyone who loves is begotten by God
and knows God. Whoever is without love does not
know God, for God is love. In this way the love of God
was revealed to us: God sent his only Son into the
world so that we might have life through him. In this
is love: not that we have loved God, but that he loved
us and sent his Son as expiation for our sins.—The
word of the Lord. ℟. **Thanks be to God.** ↓

ALLELUIA Jn 14:23   [Divine Love]

℟. **Alleluia, alleluia.**
Whoever loves me will keep my word, says the Lord,
and my Father will love him, and we will come to him.
℟. **Alleluia, alleluia.** ↓

GOSPEL Jn 15:9-17   [Love One Another]

**Jesus admonishes his disciples to continue the love he has
shown to them. The keeping of the commandments will
prove this. "You are to love one another. . . . It was I who
chose you."**

℣. The Lord be with you. ℟. **And also with you.**

✠ A reading from the holy Gospel according to John.
℟. **Glory to you, Lord.**

JESUS said to his disciples: "As the Father loves me,
so I also love you. Remain in my love. If you keep
my commandments, you will remain in my love, just
as I have kept my Father's commandments and remain in his love.

"I have told you this so that my joy may be in you
and your joy might be complete. This is my commandment: love one another as I love you. No one has
greater love than this, to lay down one's life for one's
friends. You are my friends if you do what I command
you. I no longer call you slaves, because a slave does
not know what his master is doing. I have called you
friends, because I have told you everything I have
heard from my Father. It was not you who chose me,
but I who chose you and appointed you to go and bear
fruit that will remain, so that whatever you ask the
Father in my name he may give you. This I command
you: love one another."—The Gospel of the Lord. ℟.
Praise to you, Lord Jesus Christ.   → No. 14, p. 18

PRAYER OVER THE GIFTS   [Forgiveness]

Lord,
accept our prayers and offerings.
Make us worthy of your sacraments of love
by granting us your forgiveness.
We ask this in the name of Jesus the Lord.
℟. **Amen.**   → No. 21, p. 22 (Pref. P 21-25)

COMMUNION ANT. Jn 14:15-16   [Role of the Spirit]
**If you love me, keep my commandments, says the
Lord. The Father will send you the Holy Spirit, to be
with you for ever, alleluia.** ↓

PRAYER AFTER COMMUNION   [Eucharistic Strength]

Almighty and ever-living Lord,
you restored us to life
by raising Christ from death.
Strengthen us by this Easter sacrament;
may we feel its saving power in our daily life.
We ask this through Christ our Lord.
℟. **Amen.**   → No. 32, p. 70

Optional Solemn Blessings, p. 92, and Prayers Over the People, p. 99

*"Go into the whole world and proclaim the gospel
to every creature."*

*In those states that have chosen the option, the following
Mass of the Ascension is celebrated in place of the Mass of
the 7th Sunday of Easter that appears on p. 407.*

MAY 29

ASCENSION OF THE LORD

ENTRANCE ANT. Acts 1:11   [The Lord Will Return]
**Men of Galilee, why do you stand looking in the sky?
The Lord will return, just as you have seen him as-
cend, alleluia.**   → No. 2, p. 10

OPENING PRAYER   [Joy in the Ascension]

Let us pray
   [that the risen Christ
   will lead us to eternal life]
God our Father,
make us joyful in the ascension of your Son Jesus
   Christ.
May we follow him into the new creation,
for his ascension is our glory and our hope.
We ask this through our Lord Jesus Christ, your Son,
who lives and reigns with you and the Holy Spirit,
one God, for ever and ever. ℟. **Amen.** ↓

ALTERNATIVE OPENING PRAYER   [Hope in Christ]

Let us pray
   [on this day of Ascension
   as we watch and wait for Jesus' return]
Father in heaven,
our minds were prepared for the coming of your kingdom
when you took Christ beyond our sight
so that we might seek him in his glory.
May we follow where he has led
and find our hope in his glory,
for he is Lord for ever. ℟. **Amen.** ↓

FIRST READING Acts 1:1-11   [Christ's Ascension]

**Luke recounts the life, suffering and death of Jesus and
what Jesus did the forty days after his resurrection. Jesus
promises the Holy Spirit to the apostles. Jesus then as-
cends into heaven while they watch.**

A reading from of the Acts of the Apostles

IN the first book, Theophilus, I dealt with all that
   Jesus did and taught until the day he was taken up,
after giving instructions through the Holy Spirit to the
apostles whom he had chosen. He presented himself
alive to them by many proofs after he had suffered,

appearing to them during forty days and speaking about the kingdom of God. While meeting with them, he enjoined them not to depart from Jerusalem, but to wait for "the promise of the Father about which you have heard me speak; for John baptized with water, but in a few days you will be baptized with the Holy Spirit."

When they had gathered together they asked him, "Lord, are you at this time going to restore the kingdom to Israel?" He answered them, "It is not for you to know the times or seasons that the Father has established by his own authority. But you will receive power when the Holy Spirit comes upon you, and you will be my witnesses in Jerusalem, throughout Judea and Samaria, and to the ends of the earth." When he had said this, as they were looking on, he was lifted up, and a cloud took him from their sight. While they were looking intently at the sky as he was going, suddenly two men dressed in white garments stood beside them. They said, "Men of Galilee, why are you standing there looking at the sky? This Jesus who has been taken up from you into heaven will return in the same way as you have seen him going into heaven."—The word of the Lord. ℟. **Thanks be to God.** ↓

RESPONSORIAL PSALM Ps 47　　　　[Praise to the Lord]

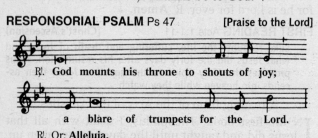

℟. **God mounts his throne to shouts of joy;**

a　blare　of　trumpets　for　the　Lord.

℟. Or: **Alleluia.**

All you peoples, clap your hands,
　　shout to God with cries of gladness.

For the Lord, the Most High, the awesome,
  is the great king over all the earth.

℟. **God mounts his throne to shouts of joy;**
  a blare of trumpets for the Lord.

℟. Or: **Alleluia.**

God mounts his throne amid shouts of joy;
  the Lord, amid trumpet blasts.
Sing praise to God, sing praise;
  sing praise to our king, sing praise.

℟. **God mounts his throne to shouts of joy;**
  a blare of trumpets for the Lord.

℟. Or: **Alleluia.**

For king of all the earth is God;
  sing hymns of praise.
God reigns over the nations,
  God sits upon his holy throne.

℟. **God mounts his throne to shouts of joy;**
  a blare of trumpets for the Lord. ↓

℟. Or: **Alleluia.** ↓

SECOND READING Eph 1:17-23   [Glorification of Jesus]

Paul speaks of Jesus as the Father of glory who is ready to
hear our prayers, to grant wisdom and knowledge.

A reading from the Letter of Saint Paul
to the Ephesians

BROTHERS and sisters: May the God of our Lord
Jesus Christ, the Father of glory, give you a Spirit
of wisdom and revelation resulting in knowledge of
him. May the eyes of your hearts be enlightened, that
you may know what is the hope that belongs to
his call, what are the riches of glory in his inheritance
among the holy ones, and what is the surpassing
greatness of his power for us who believe, in accord
with the exercise of his great might, which he worked
in Christ, raising him from the dead and seating him

at his right hand in the heavens, far above every principality, authority, power, and dominion, and every name that is named not only in this age but also in the one to come. And he put all things beneath his feet and gave him as head over all things to the church, which is his body, the fullness of the one who fills all things in every way.—The word of the Lord. ℟. **Thanks be to God.** ↓

OR

SECOND READING Eph 4:1-13 or 4:1-7, 11-13   **[Gifts]**

Our hope is in God, our strength. With Christ our head, we his people will receive the gift of wisdom and insight.

[If the "Shorter Form" is used, the indented text in brackets is omitted.]

A reading from the Letter of Saint Paul
to the Ephesians

BROTHERS and sisters, I, a prisoner for the Lord, urge you to live in a manner worthy of the call you have received, with all humility and gentleness, with patience, bearing with one another through love, striving to preserve the unity of the spirit through the bond of peace: one body and one Spirit, as you were also called to the one hope of your call; one Lord, one faith, one baptism; one God and Father of all, who is over all and through all and in all.

But grace was given to each of us according to the measure of Christ's gift.

[Therefore, it says: *He ascended on high and took prisoners captive; he gave gifts to men.* What does "he ascended" mean except that he also descended into the lower regions of the earth? The one who descended is also the one who ascended far above all the heavens, that he might fill all things.]

And he gave some as apostles, others as prophets, others as evangelists, others as pastors and teachers, to equip the holy ones for the work of ministry, for building up the body of Christ, until we all attain to the unity of faith and knowledge of the Son of God, to mature manhood, to the extent of the full stature of Christ.—The word of the Lord. ℟. **Thanks be to God.** ↓

ALLELUIA Mt 28:19a, 20b   [Christ's Abiding Presence]

℟. **Alleluia, alleluia.**
Go and teach all nations, says the Lord;
I am with you always, until the end of the world.
℟. **Alleluia, alleluia.** ↓

GOSPEL Mk 16:15-20   [Preaching the Good News]

Jesus makes his disciples apostles to preach the good news. He promises them special signs for protection on earth and then finally Jesus is taken up into heaven.

℣. The Lord be with you. ℟. **And also with you.**
✛ A reading from the holy Gospel according to Mark.
℟. **Glory to you, Lord.**

JESUS said to his disciples: "Go into the whole world and proclaim the gospel to every creature. Whoever believes and is baptized will be saved; whoever does not believe will be condemned. These signs will accompany those who believe: in my name they will drive out demons, they will speak new languages. They will pick up serpents with their hands, and if they drink any deadly thing, it will not harm them. They will lay hands on the sick, and they will recover."

So then the Lord Jesus, after he spoke to them, was taken up into heaven and took his seat at the right hand of God. But they went forth and preached everywhere, while the Lord worked with them and confirmed the word through accompanying signs.—The Gospel of the Lord. ℟. **Praise to you, Lord Jesus Christ.**

↪ No. 14, p. 18

PRAYER OVER THE GIFTS   [Rise to Heavenly Joy]

Lord,
receive our offering
as we celebrate the ascension of Christ your Son.
May his gifts help us rise with him
to the joys of heaven,
where he lives and reigns for ever and ever.
℟. **Amen.**   → No. 21, p. 22 (Pref. P 26-27)

*When Eucharistic Prayer I is used, the special Ascension
form of* In union with the whole Church *is said.*

COMMUNION ANT. Mt 28:20   [Christ's Presence]

**I, the Lord, am with you always, until the end of the
world, alleluia.** ↓

PRAYER AFTER COMMUNION   [Following Christ]

Father,
in this eucharist
we touch the divine life you give to the world.
Help us to follow Christ with love
to eternal life where he is Lord for ever and ever.
℟. **Amen.**   → No. 32, p. 70

Optional Solemn Blessings, p. 92, and Prayers Over the People, p. 99

*"Holy Father, keep them in your name
that you have given me."*

*In those states that have chosen the option, the Mass of the
Ascension that appears on p. 400 is celebrated today in place
of the following Mass of the 7th Sunday of Easter.*

JUNE 1

7th SUNDAY OF EASTER

ENTRANCE ANT. Ps 27:7-9   [Seek the Lord]

**Lord, hear my voice when I call to you. My heart has
prompted me to seek your face; I seek it, Lord; do not
hide from me, alleluia.**   ➜ No. 2, p. 10

OPENING PRAYER   [Recognizing Christ among Us]

Let us pray
  [that we may recognize
  the presence of Christ in our midst]
Father,
help us keep in mind that Christ our Savior
lives with you in glory
and promised to remain with us until the end of time.
We ask this . . . for ever and ever. ℟. **Amen.** ↓

ALTERNATIVE OPENING PRAYER   [Christ's Presence]

Let us pray
> [to our Father
> who has raised us to life in Christ]

Eternal Father,
reaching from end to end of the universe,
and ordering all things with your mighty arm:
for you, time is the unfolding of truth that already is,
the unveiling of beauty that is yet to be.
Your Son has saved us in history
by rising from the dead,
so that transcending time he might free us from death.
May his presence among us
lead to the vision of unlimited truth
and unfold the beauty of your love.
We ask this in the name of Jesus the Lord. ℟. **Amen.** ↓

FIRST READING Acts 1:15-17, 20a, 20c-26 [Choice of Matthias]

Peter discusses the question of Judas and his replacement. Two were nominated and all prayed. Then they drew lots and the choice fell to Matthias.

A reading from the Acts of the Apostles

PETER stood up in the midst of the brothers—there was a group of about one hundred and twenty persons in the one place—. He said, "My brothers, the Scripture had to be fulfilled which the Holy Spirit spoke beforehand through the mouth of David, concerning Judas, who was the guide for those who arrested Jesus. He was numbered among us and was allotted a share in this ministry.

"For it is written in the Book of Psalms:
May another take his office.

"Therefore, it is necessary that one of the men who accompanied us the whole time the Lord Jesus came and went among us, beginning from the baptism of John until the day on which he was taken up from us, become with us a witness to his resurrection." So they proposed two, Judas called Barsabbas, who was also known as Justus, and Matthias. Then they prayed, "You, Lord, who know the hearts of all, show which one of these two you have chosen to take the place in this apostolic ministry from which Judas turned away to go to his own place." Then they gave lots to them, and the lot fell upon Matthias, and he was counted with the eleven apostles.—The word of the Lord. ℟. **Thanks be to God.** ↓

RESPONSORIAL PSALM Ps 103   **[Bless the Lord]**

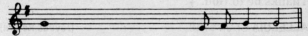

℟. **The   Lord   has   set   his   throne in heav - en.**

℟. Or: **Alleluia.**

Bless the LORD, O my soul;
   and all my being, bless his holy name.
Bless the LORD, O my soul,
   and forget not all his benefits.—℟.

For as the heavens are high above the earth,
   so surpassing is his kindness toward those who fear
      him.
As far as the east is from the west,
   so far has he put our transgressions from us.—℟.

The LORD has established his throne in heaven,
   and his kingdom rules over all.
Bless the LORD, all you his angels,
   you mighty in strength, who do his bidding.—℟. ↓

SECOND READING 1 Jn 4:11-16   **[God Dwells in Us]**
Christians must have love for one another since the God of love dwells in them. When Jesus is acknowledged, God dwells in that person. God is love.

   A reading from the first Letter of Saint John

Beloved, if God so loved us, we also must love one another. No one has ever seen God. Yet, if we love one another, God remains in us, and his love is brought to perfection in us.

This is how we know that we remain in him and he in us, that he has given us of his Spirit. Moreover, we have seen and testify that the Father sent his Son as savior of the world. Whoever acknowledges that Jesus is the Son of God, God remains in him and he in God. We have come to know and to believe in the love God has for us.

God is love, and whoever remains in love remains in God and God in him.—The word of the Lord. ℟. **Thanks be to God.** ↓

ALLELUIA Cf. Jn 14:18   [Joyous Return]
℟. **Alleluia, alleluia.**
I will not leave you orphans says the Lord.
I will come back to you, and your hearts will rejoice.
℟. **Alleluia, alleluia.** ↓

GOSPEL Jn 17:11b-19   [Jesus' Prayer for Us]
> Jesus prays for his followers. They have been looked after and have heard the gospel message from Jesus. He prays that his Father will continue to look after them and guard them from the evil one.

℣. The Lord be with you. ℟. **And also with you.**
✝ A reading from the holy Gospel according to John.
℟. **Glory to you, Lord.**

LIFTING up his eyes to heaven, Jesus prayed, saying: "Holy Father, keep them in your name that you have given me, so that they may be one just as we are one. When I was with them I protected them in your name that you gave me, and I guarded them, and none of them was lost except the son of destruction, in order that the Scripture might be fulfilled. But now I am coming to you. I speak this in the world so that they may share my joy completely. I gave them your

word, and the world hated them, because they do not belong to the world any more than I belong to the world. I do not ask that you take them out of the world but that you keep them from the evil one. They do not belong to the world any more than I belong to the world. Consecrate them in the truth. Your word is truth. As you sent me into the world, so I sent them into the world. And I consecrate myself for them, so that they also may be consecrated in truth."—The Gospel of the Lord. ℟. **Praise to you, Lord Jesus Christ.**
                                        → No. 14, p. 18

PRAYER OVER THE GIFTS   [Gifts of Love]

Lord,
accept the prayers and gifts
we offer in faith and love.
May this eucharist
bring us to your glory.
Grant this through Christ our Lord.
℟. **Amen.**   → No. 21, p. 22 (Pref. P 21-25 or P 26-27)

COMMUNION ANT. Jn 17:22   [Christian Unity]

This is the prayer of Jesus: that his believers may become one as he is one with the Father, alleluia. ↓

PRAYER AFTER COMMUNION   [Glory of Christ's Body]

God our Savior,
hear us,
and through this holy mystery give us hope
that the glory you have given Christ
will be given to the Church, his body,
for he is Lord for ever and ever.
℟. **Amen.**   → No. 32, p. 70

Optional Solemn Blessings, p. 92, and Prayers Over the People, p. 99

"They were all filled with the Holy Spirit."

JUNE 8

PENTECOST SUNDAY

VIGIL MASS

ENTRANCE ANT. See Rom 5:5; 8:11   [Love-Imparting Spirit]

The love of God has been poured into our hearts by his Spirit living in us, alleluia.   ➜ No. 2, p. 10

OPENING PRAYER   [Spirit of Peace]

Let us pray
   [that the Holy Spirit
     may bring peace and unity to all mankind]
Almighty and ever-living God,
you fulfilled the Easter promise
by sending us your Holy Spirit.
May that Spirit unite the races and nations on earth
to proclaim your glory.
Grant this . . . for ever and ever. ℟. **Amen.** ↓

OR   [New Birth in the Spirit]

God our Father,
you have given us new birth.
Strengthen us with your Holy Spirit
and fill us with your light.
Grant this . . . for ever and ever. ℟. **Amen.** ↓

412

ALTERNATIVE OPENING PRAYER   [Eliminate Division]

Let us pray

[that the flame of the Spirit will descend upon us]

Father in heaven,

fifty days have celebrated the fullness

of the mystery of your revealed love.

See your people gathered in prayer,

open to receive the Spirit's flame.

May it come to rest in our hearts

and disperse the divisions of word and tongue.

With one voice and one song

may we praise your name in joy and thanksgiving.

Grant this through Christ our Lord. ℟. **Amen.** ↓

FIRST READING

A Gn 11:1-9   [Dangers of Human Pride]

Those who put their trust in pride, and human ability, are bound to fail.

A reading from the Book of Genesis

THE whole world spoke the same language, using the same words. While the people were migrating in the east, they came upon a valley in the land of Shinar and settled there. They said to one another, "Come, let us mold bricks and harden them with fire." They used bricks for stone, and bitumen for mortar. Then they said, "Come, let us build ourselves a city and a tower with its top in the sky, and so make a name for ourselves; otherwise we shall be scattered all over the earth."

The LORD came down to see the city and the tower that the people had built. Then the LORD said: "If now, while they are one people, all speaking the same language, they have started to do this, nothing will later stop them from doing whatever they presume to do. Let us then go down there and confuse their language, so that one will not understand what another says." Thus the LORD scattered them from there all over the earth, and they stopped building the city. That is why it was called Babel, because there the LORD confused the speech of all the world. It was from that place that he scattered them all over the earth.—The word of the Lord. ℟. **Thanks be to God.** ↓

OR

B Ex 19:3-8a, 16-20b   [The Lord on Mount Sinai]
The Lord God covenants with the Israelites—they are to be a holy nation, a princely Kingdom.

A reading from the Book of Exodus

MOSES went up the mountain to God. Then the LORD called to him and said, "Thus shall you say to the house of Jacob; tell the Israelites: You have seen for yourselves how I treated the Egyptians and how I bore you up on eagle wings and brought you here to myself. Therefore, if you hearken to my voice and keep my covenant, you shall be my special possession, dearer to me than all other people, though all the earth is mine. You shall be to me a kingdom of priests, a holy nation. That is what you must tell the Israelites." So Moses went and summoned the elders of the people. When he set before them all that the LORD had ordered him to tell them, the people all answered together, "Everything the LORD has said, we will do."

On the morning of the third day there were peals of thunder and lightning, and a heavy cloud over the mountain, and a very loud trumpet blast, so that all the people in the camp trembled. But Moses led the people out of the camp to meet God, and they stationed themselves at the foot of the mountain. Mount Sinai was all wrapped in smoke, for the LORD came down upon it in fire. The smoke rose from it as though from a furnace, and the whole mountain trembled violently. The trumpet blast grew louder and louder, while Moses was speaking and God answering him with thunder.

When the LORD came down to the top of Mount Sinai, he summoned Moses to the top of the mountain.—The word of the Lord. ℟. **Thanks be to God.** ↓

OR

C Ez 37:1-14   [Life-Giving Spirit]

The prophet, in a vision, sees the power of God—the band of the living and the dead, as he describes the resurrection of the dead.

A reading from the Book of the Prophet Ezekiel

THE hand of the LORD came upon me, and he led me out in the spirit of the LORD and set me in the center of the plain, which was now filled with bones. He made me walk among the bones in every direction so that I saw how many they were on the surface of the plain. How dry they were! He asked me: Son of man, can these bones come to life? I answered, "LORD God, you alone know that." Then he said to me: Prophesy over these bones, and say to them: Dry bones, hear the word of the LORD! Thus says the Lord GOD to these bones: See! I will bring spirit into you, that you may come to life. I will put sinews upon you, make flesh grow over you, cover you with skin, and put spirit in you so that you may come to life and know that I am the LORD. I, Ezekiel, prophesied as I had been told, and even as I was prophesying I heard a noise; it was a rattling as the bones came together, bone joining bone. I saw the sinews and the flesh come upon them, and the skin cover them, but there was no spirit in them. Then the LORD said to me: Prophesy to the spirit, prophesy, son of man, and say to the spirit: Thus says the Lord GOD: From the four winds come, O spirit, and breathe into these slain that they may come to life. I prophesied as he told me, and the spirit came into them; they came alive and stood upright, a vast army. Then he said to me: Son of man, these bones are the whole house of Israel. They have been saying,

"Our bones are dried up, our hope is lost, and we are cut off." Therefore, prophesy and say to them: Thus says the Lord GOD: O my people, I will open your graves and have you rise from them, and bring you back to the land of Israel. Then you shall know that I am the LORD, when I open your graves and have you rise from them, O my people! I will put my spirit in you that you may live, and I will settle you upon your land; thus you shall know that I am the LORD. I have promised, and I will do it, says the LORD.—The word of the Lord. ℟. **Thanks be to God.** ↓

OR

D Jl 3:1-5   [Signs of the Spirit]

At the end of time, the Day of the Lord, Judgment Day, those who persevere in faith will be saved.

A reading from the Book of the Prophet Joel

THUS says the LORD: I will pour out my spirit upon all mankind. Your sons and daughters shall prophesy, your old men shall dream dreams, your young men shall see visions; even upon the servants and the handmaids, in those days, I will pour out my spirit. And I will work wonders in the heavens and on the earth, blood, fire, and columns of smoke; the sun will be turned to darkness, and the moon to blood, at the coming of the Day of the LORD, the great and terrible day. Then everyone shall be rescued who calls on the name of the LORD; for on Mount Zion there shall be a remnant, as the LORD has said, and in Jerusalem survivors whom the LORD shall call.—The word of the LORD. ℟. **Thanks be to God.** ↓

RESPONSORIAL PSALM Ps 104   [Send Out Your Spirit]

℟. **Lord, send out your Spir - it, and re-new the face of the earth.**

℟. Or: **Alleluia.**

Bless the LORD, O my soul!
 O LORD, my God, you are great indeed!
You are clothed with majesty and glory,
 robed in light as with a cloak.—℟.

How manifold are your works, O LORD!
 In wisdom you have wrought them all—
the earth is full of your creatures;
 bless the LORD, O my soul! Alleluia.—℟.

Creatures all look to you
 to give them food in due time.
When you give it to them, they gather it;
 when you open your hand, they are filled with good
  things.—℟.

If you take away their breath, they perish
 and return to their dust.
When you send forth your spirit, they are created,
 and you renew the face of the earth.—℟. ↓

SECOND READING Rom 8:22-27   [The Spirit Our Helper]
Be patient and have hope. The Spirit intercedes for us.

A reading from the Letter of Saint Paul to the Romans

B ROTHERS and sisters: We know that all creation
 is groaning in labor pains even until now; and not
only that, but we ourselves, who have the firstfruits of
the Spirit, we also groan within ourselves as we wait
for adoption, the redemption of our bodies. For in
hope we were saved. Now hope that sees is not hope.
For who hopes for what one sees? But if we hope for
what we do not see, we wait with endurance.
 In the same way, the Spirit too comes to the aid of
our weakness; for we do not know how to pray as we
ought, but the Spirit himself intercedes with inex-
pressible groanings. And the one who searches hearts
knows what is the intention of the Spirit, because he
intercedes for the holy ones according to God's will.—
The word of the Lord. ℟. **Thanks be to God.** ↓

ALLELUIA   **[Fire of God's Love]**

℟. **Alleluia, alleluia.**
Come, Holy Spirit, fill the hearts of the faithful
and kindle in them the fire of your love.
℟. **Alleluia, alleluia.** ↓

GOSPEL Jn 7:37-39   **[Prediction of the Spirit]**
**The Spirit is the source of life for those who have faith and
believe.**

℣. The Lord be with you. ℟. **And also with you.**
✤ A reading from the holy Gospel according to John.
℟. **Glory to you, Lord**.

O N the last and greatest day of the feast, Jesus stood
up and exclaimed, "Let anyone who thirsts come to
me and drink. As scripture says:
Rivers of living water will flow from within him who
believes in me." He said this in reference to the Spirit
that those who came to believe in him were to receive.
There was, of course, no Spirit yet, because Jesus had
not yet been glorified.—The Gospel of the Lord. ℟.
Praise to you, Lord Jesus Christ.   → No. 14, p. 18

PRAYER OVER THE GIFTS   **[Manifestation of Salvation]**
Lord,
send your Spirit on these gifts
and through them help the Church you love
to show your salvation to all the world.
We ask this in the name of Jesus the Lord.
℟. **Amen.**   → Pref. (P 28), p. 425

*When Eucharistic Prayer I is used, the special Pentecost form
of* In union with the whole Church *is said.*

COMMUNION ANT. Jn 7:37   **[Thirst for the Spirit]**
**On the last day of the festival, Jesus stood up and
cried aloud: If anyone is thirsty, let him come to me
and drink, alleluia.** ↓

PRAYER AFTER COMMUNION   [Eucharistic Love]

Lord,
through this eucharist,
send the Holy Spirit of Pentecost into our hearts
to keep us always in your love.
We ask this through Christ our Lord.
℟. **Amen.**   ➔ No. 32, p. 70

Optional Solemn Blessings, p. 92, and Prayers Over the People, p. 99

MASS DURING THE DAY

ENTRANCE ANT. Wis 1:7   [The Spirit in the World]

**The Spirit of the Lord fills the whole world. It holds
all things together and knows every word spoken by
man, alleluia.**

OR See Rom 5:5; 8:11   [God's Love for Us]

**The love of God has been poured into our hearts by
his Spirit living in us, alleluia.**   ➔ No. 2, p. 10

OPENING PRAYER   [Work of the Spirit]

Let us pray
   [that the Spirit will work through our lives
   to bring Christ to the world]
God our Father,
let the Spirit you sent on your Church
to begin the teaching of the gospel
continue to work in the world
through the hearts of all who believe.
We ask this through our Lord Jesus Christ, your Son,
who lives and reigns with you and the Holy Spirit,
one God, for ever and ever. ℟. **Amen.** ↓

ALTERNATIVE OPENING PRAYER   [Power of the Spirit]

Let us pray
   [in the Spirit who dwells within us]
Father of light, from whom every good gift comes,

send your Spirit into our lives
with the power of a mighty wind,
and by the flame of your wisdom
open the horizons of our minds.
Loosen our tongues to sing your praise
in words beyond the power of speech,
for without your Spirit
man could never raise his voice in words of peace
or announce the truth that Jesus is Lord,
who lives and reigns with you and the Holy Spirit,
one God, for ever and ever. ℟. **Amen.** ↓

FIRST READING Acts 2:1-11   [Coming of the Spirit]

On this day the Holy Spirit in fiery tongues descended
upon the apostles and the Mother of Jesus. Today the law
of grace and purification from sin was announced. Three
thousand were baptized.

A reading from the Acts of the Apostles

WHEN the time for Pentecost was fulfilled, they
were all in one place together. And suddenly there
came from the sky a noise like a strong driving wind,
and it filled the entire house in which they were. Then
there appeared to them tongues as of fire, which parted
and came to rest on each of them. And they were all
filled with the Holy Spirit and began to speak in different tongues, as the Spirit enabled them to proclaim.

Now there were devout Jews from every nation
under heaven staying in Jerusalem. At this sound, they
gathered in a large crowd, but they were confused because each one heard them speaking in his own language. They were astounded, and in amazement
asked, "Are not all these people who are speaking
Galileans? Then how does each of us hear them in his
native language? We are Parthians, Medes, and
Elamites, inhabitants of Mesopotamia, Judea and Cap-
padocia, Pontus and Asia, Phrygia and Pamphylia,

Egypt, and the districts of Libya near Cyrene, as well as travelers from Rome, both Jews and converts to Judaism, Cretans and Arabs, yet we hear them speaking in our own tongues of the mighty acts of God."—The word of the Lord. ℟. **Thanks be to God.** ↓

RESPONSORIAL PSALM Ps 104   [Renewal by the Spirit]

℟. **Lord, send out your Spir - it, and re-new the face of the earth.**

℟. Or: **Alleluia.**

Bless the LORD, O my soul!
  O LORD, my God, you are great indeed!
How manifold are your works, O LORD!
  the earth is full of your creatures.—℟.

If you take away their breath, they perish
  and return to their dust.
When you send forth your spirit, they are created,
  and you renew the face of the earth.—℟.

May the glory of the LORD endure forever,
  may the LORD be glad in his works!
Pleasing to him be my theme;
  I will be glad in the LORD.—℟. ↓

SECOND READING 1 Cor 12:3b-7, 12-13 [Grace of the Spirit]

No one can confess the divinity and sovereignty of Jesus unless inspired by the Holy Spirit. Different gifts and ministries are given but all for the one body with Jesus.

A reading from the first Letter of Saint Paul
to the Corinthians

BROTHERS and sisters: No one can say: "Jesus is Lord," except by the Holy Spirit. There are different kinds of spiritual gifts but the same Spirit; there are different forms of service but the same Lord; there are different workings but the same God who produces all of them in everyone. To each individual the manifestation of the Spirit is given for some benefit.

As a body is one though it has many parts, and all the parts of the body, though many, are one body, so also Christ. For in one Spirit we were all baptized into one body, whether Jews or Greeks, slaves or free persons, and we are all given to drink of one Spirit.—The word of the Lord. ℟. **Thanks be to God.** ↓

OR

SECOND READING Gal 5:16-25   [Fruits of the Spirit]

Paul's concrete advice illustrates the love which he stresses. "Good deeds" are not to be excluded from Christian life. There is no law against such virtuous actions.

A reading from the Letter of Saint Paul
to the Galatians

BROTHERS and sisters, live by the Spirit and you will certainly not gratify the desire of the flesh. For the flesh has desires against the Spirit, and the Spirit against the flesh; these are opposed to each other, so that you may not do what you want. But if you are guided by the Spirit, you are not under the law. Now the works of the flesh are obvious: immorality, impurity, lust, idolatry, sorcery, hatreds, rivalry, jealousy, outbursts of fury, acts of selfishness, dissensions, factions, occasions of envy, drinking bouts, orgies, and the like. I warn you, as I warned you before, that those who do such things will not inherit the kingdom of God. In contrast, the fruit of the Spirit is love, joy, peace, patience, kindness, generosity, faithfulness, gentleness, self-control. Against such there is no law. Now those who belong to Christ Jesus have crucified their flesh with its passions and desires. If we live in the Spirit, let us also follow the Spirit.—The word of the Lord. ℟. **Thanks be to God.** ↓

SEQUENCE (*Veni, Sancte Spiritus*)   [Come, Holy Spirit]

Come, Holy Spirit, come!
And from your celestial home
  Shed a ray of light divine!

Come, Father of the poor!
Come, source of all our store!
  Come, within our bosoms shine!

You, of comforters the best;
You, the soul's most welcome guest;
  Sweet refreshment here below;

In our labor, rest most sweet;
Grateful coolness in the heat;
  Solace in the midst of woe.

O most blessed Light divine,
Shine within these hearts of yours,
  And our inmost being fill!

Where you are not, we have naught,
Nothing good in deed or thought,
  Nothing free from taint of ill.

Heal our wounds, our strength renew;
On our dryness pour your dew;
  Wash the stains of guilt away:

Bend the stubborn heart and will;
Melt the frozen, warm the chill;
  Guide the steps that go astray.

On the faithful, who adore
And confess you, evermore
  In your sevenfold gift descend;

Give them virtue's sure reward;
Give them your salvation, Lord;
  Give them joys that never end. Amen.
  Alleluia. ↓

ALLELUIA   [Fire of God's Love]

℟. Alleluia, alleluia.
Come, Holy Spirit, fill the hearts of your faithful

and kindle in them the fire of your love.
℟. **Alleluia, alleluia.** ↓

GOSPEL Jn 20:19-23   [Christ Imparts the Spirit]

Jesus breathes on the disciples to indicate the conferring of
the Holy Spirit. Here we see the origin of power over sin,
the Sacrament of Penance. This shows the power of the
Holy Spirit in the hearts of human beings.

℣. The Lord be with you. ℟. **And also with you.**
✝ A reading from the holy Gospel according to John.
℟. **Glory to you, Lord.**

O N the evening of that first day of the week, when
the doors were locked, where the disciples were,
for fear of the Jews, Jesus came and stood in their
midst and said to them, "Peace be with you." When he
had said this, he showed them his hands and
his side. The disciples rejoiced when they saw the
Lord. Jesus said to them again, "Peace be with you. As
the Father has sent me, so I send you." And when he
had said this, he breathed on them and said
to them, "Receive the Holy Spirit. Whose sins you forgive are forgiven them, and whose sins you retain are
retained."—The Gospel of the Lord. ℟. **Praise to you,
Lord Jesus Christ.**   → No. 14, p. 18

OR

GOSPEL Jn 15:26-27; 16:12-15   [Spirit of Truth]

Jesus indicates that the Holy Spirit will bear witness to the
good news. He will guide Christians to the truth and teach
about things to come.

℣. The Lord be with you. ℟. **And also with you.**
✝ A reading from the holy Gospel according to John.
℟. **Glory to you, Lord.**

J ESUS said to his disciples: "When the Advocate
comes whom I will send you from the Father, the

Spirit of truth that proceeds from the Father, he will testify to me. And you also testify, because you have been with me from the beginning.

"I have much more to tell you, but you cannot bear it now. But when he comes, the Spirit of truth, he will guide you to all truth. He will not speak on his own, but he will speak what he hears, and will declare to you the things that are coming. He will glorify me, because he will take from what is mine and declare it to you. Everything that the Father has is mine; for this reason I told you that he will take from what is mine and declare it to you."—The Gospel of the Lord. ℟. **Praise to you, Lord Jesus Christ.**   ➜ No. 14, p. 18

PRAYER OVER THE GIFTS   [Spirit of Jesus]

Lord,
may the Spirit you promised
lead us into all truth
and reveal to us the full meaning of this sacrifice.
Grant this through Christ our Lord. ℟. **Amen.** ↓

PREFACE (P 28)   [Coming of the Spirit]

℣. The Lord be with you. ℟. **And also with you.**
℣. Lift up your hearts. ℟. **We lift them up to the Lord.**
℣. Let us give thanks to the Lord our God. ℟. **It is right to give him thanks and praise.**

Father, all-powerful and ever-living God,
we do well always and everywhere to give you thanks.
Today you sent the Holy Spirit
on those marked out to be your children
by sharing the life of your only Son,
and so you brought the paschal mystery to its completion.
Today we celebrate the great beginning of your Church
when the Holy Spirit made known to all peoples the
one true God,

and created from the many languages of man
one voice to profess one faith.
The joy of the resurrection renews the whole world,
while the choirs of heaven sing for ever to your glory:

→ No. 23, p. 23

*When Eucharistic Prayer I is used, the special Pentecost form
of In union with the whole Church is said.*

COMMUNION ANT. Acts 2:4, 11   [Filled with the Spirit]
**They were all filled with the Holy Spirit, and they
spoke of the great things God had done, alleluia.** ↓

PRAYER AFTER COMMUNION   [Vigor of the Spirit]
Father,
may the food we receive in the eucharist
help our eternal redemption.
Keep within us the vigor of your Spirit
and protect the gifts you have given to your Church.
We ask this in the name of Jesus the Lord.
℟. **Amen.**   → No. 32, p. 70

*The Blessing, p. 70, is given as usual. (At the end of the Dis-
missal the people answer: "Thanks be to God, alleluia, alleluia.")*

Optional Solemn Blessings, p. 92, and Prayers Over the People, p. 99

"Blessed be God the Father and his only-begotten Son and the Holy Spirit."

JUNE 15

TRINITY SUNDAY

ENTRANCE ANT. [Blessed Trinity]

Blessed be God the Father and his only-begotten Son and the Holy Spirit: for he has shown that he loves us.

➞ No. 2, p. 10

OPENING PRAYER [Witnessing to the Trinity]

Let us pray
[to the one God, Father, Son and Spirit,
  that our lives may bear witness to our faith]
Father,
you sent your Word to bring us truth
and your Spirit to make us holy.
Through them we come to know the mystery of your
  life.
Help us to worship you, one God in three Persons,
by proclaiming and living our faith in you.
Grant this . . . for ever and ever. ℟. **Amen.** ↓

ALTERNATIVE OPENING PRAYER [Praise to Triune God]

Let us pray
[to our God who is Father, Son, and Holy Spirit]

427

God, we praise you:
Father all-powerful, Christ Lord and Savior, Spirit of
   love.
You reveal yourself in the depths of our being,
drawing us to share in your life and your love.
One God, three Persons,
be near to the people formed in your image,
close to the world your love brings to life.
We ask you this, Father, Son, and Holy Spirit,
one God, true and living, for ever and ever. ℟. **Amen.** ↓

FIRST READING Dt 4:32-34, 39-40   [The One God]

**Moses asks the people to reflect on what has happened
and whether or not God was their sole Creator and protector. For this reason his laws and commandments must be
obeyed.**

A reading from the Book of Deuteronomy

MOSES said to the people: "Ask now of the days of
old, before your time, ever since God created
man upon the earth; ask from one end of the sky to
the other: Did anything so great ever happen before?
Was it ever heard of? Did a people ever hear the voice
of God speaking from the midst of fire, as you did, and
live? Or did any god venture to go and take a nation
for himself from the midst of another nation, by test-
ings, by signs and wonders, by war, with his strong
hand and outstretched arm, and by great terrors, all of
which the LORD, your God, did for you in Egypt before
your very eyes? This is why you must now know, and
fix in your heart, that the LORD is God in the heavens
above and on earth below, and that there is no other.
You must keep his statutes and commandments that I
enjoin on you today, that you and your children after
you may prosper, and that you may have long life on
the land which the LORD, your God, is giving you forever."—The word of the Lord. ℟. **Thanks be to God.** ↓

RESPONSORIAL PSALM Ps 33   [God's People Hopes in Him]

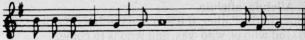

℟. **Bless-ed the peo-ple the Lord has chosen to be his own.**

Upright is the word of the LORD,
   and all his works are trustworthy.
He loves justice and right;
   of the kindness of the LORD the earth is full.—℟.

By the word of the LORD the heavens were made;
   by the breath of his mouth all their host.
For he spoke, and it was made;
   he commanded, and it stood forth.—℟.

See, the eyes of the LORD are upon those who fear him,
   upon those who hope for his kindness,
to deliver them from death
   and preserve them in spite of famine.—℟.

Our soul waits for the LORD,
   who is our help and our shield.
May your kindness, O LORD, be upon us
   who have put our hope in you.—℟. ↓

SECOND READING Rom 8:14-17   [Children of God]

   The Spirit of God makes Christians adopted children of
   God. They become at the same time heirs of God with
   Christ—to suffer with him and also be glorified.

A reading from the Letter of Saint Paul to the Romans

BROTHERS and sisters: Those who are led by the
Spirit of God are sons of God. For you did not receive
a spirit of slavery to fall back into fear, but you received
a Spirit of adoption, through whom we cry, "Abba,
Father!" The Spirit himself bears witness with our spirit
that we are children of God, and if children, then heirs,
heirs of God and joint heirs with Christ, if only we suffer
with him so that we may also be glorified with him.—
The word of the Lord. ℟. **Thanks be to God.** ↓

ALLELUIA Rv 1:8   [Triune God]

℟. **Alleluia, alleluia.**
Glory to the Father, the Son and the Holy Spirit:
to God who is, who was, and who is to come.
℟. **Alleluia, alleluia.** ↓

GOSPEL Mt 28:16-20   [Disciples of the Trinity]

At Jesus' request the eleven assembled and fell down in
homage. Jesus gives them the all pervading command to
preach and baptize all human beings. He also promises to
be with them to the end of time.

℣. The Lord be with you. ℟. **And also with you.**
✤ A reading from the holy Gospel according to Matthew. ℟. **Glory to you, Lord.**

T HE eleven disciples went to Galilee, to the mountain to which Jesus had ordered them. When they
all saw him, they worshiped, but they doubted. Then
Jesus approached and said to them, "All power in
heaven and on earth has been given to me. Go, therefore, and make disciples of all nations, baptizing them
in the name of the Father, and of the Son, and of the
Holy Spirit, teaching them to observe all that I have
commanded you. And behold, I am with you always,
until the end of the age."—The Gospel of the Lord. ℟.
Praise to you, Lord Jesus Christ.   → No. 14, p. 18

PRAYER OVER THE GIFTS   [Perfect Offering]
Lord our God,
make these gifts holy,
and through them
make us a perfect offering to you.
We ask this in the name of Jesus the Lord.
℟. **Amen.** ↓

PREFACE (P 43)   [Mystery of the One Godhead]
℣. The Lord be with you. ℟. **And also with you.**
℣. Lift up your hearts. ℟. **We lift them up to the Lord.**

℣. Let us give thanks to the Lord our God. ℟. **It is right to give him thanks and praise.**

Father, all-powerful and ever-living God,
we do well always and everywhere to give you thanks.
We joyfully proclaim our faith
in the mystery of your Godhead.
You have revealed your glory
as the glory also of your Son
and of the Holy Spirit:
three Persons equal in majesty,
undivided in splendor,
yet one Lord, one God,
ever to be adored in your everlasting glory.
And so, with all the choirs of angels in heaven
we proclaim your glory
and join in their unending hymn of praise:

→ No. 23, p. 23

COMMUNION ANT. Gal 4:6   [Abba, Father]

You are the sons of God, so God has given you the Spirit of his Son to form your hearts and make you cry out: Abba, Father. ↓

PRAYER AFTER COMMUNION   [Eternal God]

Lord God,
we worship you, a Trinity of Persons, one eternal God.
May our faith and the sacrament we receive
bring us health of mind and body.
We ask this through Christ our Lord.
℟. **Amen.**   → No. 32, p. 70

Optional Solemn Blessings, p. 92, and Prayers Over the People, p. 99

"This is my body...."

JUNE 22

THE BODY AND BLOOD OF CHRIST
(CORPUS CHRISTI)

ENTRANCE ANT. Ps 81:17   **[Finest Wheat and Honey]**

The Lord fed his people with the finest wheat and honey; their hunger was satisfied.   ➜ No. 2, p. 10

OPENING PRAYER   **[Memorial of Christ]**

Let us pray
  [to the Lord who gives himself in the eucharist,
    that this sacrament may bring us salvation and
    peace]
Lord Jesus Christ,
you gave us the eucharist
as the memorial of your suffering and death.
May our worship of this sacrament of your body and
    blood
help us to experience the salvation you won for us
and the peace of the kingdom
where you live with the Father and the Holy Spirit,
one God, for ever and ever. ℟. **Amen.** ↓

ALTERNATIVE OPENING PRAYER   [Eucharistic Love]

Let us pray
[for the willingness to make present in our world
the love of Christ shown to us in the eucharist]
Lord Jesus Christ,
we worship you living among us
in the sacrament of your body and blood.
May we offer to our Father in heaven
a solemn pledge of undivided love.
May we offer to our brothers and sisters
a life poured out in loving service of that kingdom
where you live with the Father and the Holy Spirit,
one God, for ever and ever. ℟. **Amen.** ↓

FIRST READING Ex 24:3-8   [Blood of the Covenant]

The Israelites promised to observe all the prescriptions of the Lord as related by Moses. To seal this promise Moses offered a sacrifice to the Lord and sprinkled the people with the blood offering.

A reading from the Book of Exodus

WHEN Moses came to the people and related all the words and ordinances of the LORD, they all answered with one voice, "We will do everything that the LORD has told us." Moses then wrote down all the words of the LORD and, rising early the next day, he erected at the foot of the mountain an altar and twelve pillars for the twelve tribes of Israel. Then, having sent certain young men of the Israelites to offer holocausts and sacrifice young bulls as peace offerings to the LORD, Moses took half of the blood and put it in large bowls; the other half he splashed on the altar. Taking the book of the covenant, he read it aloud to the people, who answered, "All that the LORD has said, we will heed and do." Then he took the blood and sprinkled it on the people, saying, "This is the blood of the covenant that the LORD has made with you in ac-

cordance with all these words of his."—The word of
the Lord. ℟. **Thanks be to God.** ↓

RESPONSORIAL PSALM Ps 116   [The Cup of Salvation]

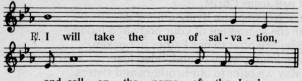

℟. I   will   take   the   cup   of   sal - va - tion,

and call   on   the   name   of   the   Lord.
℟. Or: **Alleluia.**

How shall I make a return to the LORD
   for all the good he has done for me?
The cup of salvation I will take up,
   and I will call upon the name of the LORD.

℟. **I will take the cup of salvation,
   and call on the name of the Lord.**

℟. Or: **Alleluia.**

Precious in the eyes of the LORD
   is the death of his faithful ones.
I am your servant, the son of your handmaid;
   you have loosed my bonds.

℟. **I will take the cup of salvation,
   and call on the name of the Lord.**

℟. Or: **Alleluia.**

To you will I offer sacrifice of thanksgiving,
   and I will call upon the name of the LORD.
My vows to the LORD I will pay
   in the presence of all his people.

℟. **I will take the cup of salvation,
   and call on the name of the Lord.** ↓

℟. Or: **Alleluia.** ↓

SECOND READING Heb 9:11-15   [Jesus the High Priest]

Jesus came as high priest, not offering the blood of animals but his own blood, to achieve eternal redemption. Jesus is mediator of the new covenant.

A reading from the Letter to the Hebrews

Brothers and sisters: When Christ came as high priest of the good things that have come to be, passing through the greater and more perfect tabernacle not made by hands, that is, not belonging to this creation, he entered once for all into the sanctuary, not with the blood of goats and calves but with his own blood, thus obtaining eternal redemption. For if the blood of goats and bulls and the sprinkling of a heifer's ashes can sanctify those who are defiled so that their flesh is cleansed, how much more will the blood of Christ, who through the eternal Spirit offered himself unblemished to God, cleanse our consciences from dead works to worship the living God.

For this reason he is mediator of a new covenant: since a death has taken place for deliverance from transgressions under the first covenant, those who are called may receive the promised eternal inheritance. —The word of the Lord. ℟. **Thanks be to God.** ↓

SEQUENCE (*Lauda Sion*)   [Praise of the Eucharist]

The Sequence Laud, O Zion (Lauda Sion), *or the Shorter Form beginning with the verse* Lo! the angel's food is given, *may be sung optionally before the Alleluia.*

Laud, O Zion, your salvation,
Laud with hymns of exultation,
  Christ, your king and shepherd true:
Bring him all the praise you know,
He is more than you bestow,
  Never can you reach his due.

Special theme for glad thanksgiving
Is the quick'ning and the living Bread today before you set:
From his hands of old partaken,
As we know, by faith unshaken,
  Where the Twelve at supper met.

Full and clear ring out your chanting,
Joy nor sweetest grace be wanting,
From your heart let praises burst:

For today the feast is holden,
When the institution olden
Of that supper was rehearsed.

Here the new law's new oblation,
By the new king's revelation,
Ends the form of ancient rite:

Now the new the old effaces,
Truth away the shadow chases,
Light dispels the gloom of night.

What he did at supper seated,
Christ ordained to be repeated,
His memorial ne'er to cease:

And his rule for guidance taking,
Bread and wine we hallow, making
Thus our sacrifice of peace.

This the truth each Christian learns,
Bread into his flesh he turns,
To his precious blood the wine:

Sight has fail'd, nor thought conceives,
But a dauntless faith believes,
Resting on a pow'r divine.

Here beneath these signs are hidden
Priceless things to sense forbidden;
Signs, not things are all we see:

Blood is poured and flesh is broken,
Yet in either wondrous token
Christ entire we know to be.

Whoso of this food partakes,
Does not rend the Lord nor breaks;
Christ is whole to all that taste:

Thousands are, as one, receivers,
One, as thousands of believers,
Eats of him who cannot waste.

Bad and good the feast are sharing,
Of what divers dooms preparing,
Endless death, or endless life.

Life to these, to those damnation,
See how like participation
Is with unlike issues rife.

When the sacrament is broken,
Doubt not, but believe 'tis spoken,
That each sever'd outward token
doth the very whole contain.

Nought the precious gift divides,
Breaking but the sign betides,

Jesus still the same abides,
still unbroken does remain.

The Shorter Form of the Sequence begins here.

Lo! the angel's food is given
To the pilgrim who has striven;
    See the children's bread from
    heaven,
    which on dogs may not be
    spent.
Truth the ancient types fulfill-
ing,
Isaac bound, a victim willing,
    Paschal lamb, its lifeblood
    spilling,
    manna to the fathers sent.
Very bread, good shepherd,
tend us,
Jesu, of your love befriend us,

You refresh us, you defend
us,
Your eternal goodness send
us
In the land of life to see.
You who all things can and
know,
Who on earth such food be-
stow,
    Grant us with your saints,
    though lowest,
    Where the heav'nly feast you
    show,
Fellow heirs and guests to be.
    Amen. Alleluia. ↓

ALLELUIA Jn 6:51   [Living Bread]

℞. **Alleluia, alleluia.**
I am the living bread that came down from heaven,
    says the Lord;
whoever eats this bread will live for ever.
℞. **Alleluia, alleluia.** ↓

GOSPEL Mk 14:12-16, 22-26   [The First Eucharist]

**Jesus gave instructions for the Passover supper. At this
meal he took bread and wine and changed it into his Body
and Blood and gave this Eucharist to his disciples. They all
ate and drank at Jesus' request.**

℣. The Lord be with you. ℞. **And also with you.**
✣ A reading from the holy Gospel according to Mark.
℞. **Glory to you, Lord.**

O N the first day of the Feast of Unleavened Bread,
    when they sacrificed the Passover lamb, Jesus'

disciples said to him, "Where do you want us to go and prepare for you to eat the Passover?" He sent two of his disciples and said to them, "Go into the city and a man will meet you, carrying a jar of water. Follow him. Wherever he enters, say to the master of the house, 'The Teacher says, "Where is my guest room where I may eat the Passover with my disciples?" ' Then he will show you a large upper room furnished and ready. Make the preparations for us there." The disciples then went off, entered the city, and found it just as he had told them; and they prepared the Passover.

While they were eating, he took bread, said the blessing, broke it, gave it to them, and said, "Take it; this is my body." Then he took a cup, gave thanks, and gave it to them, and they all drank from it. He said to them, "This is my blood of the covenant, which will be shed for many. Amen, I say to you, I shall not drink again the fruit of the vine until the day when I drink it new in the kingdom of God." Then, after singing a hymn, they went out to the Mount of Olives.—The Gospel of the Lord. ℟. **Praise to you, Lord Jesus Christ.**   → No. 14, p. 18

PRAYER OVER THE GIFTS   [Unity and Peace]

Lord,
may the bread and cup we offer
bring your Church the unity and peace they signify.
We ask this in the name of Jesus the Lord.
℟. **Amen.**   → No. 21, p. 22 (Pref. P 47-48)

COMMUNION ANT. Jn 6:57   [Eucharistic Life]

Whoever eats my flesh and drinks my blood will live in me and I in him, says the Lord. ↓

PRAYER AFTER COMMUNION   [Divine Life]

Lord Jesus Christ,
you give us your body and blood in the eucharist
as a sign that even now we share your life.
May we come to possess it completely in the kingdom
where you live for ever and ever.
℞. **Amen.**   ➜   No. 32, p. 70

Optional Solemn Blessings, p. 92, and Prayers Over the People, p. 99

*"You are Peter, and upon this rock
I will build my church."*

JUNE 29

STS. PETER AND PAUL APOSTLES

(13th SUNDAY IN ORDINARY TIME)
VIGIL MASS

ENTRANCE ANT. [Role of Peter and Paul]

Peter the apostle and Paul the teacher of the Gentiles have brought us to know the law of the Lord.

→ No. 2, p. 10

OPENING PRAYER [Salvation through Prayers of Apostles]

Let us pray
   [that the prayers of the apostles
   will lead us to salvation]
Lord our God,
encourage us through the prayers of Saints Peter and
   Paul.
May the apostles who strengthened the faith of the infant Church
help us on our way of salvation.
We ask this through our Lord Jesus Christ, your Son,

who lives and reigns with you and the Holy Spirit,
one God, for ever and ever. ℟. **Amen.** ↓

ALTERNATIVE OPENING PRAYER   [True to the Faith]

Let us pray
   [to be true to the faith
   which has come to us
   through the apostles Peter and Paul]
Father in heaven,
the light of your revelation brought Peter and Paul
the gift of faith in Jesus your Son.
Through their prayers
may we always give thanks for your life
given us in Christ Jesus,
and for having been enriched by him
in all knowledge and love.
We ask this through Christ our Lord. ℟. **Amen.** ↓

FIRST READING Acts 3:1-10   [The Power of Jesus' Name]

St. Peter cures the crippled man not in his own name, but in the name of Christ. We may see in this cure an image of ourselves. We are crippled by sin, but we are lifted up by Christ's power into human dignity and spiritual health.

A reading from the Acts of the Apostles

PETER and John were going up to the temple area for the three o'clock hour of prayer. And a man crippled from birth was carried and placed at the gate of the temple called "the Beautiful Gate" every day to beg for alms from the people who entered the temple. When he saw Peter and John about to go into the temple, he asked for alms. But Peter looked intently at him, as did John, and said, "Look at us." He paid attention to them, expecting to receive something from them. Peter said, "I have neither silver nor gold, but what I do have I give you: in the name of Jesus Christ the Nazarene, rise and walk." Then Peter took him by the right hand and raised him up, and immediately his feet and ankles grew strong. He leaped up, stood, and walked around, and went into the temple with them, walking and jumping and praising God. When all the people saw the man walking and praising God, they recognized him as the one who used to sit begging at the Beautiful Gate of the temple, and they were filled with amazement and astonishment at what had happened to him.—The word of the Lord. ℟. **Thanks be to God.** ↓

RESPONSORIAL PSALM Ps 19   [Creation Praises God]

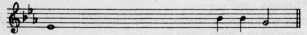

℟. Their message goes out through all the earth.

The heavens declare the glory of God,
    and the firmament proclaims his handiwork.
Day pours out the word to day,
    and night to night imparts knowledge.

℟. **Their message goes out through all the earth.**

Not a word nor a discourse
    whose voice is not heard;
through all the earth their voice resounds,
    and to the ends of the world, their message.

℟. **Their message goes out through all the earth.** ↓

SECOND READING Gal 1:11-20   [God's Call]

St. Paul explains how he and the other apostles can claim such authority for their teaching. The message comes from Christ and is delivered by those whom the Lord has chosen.

A reading from the Letter of Saint Paul to the Galatians

I want you to know, brothers and sisters, that the gospel preached by me is not of human origin. For I did not receive it from a human being, nor was I taught it, but it came through a revelation of Jesus Christ.

For you heard of my former way of life in Judaism, how I persecuted the church of God beyond measure and tried to destroy it, and progressed in Judaism beyond many of my contemporaries among my race, since I was even more a zealot for my ancestral traditions. But when God, who from my mother's womb had set me apart and called me through his grace, was pleased to reveal his Son to me, so that I might proclaim him to the Gentiles, I did not immediately consult flesh and blood, nor did I go up to Jerusalem to those who were apostles before me; rather, I went into Arabia and then returned to Damascus.

Then after three years I went up to Jerusalem to confer with Cephas and remained with him for fifteen days. But I did not see any other of the apostles, only James the brother of the Lord.—As to what I am writing to you, behold, before God, I am not lying.—The word of the Lord. ℟. **Thanks be to God.** ↓

ALLELUIA Jn 21:17   [Love for Christ]

℟. **Alleluia, alleluia.**
Lord, you know everything;
you know that I love you.
℟. **Alleluia, alleluia.** ↓

GOSPEL Jn 21:15-19   [The Primacy Bestowed on Peter]

The words of Jesus to Peter indicate the dignity bestowed on him, but also the great responsibility. Peter must tend the flock of Christ, even to the point of sacrificing his life. Today's Holy Father must do the same, and deserves our prayers.

℣. The Lord be with you. ℟. **And also with you.**
✛ A reading from the holy Gospel according to John.
℟. **Glory to you, Lord.**

JESUS revealed himself to his disciples and, when they had finished breakfast, said to Simon Peter, "Simon, son of John, do you love me more than these?" He answered him, "Yes, Lord, you know that I love you." Jesus said to him, "Feed my lambs."

He then said to him a second time, "Simon, son of
John, do you love me?" He answered him, "Yes, Lord,
you know that I love you." He said to him, "Tend my
sheep."

He said to him the third time, "Simon, son of John,
do you love me?" Peter was distressed that Jesus had
said to him a third time, "Do you love me?" and he
said to him, "Lord, you know everything; you know
that I love you." Jesus said to him, "Feed my sheep.
Amen, amen, I say to you, when you were younger,
you used to dress yourself and go where you wanted;
but when you grow old, you will stretch out your
hands, and someone else will dress you and lead you
where you do not want to go." He said this signifying
by what kind of death he would glorify God. And
when he had said this, he said to him, "Follow me."—
The Gospel of the Lord. ℟. **Praise to you, Lord Jesus
Christ.**   ➜ No. 14, p. 18

PRAYER OVER THE GIFTS   [Relying on God]

Lord,
we present these gifts
on this feast of the apostles Peter and Paul.
Help us to know our own weakness
and to rejoice in your saving power.
Grant this through Christ our Lord. ℟. **Amen.** ↓

PREFACE (P 63)   [Two Great Apostles]

℣. The Lord be with you. ℟. **And also with you.**
℣. Lift up your hearts. ℟. **We lift them up to the Lord.**
℣. Let us give thanks to the Lord our God. ℟. **It is right
to give him thanks and praise.**

Father, all-powerful and ever-living God,
we do well always and everywhere to give you thanks.
You fill our hearts with joy
as we honor your great apostles:
Peter, our leader in the faith,

and Paul, its fearless preacher.
Peter raised up the Church
from the faithful flock of Israel.
Paul brought your call to the nations,
and became the teacher of the world.
Each in his chosen way gathered into unity
the one family of Christ.
Both shared a martyr's death
and are praised throughout the world.
Now, with the apostles and all the angels and saints,
we praise you for ever: → No. 23, p. 23

COMMUNION ANT. Jn 21:15-17   [Peter's Love for Jesus]
Simon, son of John, do you love me more than these?
Lord, you know all things; you know that I love you. ↓

PRAYER AFTER COMMUNION   [Our Teacher]
Father,
you give us light by the teaching of your apostles.
In this sacrament we have received
fill us with your strength.
We ask this in the name of Jesus the Lord.
℟. **Amen.**   → No. 32, p. 70

MASS DURING THE DAY

ENTRANCE ANT.   [Friends of God]
These men, conquering all human frailty, shed their
blood and helped the Church to grow. By sharing the
cup of the Lord's suffering, they became the friends
of God.   → No. 2, p. 10

OPENING PRAYER   [True to the Apostles' Faith]
Let us pray
    [that we will remain true to
    the faith of the apostles]
God our Father,

today you give us the joy
of celebrating the feast of the apostles Peter and Paul.
Through them your Church first received the faith.
Keep us true to their teaching.
Grant this through our Lord Jesus Christ, your Son,
who lives and reigns with you and the Holy Spirit,
one God, for ever and ever. ℟. **Amen.** ↓

ALTERNATIVE OPENING PRAYER

[United with the Apostles]

Let us pray
[one with Peter and Paul in our faith
in Christ the Son of the living God]
Praise to you, the God and Father of our Lord Jesus
    Christ,
who in your great mercy
have given us new birth and hope
through the power of Christ's resurrection.
Through the prayers of the apostles Peter and Paul
may we who received this faith through their preaching
share their love in following the Lord
to the unfading inheritance
reserved for us in heaven.
We ask this in the name of Jesus the Lord. ℟. **Amen.** ↓

FIRST READING Acts 12:1-11   [A Miraculous Escape]

**The apostles are not stopped by accusations and imprison-
ment. They continue their witnessing to the Good News of
Jesus Christ. The Lord works with them and through them,
and often saves them from death. This text relates one such
incident.**

A reading from the Acts of the Apostles

IN those days, King Herod laid hands upon some
members of the church to harm them. He had
James, the brother of John, killed by the sword, and
when he saw that this was pleasing to the Jews he
proceeded to arrest Peter also.—It was the feast of Unleavened Bread.—He had him taken into custody and

put in prison under the guard of four squads of four soldiers each. He intended to bring him before the people after Passover. Peter thus was being kept in prison, but prayer by the church was fervently being made to God on his behalf.

On the very night before Herod was to bring him to trial, Peter, secured by double chains, was sleeping between two soldiers, while outside the door guards kept watch on the prison. Suddenly the angel of the Lord stood by him and a light shone in the cell. He tapped Peter on the side and awakened him, saying, "Get up quickly." The chains fell from his wrists. The angel said to him, "Put on your belt and your sandals." He did so. Then he said to him, "Put on your cloak and follow me." So he followed him out, not realizing that what was happening through the angel was real; he thought he was seeing a vision. They passed the first guard, then the second, and came to the iron gate leading out to the city, which opened for them by itself. They emerged and made their way down an alley, and suddenly the angel left him. —The word of the Lord. ℟. **Thanks be to God.** ↓

RESPONSORIAL PSALM Ps 34   [The Lord's Protection]

℟. **The angel of the Lord will rescue those who fear him.**

I will bless the LORD at all times;
  his praise shall be ever in my mouth.
Let my soul glory in the LORD;
  the lowly will hear me and be glad.

℟. **The angel of the Lord will rescue those who fear him.**

Glorify the LORD with me,
  let us together extol his name.

I sought the LORD, and he answered me
  and delivered me from all my fears.

℟. **The angel of the Lord will rescue those who fear
him.**

Look to him that you may be radiant with joy,
  and your faces may not blush with shame.
When the afflicted man called out, the LORD heard,
  and from all his distress he saved him.

℟. **The angel of the Lord will rescue those who fear
him.**

The angel of the LORD encamps
  around those who fear him, and delivers them.
Taste and see how good the LORD is;
  blessed the man who takes refuge in him.

℟. **The angel of the Lord will rescue those who fear
him.** ↓

SECOND READING 2 Tm 4:6-8, 17-18   **[A Merited Crown]**

**The apostles had to rely totally on God to guide them and
grant faith to those who heard their preaching. Their
human weakness made God's power more obvious.**

A reading from the second Letter of Saint Paul
to Timothy

I, PAUL, am already being poured out like a libation,
and the time of my departure is at hand. I have
competed well; I have finished the race; I have kept
the faith. From now on the crown of righteousness
awaits me, which the Lord, the just judge, will award
to me on that day, and not only to me, but to all who
have longed for his appearance.

The Lord stood by me and gave me strength, so that
through me the proclamation might be completed and
all the Gentiles might hear it. And I was rescued from
the lion's mouth. The Lord will rescue me from every
evil threat and will bring me safe to his heavenly king-

dom. To him be glory forever and ever. Amen.—The word of the Lord. ℟. **Thanks be to God.** ↓

ALLELUIA Mt 16:18   [The First Pope]

℟. **Alleluia, alleluia.**
You are Peter and upon this rock I will build my church,
and the gates of the netherworld shall not prevail against it.
℟. **Alleluia, alleluia.** ↓

GOSPEL Mt 16:13-19   [Peter the Rock]

To the Jews, a change of name meant a change of the very person and of that person's life. Jesus changes the name of Simon to Peter, which means "rock." He would be the human rock of firmness that would protect the word of God and would guide the whole Church.

℣. The Lord be with you. ℟. **And also with you.**

✤ A reading from the holy Gospel according to Matthew. ℟. **Glory to you, Lord.**

WHEN Jesus went into the region of Caesarea Philippi he asked his disciples, "Who do people say that the Son of Man is?" They replied, "Some say John the Baptist, others Elijah, still others Jeremiah or one of the prophets." He said to them, "But who do you say that I am?" Simon Peter said in reply, "You are the Christ, the Son of the living God." Jesus said to him in reply, "Blessed are you, Simon son of Jonah. For flesh and blood has not revealed this to you, but my heavenly Father. And so I say to you, you are Peter, and upon this rock I will build my church, and the gates of the netherworld shall not prevail against it. I will give you the keys to the kingdom of heaven. Whatever you bind on earth shall be bound in heaven; and whatever you loose on earth shall be loosed in heaven." —The Gospel of the Lord. ℟. **Praise to you, Lord Jesus Christ.**   ➜ No. 14, p. 18

PRAYER OVER THE GIFTS   [United with the Apostles]

Lord,
may your apostles join their prayers to our offering
and help us to celebrate this sacrifice in love and
  unity.
We ask this through Christ our Lord.
℟. **Amen.**   ➜ Pref. (P 63), p. 444

COMMUNION ANT. Mt 16:16, 18   [Head of the Church]

Peter said: You are the Christ, the Son of the living God. Jesus answered: You are Peter, the rock on which I will build my Church. ↓

PRAYER AFTER COMMUNION   [Renew the Church]

Lord,
renew the life of your Church
with the power of this sacrament.
May the breaking of bread
and the teaching of the apostles
keep us united in your love.
We ask this in the name of Jesus the Lord.
℟. **Amen.**   ➜ No. 32, p. 70

Optional Solemn Blessings, p. 92, and Prayers Over the People, p. 99

"A prophet is not without honor except in his native place."

JULY 6

14th SUNDAY IN ORDINARY TIME

ENTRANCE ANT. Ps 48:10-11   [God's Kindness and Justice]

Within your temple, we ponder your loving kindness, O God. As your name, so also your praise reaches to the ends of the earth; your right hand is filled with justice.   ➜ No. 2, p. 10

OPENING PRAYER   [Forgiveness]

Let us pray
[for forgiveness through the grace of Jesus Christ]
Father,
through the obedience of Jesus,
your servant and your Son,
you raised a fallen world.
Free us from sin
and bring us the joy that lasts for ever.
We ask this through our Lord Jesus Christ, your Son,
who lives and reigns with you and the Holy Spirit,
one God, for ever and ever. ℟. **Amen.** ↓

451

ALTERNATIVE OPENING PRAYER

[Serving God and Others]

Let us pray
  [for greater willingness
  to serve God and our fellow man]
Father,
in the rising of your Son
death gives birth to new life.
The sufferings he endured restored hope to a fallen
  world.
Let sin never ensnare us
with empty promises of passing joy.
Make us one with you always,
so that our joy may be holy,
and our love may give life.
We ask this through Christ our Lord. ℟. **Amen.** ↓

FIRST READING Ez 2:2-5   [God's Prophet]

**Ezekiel is selected by God to be a prophet and messenger
to the Israelites. When resisted, Ezekiel is to say: "Thus
says the Lord God!" In this way they shall see that he is a
prophet.**

A reading from the Book of the Prophet Ezekiel

A S the LORD spoke to me, the spirit entered into me
and set me on my feet, and I heard the one who
was speaking say to me: Son of man, I am sending
you to the Israelites, rebels who have rebelled against
me; they and their ancestors have revolted against me
to this very day. Hard of face and obstinate of heart
are they to whom I am sending you. But you shall say
to them: Thus says the LORD God! And whether they
heed or resist—for they are a rebellious house—they
shall know that a prophet has been among them.—
The word of the Lord. ℟. **Thanks be to God.** ↓

RESPONSORIAL PSALM Ps 123   [Eyes on God]

℟. Our eyes are fixed on the Lord, pleading for his mer-cy.

To you I lift up my eyes
   who are enthroned in heaven—
as the eyes of servants
   are on the hands of their masters.

℟. **Our eyes are fixed on the Lord,
   pleading for his mercy.**

As the eyes of a maid
   are on the hands of her mistress,
so are our eyes on the Lord, our God,
   till he have pity on us.

℟. **Our eyes are fixed on the Lord,
   pleading for his mercy.**

Have pity on us, O Lord, have pity on us,
   for we are more than sated with contempt;
our souls are more than sated
   with the mockery of the arrogant,
   with the contempt of the proud.

℟. **Our eyes are fixed on the Lord,
   pleading for his mercy.** ↓

SECOND READING 2 Cor 12:7-10   [Suffering for Christ]

**Paul is given a "thorn in the flesh." He asks God for relief
and God replies that his grace is sufficient.**

A reading from the second Letter of Saint Paul
to the Corinthians

BROTHERS and sisters: That I, Paul, might not become too elated, because of the abundance of the
revelations, a thorn in the flesh was given to me, an
angel of Satan, to beat me, to keep me from being too
elated. Three times I begged the Lord about this, that it

might leave me, but he said to me, "My grace is sufficient for you, for power is made perfect in weakness." I
will rather boast most gladly of my weaknesses, in
order that the power of Christ may dwell with me.
Therefore, I am content with weaknesses, insults,
hardships, persecutions, and constraints, for the sake
of Christ; for when I am weak, then I am strong.—The
word of the Lord. ℟. **Thanks be to God.** ↓

ALLELUIA Cf.Lk 4:18   [God's Spirit]
℟. **Alleluia, alleluia.**
The Spirit of the Lord is upon me
for he sent me to bring glad tidings to the poor.
℟. **Alleluia, alleluia.** ↓

GOSPEL Mk 6:1-6   [Spreading the Good News]
Jesus began to teach in his home synagogue. The people,
knowing Mary and Joseph, cannot understand the wisdom
Jesus shows and Jesus tells them: "No prophet is without
honor except in his native place."

℣. The Lord be with you. ℟. **And also with you.**
✛ A reading from the holy Gospel according to Mark.
℟. **Glory to you, Lord.**

JESUS departed from there and came to his native
place, accompanied by his disciples. When the sabbath came he began to teach in the synagogue, and
many who heard him were astonished. They said,
"Where did this man get all this? What kind of wisdom has been given him? What mighty deeds are
wrought by his hands! Is he not the carpenter, the son
of Mary, and the brother of James and Joses and
Judas and Simon? And are not his sisters here with
us?" And they took offense at him. Jesus said to them,
"A prophet is not without honor except in his native
place and among his own kin and in his own house."

So he was not able to perform any mighty deed there, apart from curing a few sick people by laying his hands on them. He was amazed at their lack of faith.—The Gospel of the Lord. ℟. **Praise to you, Lord Jesus Christ.**   ➜ No. 14, p. 18

PRAYER OVER THE GIFTS   [God's Glory]

Lord,
let this offering to the glory of your name
purify us and bring us closer to eternal life.
We ask this in the name of Jesus the Lord.
    ℟. **Amen.**   ➜   No. 21, p. 22 (Pref. P 29-36)

COMMUNION ANT. Ps 34:9   [The Lord's Goodness]

Taste and see the goodness of the Lord; blessed is he who hopes in God. ↓

OR Mt 11:28   [Refuge in God]

Come to me, all you that labor and are burdened, and I will give you rest, says the Lord. ↓

PRAYER AFTER COMMUNION   [Life and Salvation]

Lord,
may we never fail to praise you
for the fullness of life and salvation
you give us in this eucharist.
We ask this through Christ our Lord.
    ℟. **Amen.**   ➜ No. 32, p. 70

Optional Solemn Blessings, p. 92, and Prayers Over the People, p. 99

"Jesus summoned the Twelve and began to send them out two by two."

JULY 13

15th SUNDAY IN ORDINARY TIME

ENTRANCE ANT. Ps 17:15   [God's Face]

In my justice I shall see your face, O Lord; when your glory appears, my joy will be full.   → No. 2, p. 10

OPENING PRAYER   [Rule of Life]

Let us pray
   [that the gospel may be our rule of life]
God our Father,
your light of truth
guides us to the way of Christ.
May all who follow him
reject what is contrary to the gospel.
We ask this through our Lord Jesus Christ, your Son,
who lives and reigns with you and the Holy Spirit,
one God, for ever and ever. ℞. **Amen.** ↓

ALTERNATIVE OPENING PRAYER   [Fidelity]

Let us pray
   [to be faithful to the light we have received,
   to the name we bear]

Father,
let the light of your truth
guide us to your kingdom
through a world filled with lights contrary to your
    own.
Christian is the name and the gospel we glory in.
May your love make us what you have called us to be.
We ask this through Christ our Lord. ℟. **Amen.** ↓

FIRST READING Am 7:12-15   [God Makes a Prophet]

**Amos writes how he was chosen by God to go out and
prophesy to the people of Israel.**

A reading from the Book of the Prophet Amos

AMAZIAH, priest of Bethel, said to Amos, "Off with
you, visionary, flee to the land of Judah! There
earn your bread by prophesying, but never again
prophesy in Bethel; for it is the king's sanctuary and a
royal temple." Amos answered Amaziah, "I was no
prophet, nor have I belonged to a company of
prophets; I was a shepherd and a dresser of
sycamores. The LORD took me from following the
flock, and said to me, Go, prophesy to my people Israel."—The word of the Lord. ℟. **Thanks be to God.** ↓

RESPONSORIAL PSALM Ps 85   [The Lord's Salvation]

℟. **Lord, let us see your kindness, and grant us your sal-va-tion.**

I will hear what God proclaims;
    the LORD—for he proclaims peace.
Near indeed is his salvation to those who fear him,
    glory dwelling in our land.

℟. **Lord, let us see your kindness,
    and grant us your salvation.**

Kindness and truth shall meet;
  justice and peace shall kiss.
Truth shall spring out of the earth,
  and justice shall look down from heaven.

R̗. **Lord, let us see your kindness,
  and grant us your salvation.**

The LORD himself will give his benefits;
  our land shall yield its increase.
Justice shall walk before him,
  and prepare the way of his steps.

R̗. **Lord, let us see your kindness,
  and grant us your salvation.** ↓

SECOND READING Eph 1:3-14 or 1:3-10 [Christ's Headship]

**God chose his followers to be holy, blameless, and filled
with love—to be his adopted children in Jesus. In Jesus and
through the seal of the Holy Spirit, full redemption shall
come to humankind.**

*[If the "Shorter Form" is used, the indented text in brackets is
omitted.]*

A reading from the Letter of Saint Paul to the Ephesians

BLESSED be the God and Father of our Lord Jesus
Christ, who has blessed us in Christ with every
spiritual blessing in the heavens, as he chose us in
him, before the foundation of the world, to be holy
and without blemish before him. In love he destined
us for adoption to himself through Jesus Christ, in accord with the favor of his will, for the praise of the
glory of his grace that he granted us in the beloved. In
him we have redemption by his blood, the forgiveness
of transgressions, in accord with the riches of his
grace that he lavished upon us. In all wisdom and insight, he has made known to us the mystery of his will
in accord with his favor that he set forth in him as a
plan for the fullness of times, to sum up all things in
Christ, in heaven and on earth.

[In him we were also chosen, destined in accord with the purpose of the One who accomplishes all things according to the intention of his will, so that we might exist for the praise of his glory, we who first hoped in Christ. In him you also, who have heard the word of truth, the gospel of your salvation, and have believed in him, were sealed with the promised holy Spirit, which is the first installment of our inheritance toward redemption as God's possession, to the praise of his glory.]

The word of the Lord. ℟. **Thanks be to God.** ↓

ALLELUIA Cf. Eph 1:17-18   [Our Great Hope]

℟. **Alleluia, alleluia.**
May the Father of our Lord Jesus Christ
enlighten the eyes of our hearts,
that we may know what is the hope
that belongs to our call.
℟. **Alleluia, alleluia.** ↓

GOSPEL Mk 6:7-13   [Spreading the Gospel]

Jesus sent out the Twelve, instructing them to take only a walking stick and to preach the gospel. If they were refused a listening ear, they should leave the locality. They worked many miracles.

℣. The Lord be with you. ℟. **And also with you.**
✠ A reading from the holy Gospel according to Mark.
℟. **Glory to you, Lord.**

JESUS summoned the Twelve and began to send them out two by two and gave them authority over unclean spirits. He instructed them to take nothing for the journey but a walking stick—no food, no sack, no money in their belts. They were, however, to wear sandals but not a second tunic. He said to them, "Wherever you enter a house, stay there until you leave. Whatever place does not welcome you or listen to you, leave there and shake the dust off your feet in testimony against them." So they went off and preached repentance. The Twelve drove out many demons, and they anointed with oil many who were sick and cured them.—The Gospel of the Lord. ℟. **Praise to you, Lord Jesus Christ.**   → No. 14, p. 18

PRAYER OVER THE GIFTS   [Growth in Faith]

Lord,
accept the gifts of your Church.
May this eucharist
help us grow in holiness and faith.
We ask this in the name of Jesus the Lord.
℟. **Amen.**   → No. 21, p. 22 (Pref. P 29-36)

COMMUNION ANT. Ps 84:4-5   [The Lord's House]

The sparrow even finds a home, the swallow finds a nest wherein to place her young, near to your altars, Lord of hosts, my King, my God! How happy they who dwell in your house! For ever they are praising you. ↓

OR Jn 6:57   [Life in Jesus]

Whoever eats my flesh and drinks my blood will live in me and I in him, says the Lord. ↓

PRAYER AFTER COMMUNION   [God's Love]

Lord,
by our sharing in the mystery of this eucharist,
let your saving love grow within us.
Grant this through Christ our Lord.
℟. **Amen.**   → No. 32, p. 70

Optional Solemn Blessings, p. 92, and Prayers Over the People, p. 99

"[Jesus and the disciples] went off in the boat by themselves."

JULY 20

16th SUNDAY IN ORDINARY TIME

ENTRANCE ANT. Ps 54:6, 8   [God Our Help]
God himself is my help. The Lord upholds my life. I will offer you a willing sacrifice; I will praise your name, O Lord, for its goodness.   → No. 2, p. 10

OPENING PRAYER   [Faithful Service]
Let us pray
   [to be kept faithful in the service of God]
Lord,
be merciful to your people.
Fill us with your gifts
and make us always eager to serve you
in faith, hope, and love.
Grant this through our Lord Jesus Christ, your Son,
who lives and reigns with you and the Holy Spirit,
one God, for ever and ever. ℟. **Amen.** ↓

ALTERNATIVE OPENING PRAYER   [God's Blessing]
Let us pray
   [that God will continue to bless us
   with his compassion and love]

461

Father,
let the gift of your life
continue to grow in us,
drawing us from death to faith, hope, and love.
Keep us alive in Christ Jesus.
Keep us watchful in prayer
and true to his teaching
till your glory is revealed in us.
Grant this through Christ our Lord. ℟. **Amen.** ↓

FIRST READING Jer 23:1-6   [A True Shepherd]

Woe to those who sow evil. Their evil deeds will be punished. Good shepherds will be appointed. There will come a shoot to David in whose days Judah will be saved.

A reading from the Book of the Prophet Jeremiah

WOE to the shepherds who mislead and scatter the flock of my pasture, says the LORD. Therefore, thus says the LORD, the God of Israel, against the shepherds who shepherd my people: You have scattered my sheep and driven them away. You have not cared for them, but I will take care to punish your evil deeds. I myself will gather the remnant of my flock from all the lands to which I have driven them and bring them back to their meadow; there they shall increase and multiply. I will appoint shepherds for them who will shepherd them so that they need no longer fear and tremble; and none shall be missing, says the LORD.

Behold, the days are coming, says the LORD,
    when I will raise up a righteous shoot to David;
as king he shall reign and govern wisely,
    he shall do what is just and right in the land.
In his days Judah shall be saved,
    Israel shall dwell in security.
This is the name they give him:
    "The LORD our justice."
The word of the Lord. ℟. **Thanks be to God.** ↓

RESPONSORIAL PSALM Ps 23   [The Lord as Shepherd]

℟. **The Lord is my shep-herd; there is noth-ing I shall want.**

The LORD is my shepherd; I shall not want.
    In verdant pastures he gives me repose;
beside restful waters he leads me;
    he refreshes my soul.

℟. **The Lord is my shepherd;**
    there is nothing I shall want.

He guides me in right paths
    for his name's sake.
Even though I walk in the dark valley
    I fear no evil; for you are at my side
with your rod and your staff
    that give me courage.

℟. **The Lord is my shepherd;**
    there is nothing I shall want.

You spread the table before me
    in the sight of my foes;
you anoint my head with oil;
    my cup overflows.

℟. **The Lord is my shepherd;**
    there is nothing I shall want.

Only goodness and kindness follow me
    all the days of my life;
and I shall dwell in the house of the LORD
    for years to come.

℟. **The Lord is my shepherd;**
    there is nothing I shall want. ↓

SECOND READING Eph 2:13-18   [Access to the Father]

Paul tells the Ephesians that Christ has brought them together. Jesus has brought peace and reconciliation through
his cross.

A reading from the Letter of Saint Paul to the Ephesians

BROTHERS and sisters: In Christ Jesus you who once were far off have become near by the blood of Christ.

For he is our peace, he who made both one and broke down the dividing wall of enmity, through his flesh, abolishing the law with its commandments and legal claims, that he might create in himself one new person in place of the two, thus establishing peace, and might reconcile both with God, in one body, through the cross, putting that enmity to death by it. He came and preached peace to you who were far off and peace to those who were near, for through him we both have access in one Spirit to the Father.—The word of the Lord. ℟. **Thanks be to God.** ↓

ALLELUIA Jn 10:27   [God's Sheep]

℟. **Alleluia, alleluia.**

My sheep hear my voice, says the Lord;
I know them, and they follow me.

℟. **Alleluia, alleluia.** ↓

GOSPEL Mk 6:30-34   [Jesus the Shepherd]

Jesus called the apostles aside to rest. Still the people came, so Jesus and the apostles went to a deserted place. Yet the people came.

℣. The Lord be with you. ℟. **And also with you.**
✠ A reading from the holy Gospel according to Mark.
℟. **Glory to you, Lord.**

THE apostles gathered together with Jesus and reported all they had done and taught. He said to them, "Come away by yourselves to a deserted place and rest a while." People were coming and going in great numbers, and they had no opportunity even to eat. So they went off in the boat by themselves to a deserted place. People saw them leaving and many came to know about it. They hastened there on foot from all the towns and arrived at the place before them.

When he disembarked and saw the vast crowd, his heart was moved with pity for them, for they were like sheep without a shepherd; and he began to teach them many things.—The Gospel of the Lord. ℟. **Praise to you, Lord Jesus Christ.**   ➜ No. 14, p. 18

PRAYER OVER THE GIFTS   [Saving Gifts]

Lord,
bring us closer to salvation
through these gifts which we bring in your honor.
Accept the perfect sacrifice you have given us,
bless it as you blessed the gifts of Abel.
We ask this through Christ our Lord.
℟. **Amen.**   ➜ No. 21, p. 22 (Pref. P 29-36)

COMMUNION ANT. Ps 111:4-5   [Jesus Provides]

The Lord keeps in our minds the wonderful things he has done. He is compassion and love; he always provides for his faithful. ↓

OR Rv 3:20   [Jesus Knocks]

I stand at the door and knock, says the Lord. If anyone hears my voice and opens the door, I will come in and sit down to supper with him, and he with me. ↓

PRAYER AFTER COMMUNION   [New Life]

Merciful Father,
may these mysteries
give us new purpose
and bring us to a new life in you.
We ask this in the name of Jesus the Lord.
℟. **Amen.**   ➜ No. 32, p. 70

Optional Solemn Blessings, p. 92, and Prayers Over the People, p. 99

"Jesus took the loaves, gave thanks, and distributed them to those who were reclining."

JULY 27

17th SUNDAY IN ORDINARY TIME

ENTRANCE ANT. Ps 68:6-7, 36   [God Our Strength]

God is in his holy dwelling; he will give a home to the lonely, he gives power and strength to his people.

→ No. 2, p. 10

OPENING PRAYER   [Wise Use of Gifts]

Let us pray
  [that we will make good use of the gifts
    that God has given us]
God our Father and protector,
without you nothing is holy,
nothing has value.
Guide us to everlasting life
by helping us to use wisely
the blessings you have given to the world.
We ask this through our Lord Jesus Christ, your Son,
who lives and reigns with you and the Holy Spirit,
one God, for ever and ever. R/. **Amen.** ↓

ALTERNATIVE OPENING PRAYER   [God in the World]

Let us pray
  [for the faith to recognize God's presence
  in our world]
God our Father,
open our eyes to see your hand at work
in the splendor of creation,
in the beauty of human life.
Touched by your hand our world is holy.
Help us to cherish the gifts that surround us,
to share your blessings with our brothers and sisters,
and to experience the joy of life in your presence.
We ask this through Christ our Lord. ℞. **Amen.** ↓

FIRST READING 2 Kgs 4:42-44   [Miracle of the Loaves]

> **At the command from Elisha, the man of God, the barley
> bread was placed before the people, indicating that this
> comes from the Lord. Even though the number to be fed
> from the twenty loaves was a hundred, some was left over.**

A reading from the second Book of Kings

A MAN came from Baal-shalishah bringing to Elisha, the man of God, twenty barley loaves made
from the firstfruits, and fresh grain in the ear. Elisha
said, "Give it to the people to eat." But his servant objected, "How can I set this before a hundred people?"
Elisha insisted, "Give it to the people to eat. For thus
says the LORD, 'They shall eat and there shall be some
left over.' " And when they had eaten, there was some
left over, as the LORD had said.—The word of the
Lord. ℞. **Thanks be to God.** ↓

RESPONSORIAL PSALM Ps 145   [The Bounty of the Lord]

℞. **The hand of the Lord feeds us;   he answers all our needs.**

Let all your works give you thanks, O Lord,
  and let your faithful ones bless you.
Let them discourse of the glory of your kingdom
  and speak of your might.

℟. **The hand of the Lord feeds us;**
  he answers all our needs.

The eyes of all look hopefully to you,
  and you give them their food in due season;
you open your hand
  and satisfy the desire of every living thing.

℟. **The hand of the Lord feeds us;**
  he answers all our needs.

The Lord is just in all his ways
  and holy in all his works.
The Lord is near to all who call upon him,
  to all who call upon him in truth.

℟. **The hand of the Lord feeds us;**
  he answers all our needs. ↓

SECOND READING Eph 4:1-6   [Unity in the Spirit]

  A life worthy of the Lord consists of humility, meekness,
  patience and bearing love for one another.

A reading from the Letter of Saint Paul to the Ephesians

BROTHERS and sisters: I, a prisoner for the Lord,
urge you to live in a manner worthy of the call
you have received, with all humility and gentleness,
with patience, bearing with one another through love,
striving to preserve the unity of the spirit through the
bond of peace: one body and one Spirit, as you were
also called to the one hope of your call; one Lord, one
faith, one baptism; one God and Father of all, who is
over all and through all and in all.—The word of the
Lord. ℟. **Thanks be to God.** ↓

ALLELUIA   [God's Prophet]

℟. **Alleluia, alleluia.**
A great prophet has risen in our midst.
God has visited his people.
℟. **Alleluia, alleluia.** ↓

GOSPEL Jn 6:1-15   [Multiplication of Loaves and Fish]

> Jesus told the five thousand to sit down. He took the five
> barley loaves and a couple of dried fish, gave thanks and
> told the disciples to pass out the food.

℣. The Lord be with you. ℟. **And also with you.**
✚ A reading from the holy Gospel according to John.
℟. **Glory to you, Lord.**

JESUS went across the Sea of Galilee. A large crowd
followed him, because they saw the signs he was
performing on the sick. Jesus went up on the mountain, and there he sat down with his disciples. The
Jewish feast of Passover was near. When Jesus raised
his eyes and saw that a large crowd was coming to
him, he said to Philip, "Where can we buy enough
food for them to eat?" He said this to test him, because
he himself knew what he was going to do. Philip answered him, "Two hundred days' wages worth of food
would not be enough for each of them to have a little."
One of his disciples, Andrew, the brother of Simon
Peter, said to him, "There is a boy here who has five
barley loaves and two fish; but what good are these
for so many?" Jesus said, "Have the people recline."
Now there was a great deal of grass in that place.
  So the men reclined, about five thousand in number.
Then Jesus took the loaves, gave thanks, and distributed them to those who were reclining, and also as
much of the fish as they wanted. When they had had
their fill, he said to his disciples, "Gather the fragments left over, so that nothing will be wasted." So
they collected them, and filled twelve wicker baskets

with fragments from the five barley loaves that had
been more than they could eat. When the people saw
the sign he had done, they said, "This is truly the
Prophet, the one who is to come into the world." Since
Jesus knew that they were going to come and carry
him off to make him king, he withdrew again to the
mountain alone.—The Gospel of the Lord. ℟. **Praise to
you, Lord Jesus Christ.**   → No. 14, p. 18

PRAYER OVER THE GIFTS   [Sanctifying Mysteries]

Lord,
receive these offerings
chosen from your many gifts.
May these mysteries make us holy
and lead us to eternal joy.
Grant this through Christ our Lord.
℟. **Amen.**   → No. 21, p. 22 (Pref. P 29-36)

COMMUNION ANT. Ps 103:2   [Bless the Lord]

**O bless the Lord, my soul, and remember all his kind-
ness.** ↓

OR Mt 5:7-8   [Happy the Pure of Heart]

**Happy are those who show mercy; mercy shall be
theirs. Happy are the pure of heart, for they shall see
God.** ↓

PRAYER AFTER COMMUNION   [Memorial of Christ]

Lord,
we receive the sacrament
which celebrates the memory
of the death and resurrection of Christ your Son.
May this gift bring us closer to our eternal salvation.
We ask this through Christ our Lord.
℟. **Amen.**   → No. 32, p. 70

Optional Solemn Blessings, p. 92, and Prayers Over the People, p. 99

"The bread of God . . . comes down from heaven and gives life to the world."

AUGUST 3

18TH SUNDAY IN ORDINARY TIME

ENTRANCE ANT. Ps 70:2, 6   [God's Help]
God, come to my help. Lord, quickly give me assistance. You are the one who helps me and sets me free: Lord, do not be long in coming.   → No. 2, p. 10

OPENING PRAYER   [God's Forgiveness]
Let us pray
  [for the gift of God's forgiveness and love]
Father of everlasting goodness,
our origin and guide,
be close to us
and hear the prayers of all who praise you.
Forgive our sins and restore us to life.
Keep us safe in your love.
Grant this through our Lord Jesus Christ, your Son,
who lives and reigns with you and the Holy Spirit,
one God, for ever and ever. ℟. **Amen.** ↓

ALTERNATIVE OPENING PRAYER   [God's Kindness]

Let us pray
  [to the Father whose kindness never fails]
God our Father,
gifts without measure flow from your goodness
to bring us your peace.
Our life is your gift.
Guide our life's journey,
for only your love makes us whole.
Keep us strong in your love.
We ask this through Christ our Lord. ℞. **Amen.** ↓

FIRST READING Ex 16:2-4, 12-15   [Manna from Heaven]

**The Isrealites begin to grumble, and the Lord promises to
rain down bread from heaven and give them quail to eat at
twilight. In this they will know that the Lord is God.**

A reading from the Book of Exodus

THE whole Israelite community grumbled against
Moses and Aaron. The Israelites said to them,
"Would that we had died at the LORD's hand in the
land of Egypt, as we sat by our fleshpots and ate our
fill of bread! But you had to lead us into this desert to
make the whole community die of famine!"

Then the LORD said to Moses, "I will now rain down
bread from heaven for you. Each day the people are to
go out and gather their daily portion; thus will I test
them, to see whether they follow my instructions or
not.

"I have heard the grumbling of the Israelites. Tell
them: In the evening twilight you shall eat flesh, and
in the morning you shall have your fill of bread, so
that you may know that I, the LORD, am your God."

In the evening quail came up and covered the camp.
In the morning a dew lay all about the camp, and
when the dew evaporated, there on the surface of the
desert were fine flakes like hoarfrost on the ground.

On seeing it, the Israelites asked one another, "What is this?" for they did not know what it was. But Moses told them, "This is the bread which the LORD has given you to eat."—The word of the Lord. ℟. **Thanks be to God.** ↓

RESPONSORIAL PSALM Ps 78   [Heavenly Bread]

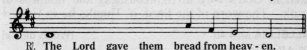

℟. The Lord gave them bread from heav - en.

What we have heard and know,
    and what our fathers have declared to us,
we will declare to the generation to come,
    the glorious deeds of the LORD and his strength
    and the wonders that he wrought.

℟. **The Lord gave them bread from heaven.**

He commanded the skies above
    and the doors of heaven he opened;
he rained manna upon them for food
    and gave them heavenly bread.

℟. **The Lord gave them bread from heaven.**

Man ate the bread of angels,
    food he sent them in abundance.
And he brought them to his holy land,
    to the mountain his right hand had won.

℟. **The Lord gave them bread from heaven.** ↓

SECOND READING Eph 4:17, 20-24   [A New Self]

Paul tells the Ephesians that they must abandon their old pagan ways and acquire a fresh, spiritual way of living—to become new people created in God's image.

A reading from the Letter of Saint Paul
to the Ephesians

BROTHERS and sisters: I declare and testify in the Lord that you must no longer live as the Gentiles do, in the futility of their minds; that is not how you learned Christ, assuming that you have heard of him and were taught in him, as truth is in Jesus, that you should put away the old self of your former way of life, corrupted through deceitful desires, and be renewed in the spirit of your minds, and put on the new self, created in God's way in righteousness and holiness of truth.—The word of the Lord. ℟. **Thanks be to God.** ↓

ALLELUIA Mt 4:4b   [Words of Life]

℟. **Alleluia, alleluia.**
One does not live on bread alone,
but on every word that comes forth from the mouth of
   God.
℟. **Alleluia, alleluia.** ↓

GOSPEL Jn 6:24-35   [Christ, True Bread from Heaven]

After feeding the multitude, Jesus and his disciples went across the lake. The people found them, and Jesus cautioned them that they were looking only for signs and food but the work of God demands faith in the One he sent.

℣. The Lord be with you. ℟. **And also with you.**
✝ A reading from the holy Gospel according to John.
℟. **Glory to you, Lord.**

WHEN the crowd saw that neither Jesus nor his disciples were there, they themselves got into boats and came to Capernaum looking for Jesus. And when they found him across the sea they said to him, "Rabbi, when did you get here?" Jesus answered them and said, "Amen, amen, I say to you, you are looking for me not because you saw signs but because you ate the loaves and were filled. Do not work for food that perishes but for the food that endures for eternal life, which the Son of Man will give you. For on him the Father, God, has set his seal." So they said to him, "What can we do to accomplish the works of God?" Jesus answered and said to them, "This is the work of

God, that you believe in the one he sent." So they said to him, "What sign can you do, that we may see and believe in you? What can you do? Our ancestors ate manna in the desert, as it is written: *He gave them bread from heaven to eat.*" So Jesus said to them, "Amen, amen, I say to you, it was not Moses who gave the bread from heaven; my Father gives you the true bread from heaven. For the bread of God is that which comes down from heaven and gives life to the world." So they said to him, "Sir, give us this bread always." Jesus said to them, "I am the bread of life; whoever comes to me will never hunger, and whoever believes in me will never thirst."—The Gospel of the Lord. ℟. **Praise to you, Lord Jesus Christ.**   → No. 14, p. 18

PRAYER OVER THE GIFTS   [Spiritual Sacrifice]

Merciful Lord,
make holy these gifts,
and let our spiritual sacrifice
make us an everlasting gift to you.
We ask this in the name of Jesus the Lord.
℟. **Amen.**   → No. 21, p. 22 (Pref. P 29-36)

COMMUNION ANT. Wis 16:20   [Bread from Heaven]

You gave us bread from heaven, Lord: a sweet-tasting bread that was very good to eat. ↓

OR Jn 6:35   [Bread of Life]

The Lord says: I am the bread of life. A man who comes to me will not go away hungry, and no one who believes in me will thirst. ↓

PRAYER AFTER COMMUNION   [Strength of New Life]

Lord,
you give us the strength of new life
by the gift of the eucharist.

Protect us with your love
and prepare us for eternal redemption.
We ask this through Christ our Lord.
℟. **Amen.**

→ No. 32, p. 70

Optional Solemn Blessings, p. 92, and Prayers Over the People, p. 99

"I am the bread of life."

AUGUST 10

19th SUNDAY IN ORDINARY TIME

ENTRANCE ANT. Ps 74:20, 19, 22, 23   [Rise Up, O God]

Lord, be true to your covenant, forget not the life of your poor ones for ever. Rise up, O God, and defend your cause; do not ignore the shouts of your enemies.

→ No. 2, p. 10

OPENING PRAYER   [Growth in God's Love]

Let us pray
  [in the Spirit
  that we may grow in the love of God]
Almighty and ever-living God,
your Spirit made us your children,
confident to call you Father.

Increase your Spirit within us
and bring us to our promised inheritance.
Grant this through our Lord Jesus Christ, your Son,
who lives and reigns with you and the Holy Spirit,
one God, for ever and ever. ℟. **Amen.** ↓

ALTERNATIVE OPENING PRAYER   [Witnesses for Christ]

Let us pray
  [that through us
   others may find the way to life in Christ]
Father,
we come, reborn in the Spirit,
to celebrate our sonship in the Lord Jesus Christ.
Touch our hearts,
help them grow toward the life you have promised.
Touch our lives,
make them signs of your love for all men.
Grant this through Christ our Lord. ℟. **Amen.** ↓

FIRST READING 1 Kgs 19:4-8   [Supernatural Food]

> Elijah, being discouraged, prayed for death. Twice an angel
> came to him and supplied him with food. Strengthened by
> food and the word of God, Elijah got up and continued his
> journey to the mountain of God, Horeb.

A reading from the first Book of Kings

ELIJAH went a day's journey into the desert, until
he came to a broom tree and sat beneath it. He
prayed for death, saying: "This is enough, O LORD!
Take my life, for I am no better than my fathers." He
lay down and fell asleep under the broom tree, but
then an angel touched him and ordered him to get up
and eat. Elijah looked and there at his head was a
hearth cake and a jug of water. After he ate and
drank, he lay down again, but the angel of the LORD
came back a second time, touched him, and ordered,
"Get up and eat, else the journey will be too long for

you!" He got up, ate, and drank; then strengthened by that food, he walked forty days and forty nights to the mountain of God, Horeb.—The word of the Lord. ℞. **Thanks be to God.** ↓

RESPONSORIAL PSALM Ps 34   [Refuge in God]

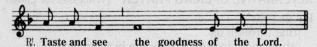

℞. **Taste and see   the goodness of   the Lord.**

I will bless the LORD at all times;
   his praise shall be ever in my mouth.
Let my soul glory in the LORD;
   the lowly will hear me and be glad.

℞. **Taste and see the goodness of the Lord.**

Glorify the LORD with me,
   let us together extol his name.
I sought the LORD, and he answered me
   and delivered me from all my fears.

℞. **Taste and see the goodness of the Lord.**

Look to him that you may be radiant with joy,
   and your faces may not blush with shame.
When the afflicted man called out, the LORD heard,
   and from all his distress he saved him.

℞. **Taste and see the goodness of the Lord.**

The angel of the LORD encamps
   around those who fear him and delivers them.
Taste and see how good the LORD is;
   blessed the man who takes refuge in him.

℞. **Taste and see the goodness of the Lord.** ↓

SECOND READING Eph 4:30—5:2 [Imitating God's Goodness]
   Paul directs the Ephesians to be kind, compassionate, and forgiving. They are to imitate God as his children and follow the way of love as Christ loved.

A reading from the Letter of Saint Paul to the Ephesians

BROTHERS and sisters: Do not grieve the Holy Spirit of God, with which you were sealed for the day of redemption. All bitterness, fury, anger, shouting, and reviling must be removed from you, along with all malice. And be kind to one another, compassionate, forgiving one another as God has forgiven you in Christ.

So be imitators of God, as beloved children, and live in love, as Christ loved us and handed himself over for us as a sacrificial offering to God for a fragrant aroma.—The word of the Lord. ℟. **Thanks be to God.** ↓

ALLELUIA Jn 6:51   [Eternal Life]

℟. **Alleluia, alleluia.**
I am the living bread that came down from heaven, says the Lord;
whoever eats this bread will live for ever.
℟. **Alleluia, alleluia.** ↓

GOSPEL Jn 6:41-51   [Jesus, the Living Bread]

The Jews question Jesus' origin, and Jesus tells them that no one can come to him unless drawn by the Father. Those who believe will have eternal life.

℣. The Lord be with you. ℟. **And also with you.**
✝ A reading from the holy Gospel according to John.
℟. **Glory to you, Lord.**

THE Jews murmured about Jesus because he said, "I am the bread that came down from heaven," and they said, "Is this not Jesus, the son of Joseph? Do we not know his father and mother? Then how can he say, 'I have come down from heaven'?" Jesus answered and said to them, "Stop murmuring among yourselves. No one can come to me unless the Father who sent me draw him, and I will raise him on the last day. It is written in the prophets: *They shall all be taught by God.* Everyone who listens to my Father and learns from him comes to me. Not that anyone has seen the Father except the one who is from God; he has seen the Father. Amen, amen, I say to you, whoever believes has eternal life. I am the bread of life. Your ancestors ate the manna in the desert, but they died; this is the bread that comes down from heaven so that one may eat it and not die. I am the living bread that came down from heaven; whoever eats this bread will live forever; and the bread that I will give is my flesh for the life of the world."—The Gospel of the Lord. ℟. **Praise to you, Lord Jesus Christ.**   ➔ No. 14, p. 18

PRAYER OVER THE GIFTS   [Sacrament of Salvation]

God of power,
giver of the gifts we bring,
accept the offering of your Church
and make it the sacrament of our salvation.
We ask this through Christ our Lord.
℟. **Amen.**   ➔ No. 21, p. 22 (Pref. P 29-36)

COMMUNION ANT. Ps 148:12-14   [Praise the Lord]
Praise the Lord, Jerusalem; he feeds you with the finest wheat. ↓

OR Jn 6:52   [The Flesh of Jesus]
The bread I shall give is my flesh for the life of the world, says the Lord. ↓

PRAYER AFTER COMMUNION   [Faithful to God's Truth]

Lord,
may the eucharist you give us
bring us to salvation
and keep us faithful to the light of your truth.
We ask this in the name of Jesus the Lord.
℟. **Amen.**   ➔ No. 32, p. 70

Optional Solemn Blessings, p. 92, and Prayers Over the People, p. 99

"Alleluia. Mary is taken up to heaven."

AUGUST 15

ASSUMPTION OF THE BLESSED VIRGIN MARY

VIGIL MASS

ENTRANCE ANT. [Mary in Glory]

All honor to you, Mary! Today you were raised above the choirs of angels to lasting glory with Christ.

➙ No. 2, p. 10

OPENING PRAYER [Mary's Help]

Let us pray
[that the Virgin Mary will help us
    with her prayers]
Almighty God,
you gave a humble virgin
the privilege of being the mother of your Son,
and crowned her with the glory of heaven.
May the prayers of the Virgin Mary
bring us to the salvation of Christ
and raise us up to eternal life.
We ask this through our Lord Jesus Christ, your Son,

481

who lives and reigns with you and the Holy Spirit,
one God, for ever and ever. ℟. **Amen.** ↓

ALTERNATIVE OPENING PRAYER   [Praying with Mary]
Let us pray
  [with Mary to the Father,
  in whose presence she now dwells]
Almighty Father of our Lord Jesus Christ,
you have revealed the beauty of your power
by exalting the lowly virgin of Nazareth
and making her the mother of our Savior.
May the prayers of this woman clothed with the sun
bring Jesus to the waiting world
and fill the void of incompletion
with the presence of her child,
who lives and reigns with you and the Holy Spirit,
one God, for ever and ever. ℟. **Amen.** ↓

FIRST READING 1 Chr 15:3-4, 15-16; 16:1-2
                                      [Procession of Glory]
  Under David's direction the Israelites brought the ark of
  the Lord to the tent prepared for it. They showed great respect for it. They offered holocausts and peace offerings.
  This becomes a figure of Mary who bore the Son of God.

  A reading from the first Book of Chronicles

D AVID assembled all Israel in Jerusalem to bring
  the ark of the LORD to the place which he had prepared for it. David also called together the sons of
Aaron and the Levites.

  The Levites bore the ark of God on their shoulders
with poles, as Moses had ordained according to the
word of the LORD.

  David commanded the chiefs of the Levites to appoint their kinsmen as chanters, to play on musical in-
struments, harps, lyres, and cymbals, to make a loud
sound of rejoicing.

They brought in the ark of God and set it within the tent which David had pitched for it. Then they offered up burnt offerings and peace offerings to God. When David had finished offering up the burnt offerings and peace offerings, he blessed the people in the name of the LORD.—The word of the Lord. ℟. **Thanks be to God.** ↓

RESPONSORIAL PSALM Ps 132   [Mary, Ark of God]

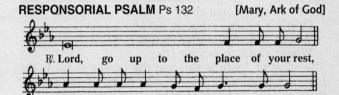

℟. Lord, go up to the place of your rest, you and the ark of your ho - li - ness.

Behold, we heard of it in Ephrathah;
  we found it in the fields of Jaar.
Let us enter into his dwelling,
  let us worship at his footstool.

℟. **Lord, go up to the place of your rest,
  you and the ark of your holiness.**

May your priests be clothed with justice;
  let your faithful ones shout merrily for joy.
For the sake of David your servant,
  reject not the plea of your anointed.

℟. **Lord, go up to the place of your rest,
  you and the ark of your holiness.**

For the LORD has chosen Zion;
  he prefers her for his dwelling.
"Zion is my resting place forever;
  in her will I dwell, for I prefer her."

℟. **Lord, go up to the place of your rest,
  you and the ark of your holiness.** ↓

SECOND READING 1 Cor 15:54b-57   [Victory Over Death]

Paul reminds the Corinthians that in life after death there is victory. Through his love for us, God has given victory over sin and death in Jesus, his Son.

A reading from the first Letter of Saint Paul
to the Corinthians

Brothers and sisters: When that which is mortal clothes itself with immortality, then the word that is written shall come about:

Death is swallowed up in victory.
Where, O death, is your victory?
Where, O death, is your sting?

The sting of death is sin, and the power of sin is the law. But thanks be to God who gives us the victory through our Lord Jesus Christ.—The word of the Lord. ℟. **Thanks be to God.** ↓

ALLELUIA Lk 11:28   [Doers of God's Word]

℟. **Alleluia, alleluia.**
Blessed are they who hear the word of God
and observe it.
℟. **Alleluia, alleluia.** ↓

GOSPEL Lk 11:27-28   [Keeping God's Word]

Mary's relationship as the mother of Jesus is unique in all of history. But Jesus reminds us that those who keep his word are most pleasing to God. In this Mary has set an example.

℣. The Lord be with you. ℟. **And also with you.**
✤ A reading from the holy Gospel according to Luke.
℟. **Glory to you, Lord.**

While Jesus was speaking, a woman from the crowd called out and said to him, "Blessed is the womb that carried you and the breasts at which you nursed." He replied, "Rather, blessed are those who hear the word of God and observe it."—The Gospel of the Lord. ℟. **Praise to you, Lord Jesus Christ.**

➜ No. 14, p. 18

PRAYER OVER THE GIFTS   [Sacrifice of Praise]

Lord,
receive this sacrifice of praise and peace
in honor of the assumption of the Mother of God.
May our offering bring us pardon
and make our lives a thanksgiving to you.
We ask this in the name of Jesus the Lord. ℟. **Amen.** ↓

PREFACE (P 59)   [Assumption—Sign of Hope]

℣. The Lord be with you. ℟. **And also with you.**
℣. Lift up your hearts. ℟. **We lift them up to the Lord.**
℣. Let us give thanks to the Lord our God. ℟. **It is right to give him thanks and praise.**

Father, all-powerful and ever-living God,
we do well always and everywhere to give you thanks
through Jesus Christ our Lord.
Today the virgin Mother of God was taken up into heaven
to be the beginning and the pattern of the Church in its perfection,
and a sign of hope and comfort for your people on their pilgrim way.
You would not allow decay to touch her body,
for she had given birth to your Son, the Lord of all life,
in the glory of the incarnation.
In our joy we sing to your glory
with all the choirs of angels: → No. 23, p. 23

COMMUNION ANT. See Lk 11:27   [Mary Carried Christ]

Blessed is the womb of the Virgin Mary; she carried the Son of the eternal Father. ↓

PRAYER AFTER COMMUNION   [Rejoice]

God of mercy,
we rejoice because Mary, the mother of our Lord,
was taken into the glory of heaven.

May the holy food we receive at this table
free us from evil.
We ask this through Christ our Lord.
℞. **Amen.**   → No. 32, p. 70

Optional Solemn Blessings, p. 92, and Prayers Over the People, p. 99

MASS DURING THE DAY

ENTRANCE ANT. Rv 12:1   [Mary's Glory]
**A great sign appeared in heaven: a woman clothed
with the sun, the moon beneath her feet, and a crown
of twelve stars on her head.**

OR   [Joy in Heaven]
**Let us rejoice in the Lord and celebrate this feast in
honor of the Virgin Mary, at whose assumption the
angels rejoice, giving praise to the Son of God.**

                                                  → No. 2, p. 10

OPENING PRAYER   [Sharing Mary's Glory]
Let us pray
  [that we will join Mary, the mother of the Lord,
  in the glory of heaven]
All-powerful and ever-living God,
you raised the sinless Virgin Mary,
Mother of your Son,
body and soul to the glory of heaven.
May we see heaven as our final goal
and come to share her glory.
We ask this through our Lord Jesus Christ, your Son,
who lives and reigns with you and the Holy Spirit,
one God, for ever and ever. ℞. **Amen.** ↓

ALTERNATIVE OPENING PRAYER   [Following Mary]
Let us pray
  [that with the help of Mary's prayers
  we too may reach our heavenly home]

Father in heaven,
all creation rightly gives you praise,
for all life and all holiness come from you.
In the plan of your wisdom
she who bore the Christ in her womb
was raised body and soul in glory to be with him in
    heaven.
May we follow her example in reflecting your holiness
and join in her hymn of endless life and praise.
We ask this through Christ our Lord. R̝. **Amen.** ↓

FIRST READING Rv 11:19a; 12:1-6a, 10ab   [Mary, the Ark]

The appearance of the Ark in this time of retribution indicates that God is now accessible—no longer hidden, but
present in the midst of his people. Filled with hatred, the
devil spares no pains to destroy Christ and his Church. The
dragon seeks to destroy the celestial woman and her Son.
Its hatred is futile.

A reading from the Book of Revelation

GOD'S temple in heaven was opened, and the ark
of his covenant could be seen in the temple.
A great sign appeared in the sky, a woman clothed
with the sun, with the moon beneath her feet, and on
her head a crown of twelve stars. She was with child
and wailed aloud in pain as she labored to give birth.
Then another sign appeared in the sky; it was a huge
red dragon, with seven heads and ten horns, and on its
heads were seven diadems. Its tail swept away a third
of the stars in the sky and hurled them down to the
earth. Then the dragon stood before the woman about
to give birth, to devour her child when she gave birth.
She gave birth to a son, a male child, destined to rule
all the nations with an iron rod. Her child was caught
up to God and his throne. The woman herself fled into
the desert where she had a place prepared by God.
Then I heard a loud voice in heaven say:
    "Now have salvation and power come,

and the kingdom of our God
and the authority of his Anointed One."
The word of the Lord. ℟. **Thanks be to God.** ↓

RESPONSORIAL PSALM Ps 45   [Mary the Queen]

℟. **The queen stands at your right hand, ar-rayed in gold.**

The queen takes her place at your right hand in gold
  of Ophir.
℟. **The queen stands at your right hand, arrayed in
  gold.**

Hear, O daughter, and see; turn your ear,
  forget your people and your father's house.
℟. **The queen stands at your right hand, arrayed in
  gold.**

So shall the king desire your beauty;
  for he is your lord.
℟. **The queen stands at your right hand, arrayed in
  gold.**

They are borne in with gladness and joy;
  they enter the palace of the king.
℟. **The queen stands at your right hand, arrayed in
  gold.** ↓

SECOND READING 1 Cor 15:20-27   [Christ the King]

**The offering of the firstfruits was the symbol of the dedica-
tion of the entire harvest to God. So the Resurrection of
Christ involves the resurrection of all who are in him. Since
his glorious Resurrection, Christ reigns in glory; he is the
Lord.**

A reading from the first Letter of Saint Paul
to the Corinthians

BROTHERS and sisters: Christ has been raised
from the dead, the firstfruits of those who have

fallen asleep. For since death came through man, the resurrection of the dead came also through man. For just as in Adam all die, so too in Christ shall all be brought to life, but each one in proper order: Christ the firstfruits; then, at his coming, those who belong to Christ; then comes the end, when he hands over the kingdom to his God and Father, when he has destroyed every sovereignty and every authority and power. For he must reign until he has put all his enemies under his feet. The last enemy to be destroyed is death, for "he subjected everything under his feet."— The word of the Lord. ℟. **Thanks be to God.** ↓

ALLELUIA   [Mary in Heaven]

℟. **Alleluia, alleluia.**
Mary is taken up to heaven;
a chorus of angels exults.
℟. **Alleluia, alleluia.** ↓

GOSPEL Lk 1:39-56   [Blessed among Women]

Mary visits her kinswoman, Elizabeth. Mary's song of thanksgiving, often called the "Magnificat," has been put together from many Old Testament phrases.

℣. The Lord be with you. ℟. **And also with you.**
✠ A reading from the holy Gospel according to Luke.
℟. **Glory to you, Lord.**

MARY set out and traveled to the hill country in haste to a town of Judah, where she entered the house of Zechariah and greeted Elizabeth. When Elizabeth heard Mary's greeting, the infant leaped in her womb, and Elizabeth, filled with the Holy Spirit, cried out in a loud voice and said, "Blessed are you among women, and blessed is the fruit of your womb. And how does this happen to me, that the mother of my Lord should come to me? For at the moment the sound of your greeting reached my ears, the infant in my womb leaped for joy. Blessed are you who believed that what was spoken to you by the Lord would be fulfilled."

And Mary said:

"My soul proclaims the greatness of the Lord;
    my spirit rejoices in God my Savior
    for he has looked upon his lowly servant.
From this day all generations will call me blessed:
    the Almighty has done great things for me,
    and holy is his Name.
He has mercy on those who fear him
    in every generation.
He has shown the strength of his arm,
    and has scattered the proud in their conceit.
He has cast down the mighty from their thrones,
    and has lifted up the lowly.
He has filled the hungry with good things,
    and the rich he has sent away empty.
He has come to the help of his servant Israel
    for he has remembered his promise of mercy,
    the promise he made to our fathers,
    to Abraham and his children for ever."

Mary remained with her about three months and then returned to her home.—The Gospel of the Lord.
℟. **Praise to you, Lord Jesus Christ.**   → No. 14, p. 18

PRAYER OVER THE GIFTS   [Living in God's Love]

Lord,
receive this offering of our service.
You raised the Virgin Mary to the glory of heaven.
By her prayers, help us to seek you
and to live in your love.
Grant this through Christ our Lord.
℟. **Amen.**   → Pref. (P 59), p. 485

COMMUNION ANT. Lk 1:48-49   [Mary Aided by Grace]
All generations will call me blessed, for the Almighty has done great things for me. ↓

PRAYER AFTER COMMUNION   [Mary's Intercession]

Lord,
may we who receive this sacrament of salvation
be led to the glory of heaven
by the prayers of the Virgin Mary.
We ask this in the name of Jesus the Lord.
℟. **Amen.**   ➜ No. 32, p. 70

Optional Solemn Blessings, p. 92, and Prayers Over the People, p. 99

"The bread that I will give is my flesh for the life of the world."

AUGUST 17

20th SUNDAY IN ORDINARY TIME

ENTRANCE ANT. Ps 84:10-11   [God Our Strength]

God, our protector, keep us in mind; always give
strength to your people. For if we can be with you
even one day, it is better than a thousand without
you.   ➜ No. 2, p. 10

OPENING PRAYER   [Joy beyond Imagining]

Let us pray
[that the love of God
may raise us beyond what we see
to the unseen glory of his kingdom]

God our Father,
may we love you in all things and above all things
and reach the joy you have prepared for us
beyond all our imagining.
We ask this through our Lord Jesus Christ, your Son,
who lives and reigns with you and the Holy Spirit,
one God, for ever and ever. ℟. **Amen.** ↓

ALTERNATIVE OPENING PRAYER [Avoiding Prejudice]

Let us pray
  [with humility and persistence]
Almighty God, ever-loving Father,
your care extends beyond the boundaries of race and
  nation
to the hearts of all who live.
May the walls, which prejudice raises between us,
crumble beneath the shadow of your outstretched
  arm.
We ask this through Christ our Lord. ℟. **Amen.** ↓

FIRST READING Prv 9:1-6 [Divine Food and Drink]

**Proverbs directing attention to young men who were to
take their places in the royal court speak of food and drink.
A diet of wisdom, however, will lead to prudent living, religious wisdom, long vision and moderation.**

A reading from the Book of Proverbs

WISDOM has built her house,
    she has set up her seven columns;
she has dressed her meat, mixed her wine,
    yes, she has spread her table.
She has sent out her maidens; she calls
    from the heights out over the city:
"Let whoever is simple turn in here;
    to the one who lacks understanding, she says,
Come, eat of my food,
    and drink of the wine I have mixed!

Forsake foolishness that you may live;
  advance in the way of understanding."
The word of the Lord. ℟. **Thanks be to God.** ↓

RESPONSORIAL PSALM Ps 34 [Taste the Lord's Goodness]

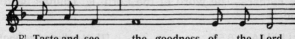

℟. **Taste and see   the goodness of   the Lord.**

I will bless the LORD at all times;
  his praise shall be ever in my mouth.
Let my soul glory in the LORD;
  the lowly will hear me and be glad.

℟. **Taste and see the goodness of the Lord.**

Glorify the LORD with me,
  let us together extol his name.
I sought the LORD, and he answered me
  and delivered me from all my fears.

℟. **Taste and see the goodness of the Lord.**

Look to him that you may be radiant with joy,
  and your faces may not blush with shame.
When the poor one called out, the LORD heard,
  and from all his distress he saved him.

℟. **Taste and see the goodness of the Lord.** ↓

SECOND READING Eph 5:15-20   [Discern God's Will]

Christians should be careful to live according to the will of the Lord. They should avoid carefree living and give praise and worship to God in the name of Jesus.

A reading from the Letter of Saint Paul to the Ephesians

BROTHERS and sisters: Watch carefully how you live, not as foolish persons but as wise, making the most of the opportunity, because the days are evil. Therefore, do not continue in ignorance, but try to understand what is the will of the Lord. And do not get drunk on wine, in which lies debauchery, but be filled with the Spirit, addressing one another in psalms and hymns and spiritual songs, singing and playing to the Lord in your hearts, giving thanks always and for everything in the name of our Lord Jesus Christ to God the Father.—The word of the Lord. ℟. **Thanks be to God.** ↓

ALLELUIA Jn 6:56   [The Lord's Indwelling]

℟. **Alleluia, alleluia.**
Whoever eats my flesh and drinks my blood
remains in me and I in him, says the Lord.
℟. **Alleluia, alleluia.** ↓

GOSPEL Jn 6:51-58   [Need for Communion]

Jesus proclaims that he is the living bread from heaven. Whoever eats of it shall live forever. When the Jews quarreled about this teaching, Jesus repeated it without any qualification.

℣. The Lord be with you. ℟. **And also with you.**
✢ A reading from the holy Gospel according to John.
℟. **Glory to you, Lord.**

JESUS said to the crowds: "I am the living bread that came down from heaven; whoever eats this bread will live forever; and the bread that I will give is my flesh for the life of the world."

The Jews quarreled among themselves, saying, "How can this man give us his flesh to eat?" Jesus said to them, "Amen, amen, I say to you, unless you eat the flesh of the Son of Man and drink his blood, you do not have life within you. Whoever eats my flesh and drinks my blood has eternal life, and I will raise him on the last day. For my flesh is true food, and my blood is true drink. Whoever eats my flesh and drinks my blood remains in me and I in him. Just as the living Father sent me and I have life because of the Father, so also the one who feeds on me will have life

because of me. This is the bread that came down from
heaven. Unlike your ancestors who ate and still died,
whoever eats this bread will live forever."—The
Gospel of the Lord. ℟. **Praise to you, Lord Jesus
Christ.**   → No. 14, p. 18

PRAYER OVER THE GIFTS   [Holy Exchange]

Lord,
accept our sacrifice
as a holy exchange of gifts.
By offering what you have given us
may we receive the gift of yourself.
We ask this in the name of Jesus the Lord.
℟. **Amen.**   → No. 21, p. 22 (Pref. P 29-36)

COMMUNION ANT. Ps 130:7   [Fullness of Redemption]

**With the Lord there is mercy, and fullness of redemp-
tion.** ↓

OR Jn 6:51-52   [Eternal Life]

**I am the living bread from heaven, says the Lord; if
anyone eats this bread he will live for ever.** ↓

PRAYER AFTER COMMUNION   [One with Christ]

God of mercy,
by this sacrament you make us one with Christ.
By becoming more like him on earth,
may we come to share his glory in heaven,
where he lives and reigns for ever and ever.
℟. **Amen.**   → No. 32, p. 70

Optional Solemn Blessings, p. 92, and Prayers Over the People, p. 99

"No one can come to me unless it is granted him by my Father."

AUGUST 24

21st SUNDAY IN ORDINARY TIME

ENTRANCE ANT. Ps 86:1-3   [Save Us]

Listen, Lord, and answer me. Save your servant who trusts in you. I call to you all day long; have mercy on me, O Lord. → No. 2, p. 10

OPENING PRAYER   [One in Mind and Heart]

Let us pray
  [that God will make us one in mind and heart]
Father,
help us to seek the values
that will bring us lasting joy in this changing world.
In our desire for what you promise
make us one in mind and heart.
Grant this through our Lord Jesus Christ, your Son,
who lives and reigns with you and the Holy Spirit,
one God, for ever and ever. ℟. **Amen.** ↓

ALTERNATIVE OPENING PRAYER   [Minds on God]

Let us pray
  [with minds fixed on eternal truth]

Lord our God,
all truth is from you,
and you alone bring oneness of heart.
Give your people the joy
of hearing your word in every sound
and of longing for your presence more than for life it-
    self.
May all the attractions of a changing world
serve only to bring us
the peace of your kingdom which this world does not
    give.
Grant this through Christ our Lord. ℞. **Amen.** ↓

FIRST READING Jos 24:1-2a, 15-17, 18b   [Serving the Lord]

Joshua admonished the Israelites to decide their allegiance
to God. They answered that they would serve the God of
their fathers who delivered them from slavery and protected them.

A reading from the Book of Joshua

JOSHUA gathered together all the tribes of Israel at
Shechem, summoning their elders, their leaders,
their judges, and their officers. When they stood in
ranks before God, Joshua addressed all the people: "If
it does not please you to serve the LORD, decide today
whom you will serve, the gods your fathers served beyond the River or the gods of the Amorites in whose
country you are dwelling. As for me and my household, we will serve the LORD."

But the people answered, "Far be it from us to forsake the LORD for the service of other gods. For it was
the LORD, our God, who brought us and our fathers up
out of the land of Egypt, out of a state of slavery. He
performed those great miracles before our very eyes
and protected us along our entire journey and among
all the peoples through whom we passed. Therefore
we also will serve the LORD, for he is our God."—The
word of the Lord. ℞. **Thanks be to God.** ↓

RESPONSORIAL PSALM Ps 34   [Refuge in God]

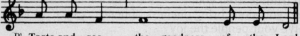

℞. Taste and see   the goodness   of   the Lord.

I will bless the LORD at all times;
  his praise shall be ever in my mouth.
Let my soul glory in the LORD;
  the lowly will hear me and be glad.

℞. **Taste and see the goodness of the Lord.**

The LORD has eyes for the just,
  and ears for their cry.
The LORD confronts the evildoers,
  to destroy remembrance of them from the earth.

℞. **Taste and see the goodness of the Lord.**

When the just cry out, the LORD hears them,
  and from all their distress he rescues them.
The LORD is close to the brokenhearted;
  and those who are crushed in spirit he saves.

℞. **Taste and see the goodness of the Lord.**

Many are the troubles of the just one,
  but out of them all the LORD delivers him;
he watches over all his bones;
  not one of them shall be broken.

℞. **Taste and see the goodness of the Lord.** ↓

SECOND READING Eph 5:21-32 or 5:2a, 25-32

[Sacrament of Marriage]

Paul gives specific directives to wives and husbands. Wives are to be submissive to their husbands as the Church submits to Christ. Husbands must love their wives as their own bodies. They are to be ever faithful to each other.

[If the "Shorter Form" is used, omit indented text in brackets.]

A reading from the Letter of Saint Paul to the Ephesians

Brothers and sisters:
    [Be subordinate to one another out of reverence

for Christ. Wives should be subordinate to their husbands as to the Lord. For the husband is head of his wife just as Christ is head of the church, he himself the savior of the body. As the church is subordinate to Christ, so wives should be subordinate to their husbands in everything.]

Live in love, as Christ loved us.* Husbands, love your wives, even as Christ loved the church and handed himself over for her to sanctify her, cleansing her by the bath of water with the word, that he might present to himself the church in splendor, without spot or wrinkle or any such thing, that she might be holy and without blemish. So also husbands should love their wives as their own bodies. He who loves his wife loves himself. For no one hates his own flesh but rather nourishes and cherishes it, even as Christ does the church, because we are members of his body.

For this reason a man shall leave his father and his mother
    and be joined to his wife,
  and the two shall become one flesh.

This is a great mystery, but I speak in reference to Christ and the church.—The word of the Lord. ℟.
Thanks be to God. ↓

ALLELUIA Jn 6:63c, 68c   [Living Words]

℟.. **Alleluia, alleluia.**
Your words, Lord, are Spirit and life;
you have the words of everlasting life.
℟.. **Alleluia, alleluia.** ↓

GOSPEL Jn 6:60-69   [Words of Life]

  Jesus emphasizes that to believe in him demands faith—a gift from his Father. Many left Jesus, but his Twelve turned and said, "Lord, to whom shall we go? You alone have the words of eternal life."

*The words "Live . . . us" are said only in the Shorter Form.

℣. The Lord be with you. ℟. **And also with you.**
✠ A reading from the holy Gospel according to John.
℟. **Glory to you, Lord.**

MANY of Jesus' disciples who were listening said, "This saying is hard; who can accept it?" Since Jesus knew that his disciples were murmuring about this, he said to them, "Does this shock you? What if you were to see the Son of Man ascending to where he was before? It is the spirit that gives life, while the flesh is of no avail. The words I have spoken to you are Spirit and life. But there are some of you who do not believe." Jesus knew from the beginning the ones who would not believe and the one who would betray him. And he said, "For this reason I have told you that no one can come to me unless it is granted him by my Father."

As a result of this, many of his disciples returned to their former way of life and no longer accompanied him. Jesus then said to the Twelve, "Do you also want to leave?" Simon Peter answered him, "Master, to whom shall we go? You have the words of eternal life. We have come to believe and are convinced that you are the Holy One of God."—The Gospel of the Lord. ℟.
Praise to you, Lord Jesus Christ.   → No. 14, p. 18

PRAYER OVER THE GIFTS   [Peace and Unity]

Merciful God,
the perfect sacrifice of Jesus Christ
made us your people.
In your love,
grant peace and unity to your Church.
We ask this through Christ our Lord.
℟. **Amen.**   → No. 21, p. 22 (Pref. P 29-36)

COMMUNION ANT. Ps 104:13-15   [Sacred Bread and Wine]

Lord, the earth is filled with your gift from heaven; man grows bread from earth, and wine to cheer his heart. ↓

OR Jn 6:55   [Eternal Life]

**The Lord says: The man who eats my flesh and drinks
my blood will live for ever; I shall raise him to life on
the last day.** ↓

PRAYER AFTER COMMUNION   [Pleasing God]

Lord,
may this eucharist increase within us
the healing power of your love.
May it guide and direct our efforts
to please you in all things.
We ask this in the name of Jesus the Lord.
℟. **Amen.**   ➔ No. 32, p. 70

Optional Solemn Blessings, p. 92, and Prayers Over the People, p. 99

"Nothing that enters one from outside can defile that person."

AUGUST 31

22nd SUNDAY IN ORDINARY TIME

ENTRANCE ANT. Ps 86:3, 5   [Call Upon God]

**I call to you all day long, have mercy on me, O Lord.
You are good and forgiving, full of love for all who
call to you.**   ➔ No. 2, p. 10

OPENING PRAYER   [Increasing Our Spiritual Gifts]

Let us pray
  [that God will increase our faith
  and bring to perfection the gifts he has given us]
Almighty God,
every good thing comes from you.
Fill our hearts with love for you,
increase our faith,
and by your constant care
protect the good you have given us.
We ask this through our Lord Jesus Christ, your Son,
who lives and reigns with you and the Holy Spirit,
one God, for ever and ever. ℟. **Amen.** ↓

ALTERNATIVE OPENING PRAYER [Desire To Please God]

Let us pray
  [to God who forgives all who call upon him]
Lord God of power and might,
nothing is good which is against your will,
and all is of value which comes from your hand.
Place in our hearts a desire to please you
and fill our minds with insight into love,
so that every thought may grow in wisdom
and all our efforts may be filled with your peace.
We ask this through Christ our Lord. ℟. **Amen.** ↓

FIRST READING Dt 4:1-2, 6-8   [Observing God's Law]

Moses warns the people that they are not to add or subtract from the statutes and decrees of the Lord. God is
looking after them directly.

A reading from the Book of Deuteronomy

MOSES said to the people: "Now, Israel, hear the
statutes and decrees which I am teaching you to
observe, that you may live, and may enter in and take
possession of the land which the LORD, the God of
your fathers, is giving you. In your observance of the

commandments of the LORD, your God, which I enjoin upon you, you shall not add to what I command you nor subtract from it. Observe them carefully, for thus will you give evidence of your wisdom and intelligence to the nations, who will hear of all these statutes and say, 'This great nation is truly a wise and intelligent people.' For what great nation is there that has gods so close to it as the LORD, our God, is to us whenever we call upon him? Or what great nation has statutes and decrees that are as just as this whole law which I am setting before you today?"—The word of the Lord. ℟. **Thanks be to God.** ↓

RESPONSORIAL PSALM Ps 15   [Practicing Justice]

℟. The one who does jus - tice will live in the presence of the Lord.

Whoever walks blamelessly and does justice;
  who thinks the truth in his heart
  and slanders not with his tongue.

℟. **The one who does justice will live in the presence of the Lord.**

Who harms not his fellow man,
  nor takes up a reproach against his neighbor;
by whom the reprobate is despised,
  while he honors those who fear the LORD.

℟. **The one who does justice will live in the presence of the Lord.**

Who lends not his money at usury
  and accepts no bribe against the innocent.
Whoever does these things
  shall never be disturbed.

℟. **The one who does justice will live in the presence of the Lord.** ↓

SECOND READING Jas 1:17-18, 21b-22, 27

[Act on God's Word]

Everything worthwhile comes from God. Christians should welcome God's word, listen and act upon it.

A reading from the Letter of Saint James

DEAREST brothers and sisters: All good giving and every perfect gift is from above, coming down from the Father of lights, with whom there is no alteration or shadow caused by change. He willed to give us birth by the word of truth that we may be a kind of firstfruits of his creatures.

Humbly welcome the word that has been planted in you and is able to save your souls.

Be doers of the word and not hearers only, deluding yourselves.

Religion that is pure and undefiled before God and the Father is this: to care for orphans and widows in their affliction and to keep oneself unstained by the world.—The word of the Lord. ℟. **Thanks be to God.** ↓

ALLELUIA Jas 1:18   **[Firstfruits]**

℟. **Alleluia, alleluia.**
The Father willed to give us birth by the word of truth, that we may be a kind of firstfruits of his creatures.
℟. **Alleluia, alleluia.** ↓

GOSPEL Mk 7:1-8, 14-15, 21-23   **[Sin Comes from the Heart]**

Jesus condemned lip service. It is wicked thoughts from the heart that really make a person impure.

℣. The Lord be with you. ℟. **And also with you.**
✛ A reading from the holy Gospel according to Mark.
℟. **Glory to you, Lord.**

WHEN the Pharisees with some scribes who had come from Jerusalem gathered around Jesus, they observed that some of his disciples ate their meals with unclean, that is, unwashed, hands.—For the Pharisees and, in fact, all Jews, do not eat without carefully washing their hands, keeping the tradition of the elders. And on coming from the marketplace they do not eat without purifying themselves. And there are many other things that they have traditionally observed, the purification of cups and jugs and kettles and beds.—So the Pharisees and scribes questioned him, "Why do your disciples not follow the tradition of the elders but instead eat a meal with unclean hands?" He responded, "Well did Isaiah prophesy about you hypocrites, as it is written:

This people honors me with their lips,
    but their hearts are far from me;
in vain do they worship me,
    teaching as doctrines human precepts.

You disregard God's commandment but cling to human tradition." He summoned the crowd again and said to them, "Hear me, all of you, and understand. Nothing that enters one from outside can defile that person; but the things that come out from within are what defile.

"From within people, from their hearts, come evil thoughts, unchastity, theft, murder, adultery, greed, malice, deceit, licentiousness, envy, blasphemy, arrogance, folly. All these evils come from within and they defile."—The Gospel of the Lord. ℟. **Praise to you, Lord Jesus Christ.**   ➜ No. 14, p. 18

PRAYER OVER THE GIFTS   [Promise of Salvation]

Lord,
may this holy offering
bring us your blessing
and accomplish within us
its promise of salvation.
Grant this through Christ our Lord.
℟. **Amen.**   ➜ No. 21, p. 22 (Pref. P 29-36)

COMMUNION ANT. Ps 31:20   [God's Kindness]

O Lord, how great is the depth of the kindness which you have shown to those who love you. ↓

OR Mt 5:9-10   [Happy the Peacemakers]

Happy are the peacemakers; they shall be called sons of God. Happy are they who suffer persecution for justice' sake; the kingdom of heaven is theirs. ↓

PRAYER AFTER COMMUNION   [Serving God in Others]

Lord,
you renew us at your table with the bread of life.
May this food strengthen us in love
and help us to serve you in each other.
We ask this in the name of Jesus the Lord.
℟. **Amen.**   → No. 32, p. 70

Optional Solemn Blessings, p. 92, and Prayers Over the People, p. 99

" 'Ephphatha!'—that is, 'Be opened!' "

SEPTEMBER 7

23rd SUNDAY IN ORDINARY TIME

ENTRANCE ANT. Ps 119:137, 124   [Plea for Mercy]

Lord, you are just, and the judgments you make are right. Show mercy when you judge me, your servant.
→ No. 2, p. 10

OPENING PRAYER   [Christian Freedom]

Let us pray
   [that we may realize the freedom God has given us
   in making us his sons and daughters]
God our Father,
you redeem us
and make us your children in Christ.
Look upon us,
give us true freedom
and bring us to the inheritance you promised.
Grant this through our Lord Jesus Christ, your Son,
who lives and reigns with you and the Holy Spirit,
one God, for ever and ever. ℟. **Amen.** ↓

ALTERNATIVE OPENING PRAYER   [Appreciation of Life]

Let us pray
   [to our just and merciful God]
Lord our God,
in you justice and mercy meet.
With unparalleled love you have saved us from death
and drawn us into the circle of your life.
Open our eyes to the wonders this life sets before us,
that we may serve you free from fear
and address you as God our Father.
We ask this through Christ our Lord. ℟. **Amen.** ↓

FIRST READING Is 35:4-7a   [The Messiah's Coming]

**Isaiah speaks of the Messiah's coming. At that time God will
come to save his people and bring many blessings to them.**

A reading from the Book of the Prophet Isaiah

THUS says the LORD:
   Say to those whose hearts are frightened:
      Be strong, fear not!
Here is your God,
   he comes with vindication;
with divine recompense
   he comes to save you.

Then will the eyes of the blind be opened,
  the ears of the deaf be cleared;
then will the lame leap like a stag,
  then the tongue of the dumb will sing.
Streams will burst forth in the desert,
  and rivers in the steppe.
The burning sands will become pools,
  and the thirsting ground, springs of water.
The word of the Lord. ℟. **Thanks be to God.** ↓

RESPONSORIAL PSALM Ps 146 [The Lord's Saving Deeds]

℟. **Praise the Lord, my soul!**
℟. Or: **Alleluia.**

The God of Jacob keeps faith forever,
  secures justice for the oppressed,
  gives food to the hungry.
The LORD sets captives free.

℟. **Praise the Lord, my soul!**

℟. Or: **Alleluia.**

The LORD gives sight to the blind;
  the LORD raises up those that were bowed down.
The LORD loves the just;
  the LORD protects strangers.

℟. **Praise the Lord, my soul!**

℟. Or: **Alleluia.**

The fatherless and the widow the LORD sustains,
  but the way of the wicked he thwarts.
The LORD shall reign forever;
  your God, O Zion, through all generations. Alleluia.

℟. **Praise the Lord, my soul!** ↓

℟. Or: **Alleluia.** ↓

SECOND READING Jas 2:1-5   [No Favoritism with God]

James warns the Christians about showing favoritism to
the rich. No one is in a position to judge. God chose those
who were poor according to worldly standards to become
rich in faith.

A reading from the Letter of James

MY brothers and sisters, show no partiality as you
adhere to the faith in our glorious Lord Jesus
Christ. For if a man with gold rings and fine clothes
comes into your assembly, and a poor person in
shabby clothes also comes in, and you pay attention to
the one wearing the fine clothes and say, "Sit here,
please," while you say to the poor one, "Stand there,"
or "Sit at my feet," have you not made distinctions
among yourselves and become judges with evil de-
signs?

Listen, my beloved brothers and sisters. Did not
God choose those who are poor in the world to be rich
in faith and heirs of the kingdom that he promised to
those who love him?—The word of the Lord. ℟.
Thanks be to God. ↓

ALLELUIA Cf. Mt 4:23   [The Healer]

℟. **Alleluia, alleluia.**
Jesus proclaimed the Gospel of the kingdom
and cured every disease among the people.
℟. **Alleluia, alleluia.** ↓

GOSPEL Mk 7:31-37   [Cure of a Deaf-Mute]

The people brought to Jesus a deaf and dumb man to be
cured. Taking him aside, Jesus cured him, asking him to
keep this a secret. But the man proclaimed the cure all the
more. The people were amazed at this power.

℣. The Lord be with you. ℟. **And also with you.**
✝ A reading from the holy Gospel according to Mark.
℟. **Glory to you, Lord.**

Again Jesus left the district of Tyre and went by way of Sidon to the Sea of Galilee, into the district of the Decapolis. And people brought to him a deaf man who had a speech impediment and begged him to lay his hand on him. He took him off by himself away from the crowd. He put his finger into the man's ears and, spitting, touched his tongue; then he looked up to heaven and groaned, and said to him, *"Ephphatha!"*—that is, "Be opened!"—And immediately the man's ears were opened, his speech impediment was removed, and he spoke plainly. He ordered them not to tell anyone. But the more he ordered them not to, the more they proclaimed it. They were exceedingly astonished and they said, "He has done all things well. He makes the deaf hear and the mute speak."—The Gospel of the Lord. ℟. **Praise to you, Lord Jesus Christ.**   → No. 14, p. 18

PRAYER OVER THE GIFTS   [True Worship]

God of peace and love,
may our offering bring you true worship
and make us one with you.
Grant this through Christ our Lord.
℟. **Amen.**   → No. 21, p. 22 (Pref. P 29-36)

COMMUNION ANT. Ps 42:2-3   [Longing for God]

Like a deer that longs for running streams, my soul longs for you, my God. My soul is thirsting for the living God. ↓

OR Jn 8:12   [The Light of Life]

I am the light of the world, says the Lord; the man who follows me will have the light of life. ↓

PRAYER AFTER COMMUNION   [Word and Sacrament]

Lord,
your word and your sacrament
give us food and life.

May this gift of your Son
lead us to share his life for ever.
We ask this through Christ our Lord.
℟. **Amen.**   → No. 32, p. 70

Optional Solemn Blessings, p. 92, and Prayers Over the People, p. 99

"God so loved the world that he gave his only Son."

SEPTEMBER 14

TRIUMPH OF THE CROSS
(24th SUNDAY IN ORDINARY TIME)

ENTRANCE ANT. See Gal 6:14   [Glory in the Cross]
**We should glory in the cross of our Lord Jesus Christ,
for he is our salvation, our life and our resurrection;
through him we are saved and made free.**

                                                → No. 2, p. 10

OPENING PRAYER   [Gift of Redemption]

Let us pray
    [that the death of Christ on the cross
    will bring us to the glory of the resurrection]
God our Father,
in obedience to you

your only Son accepted death on the cross
for the salvation of mankind.
We acknowledge the mystery of the cross on earth.
May we receive the gift of redemption in heaven.
We ask this through our Lord Jesus Christ, your Son,
who lives and reigns with you and the Holy Spirit,
one God, for ever and ever. ℟. **Amen.** ↓

FIRST READING   Nm 21:4b-9   [The Bronze Serpent]

**The bronze serpent raised on high is a healing force for all
the afflicted who look upon it.**

A reading from the Book of Numbers

WITH their patience worn out by the journey, the
people complained against God and Moses,
"Why have you brought us up from Egypt to die in
this desert, where there is no food or water? We are
disgusted with this wretched food!"

In punishment the LORD sent among the people
saraph serpents, which bit the people so that many of
them died. Then the people came to Moses and said,
"We have sinned in complaining against the LORD and
you. Pray the LORD to take the serpents from us." So
Moses prayed for the people, and the LORD said to
Moses, "Make a saraph and mount it on a pole, and if
any who have been bitten look at it, they will live."
Moses accordingly made a bronze serpent and mounted
it on a pole, and whenever anyone who had been bitten
by a serpent looked at the bronze serpent, he lived.—
The word of the Lord. ℟. **Thanks be to God.** ↓

RESPONSORIAL PSALM   Ps 78   [Remember God's Works]

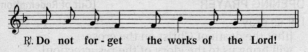

℟. Do not for-get the works of the Lord!

Hearken, my people, to my teaching;
    incline your ears to the words of my mouth.

I will open my mouth in a parable,
　I will utter mysteries from of old.

℟. **Do not forget the works of the Lord!**

While he slew them they sought him
　and inquired after God again,
remembering that God was their rock
　and the Most High God, their redeemer.

℟. **Do not forget the works of the Lord!**

But they flattered him with their mouths
　and lied to him with their tongues,
though their hearts were not steadfast toward him,
　nor were they faithful to his covenant.

℟. **Do not forget the works of the Lord!**

Yet he, being merciful, forgave their sin
　and destroyed them not;
often he turned back his anger
　and let none of his wrath be roused.

℟. **Do not forget the works of the Lord!** ↓

SECOND READING　Phil 2:6-11　　[Christ Humbled Himself]

　Jesus' death on the cross began his rise to exaltation: Jesus
　Christ is Lord!

A reading from the letter of Saint Paul to the Philippians

B ROTHERS and sisters:
　Christ Jesus, though he was in the form of God,
　　did not regard equality with God
　　something to be grasped.
　Rather, he emptied himself,
　　taking the form of a slave,
　　coming in human likeness;
　　and found human in appearance,
　　he humbled himself,
　　becoming obedient to the point of death,
　　even death on a cross.

Because of this, God greatly exalted him
   and bestowed on him the name
   which is above every name,
   that at the name of Jesus
   every knee should bend,
   of those in heaven and on earth and under the
      earth,
   and every tongue confess that
   Jesus Christ is Lord,
   to the glory of God the Father.
The word of the Lord. ℟. **Thanks be to God.** ↓

ALLELUIA   [Power of the Cross]
℟. **Alleluia, alleluia.**
We adore you, O Christ, and we bless you,
because by your Cross you have redeemed the world.
℟. **Alleluia, alleluia.** ↓

GOSPEL Jn 3:13-17   [Lifted Up on the Cross]
**Moses' lifting up the serpent in the desert had the salutary
effect of healing. The lifting up of the Son of Man on the
cross had the saving effect of redemption.**

℣. The Lord be with you. ℟. **And also with you.**
✝ A reading from the holy Gospel according to John.
℟. **Glory to you, Lord.**

JESUS said to Nicodemus: "No one has gone up to
heaven except the one who has come down from
heaven, the Son of Man. And just as Moses lifted up
the serpent in the desert, so must the Son of Man be
lifted up, so that everyone who believes in him may
have eternal life."

For God so loved the world that he gave his only
Son, so that he who believes in him might not perish
but might have eternal life. For God did not send his
Son into the world to condemn the world, but that the
world might be saved through him.—The Gospel of

the Lord. ℟. **Praise to you, Lord Jesus Christ.**

➜ No. 14, p. 18

PRAYER OVER THE GIFTS   [Forgiveness]

Lord,
may this sacrifice once offered on the cross
to take away the sins of the world
now free us from our sins.
We ask this through Christ our Lord.
℟. **Amen.** ↓

PREFACE (P 46)   [Saved through the Cross]

℣. The Lord be with you. ℟. **And also with you.**
℣. Lift up your hearts. ℟. **We lift them up to the Lord.**
℣. Let us give thanks to the Lord our God. ℟. **It is right
to give him thanks and praise.**

Father, all-powerful and ever-living God,
we do well always and everywhere to give you thanks.
You decreed that man should be saved through the
    wood of the cross.
The tree of man's defeat became his tree of victory;
where life was lost, there life has been restored
through Christ our Lord.
Through him the choirs of angels
and all the powers of heaven
praise and worship your glory.
May our voices blend with theirs
as we join in their unending hymn: ➜ No. 23, p. 23

COMMUNION ANT. Jn 12:32   [Union with Christ]

**When I am lifted up from the earth, I will draw all
men to myself, says the Lord.** ↓

PRAYER AFTER COMMUNION   [Holy Bread of Life]

Lord Jesus Christ,
you are the holy bread of life.
Bring to the glory of the resurrection

the people you have redeemed by the wood of the
   cross.
We ask this through Christ our Lord.
℟. **Amen.**   ➜ No. 32, p. 70

Optional Solemn Blessings, p. 92, and Prayers Over the People, p. 99

*"Whoever receives one child such as this in my name,
receives me."*

SEPTEMBER 21

25th SUNDAY IN ORDINARY TIME

ENTRANCE ANT.   [Savior of All]
**I am the Savior of all people, says the Lord. Whatever
their troubles, I will answer their cry, and I will always be their Lord.**   ➜ No. 2, p. 10

OPENING PRAYER   [Growth in Love]
Let us pray
   [that we will grow in the love of God
   and of one another]
Father,
guide us, as you guide creation

according to your law of love.
May we love one another
and come to perfection
in the eternal life prepared for us.
Grant this through our Lord Jesus Christ, your Son,
who lives and reigns with you and the Holy Spirit,
one God, for ever and ever. ℟. **Amen.** ↓

ALTERNATIVE OPENING PRAYER   [Mutual Love]

Let us pray
  [to the Lord who is a God of love to all peoples]
Father in heaven,
the perfection of justice is found in your love
and all mankind is in need of your law.
Help us to find this love in each other
that justice may be attained
through obedience to your law.
We ask this through Christ our Lord. ℟. **Amen.** ↓

FIRST READING Wis 2:12, 17-20   [The Just Are Persecuted]

**The wicked detest the just one because the person of God
disturbs their conscience. They are anxious to do away
with the good, saying that God will care for them if they
are really his.**

A reading from the Book of Wisdom

THE wicked say:
  Let us beset the just one, because he is obnoxious
    to us;
  he sets himself against our doings,
reproaches us for transgressions of the law
  and charges us with violations of our training.
Let us see whether his words be true;
  let us find out what will happen to him.
For if the just one be the son of God, God will defend
    him
  and deliver him from the hand of his foes.

With revilement and torture let us put the just one to
    the test
  that we may have proof of his gentleness
  and try his patience.
Let us condemn him to a shameful death;
  for according to his own words, God will take care
    of him.
The word of the Lord. ℟. **Thanks be to God.** ↓

RESPONSORIAL PSALM Ps 54   [God Our Helper]

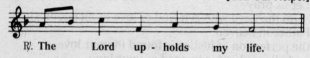

℟. **The   Lord   up - holds   my   life.**

O God, by your name save me,
  and by your might defend my cause.
O God, hear my prayer;
  hearken to the words of my mouth.

℟. **The Lord upholds my life.**

For the haughty have risen up against me,
  the ruthless seek my life;
  they set not God before their eyes.

℟. **The Lord upholds my life.**

Behold, God is my helper;
  the Lord sustains my life.
Freely will I offer you sacrifice;
  I will praise your name, O LORD, for its goodness.

℟. **The Lord upholds my life.** ↓

SECOND READING Jas 3:16—4:3   [Avoiding Conflicts]
  **Wisdom begets innocence. It is peace-loving, kind, docile,
  impartial, and sincere. The inner cravings of human beings
  lead to murder, envy and squandering.**

A reading from the Letter of Saint James

BELOVED: Where jealousy and selfish ambition
exist, there is disorder and every foul practice. But

the wisdom from above is first of all pure, then peaceable, gentle, compliant, full of mercy and good fruits, without inconstancy or insincerity. And the fruit of righteousness is sown in peace for those who cultivate peace.

Where do the wars and where do the conflicts among you come from? Is it not from your passions that make war within your members? You covet but do not possess. You kill and envy but you cannot obtain; you fight and wage war. You do not possess because you do not ask. You ask but do not receive, because you ask wrongly, to spend it on your passions.—The word of the Lord. ℟. **Thanks be to God.** ↓

ALLELUIA Cf. 2 Thes 2:14   [Shared Glory]

℟. **Alleluia, alleluia.**
God has called us through the Gospel
to possess the glory of our Lord Jesus Christ.
℟. **Alleluia, alleluia.** ↓

GOSPEL Mk 9:30-37   [Service of Others]

Jesus tells his trusted disciples of his forthcoming sufferings, death and resurrection. Then he tells the Twelve about humility. To rank first, one must remain the last and be the servant of all.

℣. The Lord be with you. ℟. **And also with you.**
✤ A reading from the holy Gospel according to Mark.
℟. **Glory to you, Lord.**

JESUS and his disciples left from there and began a journey through Galilee, but he did not wish anyone to know about it. He was teaching his disciples and telling them, "The Son of Man is to be handed over to men and they will kill him, and three days after his death the Son of Man will rise." But they did not understand the saying, and they were afraid to question him.

They came to Capernaum and, once inside the house, he began to ask them, "What were you arguing about on the way?" But they remained silent. They had been discussing among themselves on the way who was the greatest. Then he sat down, called the Twelve, and said to them, "If anyone wishes to be first, he shall be the last of all and the servant of all." Taking a child, he placed it in their midst, and putting his arms around it, he said to them, "Whoever receives one child such as this in my name, receives me; and whoever receives me, receives not me but the One who sent me."—The Gospel of the Lord. ℟. **Praise to you, Lord Jesus Christ.**   → No. 14, p. 18

PRAYER OVER THE GIFTS   [Gifts Become Eucharist]

Lord,
may these gifts which we now offer
to show our belief and our love
be pleasing to you.
May they become for us
the eucharist of Jesus Christ your Son,
who is Lord for ever and ever.
℟. **Amen.**   → No. 21, p. 22 (Pref. P 29-36)

COMMUNION ANT. Ps 119:4-5   [Keeping God's Commands]

You have laid down your precepts to be faithfully kept. May my footsteps be firm in keeping your commands. ↓

OR Jn 10:14   [The Good Shepherd]

I am the Good Shepherd, says the Lord; I know my sheep, and mine know me. ↓

PRAYER AFTER COMMUNION   [The Eucharist in Action]

Lord,
help us with your kindness.
Make us strong through the eucharist.

May we put into action
the saving mystery we celebrate.
We ask this in the name of Jesus the Lord.
℞. **Amen.**   → No. 32, p. 70

Optional Solemn Blessings, p. 92, and Prayers Over the People, p. 99

"Whoever is not against us is for us."

SEPTEMBER 28

26th SUNDAY IN ORDINARY TIME

ENTRANCE ANT. Dn 3:31, 29, 30, 43, 42   [God's Kindness]

O Lord, you had just cause to judge men as you did:
because we sinned against you and disobeyed your
will. But now show us your greatness of heart, and
treat us with your unbounded kindness. → No. 2, p. 10

OPENING PRAYER   [God's Forgiveness]

Let us pray
    [for God's forgiveness
    and for the happiness it brings]
Father,
you show your almighty power
in your mercy and forgiveness.

Continue to fill us with your gifts of love.
Help us to hurry toward the eternal life you promise
and come to share in the joys of your kingdom.
Grant this through our Lord Jesus Christ, your Son,
who lives and reigns with you and the Holy Spirit,
one God, for ever and ever. ℟. **Amen.** ↓

ALTERNATIVE OPENING PRAYER   [Radiating Christ]

Let us pray
  [for the peace of the kingdom
  which we have been promised]
Father of our Lord Jesus Christ,
in your unbounded mercy
you have revealed the beauty of your power
through your constant forgiveness of our sins.
May the power of this love be in our hearts
to bring your pardon and your kingdom to all we
  meet.
We ask this through Christ our Lord. ℟. **Amen.** ↓

FIRST READING Nm 11:25-29   [Prophets Chosen by God]

The Lord empowered seventy elders with the gift of prophecy. Eldad and Medad were absent but they also received the gift. Some elders complained but Moses replied that it would be even more wonderful if all the people were prophets.

A reading from the Book of Numbers

THE LORD came down in the cloud and spoke to Moses. Taking some of the spirit that was on Moses, the LORD bestowed it on the seventy elders; and as the spirit came to rest on them, they prophesied.

Now two men, one named Eldad and the other Medad, were not in the gathering but had been left in the camp. They too had been on the list, but had not gone out to the tent; yet the spirit came to rest on them also, and they prophesied in the camp. So, when a young man quickly told Moses, "Eldad and Medad are prophesying in the camp," Joshua, son of Nun, who from his youth had been Moses' aide, said, "Moses, my lord, stop them." But Moses answered him, "Are you jealous for my sake? Would that all the people of the LORD were prophets! Would that the LORD might bestow his spirit on them all!"—The word of the Lord. ℟. **Thanks be to God.** ↓

RESPONSORIAL PSALM Ps 19   [God's Law]

℟. **The precepts of the Lord give joy to the heart.**

The law of the LORD is perfect,
    refreshing the soul;
the decree of the LORD is trustworthy,
    giving wisdom to the simple.

℟. **The precepts of the Lord give joy to the heart.**

The fear of the LORD is pure,
    enduring forever;
the ordinances of the LORD are true,
    all of them just.

℟. **The precepts of the Lord give joy to the heart.**

Though your servant is careful of them,
    very diligent in keeping them,
yet who can detect failings?
    Cleanse me from my unknown faults!

℟. **The precepts of the Lord give joy to the heart.**

From wanton sin especially, restrain your servant;
    let it not rule over me.
Then shall I be blameless and innocent
    of serious sin.

℟. **The precepts of the Lord give joy to the heart.** ↓

SECOND READING Jas 5:1-6   [Injustice of the Rich]

James deplores the injustice committed by the rich. He speaks of their pending miseries, their wanton luxury, wages withheld from workers. All these will stand as witness for greed.

A reading from the Letter of Saint James

COME now, you rich, weep and wail over your impending miseries. Your wealth has rotted away, your clothes have become moth-eaten, your gold and silver have corroded, and that corrosion will be a testimony against you; it will devour your flesh like a fire. You have stored up treasure for the last days. Behold, the wages you withheld from the workers who harvested your fields are crying aloud; and the cries of the harvesters have reached the ears of the Lord of hosts. You have lived on earth in luxury and pleasure; you have fattened your hearts for the day of slaughter. You have condemned; you have murdered the righteous one; he offers you no resistance.—The word of the Lord. ℟. **Thanks be to God.** ↓

ALLELUIA Cf. Jn 17:17b, 17a   [Holy in the Truth]
℟. **Alleluia, alleluia.**
Your word, O Lord, is truth;
consecrate us in the truth.
℟. **Alleluia, alleluia.** ↓

GOSPEL Mk 9:38-43, 45, 47-48   [Everyone Can Proclaim Christ]
Jesus reminds his followers that nothing done in his name will go unrewarded. But anyone who deceives a simple believer will be severely punished.

℣. The Lord be with you. ℟. **And also with you.**
✝ A reading from the holy Gospel according to Mark.
℟. **Glory to you, Lord.**

AT that time, John said to Jesus, "Teacher, we saw someone driving out demons in your name, and we tried to prevent him because he does not follow us." Jesus replied, "Do not prevent him. There is no one who performs a mighty deed in my name who can at the same time speak ill of me. For whoever is not against us is for us. Anyone who gives you a cup of water to drink because you belong to Christ, amen, I say to you, will surely not lose his reward.

"Whoever causes one of these little ones who believe in me to sin, it would be better for him if a great millstone were put around his neck and he were thrown into the sea. If your hand causes you to sin, cut it off. It is better for you to enter into life maimed than with two hands to go into Gehenna, into the unquenchable fire. And if your foot causes you to sin, cut it off. It is better for you to enter into life crippled than with two feet to be thrown into Gehenna. And if your eye causes you to sin, pluck it out. Better for you to enter into the kingdom of God with one eye than with two eyes to be thrown into Gehenna, where 'their worm does not die, and the fire is not quenched.' "— The Gospel of the Lord. ℟. **Praise to you, Lord Jesus Christ.**

→ No. 14, p. 18

PRAYER OVER THE GIFTS   [Offering as a Blessing]

God of mercy,
accept our offering
and make it a source of blessing for us.
We ask this in the name of Jesus the Lord.
℟. **Amen.**   → No. 21, p. 22 (Pref. P 29-36)

COMMUNION ANT. Ps 119:49-50   [Words of Hope]

O Lord, remember the words you spoke to me, your servant, which made me live in hope and consoled me when I was downcast. ↓

OR 1 Jn 3:16   [Offering of Self]

This is how we know what love is: Christ gave up his life for us; and we too must give up our lives for our brothers. ↓

PRAYER AFTER COMMUNION　　[Union with Christ]

Lord,
may this eucharist
in which we proclaim the death of Christ
bring us salvation
and make us one with him in glory,
for he is Lord for ever and ever.

℟. **Amen.**　　　　　　　　　　→ No. 32, p. 70

Optional Solemn Blessings, p. 92, and Prayers Over the People, p. 99

"A man shall leave his father and mother and be joined to his wife, and the two shall become one flesh."

OCTOBER 5

27th SUNDAY IN ORDINARY TIME

ENTRANCE ANT. Est 13:9, 10-11　　[Lord of All]

O Lord, you have given everything its place in the world, and no one can make it otherwise. For it is your creation, the heavens and the earth and the stars: you are the Lord of all.　　→ No. 2, p. 10

OPENING PRAYER　　[Peace and Salvation]

Let us pray
[that God will forgive our failings
and bring us peace]

Father,
your love for us
surpasses all our hopes and desires.
Forgive our failings,
keep us in your peace
and lead us in the way of salvation.
We ask this through our Lord Jesus Christ, your Son,
who lives and reigns with you and the Holy Spirit,
one God, for ever and ever. ℟. **Amen.** ↓

ALTERNATIVE OPENING PRAYER   [Christian Courage]

Let us pray
   [before the face of God,
   in trusting faith]
Almighty and eternal God,
Father of the world to come,
your goodness is beyond what our spirit can touch
and your strength is more than the mind can bear.
Lead us to seek beyond our reach
and give us the courage to stand before your truth.
We ask this through Christ our Lord. ℟. **Amen.** ↓

FIRST READING Gn 2:18-24   [Man's Companion]

God, knowing that man needs companionship, created animals and birds and finally placed Adam in a deep sleep and took one of his ribs, forming a woman.

A reading from the Book of Genesis

THE LORD God said: "It is not good for the man to be alone. I will make a suitable partner for him." So the LORD God formed out of the ground various wild animals and various birds of the air, and he brought them to the man to see what he would call them; whatever the man called each of them would be its name. The man gave names to all the cattle, all the birds of the air, and all wild animals; but none proved to be the suitable partner for the man.

So the L<small>ORD</small> God cast a deep sleep on the man, and while he was asleep, he took out one of his ribs and closed up its place with flesh. The L<small>ORD</small> God then built up into a woman the rib that he had taken from the man. When he brought her to the man, the man said:

"This one, at last, is bone of my bones
    and flesh of my flesh;
this one shall be called 'woman,'
    for out of 'her man' this one has been taken."

That is why a man leaves his father and mother and clings to his wife, and the two of them become one flesh.—The word of the Lord. ℟. **Thanks be to God.** ↓

RESPONSORIAL PSALM Ps 128   [Fear of the Lord]

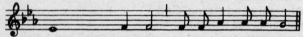

℟. May the Lord bless us   all the days of our lives.

Blessed are you who fear the L<small>ORD</small>,
    who walk in his ways!
For you shall eat the fruit of your handiwork;
    blessed shall you be, and favored.

℟. **May the Lord bless us**
    all the days of our lives.

Your wife shall be like a fruitful vine
    in the recesses of your home;
your children like olive plants
    around your table.

℟. **May the Lord bless us**
    all the days of our lives.

Behold, thus is the man blessed
    who fears the L<small>ORD</small>.
The L<small>ORD</small> bless you from Zion:
    may you see the prosperity of Jerusalem
    all the days of your life.

℟. **May the Lord bless us**
    all the days of our lives.

May you see your children's children.
 Peace be upon Israel!

℟. **May the Lord bless us
 all the days of our lives.** ↓

SECOND READING Heb 2:9-11   [Christ Our Brother]

> To suffer, Jesus took a human body. In this way God made
> our leader perfect through suffering, bringing salvation. All
> who are consecrated have thereby a common Father and
> become brothers and sisters.

A reading from the Letter to the Hebrews

B ROTHERS and sisters: He "for a little while" was
  made "lower than the angels," that by the grace of
God he might taste death for everyone.

 For it was fitting that he, for whom and through
whom all things exist, in bringing many children to
glory, should make the leader to their salvation perfect through suffering. He who consecrates and those
who are being consecrated all have one origin. Therefore, he is not ashamed to call them "brothers."—The
word of the Lord. ℟. **Thanks be to God.** ↓

ALLELUIA 1 Jn 4:12   [Love One Another]

℟. **Alleluia, alleluia.**
If we love one another, God remains in us
and his love is brought to perfection in us.
℟. **Alleluia, alleluia.** ↓

GOSPEL Mk 10:2-16 or 10:2-12   [Unity of Marriage]

> The Pharisees, knowing the permission of Moses about di-
> vorce, test Jesus, but he recalls the reason for the com-
> mand and reminds them of God's intention for the unity of
> marriage. Divorce followed by remarriage is adultery.
> (Jesus then speaks about his love for little children and
> their innocence.)

*[If the "Shorter Form" is used, the indented text in brackets is
omitted.]*

℣. The Lord be with you. ℟. **And also with you.**

✝ A reading from the holy Gospel according to Mark.
℟. **Glory to you, Lord.**

T HE Pharisees approached Jesus and asked, "Is it
lawful for a husband to divorce his wife?" They
were testing him. He said to them in reply, "What did
Moses command you?" They replied, "Moses permitted a husband to write a bill of divorce and dismiss
her." But Jesus told them, "Because of the hardness of
your hearts he wrote you this commandment. But
from the beginning of creation, *God made them male
and female. For this reason a man shall leave his
father and mother and be joined to his wife, and the
two shall become one flesh.* So they are no longer two
but one flesh. Therefore what God has joined together, no human being must separate." In the house
the disciples again questioned Jesus about this. He
said to them, "Whoever divorces his wife and marries
another commits adultery against her; and if she divorces her husband and marries another, she commits
adultery."

[And people were bringing children to him that
he might touch them, but the disciples rebuked
them. When Jesus saw this he became indignant
and said to them, "Let the children come to me;
do not prevent them, for the kingdom of God belongs to such as these. Amen, I say to you, whoever does not accept the kingdom of God like a
child will not enter it." Then he embraced them
and blessed them, placing his hands on them.]

The Gospel of the Lord. ℟. **Praise to you, Lord Jesus
Christ.**   → No. 14, p. 18

PRAYER OVER THE GIFTS   [Fullness of Redemption]

Father,
receive these gifts

which our Lord Jesus Christ
has asked us to offer in his memory.
May our obedient service
bring us to the fullness of your redemption.
We ask this in the name of Jesus the Lord.
R̠. **Amen.**   ➔ No. 21, p. 22 (Pref. P 29-36)

COMMUNION ANT. Lam 3:25   [Hope in the Lord]
The Lord is good to those who hope in him, to those
who are searching for his love. ↓

OR See 1 Cor 10:17   [One Bread, One Body]
Because there is one bread, we, though many, are one
body, for we all share in the one loaf and in the one
cup. ↓

PRAYER AFTER COMMUNION   [Eucharistic Life]

Almighty God,
let the eucharist we share
fill us with your life.
May the love of Christ
which we celebrate here
touch our lives and lead us to you.
We ask this in the name of Jesus the Lord.
R̠. **Amen.**   ➔ No. 32, p. 70

Optional Solemn Blessings, p. 92, and Prayers Over the People, p. 99

*"Sell what you have, and give to the poor . . .
then come, follow me."*

OCTOBER 12
28th SUNDAY IN ORDINARY TIME

ENTRANCE ANT. Ps 130:3-4   **[A Forgiving God]**

If you, O Lord, laid bare our guilt, who could endure
it? But you are forgiving, God of Israel. ➔ No. 2, p. 10

OPENING PRAYER   **[Love in Action]**

Let us pray
   [that God will help us to love one another]
Lord,
our help and guide,
make your love the foundation of our lives.
May our love for you express itself
in our eagerness to do good for others.
Grant this through our Lord Jesus Christ, your Son,
who lives and reigns with you and the Holy Spirit,
one God, for ever and ever. ℟. **Amen.** ↓

ALTERNATIVE OPENING PRAYER   **[Sincerity]**

Let us pray
   [in quiet for the grace of sincerity]

Father in heaven,
the hand of your loving kindness
powerfully yet gently guides all the moments of our day.
Go before us in our pilgrimage of life,
anticipate our needs and prevent our falling.
Send your Spirit to unite us in faith,
that sharing in your service,
we may rejoice in your presence.
We ask this through Christ our Lord. ℟. **Amen.** ↓

FIRST READING Wis 7:7-11   [Riches of Wisdom]

> To what can Wisdom be compared in value? She is above
> all desires because in her all good things are found—
> countless riches.

A reading from the Book of Wisdom

I PRAYED, and prudence was given me;
I pleaded, and the spirit of wisdom came to me.
I preferred her to scepter and throne,
and deemed riches nothing in comparison with her,
    nor did I liken any priceless gem to her;
because all gold, in view of her, is a little sand,
    and before her, silver is to be accounted mire.
Beyond health and comeliness I loved her,
and I chose to have her rather than the light,
    because the splendor of her never yields to sleep.
Yet all good things together came to me in her company,
    and countless riches at her hands.
The word of the Lord. ℟. **Thanks be to God.** ↓

RESPONSORIAL PSALM Ps 90   [Filled with God's Love]

℟. **Fill us with your love, O Lord, and we will sing for joy!**

Teach us to number our days aright,
    that we may gain wisdom of heart.

Return, O Lord! How long?
  Have pity on your servants!

℟. **Fill us with your love, O Lord,**
  and we will sing for joy!

Fill us at daybreak with your kindness,
  that we may shout for joy and gladness all our days.
Make us glad, for the days when you afflicted us,
  for the years when we saw evil.

℟. **Fill us with your love, O Lord,**
  and we will sing for joy!

Let your work be seen by your servants
  and your glory by their children;
and may the gracious care of the Lord our God be
  ours;
  prosper the work of our hands for us!
  Prosper the work of our hands!

℟. **Fill us with your love, O Lord,**
  and we will sing for joy! ↓

SECOND READING Heb 4:12-13   [God's Living Word]

God's word is penetrating and sharp. Nothing is hidden
from God, and all must render an account to him.

A reading from the Letter to the Hebrews

B ROTHERS and sisters: Indeed the word of God is
living and effective, sharper than any two-edged
sword, penetrating even between soul and spirit,
joints and marrow, and able to discern reflections and
thoughts of the heart. No creature is concealed from
him, but everything is naked and exposed to the eyes
of him to whom we must render an account.—The
word of the Lord. ℟. **Thanks be to God.** ↓

ALLELUIA Mt 5:3   [Poor in Spirit]

℟. **Alleluia, alleluia.**
Blessed are the poor in spirit,

for theirs is the kingdom of heaven.

℟. **Alleluia, alleluia.** ↓

GOSPEL Mk 10:17-30 or 10:17-27   [All for God]

A rich man asks Jesus what he must do to be saved. Jesus answers—keep the commandments. The man says that he does. One thing more, then, Jesus lovingly continues— sell what you have and give to the poor. The man left. Jesus added how hard it is for a rich person to get to heaven.

[If the "Shorter Form" is used, the indented text in brackets is omitted.]

℣. The Lord be with you. ℟. **And also with you.**

✤ A reading from the holy Gospel according to Mark.

℟. **Glory to you, Lord.**

AS Jesus was setting out on a journey, a man ran up, knelt down before him, and asked him, "Good teacher, what must I do to inherit eternal life?" Jesus answered him, "Why do you call me good? No one is good but God alone. You know the commandments: *You shall not kill; you shall not commit adultery; you shall not steal; you shall not bear false witness; you shall not defraud; honor your father and your mother.*" He replied and said to him, "Teacher, all of these I have observed from my youth." Jesus, looking at him, loved him and said to him, "You are lacking in one thing. Go, sell what you have, and give to the poor and you will have treasure in heaven; then come, follow me." At that statement his face fell, and he went away sad, for he had many possessions.

Jesus looked around and said to his disciples, "How hard it is for those who have wealth to enter the king- dom of God!" The disciples were amazed at his words. So Jesus again said to them in reply, "Children, how hard it is to enter the kingdom of God! It is easier for a camel to pass through the eye of a needle than for one who is rich to enter the kingdom of God." They were exceedingly astonished and said among themselves, "Then who can be saved?" Jesus looked at them and said, "For human beings it is impossible, but not for God. All things are possible for God."

[Peter began to say to him, "We have given up everything and followed you." Jesus said, "Amen, I say to you, there is no one who has given up house or brothers or sisters or mother or father or children or lands for my sake and for the sake of the gospel who will not receive a hundred times more now in this present age: houses and brothers and sisters and mothers and children and lands, with persecutions, and eternal life in the age to come."]

The Gospel of the Lord. ℟. **Praise to you, Lord Jesus Christ.**   ➞ No. 14, p. 18

PRAYER OVER THE GIFTS   [Faith and Love]

Lord,
accept the prayers and gifts
we offer in faith and love.
May this eucharist bring us to your glory.
We ask this in the name of Jesus the Lord.
℟. **Amen.**   ➞ No. 21, p. 22 (Pref. P 29-36)

COMMUNION ANT. Ps 34:11   [God's Providence]

The rich suffer want and go hungry, but nothing shall be lacking to those who fear the Lord. ↓

OR 1 Jn 3:2   [Vision of God]

When the Lord is revealed we shall be like him, for we shall see him as he is. ↓

PRAYER AFTER COMMUNION   [Christ's Life]

Almighty Father,
may the body and blood of your Son

give us a share in his life,
for he is Lord for ever and ever.
℞. **Amen.**

➜ No. 32, p. 70

Optional Solemn Blessings, p. 92, and Prayers Over the People, p. 99

"To sit at my right or at my left is not mine to give."

OCTOBER 19

29th SUNDAY IN ORDINARY TIME

ENTRANCE ANT. Ps 17:6, 8   [Refuge in God]

**I call upon you, God, for you will answer me; bend
your ear and hear my prayer. Guard me as the pupil
of your eye; hide me in the shade of your wings.**

➜ No. 2, p. 10

OPENING PRAYER   [Faithful Service]

Let us pray
    [for the gift of simplicity and joy
    in our service of God and man]
Almighty and ever-living God,
our source of power and inspiration,
give us strength and joy
in serving you as followers of Christ,

who lives and reigns with you and the Holy Spirit,
one God, for ever and ever. ℟. **Amen.** ↓

ALTERNATIVE OPENING PRAYER　　[Spiritual Sight]

Let us pray
　[to the Lord who bends close to hear our prayer]
Lord our God, Father of all,
you guard us under the shadow of your wings
and search into the depths of our hearts.
Remove the blindness that cannot know you
and relieve the fear that would hide us from your
　sight.
We ask this through Christ our Lord. ℟. **Amen.** ↓

FIRST READING　Is 53:10-11　　[The Servant of Yahweh]

**The suffering servant speaks of his life as a sin offering
that his people may prosper enjoying a long life. Through
his suffering he will bear the guilt of many.**

A reading from the Book of the Prophet Isaiah

THE LORD was pleased
　to crush him in infirmity.
If he gives his life as an offering for sin,
　he shall see his descendants in a long life,
　　and the will of the LORD shall be accomplished
　　　through him.
Because of his affliction
　he shall see the light in fullness of days;
through his suffering, my servant shall justify many,
　and their guilt he shall bear.
The word of the Lord. ℟. **Thanks be to God.** ↓

RESPONSORIAL PSALM　Ps 33　　[Trust in God]

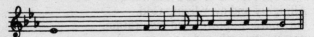

℟. **Lord, let your mercy be on us,　as we place our trust in you.**

Upright is the word of the LORD,
    and all his works are trustworthy.
He loves justice and right;
    of the kindness of the LORD the earth is full.

℞. **Lord, let your mercy be on us,**
    as we place our trust in you.

See, the eyes of the LORD are upon those who fear him,
    upon those who hope for his kindness,
to deliver them from death
    and preserve them in spite of famine.

℞. **Lord, let your mercy be on us,**
    as we place our trust in you.

Our soul waits for the LORD,
    who is our help and our shield.
May your kindness, O LORD, be upon us,
    who have put our hope in you.

℞. **Lord, let your mercy be on us,**
    as we place our trust in you. ↓

SECOND READING Heb 4:14-16   [Jesus Our High Priest]

Jesus Christ, the Son of God, is the high priest who shares
all our weaknesses, except sin. His mercy comes to all who
seek it.

A reading from the Letter to the Hebrews

BROTHERS and sisters: Since we have a great high
priest who has passed through the heavens, Jesus,
the Son of God, let us hold fast to our confession. For
we do not have a high priest who is unable to sympathize with our weaknesses, but one who has similarly
been tested in every way, yet without sin. So let us
confidently approach the throne of grace to receive
mercy and to find grace for timely help.—The word of
the Lord. ℞. **Thanks be to God.** ↓

ALLELUIA Mk 10:45 [Divine Ransom]

℟. **Alleluia, alleluia.**
The Son of Man came to serve
and to give his life as a ransom for many.
℟. **Alleluia, alleluia.** ↓

GOSPEL Mk 10:35-45 or 10:42-45 [Greatness in Serving]

James and John request a special honor in the kingdom of
heaven. Jesus reminds them and the other ten that anyone
who aspires to greatness must be prepared to serve first.

*[If the "Shorter Form" is used, the indented text in brackets is
omitted.]*

℣. The Lord be with you. ℟. **And also with you.**
✠ A reading from the holy Gospel according to Mark.
℟. **Glory to you, Lord.**

[JAMES and John, the sons of Zebedee,
came to Jesus and said to him, "Teacher,
we want you to do for us whatever we ask of
you." He replied, "What do you wish me to do
for you?" They answered him, "Grant that in
your glory we may sit one at your right and the
other at your left." Jesus said to them, "You do
not know what you are asking. Can you drink
the cup that I drink or be baptized with the
baptism with which I am baptized?" They said
to him, "We can." Jesus said to them, "The cup
that I drink, you will drink, and with the baptism with which I am baptized, you will be baptized; but to sit at my right or at my left is not
mine to give but is for those for whom it has
been prepared." When the ten heard this, they
became indignant at James and John.]
Jesus summoned the Twelve and said to them, "You
know that those who are recognized as rulers over the
Gentiles lord it over them, and their great ones make
their authority over them felt. But it shall not be so

among you. Rather, whoever wishes to be great among you will be your servant; whoever wishes to be first among you will be the slave of all. For the Son of Man did not come to be served but to serve and to give his life as a ransom for many."—The Gospel of the Lord. ℟.
Praise to you, Lord Jesus Christ.   ➜ No. 14, p. 18

PRAYER OVER THE GIFTS   [Lives of Service]

Lord God,
may the gifts we offer
bring us your love and forgiveness
and give us freedom to serve you with our lives.
We ask this in the name of Jesus the Lord.
℟. **Amen.**   ➜ No. 21, p. 22 (Pref. P 29-36)

COMMUNION ANT. Ps 33:18-19   [Divine Protection]

See how the eyes of the Lord are on those who fear him, on those who hope in his love, that he may rescue them from death and feed them in time of famine. ↓

OR Mk 10:45   [Christ Our Ransom]

The Son of Man came to give his life as a ransom for many. ↓

PRAYER AFTER COMMUNION   [Fidelity]

Lord,
may this eucharist help us to remain faithful.
May it teach us the way to eternal life.
Grant this through Christ our Lord.
℟. **Amen.**   ➜ No. 32, p. 70

Optional Solemn Blessings, p. 92, and Prayers Over the People, p. 99

"Jesus, son of David, have pity on me."

OCTOBER 26
30th SUNDAY IN ORDINARY TIME

ENTRANCE ANT. Ps 105:3-4   [Seek the Lord]

Let hearts rejoice who search for the Lord. Seek the Lord and his strength, seek always the face of the Lord. → No. 2, p. 10

OPENING PRAYER   [Doing God's Will]

Let us pray
  [for the strength to do God's will]
Almighty and ever-living God,
strengthen our faith, hope, and love.
May we do with loving hearts
what you ask of us
and come to share the life you promise.
We ask this through our Lord Jesus Christ, your Son,
who lives and reigns with you and the Holy Spirit,
one God, for ever and ever. ℟. **Amen.** ↓

ALTERNATIVE OPENING PRAYER   [Faith and Love]

Let us pray
  [in humble hope for salvation]
Praised be you, God and Father of our Lord Jesus Christ.

542

There is no power for good
which does not come from your covenant,
and no promise to hope in
that your love has not offered.
Strengthen our faith to accept your covenant
and give us the love to carry out your command.
We ask this through Christ our Lord. ℟. **Amen.** ↓

FIRST READING Jer 31:7-9   [God's Deliverance]

>Jeremiah's hymn opens with joy for God has bestowed sal-
>vation on his people. He has delivered his people and will
>guide and bless them so none will go astray.

A reading from the Book of the Prophet Jeremiah

T HUS says the LORD:
Shout with joy for Jacob,
exult at the head of the nations;
proclaim your praise and say:
The LORD has delivered his people,
the remnant of Israel.
Behold, I will bring them back
from the land of the north;
I will gather them from the ends of the world
with the blind and the lame in their midst,
the mothers and those with child;
they shall return as an immense throng.
They departed in tears,
but I will console them and guide them;
I will lead them to brooks of water,
on a level road, so that none shall stumble.
For I am a father to Israel,
Ephraim is my first-born.
The word of the Lord. ℟. **Thanks be to God.** ↓

RESPONSORIAL PSALM Ps 126   [God's Mighty Works]

℟. **The Lord has done great things for us; we are filled with joy.**

When the LORD brought back the captives of Zion,
  we were like men dreaming.
Then our mouth was filled with laughter,
  and our tongue with rejoicing.

℟. **The Lord has done great things for us;**
  we are filled with joy.

Then they said among the nations,
  "The LORD has done great things for them."
The LORD has done great things for us;
  we are glad indeed.

℟. **The Lord has done great things for us;**
  we are filled with joy.

Restore our fortunes, O LORD,
  like the torrents in the southern desert.
Those that sow in tears
  shall reap rejoicing.

℟. **The Lord has done great things for us;**
  we are filled with joy.

Although they go forth weeping,
  carrying the seed to be sown,
they shall come back rejoicing,
  carrying their sheaves.

℟. **The Lord has done great things for us;**
  we are filled with joy. ↓

SECOND READING Heb 5:1-6   [Christ the Mediator]

Every high priest is designated by God. He is selected from among the people to be their mediator with God. No one takes this honor by himself.

A reading from the Letter to the Hebrews

BROTHERS and sisters: Every high priest is taken from among men and made their representative before God, to offer gifts and sacrifices for sins. He is able to deal patiently with the ignorant and erring, for he himself is beset by weakness and so, for this reason, must make sin offerings for himself as well as for the people. No one takes this honor upon himself but only when called by God, just as Aaron was. In the same way, it was not Christ who glorified himself in becoming high priest, but rather the one who said to him:

You are my son:
this day I have begotten you;
just as he says in another place:

You are a priest forever
according to the order of Melchizedek.

The word of the Lord. ℟. **Thanks be to God.** ↓

ALLELUIA Cf. 2 Tm 1:10   [Divine Life]

℟. **Alleluia, alleluia.**
Our Savior Jesus Christ destroyed death
and brought life to light through his Gospel.
℟. **Alleluia, alleluia.** ↓

GOSPEL Mk 10:46-52   [Healing of a Blind Man]

Bartimaeus, a blind man, hearing Jesus called out loudly, "Jesus, son of David, have pity on me!" Jesus summoned him and, seeing his faith, cured him. Bartimaeus followed Jesus.

℣. The Lord be with you. ℟. **And also with you.**
✛ A reading from the holy Gospel according to Mark.
℟. **Glory to you, Lord.**

A S Jesus was leaving Jericho with his disciples and a sizable crowd, Bartimaeus, a blind man, the son of Timaeus, sat by the roadside begging. On hearing that it was Jesus of Nazareth, he began to cry out and say, "Jesus, son of David, have pity on me." And many rebuked him, telling him to be silent. But he kept calling out all the more, "Son of David, have pity on me." Jesus stopped and said, "Call him." So they called the blind man, saying to him, "Take courage; get up, Jesus is calling you." He threw aside his cloak, sprang up, and came to Jesus. Jesus said to him in reply, "What do you want me to do for you?" The blind man replied to him, "Master, I want to see." Jesus told him, "Go your way; your faith has saved you." Immediately he received his sight and followed him on the way.— The Gospel of the Lord. ℟. **Praise to you, Lord Jesus Christ.**   ➡ No. 14, p. 18

PRAYER OVER THE GIFTS   [Glorifying God]

Lord God of power and might,
receive the gifts we offer
and let our service give you glory.
Grant this through Christ our Lord.
℟. **Amen.**   ➡ No. 21, p. 22 (Pref. P 29-36)

COMMUNION ANT. Ps 20:6   [Victory of God]

We will rejoice at the victory of God and make our boast in his great name. ↓

OR Eph 5:2   [Christ's Offering for Us]

Christ loved us and gave himself up for us as a fragrant offering to God. ↓

PRAYER AFTER COMMUNION   [Effective Communion]

Lord,
bring to perfection within us
the communion we share in this sacrament.
May our celebration have an effect in our lives.
We ask this in the name of Jesus the Lord.
℟. **Amen.**   ➡ No. 32, p. 70

Optional Solemn Blessings, p. 92, and Prayers Over the People, p. 99

"Blessed are the clean of heart, for they will see God."

NOVEMBER 1

ALL SAINTS

ENTRANCE ANT. [Honoring All the Saints]

Let us all rejoice in the Lord and keep a festival in honor of all the saints. Let us join with the angels in joyful praise to the Son of God. → No. 2, p. 10

OPENING PRAYER [Forgiveness and Love]

Let us pray
[that the prayers of all the saints
will bring us forgiveness for our sins]
Father, all-powerful and ever-living God,
today we rejoice in the holy men and women
of every time and place.
May their prayers bring us your forgiveness and love.
We ask this . . . for ever and ever. ℟. **Amen.** ↓

ALTERNATIVE OPENING PRAYER
[Sharing the Saints' Peace]

Let us pray
[as we rejoice and keep festival
in honor of all the saints]

547

God our Father,
source of all holiness,
the work of your hands is manifest in your saints,
the beauty of your truth is reflected in their faith.
May we who aspire to have part in their joy
be filled with the Spirit that blessed their lives,
so that having shared their faith on earth
we may also know their peace in your kingdom.
Grant this through Christ our Lord. ℟. **Amen.** ↓

FIRST READING Rv 7:2-4, 9-14 [A Huge Crowd of Saints]

The elect give thanks to God and the Lamb who saved them. The whole court of heaven joins the acclamation of the saints.

A reading from the Book of Revelation

I, JOHN, saw another angel come up from the East, holding the seal of the living God. He cried out in a loud voice to the four angels who were given power to damage the land and the sea, "Do not damage the land or the sea or the trees until we put the seal on the foreheads of the servants of our God." I heard the number of those who had been marked with the seal, one hundred and forty-four thousand marked from every tribe of the Israelites.

After this I had a vision of a great multitude, which no one could count, from every nation, race, people, and tongue. They stood before the throne and before the Lamb, wearing white robes and holding palm branches in their hands. They cried out in a loud voice:

"Salvation comes from our God,
who is seated on the throne,
and from the Lamb."

All the angels stood around the throne and around the elders and the four living creatures. They prostrated themselves before the throne, worshiped God, and exclaimed:

"Amen. Blessing and glory, wisdom and thanksgiving,
honor, power, and might
be to our God forever and ever. Amen."

Then one of the elders spoke up and said to me, "Who
are these wearing white robes, and where did they come
from?" I said to him, "My lord, you are the one who
knows." He said to me, "These are the ones who have
survived the time of great distress; they have washed
their robes and made them white in the blood of the
Lamb."—The word of the Lord. ℟. **Thanks be to God.** ↓

RESPONSORIAL PSALM Ps 24   [Longing To See God]

℟. Lord, this is the peo-ple that longs to see your face.

The LORD's are the earth and its fullness;
the world and those who dwell in it.
For he founded it upon the seas
and established it upon the rivers.

℟. **Lord, this is the people that longs to see your face.**

Who can ascend the mountain of the LORD?
or who may stand in his holy place?
One whose hands are sinless, whose heart is clean,
who desires not what is vain.

℟. **Lord, this is the people that longs to see your face.**

He shall receive a blessing from the LORD,
a reward from God his savior.
Such is the race that seeks for him,
that seeks the face of the God of Jacob.

℟. **Lord, this is the people that longs to see your
face.** ↓

SECOND READING 1 Jn 3:1-3   [We Shall See God]

God's gift of love has been the gift of His only Son as Savior of the world. It is this gift that has made it possible for us to be called the children of God.

A reading from the first Letter of Saint John

BELOVED: See what love the Father has bestowed on us that we may be called the children of God. Yet so we are. The reason the world does not know us is that it did not know him. Beloved, we are God's children now; what we shall be has not yet been revealed. We do know that when it is revealed we shall be like him, for we shall see him as he is. Everyone who has this hope based on him makes himself pure, as he is pure.—The word of the Lord. ℟. **Thanks be to God.** ↓

ALLELUIA Mt 11:28   [Rest in Christ]

℟. **Alleluia, alleluia.**
Come to me, all you who labor and are burdened,
and I will give you rest, says the Lord.
℟. **Alleluia, alleluia.** ↓

GOSPEL Mt 5:1-12a   [The Beatitudes]

Jesus is meant to be the new Moses proclaiming the new revelation on a new Mount Sinai. This is the proclamation of the reign, or the "Good News." Blessings are pronounced on those who do not share the values of the world.

℣. The Lord be with you. ℟. **And also with you.**
✚ A reading from the holy Gospel according to Matthew. ℟. **Glory to you, Lord.**

WHEN Jesus saw the crowds, he went up the mountain, and after he had sat down, his disciples came to him. He began to teach them, saying:
    "Blessed are the poor in spirit,
        for theirs is the kingdom of heaven.
    Blessed are they who mourn,
        for they will be comforted.

Blessed are the meek,
　for they will inherit the land.
Blessed are they who hunger and thirst for righ-
　　teousness,
　for they will be satisfied.
Blessed are the merciful,
　for they will be shown mercy.
Blessed are the clean of heart,
　for they will see God.
Blessed are the peacemakers,
　for they will be called children of God.
Blessed are they who are persecuted for the sake of
　　righteousness,
　for theirs is the kingdom of heaven.
Blessed are you when they insult you and persecute
you and utter every kind of evil against you falsely because of me. Rejoice and be glad, for your reward will
be great in heaven."—The Gospel of the Lord. R̠.
Praise to you, Lord Jesus Christ.   → No. 14, p. 18

PRAYER OVER THE GIFTS   [The Saints' Concern for Us]
Lord,
receive our gifts in honor of the holy men and women
who live with you in glory.
May we always be aware
of their concern to help and save us.
We ask this in the name of Jesus the Lord. R̠. **Amen.** ↓

PREFACE (P 71)   [Saints Give Us Help and Encouragement]

℣. The Lord be with you. R̠. **And also with you.**
℣. Lift up your hearts. R̠. **We lift them up to the Lord.**
℣. Let us give thanks to the Lord our God. R̠. **It is right
to give him thanks and praise.**

Father, all-powerful and ever-living God,
we do well always and everywhere to give you thanks.
Today we keep the festival of your holy city,

the heavenly Jerusalem, our mother.
Around your throne
the saints, our brothers and sisters,
sing your praise for ever.
Their glory fills us with joy,
and their communion with us in your Church
gives us inspiration and strength,
as we hasten on our pilgrimage of faith,
eager to meet them.
With their great company and all the angels
we praise your glory
as we cry out with one voice: ➜ No. 23, p. 23

COMMUNION ANT. Mt 5:8-10   [The Saints: Children of God]

**Happy are the pure of heart for they shall see God.
Happy the peacemakers; they shall be called sons of
God. Happy are they who suffer persecution for jus-
tice' sake; the kingdom of heaven is theirs.** ↓

PRAYER AFTER COMMUNION   [Reflectors of God's Glory]

Father, holy one,
we praise your glory reflected in the saints.
May we who share at this table
be filled with your love
and prepared for the joy of your kingdom,
where Jesus is Lord for ever and ever.
℞. **Amen.**   ➜ No. 32, p. 70

Optional Solemn Blessings, p. 92, and Prayers Over the People, p. 99

"Give them eternal rest, O Lord . . ."

NOVEMBER 2

ALL SOULS

(31st SUNDAY IN ORDINARY TIME)

Even when November 2 falls on a Sunday, All Souls Day is celebrated with the following Masses.

1

ENTRANCE ANT. 1 Thes 4:14; 1 Cor 15:22   **[Life in Christ]**

Just as Jesus died and rose again, so will the Father bring with him those who have died in Jesus. Just as in Adam all men die, so in Christ all will be made alive.   → No. 2, p. 10

OPENING PRAYER   **[For All the Departed]**

Let us pray
   [for all our departed brothers and sisters]
Merciful Father,
hear our prayers and console us.
As we renew our faith in your Son,
whom you raised from the dead,
strengthen our hope that all our departed brothers
   and sisters

will share in his resurrection,
who lives and reigns with you and the Holy Spirit,
one God, for ever and ever. ℟. **Amen.** ↓

*The readings found in Masses 2 and 3 may also be used, as
well as those listed on p. 567.*

FIRST READING Wis 3:1-9   [In God's Care]

This is one of the clearest texts of the Old Testament about
God's future vindication of the just. It is not as clear as
later New Testament texts, but it does emphatically proclaim existence after death and our vision of God.

A reading from the Book of Wisdom

THE souls of the just are in the hand of God,
   and no torment shall touch them.
They seemed, in the view of the foolish, to be dead;
   and their passing away was thought an affliction
   and their going forth from us, utter destruction.
But they are in peace.
For if in the sight of others, indeed, they be punished,
   yet is their hope full of immortality;
chastised a little, they shall be greatly blessed,
   because God tried them
   and found them worthy of himself.
As gold in the furnace, he proved them,
   and as sacrificial offerings he took them to himself.
In the time of their visitation they shall shine,
   and shall dart about as sparks through stubble;
they shall judge nations and rule over peoples,
   and the LORD shall be their King forever.
Those who trust in him shall understand truth,
   and the faithful shall abide with him in love:
because grace and mercy are with his holy ones,
   and his care is with his elect.
The word of the Lord. ℟. **Thanks be to God.** ↓

RESPONSORIAL PSALM Ps 23 [Fearing No Evil]

℟. **The Lord is my shep-herd; there is noth-ing I shall want.**

℟. Or: **Though I walk in the valley of darkness,**
     I fear no evil, for you are with me.

The LORD is my shepherd; I shall not want.
    In verdant pastures he gives me repose;
beside restful waters he leads me;
    he refreshes my soul.

℟. **The Lord is my shepherd;**
     there is nothing I shall want.

℟. Or: **Though I walk in the valley of darkness,**
     I fear no evil, for you are with me.

He guides me in right paths
    for his name's sake.
Even though I walk in the dark valley
    I fear no evil; for you are at my side
with your rod and your staff
    that give me courage.

℟. **The Lord is my shepherd;**
     there is nothing I shall want.

℟. Or: **Though I walk in the valley of darkness,**
     I fear no evil, for you are with me.

You spread the table before me
    in the sight of my foes;
you anoint my head with oil;
    my cup overflows.

℟. **The Lord is my shepherd;**
     there is nothing I shall want.

℟. Or: **Though I walk in the valley of darkness,**
     I fear no evil, for you are with me.

Only goodness and kindness follow me
    all the days of my life;

and I shall dwell in the house of the LORD
   for years to come.

℟. **The Lord is my shepherd;**
   there is nothing I shall want. ↓

℟. Or: **Though I walk in the valley of darkness,**
   I fear no evil, for you are with me. ↓

SECOND READING 1 Cor 15:51-57

[O Death, Where Is Your Victory?]

St. Paul tells us that our risen body will be a body so changed by the power of God as to be immortal. Christ died for sin which is the cause of our death; he rose from the dead to be the cause of our resurrection.

A reading from the first Letter of Saint Paul
to the Corinthians

BROTHERS and sisters: Behold, I tell you a mystery. We shall not all fall asleep, but we will all be changed, in an instant, in the blink of an eye, at the last trumpet. For the trumpet will sound, the dead will be raised incorruptible, and we shall be changed. For that which is corruptible must clothe itself with incorruptibility, and that which is mortal must clothe itself with immortality. And when this which is corruptible clothes itself with incorruptibility and this which is mortal clothes itself with immortality, then the word that is written shall come about:
   Death is swallowed up in victory.
   Where, O death, is your victory?
   Where, O death, is your sting?
The sting of death is sin, and the power of sin is the law. But thanks be to God who gives us the victory through our Lord Jesus Christ.—The word of the Lord. ℟. **Thanks be to God.** ↓

ALLELUIA Mt 25:34   [Inherit the Kingdom]
℟. **Alleluia, alleluia.**
Come, you who are blessed by my Father;

inherit the kingdom prepared for you
from the foundation of the world.
℟. **Alleluia, alleluia.** ↓

GOSPEL Jn 6:37-40   [Eternal Life for Believers]

> Jesus here indicates that God wills to save all people.
> Everyone who approaches the Son and believes in him will
> be raised up on the last day to the glory of eternal life.

℣. The Lord be with you. ℟. **And also with you.**
✠ A reading from the holy Gospel according to John.
℟. **Glory to you, Lord.**

JESUS said to the crowds: "Everything that the
Father gives me will come to me, and I will not reject anyone who comes to me, because I came down
from heaven not to do my own will but the will of the
one who sent me. And this is the will of the one who
sent me, that I should not lose anything of what he
gave me, but that I should raise it on the last day. For
this is the will of my Father, that everyone who sees
the Son and believes in him may have eternal life, and
I shall raise him up on the last day."—The Gospel of
the Lord. ℟. **Praise to you, Lord Jesus Christ.**

→ No. 14, p. 18

PRAYER OVER THE GIFTS   [United in Christ's Love]
Lord,
we are united in this sacrament
by the love of Jesus Christ.
Accept these gifts
and receive our brothers and sisters
into the glory of your Son,
who is Lord for ever and ever.
℟. **Amen.**   → No. 21, p. 22 (Pref. P 77-81)

COMMUNION ANT. Jn 11:25-26 [The Resurrection and the Life]
**I am the resurrection and the life, says the Lord. If
anyone believes in me, even though he dies, he will**

live. Anyone who lives and believes in me will not
die. ↓

PRAYER AFTER COMMUNION   [Christ's Peace]
Lord God,
may the death and resurrection of Christ
which we celebrate in this eucharist
bring the departed faithful to the peace of your eternal
   home.
We ask this in the name of Jesus the Lord.
R︞. **Amen.**   → No. 32, p. 70

Optional Solemn Blessings, p. 92, and Prayers Over the People, p. 99

ALL SOULS
2

ENTRANCE ANT. See 4 Ezr 2:34-35   [Eternal Rest]
**Give them eternal rest, O Lord, and may your light
shine on them for ever.**   → No. 2, p. 10

OPENING PRAYER   [For All the Departed]
Let us pray
   [for all our departed brothers and sisters]
Lord God,
you are the glory of believers
and the life of the just.
Your Son redeemed us
by dying and rising to life again.
Since our departed brothers and sisters believed in the
   mystery of our resurrection,
let them share the joys and blessings of the life to
   come.
We ask this through our Lord Jesus Christ, your Son,
who lives and reigns with you and the Holy Spirit,
one God, for ever and ever. R︞. **Amen.** ↓

*The readings found in Masses 1 and 3 may also be used, as
well as those listed on p. 567.*

FIRST READING Wis 4:7-15   [The Just Are with God]

In contrast to the illusions of worldly wisdom, the "hope" of those who have known and believed in God is "full of immortality." After being tried by God they will reap their reward.

A reading from the Book of Wisdom

THE just man, though he die early,
  shall be at rest.
For the age that is honorable comes not
    with the passing of time,
  nor can it be measured in terms of years.
Rather, understanding is the hoary crown for men,
  and an unsullied life, the attainment of old age.
He who pleased God was loved;
  he who lived among sinners was transported—
snatched away, lest wickedness pervert his mind
  or deceit beguile his soul;
for the witchery of paltry things obscures what is right
  and the whirl of desire transforms the innocent mind.
Having become perfect in a short while,
  he reached the fullness of a long career;
for his soul was pleasing to the LORD,
  therefore he sped him out of the midst of wickedness.
But the people saw and did not understand,
  nor did they take this into account.
The word of the Lord. ℟. **Thanks be to God.** ↓

RESPONSORIAL PSALM Ps 25   [Preserve My Life]

℟. To   you,   O   Lord,   I   lift   my   soul.
    ℟. Or: No one who waits for you, O Lord, will ever be
        put to shame.

Remember that your compassion, O LORD,
  and your love are from of old.

In your kindness remember me,
  because of your goodness, O LORD.

℞. **To you, O Lord, I lift my soul.**

℞. Or: **No one who waits for you, O Lord, will ever be
       put to shame.**

Relieve the troubles of my heart,
  and bring me out of my distress.
Put an end to my affliction and my suffering;
  and take away all my sins.

℞. **To you, O Lord, I lift my soul.**

℞. Or: **No one who waits for you, O Lord, will ever be
       put to shame.**

Preserve my life, and rescue me;
  let me not be put to shame, for I take refuge in you.
Let integrity and uprightness preserve me,
  because I wait for you, O LORD.

℞. **To you, O Lord, I lift my soul.** ↓

℞. Or: **No one who waits for you, O Lord, will ever be
       put to shame.** ↓

SECOND READING Phil 3:20-21   [Citizenship in Heaven]

   While toiling for the building up of this earth, Christians
   know that their ultimate citizenship is in heaven. Salvation
   does not lie in the body but in Christ, who at his second
   coming will transform the body of all his faithful to be like
   his glorious body.

A reading from the Letter of Saint Paul
to the Philippians

BROTHERS and sisters: Our citizenship is in heaven,
and from it we also await a savior, the Lord Jesus
Christ. He will change our lowly body to conform with
his glorified body by the power that enables him also
to bring all things into subjection to himself.—The
word of the Lord. ℞. **Thanks be to God.** ↓

ALLELUIA Jn 11:25a, 26   [No Death for Believers]

℟. **Alleluia, alleluia.**

I am the resurrection and the life, says the Lord;
whoever believes in me, will never die.

℟. **Alleluia, alleluia.** ↓

GOSPEL Jn 11:17-27   [Rising with Christ]

Amid the human continuous quest for immortality, there is
only one who can impart it to us: Jesus, "the resurrection
and the life." And this immortality will be coupled with a
joy without end.

℣. The Lord be with you. ℟. **And also with you.**

✠ A reading from the holy Gospel according to John.

℟. **Glory to you, Lord.**

WHEN Jesus arrived in Bethany, he found that
Lazarus had already been in the tomb for four
days. Now Bethany was near Jerusalem, only about two
miles away. Many of the Jews had come to Martha and
Mary to comfort them about their brother. When
Martha heard that Jesus was coming, she went to meet
him; but Mary sat at home. Martha said to Jesus, "Lord,
if you had been here, my brother would not have died.
But even now I know that whatever you ask of God,
God will give you." Jesus said to her, "Your brother will
rise." Martha said to him, "I know he will rise, in the resurrection on the last day." Jesus told her, "I am the resurrection and the life; he who believes in me, even if he
dies, will live, and he who lives and believes in me will
never die. Do you believe this?" She said to him, "Yes,
Lord. I have come to believe that you are the Christ, the
Son of God, the one who is coming into the world."—
The Gospel of the Lord. ℟. **Praise to you, Lord Jesus
Christ.**   → No. 14, p. 18

PRAYER OVER THE GIFTS   [Pardon and Peace]

All-powerful Father,
may this sacrifice wash away

the sins of our departed brothers and sisters in the
   blood of Christ.
You cleansed them in the waters of baptism.
In your loving mercy grant them pardon and peace.
We ask this in the name of Jesus the Lord.
R̷. **Amen.**   ➜   No. 21, p. 22 (Pref. P 77-81)

COMMUNION ANT. See 4 Ezr 2:35, 34   [Eternal Light]
**May eternal light shine on them, O Lord, with all your
saints for ever, for you are rich in mercy. Give them
eternal rest, O Lord, and may perpetual light shine on
them for ever, for you are rich in mercy.** ↓

PRAYER AFTER COMMUNION   [For All the Departed]
Lord,
in this sacrament you give us your crucified and risen
   Son.
Bring to the glory of the resurrection our departed
   brothers and sisters
who have been purified by this holy mystery.
Grant this through Christ our Lord.
R̷. **Amen.**   ➜   No. 32, p. 70

Optional Solemn Blessings, p. 92, and Prayers Over the People, p. 99

————————————————

ALL SOULS
3

ENTRANCE ANT. Rom 8:11   [New Life through the Spirit]
**God, who raised Jesus from the dead, will give new
life to our own mortal bodies through his Spirit living
in us.**   ➜   No. 2, p. 10

OPENING PRAYER   [For All the Departed]
Let us pray
   [for all our departed brothers and sisters]
God, our creator and redeemer,
by your power Christ conquered death

and returned to you in glory.
May all your people who have gone before us in faith
share his victory
and enjoy the vision of your glory for ever.
We ask this through our Lord Jesus Christ, your Son,
who lives and reigns with you and the Holy Spirit,
one God, for ever and ever. ℟. **Amen.** ↓

*The readings found in Masses 1 and 2 may also be used, as
well as those listed on p. 567.*

FIRST READING Is 25:6-9   [Death Has Been Destroyed]

**This is the earliest statement of the doctrine that prayers
and sacrifices for the dead are beneficial. It is a holy and
pious thought to think of the dead.**

A reading from the Book of the Prophet Isaiah

O N this mountain the LORD of hosts
   will provide for all peoples.
On this mountain he will destroy
   the veil that veils all peoples,
the web that is woven over all nations;
   he will destroy death forever.
The Lord GOD will wipe away
   the tears from all faces;
the reproach of his people he will remove
   from the whole earth; for the LORD has spoken.
   On that day it will be said:
"Behold our God, to whom we looked to save us!
   This is the LORD for whom we looked;
   let us rejoice and be glad that he has saved us!"
The word of the Lord. ℟. **Thanks be to God.** ↓

RESPONSORIAL PSALM Ps 27   [Union with God]

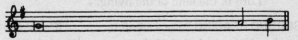

℟. **The   Lord   is   my   light   and   my   sal - va - tion.**

℟. Or: **I believe that I shall see the good things of the Lord
      in the land of the living.**

The LORD is my light and my salvation;
   whom should I fear?
The LORD is my life's refuge;
   of whom should I be afraid?

℟. **The Lord is my light and my salvation.**

℟. Or: **I believe that I shall see the good things of the
      Lord in the land of the living.**

One thing I ask of the LORD;
   this I seek:
to dwell in the house of the LORD
   all the days of my life,
that I may gaze on the loveliness of the LORD
   and contemplate his temple.

℟. **The Lord is my light and my salvation.**

℟. Or: **I believe that I shall see the good things of the
      Lord in the land of the living.**

Hear, O LORD, the sound of my call;
   have pity on me and answer me.
Your presence, O LORD, I seek!
   Hide not your face from me.

℟. **The Lord is my light and my salvation.**

℟. Or: **I believe that I shall see the good things of the
      Lord in the land of the living.**

I believe that I shall see the bounty of the LORD
   in the land of the living.
Wait for the LORD with courage;
   be stouthearted and wait for the LORD!

℟. **The Lord is my light and my salvation.** ↓

℟. Or: **I believe that I shall see the good things of the
      Lord in the land of the living.** ↓

SECOND READING 2 Cor 4:14—5:1   [Eternal Glory]

**In addition to faith in Jesus there is also need of good
works. These will accompany the doers after death to their
advantage. Happy are the dead who die thus in the Lord.**

A reading from the second Letter of Saint Paul
to the Corinthians

BROTHERS and sisters: We know that the One who raised the Lord Jesus will raise us also with Jesus and place us with you in his presence. Everything indeed is for you, so that the grace bestowed in abundance on more and more people may cause the thanksgiving to overflow for the glory of God. Therefore, we are not discouraged; rather, although our outer self is wasting away, our inner self is being renewed day by day. For this momentary light affliction is producing for us an eternal weight of glory beyond all comparison, as we look not to what is seen but to what is unseen; for what is seen is transitory, but what is unseen is eternal. For we know that if our earthly dwelling, a tent, should be destroyed, we have a building from God, a dwelling not made with hands, eternal in heaven.—The word of the Lord. ℟. **Thanks be to God.** ↓

ALLELUIA Cf. Jn 3:16   [Faith unto Life]
℟. **Alleluia, alleluia.**
God so loved the world that he gave his only Son
so that everyone who sees the Son and believes in him
may have eternal life.
℟. **Alleluia, alleluia.** ↓

GOSPEL Jn 14:1-6   [A Place for Us]
Jesus is our way, truth and life who has preceded us to our Father's heavenly house in order to prepare a place also for us. If we trust in him we will safely reach our home at our journey's end.

℣. The Lord be with you. ℟. **And also with you.**
✤ A reading from the holy Gospel according to John.
℟. **Glory to you, Lord.**

JESUS said to his disciples: "Do not let your hearts be troubled. You have faith in God; have faith also in me. In my Father's house there are many dwelling places. If there were not, would I have told you that I am going to prepare a place for you? And if I go and prepare a place for you, I will come back again and take you to myself, so that where I am you also may be. Where I am going you know the way." Thomas said to him, "Master, we do not know where you are going; how can we know the way?" Jesus said to him, "I am the way and the truth and the life. No one comes to the Father except through me."—The Gospel of the Lord. ℟. **Praise to you, Lord Jesus Christ.**

→ No. 14, p. 18

PRAYER OVER THE GIFTS   [Eternal Life]

Lord,
in your kindness accept these gifts for our departed
  brothers and sisters
and for all who sleep in Christ.
May his perfect sacrifice
free them from the power of death
and give them eternal life.
We ask this in the name of Jesus the Lord.
℟. **Amen.**   → No. 21, p. 22 (Pref. P 77-81)

COMMUNION ANT. Phil 3:20-21   [Copies of Christ's Body]

We are waiting for our Savior, the Lord Jesus Christ; he will transfigure our lowly bodies into copies of his own glorious body. ↓

PRAYER AFTER COMMUNION   [Peace and Forgiveness]

Lord,
may our sacrifice bring peace and forgiveness
to our brothers and sisters who have died.
Bring the new life given to them in baptism
to the fullness of eternal joy.
We ask this through Christ our Lord.
℟. **Amen.**   → No. 32, p. 70

Optional Solemn Blessings, p. 92, and Prayers Over the People, p. 99

OTHER POSSIBLE READINGS

Second Reading: Rom 5:5-11; Rom 5:17-21; Rom 6:3-9; Rom 8:14-23; Rom 8:31b-35, 37-39; Rom 14:7-9, 10c-12; 2 Cor 5:1, 6-10; 2 Tm 2:8-13.

Gospel: Mt 5:1-12a; Mt 11:25-30; Mt 25:31-46; Lk 7:11-17; Lk 23:44-46, 50, 52-53; 24:1-6a; Lk 24:13-16, 28-35; Jn 5:24-29; Jn 6:51-59; Jn 11:32-45.

The Readings and Responsorial Psalms given in the Masses for the Dead may also be used.

"Stop making my Father's house a marketplace."

NOVEMBER 9

DEDICATION OF ST. JOHN LATERAN
(32nd SUNDAY IN ORDINARY TIME)

ENTRANCE ANT. Rv 21: 2   [The New Jerusalem]

I saw the holy city, new Jerusalem, coming down from God out of heaven, like a bride adorned in readiness for her husband.   ➜ No. 2, p. 10

OPENING PRAYER   [A Temple of People]

God our Father,
from living stones, your chosen people,
you built an eternal temple to your glory.
Increase the spiritual gifts you have given to your
    Church,
so that your faithful people may continue to grow
into the new and eternal Jerusalem.
We ask this through our Lord Jesus Christ, your Son,
who lives and reigns with you and the Holy Spirit,
one God, for ever and ever. ℟. **Amen.** ↓

OR   [A Church of People]

Father,
you called your people to be your Church.
As we gather together in your name,
may we love, honor, and follow you
to eternal life in the kingdom you promise.
Grant this through our Lord Jesus Christ, your Son
who lives and reigns with you and the Holy Spirit,
one God, for ever and ever. ℟. **Amen.** ↓

FIRST READING Ez 47:1-2, 8-9, 12   [Life-Giving Temple]

> This text is a figure of the life that flows from the new temple
> (which signifies our churches and the Body of Christ) and
> from the new worship brought by Christ. It will overflow the
> earth, producing trees, herbs, and fruits that will become the
> food and medicine of human beings. Water is a sign and
> promise of life.

A reading from the Book of the Prophet Ezekiel

THE angel brought me back to the entrance of the
temple, and I saw water flowing out from beneath
the threshold of the temple toward the east, for the fa-
cade of the temple was toward the east; the water
flowed down from the southern side of the temple, south
of the altar. He led me outside by the north gate, and
around to the outer gate facing the east, where I saw
water trickling from the southern side. He said to me,

"This water flows into the eastern district down upon the Arabah, and empties into the sea, the salt waters, which it makes fresh. Wherever the river flows, every sort of living creature that can multiply shall live, and there shall be abundant fish, for wherever this water comes the sea shall be made fresh. Along both banks of the river, fruit trees of every kind shall grow; their leaves shall not fade, nor their fruit fail. Every month they shall bear fresh fruit, for they shall be watered by the flow from the sanctuary. Their fruit shall serve for food, and their leaves for medicine."—The word of the Lord. ℟. **Thanks be to God.** ↓

RESPONSORIAL PSALM Ps 46   [God in Its Midst]

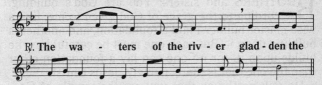

℟. The waters of the river gladden the city of God, the holy dwelling of the Most High.

God is our refuge and our strength,
    an ever-present help in distress.
Therefore we fear not, though the earth be shaken
    and mountains plunge into the depths of the sea.

℟. **The waters of the river gladden the city of God, the holy dwelling of the Most High.**

There is a stream whose runlets gladden the city of God,
    the holy dwelling of the Most High.
God is in its midst; it shall not be disturbed;
    God will help it at the break of dawn.

℟. **The waters of the river gladden the city of God, the holy dwelling of the Most High.**

The LORD of hosts is with us;
    our stronghold is the God of Jacob.

Come! behold the deeds of the LORD,
   the astounding things he has wrought on earth.

℟. **The waters of the river gladden the city of God,
   the holy dwelling of the Most High.** ↓

SECOND READING 1 Cor 3:9c-11, 16-17   [God's Building]

Paul elaborates on the temple figure, of which your parish
church is a sign. God's people can only be a solid building,
in which the Spirit of God dwells, if it is built on the solid
foundation that is Christ.

A reading from the first letter of Saint Paul
to the Corinthians

BROTHERS and sisters: You are God's building.
According to the grace of God given to me, like a
wise master builder I laid a foundation, and another is
building upon it. But each one must be careful how he
builds upon it, for no one can lay a foundation other
than the one that is there, namely, Jesus Christ.

Do you not know that you are the temple of God,
and that the Spirit of God dwells in you? If anyone de-
stroys God's temple, God will destroy that person; for
the temple of God, which you are, is holy.—The word
of the Lord. ℟. **Thanks be to God.** ↓

ALLELUIA 2 Chr 7:16   [Consecrated House]

℟. **Alleluia, alleluia.**
I have chosen and consecrated this house, says the
   Lord,
that my name may be there forever.
℟. **Alleluia, alleluia.** ↓

GOSPEL Jn 2:13-22   [Jesus: Living Temple]

John wants to teach that Jesus put an end to the old way
of worship (in the temple), and inaugurated a new worship, "in Spirit and truth." This transition was accomplished by Jesus' death and resurrection.

℣. The Lord be with you. ℟. **And also with you.**

✢ A reading from the holy Gospel according to John.
℟. **Glory to you, Lord.**

SINCE the Passover of the Jews was near, Jesus went up to Jerusalem. He found in the temple area those who sold oxen, sheep, and doves, as well as the money changers seated there. He made a whip out of cords and drove them all out of the temple area, with the sheep and oxen, and spilled the coins of the money changers and overturned their tables, and to those who sold doves he said, "Take these out of here, and stop making my Father's house a marketplace." His disciples recalled the words of Scripture, *Zeal for your house will consume me.* At this the Jews answered and said to him, "What sign can you show us for doing this?" Jesus answered and said to them, "Destroy this temple and in three days I will raise it up." The Jews said, "This temple has been under construction for forty-six years, and you will raise it up in three days?" But he was speaking about the temple of his body. Therefore, when he was raised from the dead, his disciples remembered that he had said this, and they came to believe the Scripture and the word Jesus had spoken.—The Gospel of the Lord. ℟. **Praise to you, Lord Jesus Christ.**   → No. 14, p. 18

PRAYER OVER THE GIFTS   [Answered Prayers]

Lord, receive our gifts.
May we who share this sacrament
experience the life and power it promises,
and hear the answer to our prayers.
We ask this in the name of Jesus the Lord. ℟. **Amen.** ↓

PREFACE (P 53)   [A House of Prayer]

℣. The Lord be with you. ℟. **And also with you.**
℣. Lift up your hearts. ℟. **We lift them up to the Lord.**

℣. Let us give thanks to the Lord our God. ℟. **It is right to give him thanks and praise.**

Father, all-powerful and ever-living God,
we do well always and everywhere to give you thanks.
Your house is a house of prayer,
and your presence makes it a place of blessing.
You give us grace upon grace
to build the temple of your Spirit,
creating its beauty from the holiness of our lives.
Your house of prayer
is also the promise of the Church in heaven.
Here your love is always at work,
preparing the Church on earth
for its heavenly glory
as the sinless bride of Christ,
the joyful mother of a great company of saints.
Now, with the saints and all the angels
we praise you for ever.   → No. 23, p. 23

COMMUNION ANT. 1 Pt 2:5   [A Spiritual House]
**Like living stones let yourselves be built on Christ as
a spiritual house, a holy priesthood.** ↓

PRAYER AFTER COMMUNION [Temple of God's Presence]
Father,
you make your Church on earth
a sign of the new and eternal Jerusalem.
By sharing in this sacrament
may we become the temple of your presence
and the home of your glory.
Grant this in the name of Jesus the Lord.
℟. **Amen.**   → No. 32, p. 70

Optional Solemn Blessings, p. 92, and Prayers Over the People, p. 99

*"The sun will be darkened. . . . And then they will see
'the Son of Man. . . .' "*

NOVEMBER 16

33rd SUNDAY IN ORDINARY TIME

ENTRANCE ANT. Jer 29:11, 12, 14   [God Hears Us]

**The Lord says: my plans for you are peace and not
disaster; when you call to me, I will listen to you, and
I will bring you back to the place from which I exiled
you.**   ➜ No. 2, p. 10

OPENING PRAYER   [Faithful Service]

Let us pray
    [that God will help us to be faithful]
Father of all that is good,
keep us faithful in serving you,
for to serve you is our lasting joy.
We ask this through our Lord Jesus Christ, your Son,
who lives and reigns with you and the Holy Spirit,
one God, for ever and ever. ℞. **Amen.** ↓

ALTERNATIVE OPENING PRAYER   [God's Truth]

Let us pray
    [with hearts that long for peace]

573

Father in heaven,
ever-living source of all that is good,
from the beginning of time you promised man salvation
through the future coming of your Son, our Lord
 Jesus Christ.
Help us to drink of his truth
and expand our hearts with the joy of his promises,
so that we may serve you in faith and in love
and know for ever the joy of your presence.
We ask this through Christ our Lord. ℟. **Amen.** ↓

FIRST READING Dn 12:1-3   [The Last Judgment]

Daniel describes events that will occur at the end of the
world. It will be a time of distress, but the just will live forever in glory while others shall endure horror and disgrace.

A reading from the Book of the Prophet Daniel

IN those days, I, Daniel,
 heard this word of the Lord:
"At that time there shall arise
  Michael, the great prince,
  guardian of your people;
it shall be a time unsurpassed in distress
  since nations began until that time.
At that time your people shall escape,
  everyone who is found written in the book.

"Many of those who sleep in the dust of the earth shall
    awake;
  some shall live forever,
  others shall be an everlasting horror and disgrace.

"But the wise shall shine brightly
  like the splendor of the firmament,
and those who lead the many to justice
  shall be like the stars forever."
The word of the Lord. ℟. **Thanks be to God.** ↓

RESPONSORIAL PSALM Ps 16   [God Our Hope]

℟. **You are my in-her-i-tance, O Lord!**

O LORD, my allotted portion and my cup,
  you it is who hold fast my lot.
I set the LORD ever before me;
  with him at my right hand I shall not be disturbed.

℟. **You are my inheritance, O Lord!**

Therefore my heart is glad and my soul rejoices,
  my body, too, abides in confidence;
because you will not abandon my soul to the nether-
    world,
  nor will you suffer your faithful one to undergo cor-
    ruption.

℟. **You are my inheritance, O Lord!**

You will show me the path to life,
  fullness of joys in your presence,
  the delights at your right hand forever.

℟. **You are my inheritance, O Lord!** ↓

SECOND READING Heb 10:11-14, 18   [Jesus in Glory]

**Jesus, unlike the other priests, offered only one sacrifice
for sin and took his place forever at God's right hand. He
has perfected those who are being sanctified.**

A reading from the Letter to the Hebrews

BROTHERS and sisters: Every priest stands daily at
his ministry, offering frequently those same sacrifices that can never take away sins. But this one offered one sacrifice for sins, and took his seat forever
at the right hand of God; now he waits until his enemies are made his footstool. For by one offering he
has made perfect forever those who are being consecrated.

Where there is forgiveness of these, there is no longer offering for sin.—The word of the Lord. ℟. **Thanks be to God.** ↓

ALLELUIA Lk 21:36   [Be Vigilant]

℟. **Alleluia, alleluia.**

Be vigilant at all times
and pray that you have the strength to stand before
   the Son of Man.

℟. **Alleluia, alleluia.** ↓

GOSPEL Mk 13:24-32   [The Last Judgment]

Jesus tells about the end of the world—the darkening of the sun, moon and stars. Then the Son of Man will come in glory. Learn from the signs of the fig tree. No one knows the exact time of this happening.

℣. The Lord be with you. ℟. **And also with you.**

✛ A reading from the holy Gospel according to Mark.

℟. **Glory to you, Lord.**

JESUS said to his disciples: "In those days after that tribulation the sun will be darkened, and the moon will not give its light, and the stars will be falling from the sky, and the powers in the heavens will be shaken.

"And then they will see 'the Son of Man coming in the clouds' with great power and glory, and then he will send out the angels and gather his elect from the four winds, from the end of the earth to the end of the sky.

"Learn a lesson from the fig tree. When its branch becomes tender and sprouts leaves, you know that summer is near. In the same way, when you see these things happening, know that he is near, at the gates. Amen, I say to you, this generation will not pass away until all these things have taken place. Heaven and earth will pass away, but my words will not pass away.

"But of that day or hour, no one knows, neither the angels in heaven, nor the Son, but only the Father."— The Gospel of the Lord. ℟. **Praise to you, Lord Jesus Christ.**   ➜ No. 14, p. 18

PRAYER OVER THE GIFTS   [Eternal Life]

Lord God,
may the gifts we offer
increase our love for you
and bring us to eternal life.
We ask this in the name of Jesus the Lord.
℟. **Amen.**   ➜ No. 21, p. 22 (Pref. P 29-36)

COMMUNION ANT. Ps 73:28   [Hope in God]

It is good for me to be with the Lord and to put my hope in him. ↓

OR Mk 11:23, 24   [Believing Prayer]

I tell you solemnly, whatever you ask for in prayer, believe that you have received it, and it will be yours, says the Lord. ↓

PRAYER AFTER COMMUNION   [Growth in Love]

Father,
may we grow in love
by the eucharist we have celebrated
in memory of the Lord Jesus,
who is Lord for ever and ever.
℟. **Amen.**   ➜ No. 32, p. 70

Optional Solemn Blessings, p. 92, and Prayers Over the People, p. 99

"My kingdom does not belong to this world."

NOVEMBER 23

CHRIST THE KING

ENTRANCE ANT. Rv 5:12; 1:6   [Christ's Glory]

The Lamb who was slain is worthy to receive strength and divinity, wisdom and power and honor: to him be glory and power for ever.   → No. 2, p. 10

OPENING PRAYER   [King of the Universe]

Let us pray
   [that all men will acclaim Jesus as Lord]
Almighty and merciful God,
you break the power of evil
and make all things new
in your Son Jesus Christ, the King of the universe.
May all in heaven and earth acclaim your glory
and never cease to praise you.
We ask this . . . for ever and ever. ℟. **Amen.** ↓

ALTERNATIVE OPENING PRAYER   [Spiritual Kingdom]

Let us pray
   [that the kingdom of Christ
   may live in our hearts and come to our world]

Father all-powerful, God of love,
you have raised our Lord Jesus Christ from death to
    life,
resplendent in glory as King of creation.
Open our hearts,
free all the world to rejoice in his peace,
to glory in his justice, to live in his love.
Bring all mankind together in Jesus Christ your Son,
whose kingdom is with you and the Holy Spirit,
one God, for ever and ever. ℟. **Amen.** ↓

FIRST READING Dn 7:13-14   [Everlasting Kingship]

**Daniel foresees the coming of the Son of Man. He receives
all honor and glory. All peoples of every nation serve him.
His kingship shall last forever.**

A reading from the Book of the Prophet Daniel

A S the visions during the night continued, I saw
    one like a Son of man coming,
    on the clouds of heaven;
when he reached the Ancient One
    and was presented before him,
the one like a Son of man received dominion, glory,
        and kingship;
    all peoples, nations, and languages serve him.
His dominion is an everlasting dominion
    that shall not be taken away,
    his kingship shall not be destroyed.
The word of the Lord. ℟. **Thanks be to God.** ↓

RESPONSORIAL PSALM Ps 93   [The Lord Is King]

℟. **The Lord is king; he is robed in maj - es - ty.**

The LORD is king, in splendor robed;
    robed is the LORD and girt about with strength.

℟. **The Lord is king;**
    he is robed in majesty.

And he has made the world firm,
    not to be moved.
Your throne stands firm from of old;
    from everlasting you are, O LORD.

℟. **The Lord is king;**
    he is robed in majesty.

Your decrees are worthy of trust indeed;
    holiness befits your house,
    O LORD, for length of days.

℟. **The Lord is king;**
    he is robed in majesty. ↓

SECOND READING Rv 1:5-8   [The Alpha and the Omega]

By the shedding of his blood, Jesus has made us a royal
nation of priests to serve God. The Lord God is the Alpha
and Omega—the beginning and the end. He is Almighty.

A reading from the Book of Revelation

JESUS Christ is the faithful witness, the firstborn of
the dead and ruler of the kings of the earth. To him
who loves us and has freed us from our sins by his
blood, who has made us into a kingdom, priests for
his God and Father, to him be glory and power forever
and ever. Amen.

Behold, he is coming amid the clouds,
    and every eye will see him,
    even those who pierced him.
All the peoples of the earth will lament him.
    Yes. Amen.

"I am the Alpha and the Omega," says the Lord God,
"the one who is and who was and who is to come, the
almighty."—The word of the Lord. ℟. **Thanks be to**
God. ↓

ALLELUIA Mk 11:9, 10   [Son of David]

℟. **Alleluia, alleluia.**
Blessed is he who comes in the name of the Lord!

Blessed is the kingdom of our father David that is to
  come!

℟. **Alleluia, alleluia.** ↓

GOSPEL Jn 18:33b-37   [Christ's Kingdom]

  Before Pilate, Jesus admits that he is a king but that his
  kingdom is not of this world. Jesus says that he came into
  the world to testify to the truth.

℣. The Lord be with you. ℟. **And also with you.**

✛ A reading from the holy Gospel according to John.

℟. **Glory to you, Lord.**

PILATE said to Jesus, "Are you the King of the
     Jews?" Jesus answered, "Do you say this on your
own or have others told you about me?" Pilate answered, "I am not a Jew, am I? Your own nation and
the chief priests handed you over to me. What have
you done?" Jesus answered, "My kingdom does not
belong to this world. If my kingdom did belong to this
world, my attendants would be fighting to keep me
from being handed over to the Jews. But as it is, my
kingdom is not here." So Pilate said to him, "Then you
are a king?" Jesus answered, "You say I am a king.
For this I was born and for this I came into the world,
to testify to the truth. Everyone who belongs to the
truth listens to my voice."—The Gospel of the Lord. ℟.
Praise to you, Lord Jesus Christ.   → No. 14, p. 18

PRAYER OVER THE GIFTS   [Unity and Peace]

Lord,
we offer you the sacrifice
by which your Son reconciles mankind.
May it bring unity and peace to the world.
We ask this through Christ our Lord.

℟. **Amen.** ↓

PREFACE (P 51)   [Marks of Christ's Kingdom]

℣. The Lord be with you. ℟. **And also with you.**

℣. Lift up your hearts. ℟. **We lift them up to the Lord.**

℣. Let us give thanks to the Lord our God. ℟. **It is right to give him thanks and praise.**

Father, all-powerful and ever-living God,
we do well always and everywhere to give you thanks.
You anointed Jesus Christ, your only Son, with the oil
   of gladness,
as the eternal priest and universal king.
As priest he offered his life on the altar of the cross
and redeemed the human race
by his one perfect sacrifice of peace.
As king he claims dominion over all creation,
that he may present to you, his almighty Father,
an eternal and universal kingdom:
a kingdom of truth and life,
a kingdom of holiness and grace,
a kingdom of justice, love, and peace.
And so, with all the choirs of angels in heaven
we proclaim your glory
and join in their unending hymn of praise:

→ No. 23, p. 23

COMMUNION ANT. Ps 29:10-11   **[Gift of Peace]**
**The Lord will reign for ever and will give his people
the gift of peace.** ↓

PRAYER AFTER COMMUNION   **[Joy of Christ's Kingdom]**
Lord,
you give us Christ, the King of all creation,
as food for everlasting life.
Help us to live by his gospel
and bring us to the joy of his kingdom,
where he lives and reigns for ever and ever.
℟. **Amen.**   → No. 32, p. 70

Optional Solemn Blessings, p. 92, and Prayers Over the People, p. 99

SAINT JOSEPH
HYMNAL

Praise My Soul, The King of Heaven

1

F. Lyte

John Goss

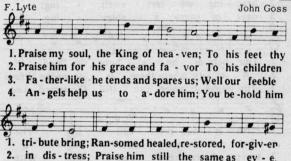

1. Praise my soul, the King of hea - ven; To his feet thy
2. Praise him for his grace and fa - vor To his children
3. Fa - ther-like he tends and spares us; Well our feeble
4. An - gels help us to a - dore him; You be -hold him

1. tri - bute bring; Ran-somed healed, re-stored, for-giv-en
2. in dis - tress; Praise him still the same as ev - e.
3. frame he knows; In his hand he gen - tly bears us,
4. face to face; Sun and moon, bow down be-fore him,

1. Ev - er -more his prais - es sing: Al - le - lu - ia!
2. Slow to chide, and swift to bless: Al - le - lu - ia!
3. Res -cues us from all our foes: Al - le - lu - ia!
4. Dwell-ers all in time and space. Al - le - lu - ia!

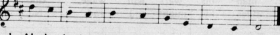

1. Al - le - lu - ia! Praise the ev - er - last - ing King.
2. Al - le - lu - ia! Glo - rious in his faith -ful -ness.
3. Al - le - lu - ia! Wide - ly yet his mer - cy flows.
4. Al - le - lu - ia! Praise with us the God of grace.

A Mighty Fortress Is Our God

Cyr de Brant

M. Luther

1. A might-y for - tress is our God, A
2. Here Crys-tal ri - vers flow a - long, Their
3. Thy ways and works, Cre - a - tor, Lord, Make

1. bul - wark nev - er fail - ing,
2. brac - ing wa - ters swell - ing;
3. days of peace a - chiev - ing.

1. Our help -er he a - bove the flood Of
2. A ci - ty where there is no wrong Where
3. Thy might-y voice can still the sword And

1. earth - ly woe pre - vail - ing. The
2. God and saints are dwell - ing. If
3. ways of wrath pre - vail - ing. With

1. earth and rag - ing sea, Re-
2. kings and ru - lers rage, And
3. faith and trust in God, Who

1. lease their pow - ers free; God
2. man his wars will wage, God
3. rules by might and rod, No

1. wat -ches from the height and shields us with his
2. is our hope and shield. Just rea - son ne'er to
3. man need ev - er fear, The God of Hosts is

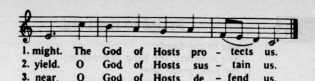

1. might.	The	God	of	Hosts	pro – tects	us.
2. yield.	O	God	of	Hosts	sus – tain	us.
3. near.	O	God	of	Hosts	de – fend	us.

Praise God from Whom All Blessings Flow

3

1. Praise God, from whom all blessings flow;
   Praise him, all creatures here below;
   Praise him above, ye heav'nly host:
   Praise Father, Son, and Holy Ghost.

2. All people that on earth do dwell.
   Sing to the Lord with cheerful voice;
   Him serve with mirth, his praise forth tell,
   Come ye before him and rejoice.

3. Know that the Lord is God indeed:
   Without our aid he did us make;
   We are his flock, he doth us feed.
   And for his sheep he doth us take.

4. O enter then his gates with praise,
   Approach with joy his courts unto;
   Praise, laud, and bless his name always,
   For it is seemly so to do. Amen.

Faith of Our Fathers

4

1. Faith of our fathers! living still,
   In spite of dungeon, fire, and sword:
   O how our hearts beat high with joy,
   Whene'er we hear that glorious word!

Refrain: Faith of our fathers holy faith,
            We will be true to thee till death.

2. Faith of our fathers! We will love
   Both friend and foe in all our strife,
   And preach thee too, as love knows how,
   By kindly words and virtuous life.

3. Faith of our fathers! Mary's prayers
   Shall keep our country close to thee:
   And through the truth that comes from God.
   O we shall prosper and be free.

5   Praise to the Lord

1. Praise to the Lord,
     The almighty, the King of creation;
   O my soul, praise him,
     For he is our health and salvation;
   Hear the great throng,
     Joyous with praises and song,
   Sounding in glad adoration.

2. Praise to the Lord,
     Who doth prosper thy way and defend thee;
   Surely his goodness
     And mercy shall ever attend thee;
   Ponder anew
     What the almighty can do,
   Who with his love doth befriend thee.

3. Praise to the Lord,
     O, let all that is in me adore him!
   All that hath breath join
     In our praises now to adore him!
   Let the "Amen"
     Sung by all people again
   Sound as we worship before him. Amen.

6   God Father Praise and Glory

1. God Father, praise and glory
     Thy children bring to thee.
   Good will and peace to mankind
     Shall now forever be.

   Refrain: O most Holy Trinity,
     Undivided Unity; Holy God,
       Mighty God, God immortal be adored.

2. And thou, Lord Coeternal,
     God's sole begotten Son;
   O Jesus, King anointed,
     Who hast redemption won. *Refrain*

3. O Holy Ghost, Creator,
     Thou gift of God most high;
   Life, love and sacred Unction
     Our weakness thou supply. *Refrain*

588

Now Thank We All Our God   7

1. Now thank we all our God,
      With heart and hands and voices,
   Who wondrous things hath done,
      In whom his world rejoices;
   Who from our mother's arms
      Hath blessed us on our way
   With countless gifts of love,
      And still is ours today.

2. All praise and thanks to God,
      The Father now be given,
   The Son, and him who reigns
      With them in highest heaven,
   The one eternal God
      Whom earth and heav'n adore;
   For thus it was, is now,
      And shall be ever more.

The Church's One Foundation   8

1

The Church's one foundation
Is Jesus Christ her Lord.
She is his new creation,
By water and the Word;
From heav'n he came and sought her,
To be his holy bride;
With his own blood he bought her,
And for her life he died.

2

Elect from ev'ry nation,
Yet one o'er all the earth.
Her charter of salvation,
One Lord, one faith, one birth;
One holy Name she blesses,
Partakes one holy food;
And to one hope she presses,
With ev'ry grace endued.

3

Mid toil and tribulation,
And tumult of her war.
She waits the consummation
Of peace for evermore;
Till with the vision glorious
Her loving eyes are blest,
And the great Church victorious
Shall be the Church at rest.

589

9 O King of Might and Splendor

Dom Gregory Murray, O.S.B.

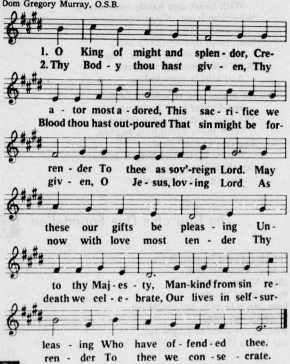

1. O King of might and splen-dor, Cre-a-tor most a-dored, This sac-ri-fice we ren-der To thee as sov'-reign Lord. May these our gifts be pleas-ing Un-to thy Maj-es-ty, Man-kind from sin re-leas-ing Who have of-fend-ed thee.

2. Thy Bod-y thou hast giv-en, Thy Blood thou hast out-poured That sin might be for-giv-en, O Je-sus, lov-ing Lord. As now with love most ten-der Thy death we cel-e-brate, Our lives in self-sur-ren-der To thee we con-se-crate.

10 Praise the Lord of Heaven

Praise the Lord of Heaven,
  Praise Him in the height.
Praise Him all ye angels,
Praise Him stars and light;
  Praise Him skies and waters
  which above the skies
When His word commanded,
  Mighty did arise,

Praise Him man and maiden,
  Princes and all kings,
Praise Him hills and mountains,
  All created things;
Heav'n and earth He fashioned
  mighty oceans raised;
This day and forever
  His name shall be praised.

Alleluia! Alleluia! Hearts and Voices

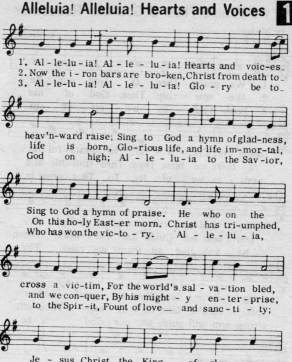

1. Al - le - lu - ia! Al - le - lu - ia! Hearts and voic - es
2. Now the i - ron bars are bro - ken, Christ from death to
3. Al - le - lu - ia! Al - le - lu - ia! Glo - ry be to

heav'n-ward raise; Sing to God a hymn of glad-ness,
life is born, Glo-rious life, and life im - mor-tal,
God on high; Al - le - lu - ia to the Sav - ior,

Sing to God a hymn of praise. He who on the
On this ho-ly East - er morn. Christ has tri-umphed,
Who has won the vic - to - ry. Al - le - lu - ia,

cross a vic-tim, For the world's sal - va - tion bled,
and we con-quer, By his might - y en - ter - prise,
to the Spir - it, Fount of love _ and sanc - ti - ty;

Je - sus Christ, the King of glo - ry,
We with him to life e - ter - nal
Al - le - lu - ia! Al - le - lu - ia!

Now is ris - en from the dead.
By his re - sur - rec - tion rise.
To the Tri - une Ma - jes - ty.

Ps. 26:12
Tr. Julia B. Cady

E. Kremser

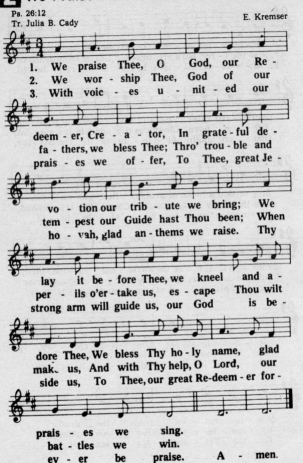

1. We praise Thee, O God, our Re-
2. We wor-ship Thee, God of our
3. With voic-es u-nit-ed our

deem-er, Cre-a-tor, In grate-ful de-
fa-thers, we bless Thee; Thro' trou-ble and
prais-es we of-fer, To Thee, great Je-

vo-tion our trib-ute we bring; We
tem-pest our Guide hast Thou been; When
ho-vah, glad an-thems we raise. Thy

lay it be-fore Thee, we kneel and a-
per-ils o'er-take us, es-cape Thou wilt
strong arm will guide us, our God is be-

dore Thee, We bless Thy ho-ly name, glad
make us, And with Thy help, O Lord, our
side us, To Thee, our great Re-deem-er for-

prais-es we sing.
bat-tles we win.
ev-er be praise. A-men.

Rejoice, the Lord is King

13

C. Wesley, alt.

J. Darwall, 1770

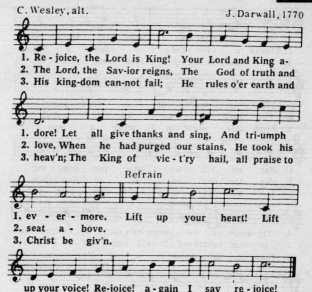

1. Re - joice, the Lord is King! Your Lord and King a-
2. The Lord, the Sav-ior reigns, The God of truth and
3. His king-dom can-not fail; He rules o'er earth and

1. dore! Let all give thanks and sing, And tri-umph
2. love, When he had purged our stains, He took his
3. heav'n; The King of vic - t'ry hail, all praise to

Refrain

1. ev - er - more. Lift up your heart! Lift
2. seat a - bove.
3. Christ be giv'n.

up your voice! Re-joice! a - gain I say re - joice!

We Gather Together

14

(Same Melody as Hymn No. 12)

1. We gather together to ask the Lord's blessing;
   He chastens and hastens his will to make known;
   The wicked oppressing now cease from distressing:
   Sing praises to his name; he forgets not his own.

2. Beside us to guide us, our God with us joining,
   Ordaining, maintaining his kingdom divine;
   So from the beginning the fight we were winning:
   Thou Lord, wast at our side: all glory be thine.

3. We all do extol thee, thou leader triumphant,
   And pray that thou still our defender wilt be.
   Let thy congregation escape tribulation:
   Thy name be ever praised! O Lord, make us free!

15 ## Lord, Dismiss Us with Thy Blessing

1. Lord dis-miss us with thy bless-ing;
2. Thanks to thee and a-dor-a-tion
3. O when, Lord, thy love shall call us,

1. Fill our hearts with joy and peace;
2. For the scrip-tures' joy-ful sound,
3. From this world of strife a-way,

1. May we all, thy love pos-sess-ing,
2. May the fruit of thy re-demp-tion
3. Let not fear of death ap-pall us

1. Tri-umph in re-deem-ing grace: O re-fresh us,
2. In our hearts and lives a-bound; Ev-er faith-ful,
3. Glad thy sum-mons to o-bey: May we ev-er

1. O re-fresh us, and the world its tur-moil cease.
2. ev-er faith-ful to the ways of truth be found.
3. May we ev-er reign with thee in end-less day.

16 ## Holy, Holy, Holy

1. Holy, holy, holy! Lord God almighty.
   Early in the morning our song shall rise to thee:
   Holy, holy, holy! Merciful and mighty.
   God in three persons, blessed Trinity.

2. Holy, holy, holy! Lord God almighty.
   All thy works shall praise thy name in earth and
       sky and sea;
   Holy, holy, holy! Merciful and mighty.
   God in three persons, blessed Trinity.

594

3. Holy, holy, holy! All thy saints adore thee,
   Praising thee in glory, with thee to ever be;
   Cherubim and Seraphim, falling down before thee,
   Which wert and art and evermore shall be.

To Jesus Christ, Our Sovereign King

17

1. To Jesus Christ, our sov'reign King,
   Who is the world's Salvation,
   All praise and homage do we bring
   And thanks and adoration.

2. Your reign extend, O King benign,
   To ev'ry land and nation;
   For in your kingdom, Lord divine,
   Alone we find salvation.

3. To you and to your Church, great King,
   We pledge our heart's oblation;
   Until before your throne we sing
   In endless jubilation.

Refrain:

Christ Jesus, Victor! Christ Jesus, Ruler!
Christ Jesus, Lord and Redeemer!

Father, We Thank Thee

18

1. Father, we thank thee who has planted
   The Holy Name within our hearts,
   Knowledge and faith and life immortal
   Jesus thy Son to us imparts.
   Thou, Lord, didst make all for thy pleasure,
   Didst give man food for all his days.
   Giving in Christ the Bread eternal;
   Thine is the power, be thine the praise.

2. Watch o'er thy Church, O Lord, in mercy,
   Save it from evil, guard it still,
   Perfect it in thy love, unite it,
   Cleansed and conformed, unto thy will.
   As grain, once scatter'd on the hillside,
   Was in this broken bread made one,
   So from all lands thy Church be gather'd
   Into thy Kingdom by the Son. Amen.

19   Crown Him with Many Crowns

1. Crown him with many crowns,
   The Lamb upon his throne;
   Hark how the heav'ly anthem drowns
   All music but its own;

   Awake my soul, and sing
   Of him who died for thee,
   And hail him as thy matchless King
   Through all eternity.

2. Crown him of lords the Lord,
   Who over all doth reign,
   Who once on earth, the incarnate Word,
   For ransomed sinners slain,

   Now lives in realms of light,
   Where saints with angels sing
   Their songs before him day and night,
   Their God, Redeemer, King.

20   O Perfect Love

1. O perfect love, all human thought transcending,
   Lowly we kneel in prayer before thy throne,
   That theirs may be the love that knows no ending,
   Whom thou for evermore dost join in one.

2. O perfect Life, be thou their full assurance
   Of tender charity and steadfast faith,
   Of patient hope, and quiet, brave endurance,
   With child-like trust that fears not pain nor death.

21   On Jordan's Bank

1. On Jordan's bank the Baptist's cry
   Announces that the Lord is nigh
   Awake and hearken, for he brings
   Glad tidings of the King of Kings.

2. Then cleansed be ev'ry breast from sin;
   Make straight the way of God within,
   Oh, let us all our hearts prepare
   For Christ to come and enter there.

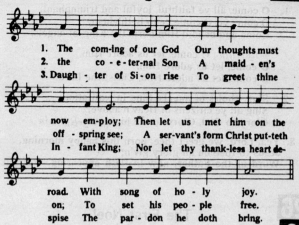

1. The com-ing of our God   Our thoughts must
2. the co - e - ter-nal Son   A maid - en's
3. Daugh - ter of Si - on rise   To greet thine

now em-ploy; Then let us met him on the
off - spring see; A ser-vant's form Christ put-teth
In - fant King; Nor let thy thank-less heart de-

road. With song of ho - ly joy.
on; To set his peo - ple free.
spise The par - don he doth bring.

O Come, O Come, Emmanuel

23

John M. Neale, Tr.   Melody adapted by T. Helmore

O come, O come, Emmanuel,
And ransom captive Israel,
That mourns in lowly exile here,
Until the Son of God appear.

       Refrain: **Rejoice! Rejoice! O Israel,**
       To thee shall come Emmanuel.

Come, Thou Long Expected Jesus

24

1. Come, thou long expected Jesus,
   Born to set thy people free;
   From our sins and fears release us,
   Let us find our rest in thee.

2. Israel's strength and consolation,
   Hope of all the earth thou art;
   dear desire of every nation,
   Joy of every longing heart.

3. Born thy people to deliver,
   Born a child and yet a king.
   Born to reign in us for ever,
   Now thy gracious kingdom bring.

25 O Come, All Ye Faithful

1. O come, all ye faithful, joyful and triumphant,
   O come ye, O come ye to Bethlehem;
   Come and behold Him born, the King of angels.

   —*Refrain:* O come, let us adore Him,
   O come, let us adore Him,
   O come, let us adore Him, Christ the Lord.

2. Sing, choirs of angels, Sing in exultation,
   Sing all ye citizens of Heav'n above;
   Glory to God, Glory to the highest. —*Refrain*

3. Yea, Lord, we greet thee, born this happy morning,
   Jesus to thee be all glory giv'n;
   Word of the Father, now in flesh appearing.—Refrain

26 The First Noel

1. The first Noel the angel did say,
   Was to certain poor shepherds in fields as they lay;
   In fields where they lay keeping their sheep
   On a cold winter's night that was so deep.

   —*Refrain:* Noel, Noel, Noel, Noel,
   Born is the King of Israel.

2. They looked up and saw a star,
   Shining in the east, beyond them far,
   And to the earth it gave great light,
   And so it continued both day and night. —*Refrain*

4. This star drew nigh to the northwest,
   O'er Bethlehem it took its rest,
   And there it did stop and stay,
   Right over the place where Jesus lay. *Refrain*

5. Then entered in those wise men three,
   Full reverently upon their knee,
   And offered there, in his presence,
   Their gold and myrrh and frankincense. *Refrain*

A Child Is Born in Bethlehem
Three Magi Kings

27

Carlton

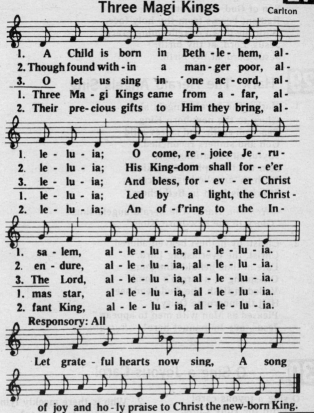

1. A Child is born in Beth-le-hem, al-
2. Though found with-in a man-ger poor, al-
3. O let us sing in one ac-cord, al-
1. Three Ma-gi Kings came from a-far, al-
2. Their pre-cious gifts to Him they bring, al-

1. le-lu-ia; O come, re-joice Je-ru-
2. le-lu-ia; His King-dom shall for-e'er
3. le-lu-ia; And bless, for-ev-er Christ
1. le-lu-ia; Led by a light, the Christ-
2. le-lu-ia; An of-f'ring to the In-

1. sa-lem, al-le-lu-ia, al-le-lu-ia.
2. en-dure, al-le-lu-ia, al-le-lu-ia.
3. The Lord, al-le-lu-ia, al-le-lu-ia.
1. mas star, al-le-lu-ia, al-le-lu-ia.
2. fant King, al-le-lu-ia, al-le-lu-ia.

Responsory: All

Let grate-ful hearts now sing, A song

of joy and ho-ly praise to Christ the new-born King.

Silent Night

28

Silent night, holy night!
All is calm, all is bright.
'Round yon Virgin Mother and
Child,
Holy Infant so tender and mild:
Sleep in heavenly peace,
Sleep in heavenly peace!

Silent night, holy night!
Shepherds quake at the sight!
Glories stream from heaven afar,
Heav'nly hosts sing Alleluia:
Christ, the Savior is born,
Christ, the Savior is born!

599

3. Silent night, holy night,
    Son of God, lov's pure light
    Radiant beams from thy holy face,
    With the dawn of redeeming grace,
    Jesus, Lord, at thy birth,
    Jesus Lord, at thy birth.

29 Hark! The Herald Angels Sing

1. Hark! The herald angels sing,
    Glory to the new-born King,
    Peace on earth, and mercy mild
    God and sinners reconciled."
    Joyful all ye nations rise,
    Join the triumph of the skies.
    With th' angelic host proclaim,
    "Christ is born in Bethlehem."

    —*Refrain.* Hark! The herald angels sing,
    "Glory to the new-born King."

2. Christ, by highest heaven adored,
    Christ, the everlasting Lord.
    Late in time behold Him come,
    Off-spring of a virgin's womb.
    Veiled in flesh, the God-head see;
    Hail th' incarnate Deity!
    Pleased as Man with men to appear,
    Jesus, our Immanuel here! —*Refrain.*

30 O Sing a Joyous Carol

O sing a joyous carol
    Unto the Holy Child,
And praise with gladsome
        voices
    His mother undefiled.
Our gladsome voices greeting
    Shall hail our Infant King;
And our sweet Lady listens
    When joyful voices sing.

2. Who is there meekly lying
        In yonder stable poor?
Dear children, it is Jesus;
    He bids you now adore.
Who is there kneeling by him
    In Virgin beauty fair?
It is our Mother Mary,
    She bids you all draw near.

600

Joy to the World

Joy to the world! The Lord is come;
　Let earth receive her King;
Let every heart prepare him room,
　And heav'n and nature sing,
And heav'n and nature sing,
　And heaven, and heaven and
　　nature sing.

Joy to the world! the Savior reigns;
　Let men their songs employ,
While fields and floods,
　Rocks, hills, and plains,
Repeat the sounding joy,
　Repeat the sounding joy,
Repeat, repeat the sounding joy.

O Come Little Children

O come little children, O come one and all
Draw near to the crib here in Bethlehem's stall
And see what a bright ray of heaven's delight,
Our Father has sent on this thrice holy night.

He lies there, O Children, on hay and straw,
Dear Mary and Joseph regard Him with awe,
The shepherds, adoring, how humbly in pray'r
Angelical choirs with song rend the air.

O children bend low and adore Him today,
O lift up your hands like the shepherds, and pray
Sing joyfully children, with hearts full of love
In jubilant song join the angels above.

A Great and Mighty Wonder

A great and mighty wonder!
A full and holy cure!
The Virgin bears the Infant
With Virgin honor pure!

　Refrain:
　Repeat the hymn again!
　To God on high be glory,
　And peace on earth to men.

The Word becomes incarnate,
And yet remains on high;
And cherubim sing anthems
To shepherds from the sky　Refrain:

34   Good Christian Men Rejoice

Tr. John Mason Neale   German

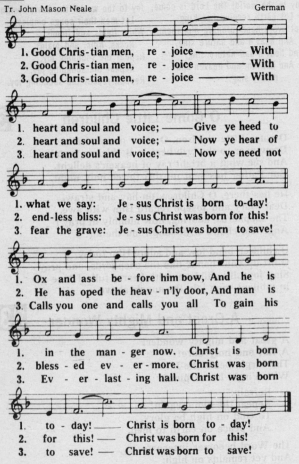

1. Good Chris-tian men, re - joice ——— With
2. Good Chris-tian men, re - joice ——— With
3. Good Chris-tian men, re - joice ——— With

1. heart and soul and voice; ——— Give ye heed to
2. heart and soul and voice; ——— Now ye hear of
3. heart and soul and voice; ——— Now ye need not

1. what we say: Je - sus Christ is born to-day!
2. end-less bliss: Je - sus Christ was born for this!
3. fear the grave: Je - sus Christ was born to save!

1. Ox and ass be - fore him bow, And he is
2. He has oped the heav - n'ly door, And man is
3. Calls you one and calls you all To gain his

1. in the man - ger now. Christ is born
2. bless - ed ev - er - more. Christ was born
3. Ev - er - last - ing hall. Christ was born

1. to - day! ——— Christ is born to - day!
2. for this! ——— Christ was born for this!
3. to save! ——— Christ was born to save!

602

Angels We Have Heard on High

1. Angels we have heard on high,
    Sweetly singing o'er our plains,
    And the mountains in reply
    Echoing their joyous strains.

    Refrain: Gloria in excelsis Deo. (Repeat)

2. Shepherds, why this jubilee,
    Why your rapturous song prolong?
    What the gladsome tidings be
    Which inspire your heav'nly song? —*Refrain*

3. Come to Bethlehem and see
    Him whose birth the angels sing;
    Come, adore on bended knee
    Christ the Lord, the new-born King. —*Refrain*

Away in a Manger

1. Away in a manger, no crib for his bed,
    The little Lord Jesus laid down his sweet head.
    The stars in the bright sky looked down where he lay,
    The little Lord Jesus asleep on the hay.

2. The cattle are lowing, the baby awakes,
    But little Lord Jesus no crying he makes.
    I love thee, Lord Jesus! Look down from the sky,
    And stay by my side until morning is nigh.

3. Be near me Lord Jesus, I ask thee to stay
    Close by me forever, and love me I pray
    Bless all the dear children in thy tender care,
    And fit us for heaven to live wth thee there.

O Little Town of Bethlehem

O little town of Bethlehem,
How still we see thee lie!
Above the deep and dreamless sleep
The silent stars go by;
Yet in the dark streets shineth
The everlasting Light;
The hopes and fears of all the years
Are met in thee tonight.

For Christ is born of Mary,
And gathered all above,
While mortals sleep, the angels keep
Their watch of wondering love.
O morning stars, together
Proclaim the holy birth!
And praising sing to God the King
And peace to men on earth.

O holy Child of Bethlehem!
Descend on us we pray;
Cast out our sin, and enter in,
Be born in us today.
We hear the Christmas angels,
The great glad tidings tell;
O come to us, abide with us,
Our Lord Emmanuel.

38   What Child Is This

What child is this, who laid to rest,
On Mary's lap is sleeping?
Whom angels greet with anthem's sweet,
While shepherds watch are keeping?

Refrain. This, this is Christ the King,
whom shepherds guard and angels sing:
Haste, haste to bring him laud,
The Babe, the Son of Mary.

Why lies he in such mean estate
Where ox and ass are feeding?
Good Christian fear, for sinner's here
The silent Word is pleading:

So bring him incense, gold, and myrrh,
Come peasant, king to own him,
The King of kings salvation brings,
Let loving hearts enthrone him.

604

As with Gladness Men of Old

1. As with gladness men of old
   Did the guiding star behold,
   As with joy they hailed its light.
   Leading onward, beaming bright,
   So, most gracious Lord, may we
   Evermore beled to thee.

2. As with joyful steps they sped
   To that lowly manger bed,
   There to bend the knee before
   him, whom heav'n and earth adore,
   So may we, our worship pay.
   For the blessing of this day.

We Three Kings

1. We three kings of Orient are
   Bearing gifts we traverse afar,
   Field and fountain, moor and mountain,
   Following yonder Star.

   Refrain: O Star of wonder, Star of night,
   Star with royal beauty bright,
   Westward leading, still proceeding,
   Guide us to thy perfect light,

2. Born a king on Bethlehem's plain,
   Gold I bring to crown Him again,
   King forever, ceasing never,
   Over us all to reign. —*Refrain*

3. Frankincense to offer have I
   Incense owns a Deity high,
   Prayer and praising, all men raising.
   Worship Him, God most High. —*Refrain*

4. Myrrh is mine, its bitter perfume
   Breathes a life of gathering gloom:
   Sorrowing, sighing, bleeding, dying.
   Sealed in the stone-cold tomb. —*Refrain*

5. Glorious now behold Him arise,
   King and God and Sacrifice,
   Alleluia, Alleluia,
   Earth to the heavens replies. —*Refrain*

41 Of the Father's Love Begotten

1. Of the Father's love begotten
   Ere the worlds began to be,
   He is Alpha and Omega,
   He the source, the ending He,
   Of the things that are, that have been
   And that future years shall see,
   Refrain: Ever more and ever more.

2. O that birth for ever blessed,
   When the Virgin, full of grace,
   By the Holy Ghost conceiving,
   Bore the Savior of our race;
   And the Babe, the world's Redeemer,
   First reveal'd His sacred face. *(Refrain)*

42 To the Name

1. To the name that brings salvation
   Honor worship let us pay,
   Which for many a generation
   Had in God's fore-knowledge lay,
   But with holy exultation
   We may sing aloud today.

2. 'Tis the name for adoration
   'Tis the name of victory
   'Tis the name for meditation
   In this vale of misery,
   'Tis the name of veneration
   By the citizens on high.

43 Holy God, We Praise Thy Name

1. Holy God, we praise Thy Name!
     Lord of all, we bow before Thee!
   All on earth Thy sceptre claim,
     All in heaven above adore Thee.
   Infinite Thy vast domain,
     Everlasting is Thy reign. *Repeat last two lines*

2. Hark! the loud celestial hymn,
     Angel choirs above are raising;
   Cherubim and seraphim,
     In unceasing chorus praising,
   Fill the heavens with sweet accord;
     Holy, holy, holy Lord! *Repeat last two lines*

606

Lord, Who throughout These 40 Days

1. Lord, who throughout these forty days
   For us did fast and pray,
   Teach us with you to mourn our sins,
   And close by you to stay.

2. And through these days of penitence,
   And through your Passiontide,
   Yea, evermore, in life and death,
   Jesus! with us abide.

3. Abide with us, that so, this life
   Of suff'ring over past,
   An Easter of unending joy
   We may attain at last! Amen.

When I Behold the Wondrous Cross 45

1. When I ___ be-hold the won-drous cross
   On which the prince of glo-ry died,—
   My rich-est gain I count_ but loss,
   And pour con-tempt on all_ my pride.

2. For-bid_ it, Lord, that I should boast,
   Save in the death of Christ, my God;—
   The vain things that at-tract_ me most,
   I sac-ri-fice them to_ his blood.

3. See from_ his head, his hands, his feet,
   What grief and love flow min-gled down;—
   Did e'er such love that sor-row meet,
   Or thorns com-pose so rich_ a crown?

4. Were all_ the realms of na-ture mine,
   It would be off-'ring far_ too small;—
   Love so a-maz-ing, so_ di-vine,
   De-mands my soul, my life,_ my all.

46

O Sacred Head Surrounded

1. O sacred Head surrounded
   By crown of piercing thorn!
   O bleeding Head, so wounded,
   Reviled, and put to scorn!
   Death's pallid hue comes ov'r you,
   The glow of life decays,
   Yet angel hosts adore you,
   And tremble as they gaze.

2. I see your strength and vigor
   All fading in the strife,
   And death with cruel rigor,
   Bereaving you of life.
   O agony and dying!
   O love to sinners free!
   Jesus, all grace supplying,
   O turn your face on me.

47

Redeemer, King And Savior

(Tune as above, no. 46)

1. Redeemer, King and Savior
   Your death we celebrate
   So good, yet born our brother,
   You live in human state.

   O Savior, in your dying
   You do your Father's will,
   Give us the strength to suffer
   To live for others still.

2. Your dying and your rising
   Give hope and life to all.
   Your faithful way of giving
   Embraces great and small.
   Help us to make our journey,
   To walk your glorious way,
   And from the night of dying
   To find a joy-filled day.

608

Where Charity and Love Prevail 48

1. Where char - i - ty and love pre - vail
2. With grate - ful joy and ho - ly fear
3. For - give we now each oth - er's faults
4. Let strife a - mong us be un - known,
5. Let us re - call that in our midst
6. No race nor creed can love ex - clude

1. There God is ev - er found;
2. His char - i - ty we learn;
3. As we our faults con - fess;
4. Let all con - ten - tion cease;
5. Dwells God's be - got - ten Son;
6. If hon - ored be God's Name;

1. Brought here to - geth - er by Christ's love
2. Let us with heart and mind and soul
3. And let us love each oth - er well
4. Be his the glo - ry that we seek,
5. As mem - bers of his Bod - y joined
6. Our broth - er - hood em - brac - es all

1. By love are we thus bound.
2. Now love him in re - turn.
3. In Chris - tian ho - li - ness.
4. Be ours his ho - ly peace.
5. We are in him made one.
6. Whose Fa - ther is the same.

609

O Faithful Cross

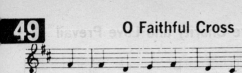

1. O faith-ful Cross, O no-blest tree! In
2. Thou tree of glo-ry, tree of life, Dost
3. Thou, thou a-lone were well es-teemed To

all the woods there's none like thee! No earth-ly
mark the world's most might-y strife. For once had
bear the Lamb who man re-deemed; Thy spread-ing

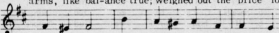

groves, no shad-y bowers. Pro-duce such leaves, such
been the sigh of shame, For Je-sus now the
arms, like bal-ance true; Weighed out the price for

fruit, such flowers. Sweet are the nails and sweet the
world doth claim. Lo, from the cross, his al-tar
sin-ners due. And on thy al-tar, meek-ly

wood That bears a load so sweet, so good!
throne, He gent-ly draws and rules his own.
laid, The Lamb of God a-tone-ment made.

O God, Our Help in Ages Past

1.

O God, our help in ages past,
Our hope for years to
come,
Our shelter from the stormy
blast,
And our eternal home.

2.

Under the shadow of Thy
throne,
Thy saints have dwelt
secure.
Sufficient is Thine arm
alone,
And our defense is sure.

3.

A thousand ages in Thy
sight,
Are like an evening gone:
Short as the watch that
ends the night,
Before the rising sun.

4.

O God, our help in ages past,
Our hope for years to
come,
Be Thou our guide while
troubles last,
And our eternal home.

I. Watts.

Were You There

1. Were you there when they cru-ci-fied my Lord?
2. Were you there when they nailed him to the tree?
3. Were you there when they laid him in the tomb?

1. Lord? Were you there when they
2. tree? Were you there when they
3. tomb? Were you there when they

1. cru-ci-fied my Lord?
2. nailed him to the tree?
3. laid him in the tomb?

Oh _____

Some-times it caus-es me to

trem-ble, trem-ble, trem-ble.

1. Were you
2. Were you
3. Were you

1. there when they cru-ci-fied my Lord?
2. there when they nailed him to the tree?
3. there when they laid him in the tomb?

52 At the Cross Her Station Keeping

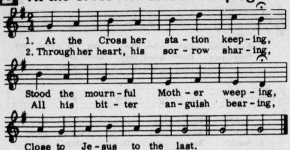

1. At the Cross her sta - tion keep - ing,
2. Through her heart, his sor - row shar - ing,

Stood the mourn - ful Moth - er weep - ing,
All his bit - ter an - guish bear - ing,

Close to Je - sus to the last.
Now at length the sword has passed. A - men.

3 Oh, how sad and sore distressed
Was that Mother highly blessed
of the sole begotten One!

4 Christ above in torment hangs,
She beneath beholds the pangs
Of her dying, glorious Son.

5 Is there one who would not weep
'Whelmed in miseries so deep
Christ's dear Mother to behold?

6 Can the human heart refrain
From partaking in her pain,
In that mother's pain unto'd?

7 Bruised, derided, cursed, defiled,
She beheld her tender Child,
All with bloody scourges rent.

8 For the sins of His own nation
Saw Him hang in desolation
Till His spirit forth He sent.

9 O sweet Mother! fount of love,
Touch my spirit from above,
Make my heart with yours accord

10 Make me feel as you have felt.
Make my soul to glow and melt
With the love of Christ, my Lord.

11 Holy Mother, pierce me through,
In my heart each wound renew
Of my Savior crucified

12 Let me share with you His pain,
Who for all our sins was slain,
Who for me in torments died.

13 Let me mingle tears with you
Mourning Him Who mourned for
me,
All the days that I may live.

14 By the Cross with you to stay,
There with you to weep and pray,
Is all I ask of you to give.

15 Virgin of all virgins blest!
Listen to my fond request
Let me share your grief divine.

16 Let me, to my latest breath
In my body bear the death
Of that dying Son of yours

17 Wounded with His every wound,
Steep my soul till it has swooned
In His very blood away

18 Be to me, O Virgin, nigh,
Lest in flames I burn and die,
In His awful judgment day

19 Christ, when You shall call me
hence,
Be Your Mother my defense,
Be Your Cross my victory

20 While my body here decays,
May my soul Your goodness
praise,
Safe in heaven eternally.
Amen Alleluia

612

Jesus Christ Is Risen Today

1. Jesus Christ is ris'n today, **alleluia!**
   Our triumphant holy day, **alleluia.**
   Who did once upon the cross, **alleluia!**
   Suffer to redeem our loss, alleluia.

2. Hymns of praise then let us sing, **alleluia!**
   Unto Christ our heav'nly King, **alleluia!**
   Who endured the cross and grave, **alleluia.**
   Sinners to redeem and save, **alleluia!**

3. Sing we to our God above, **alleluia!**
   Praise eternal as his love, **alleluia!**
   Praise him, all ye heav'nly host, **alleluia.**
   Father, Son and Holy Ghost, **alleluia!**

At the Lamb's High Feast We Sing

1. At the Lamb's high feast we sing
   Praise to our victor'ous King,
   Who has washed us in the tide
   Flowing from his pierced side;
   Praise we him whose love divine
   Gives the guests his Blood for wine,
   Gives his Body for the feast,
   Love the Victim, Love the Priest.

2. When the Paschal blood is poured,
   Death's dark Angel sheathes his sword;
   Israel's hosts triumphant go
   Through the wave that drowns the foe
   Christ, the Lamb whose Blood was shed,
   Paschal victim, Paschal bread;
   With sincerity and love
   Eat we Manna from above.

55 All Glory, Laud and Honor

Tr. John Mason Neale, 1851   Melchior Teschner, pub. 1615

1. All glo-ry, laud, and hon--or To
3. The com-pa-ny of an--gels Are
5. To thee be-fore thy Pas--sion They

1. thee, Re-deem-er, King! To whom the lips of
3. prais-ing thee on high; And mor-tal men and
5. sang their hymns of praise: To thee, now nigh ex-

1. chil-dren Made glad ho-san-nas ring. ★
3. all things Cre-a-ted make re-ply. ★
5. alt-ed, Our mel-o-dy we raise. ★

2. Thou art the King of Is-ra-el, Thou
4. The peo-ple of the He-brews With
6. Thou didst ac-cept their prais-es: Ac-

2. Dav-id's roy-al Son, Who in the Lord's Name
4. palms be-fore thee went: Our praise and prayer and
6. cept the praise we bring, Who in all good de-

2. com-est, The King and Bless-ed One. ★
4. an-thems Be-fore thee we pre-sent. ★
6. light-est, thou good and gra-cious King. ★

★ Refrain: after each stanza except the first.

Christ the Lord Is Risen Today

Tr. Jane E. Leeson, 1807-1882   Traditional

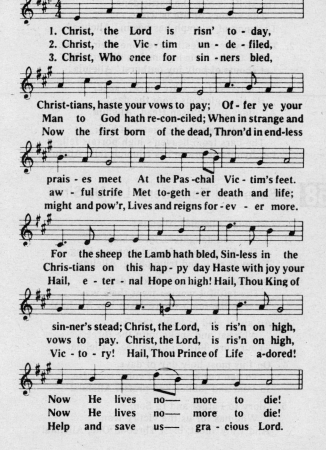

1. Christ, the Lord is risn' to-day,
2. Christ, the Vic-tim un-de-filed,
3. Christ, Who once for sin-ners bled,

Christ-tians, haste your vows to pay; Of-fer ye your
Man to God hath re-con-ciled; When in strange and
Now the first born of the dead, Thron'd in end-less

prais-es meet At the Pas-chal Vic-tim's feet.
aw-ful strife Met to-geth-er death and life;
might and pow'r, Lives and reigns for-ev-er more.

For the sheep the Lamb hath bled, Sin-less in the
Chris-tians on this hap-py day Haste with joy your
Hail, e-ter-nal Hope on high! Hail, Thou King of

sin-ner's stead; Christ, the Lord, is risn' on high,
vows to pay. Christ, the Lord, is risn' on high,
Vic-to-ry! Hail, Thou Prince of Life a-dored!

Now He lives no—— more to die!
Now He lives no—— more to die!
Help and save us—— gra-cious Lord.

57 The Strife is O'er

Alleluia! Alleluia! Alleluia!

1. The strife is o'er, the battle done!
      The victory of life is won!
   The song of triumph has begun! Alleluia!

2. The powers of death have done their worst,
      But Christ their legions has dispersed;
   Let shouts of holy joy outburst! Alleluia!

3. The three sad days are quickly sped,
      He rises glor'ous from the dead;
   All glory to our risen Head! Alleluia!

4. He closed the yawning gates of hell;
      The bars from heaven's high portals fell;
   Let hymns of praise His triumph tell! Alleluia!

58 O Sons and Daughters, Let Us Sing!

Alleluia! Alleluia! Alleluia!

1. O sons and daughters, let us sing!
      The King of heav'n, the glorious King,
   Today is ris'n and triumphing. Alleluia!

2. On Easter morn, at break of day,
      The faithful women went their way
   To seek the tomb where Jesus lay. Alleluia!

3. An angel clad in white they see,
      Who sat and spoke unto the three,
   "Your Lord doth go to Galilee." Alleluia!

4. On this most holy day of days,
      To you our hearts and voice we raise,
   In laud and jubilee and praise. Alleluia!

5. Glory to Father and to Son,
      Who has for us the vict'ry won
   And Holy Ghost; blest Three in One. Alleluia!

1. Christ the Lord is ris'n a - gain!
2. He who gave for us his life,
3. He who bore all pain and loss

Christ has bro - ken ev - 'ry chain!
Who for us en - dured the strife,
Com - fort - less up - on the Cross,

Hark, the an - gels shout for joy,
Is our Pas - chal Lamb to - day!
Lives in glo - ry now on high,

Sing - ing ev - er - more on high, —
We too sing for joy and say, —
Pleads for us and hears our cry, —

Al - le - lu - ia, Al - le - lu -

SING WE TRIUMPHANT HYMNS OF PRAISE **60**

1. Sing we triumphant hymns of praise
   To greet our Lord these festive days.
   Alleluia, alleluia!
   Who by a road before untrod
   Ascended to the throne of God.
   Alleluia, alleluia, alleluia, alleluia.

2. In wond'ring awe His faithful band
   Upon the Mount of Olives stand.
   Alleluia, alleluia!
   And with the Virgin Mother see
   Their Lord ascend in majesty.
   Alleluia, alleluia, alleluia, alleluia.

61 All Hail, Adored Trinity

All hail, adored Trinity:
All hail, eternal Unity,
O God the Father, God the Son,
And God the Spirit, ever One.

2. Three Persons praise we evermore,
And One, Eternal God adore;
In thy sure mercy ever kind,
May we our true protection find.

3. O Trinity! O Unity!
Be present as we worship thee;
And with the songs the angels sing
Unite the hymns of praise we bring.

62 Lift Up, Ye Princes of the Sky

1. Lift up, ye prin - ces of the sky; Lift
2. Lift up your por - tals, lift them high; Ye

1. up your por - tals, lift them high; And
2. prin - ces of the con - quered sky, And

1. you, O ev - er - last - ing gates, Back
2. you, O ev - er - last - ing gates, Back

1. on your gold - en hin - ges fly, For
2. on your gold - en hin - ges fly, For

1. lo, the King of glo - ry waits To
2. lo, the King of glo - ry waits The

1. en - ter in with vic - to - ry.
2. Lord of hosts, the Lord most high.

618

1. Come, Ho‐ly Ghost, Cre‐a‐tor come From
2. Thou who art called the Par‐a‐clete, Best
3. O guide our minds with thy bless'd light With
4. All glo‐ry to the Fa‐ther, be, With

thy bright heav'n‐ly throne, Come
gift of God a‐bove, The
love our hearts in‐flame; And
his co‐e‐qual Son; The

take pos‐ses‐sion of our souls, And
liv‐ing spring, the liv‐ing fire, Sweet
with thy strength which ne'er de‐cays, Con‐
same to thee, great Par‐a‐clete, While

make them all thy own.
unc‐tion and true love.
form our mor‐tal frame.
end‐less a‐ges run.

Creator Spirit, Lord of Grace   64

Creator Spirit, Lord of Grace,
Make thou our hearts thy dwelling place;
And, with thy might celestial, aid
The souls of those whom thou hast made.

O to our souls thy light impart,
And give thy love to every heart;
Turn all our weakness into might,
O thou the source of life and light.

To God the Father let us sing,
To God the Son, our risen king;
And equally with thee adore
The Spirit, God forevermore.

Come Down, O Love Divine

1. Come down, I Love di - vine,
2. O let it free - ly burn,
3. And so the yearn - ing strong,

1. Seek thou this soul of mine, And
2. Till earth - ly pas - sions turn To
3. With which the soul will long, Shall

1. vis - it it with thine own ar - dour glow - ing;
2. dust and ash - es in its heat con - sum - ing;
3. far out - pass the pow'r of hu - man tell - ing;

1. O Com - fort - er, draw near, With - in my
2. And let thy glo - rious light Shine ev - er
3. For none can guess its grace, Till he be -

1. heart ap - pear, And kin - dle it, thy
2. on my sight, And clothe me round, the
3. come the place Where - in the Ho - ly

1. ho - ly flame be - stow - ing.
2. while my path il - lum - ing.
3. Spir - it makes his dwell - ing.

Come Holy Ghost, Creator Blest

1. Come, Holy Ghost, Creator blest,
   And in our hearts take up thy rest;
   Come with thy grace and heav'nly aid
   To fill the hearts which thou hast made,
   To fill the hearts which thou hast made.

2. O Comforter, to thee we cry,
   Thou heav'nly gift of God most high;
   Thou fount of life and fire of love
   And sweet anointing from above,
   And sweet anointing from above.

3. Praise we the Father, and the Son,
   And the blest Spirit with them one;
   And may the Son on us bestow
   The gifts that from the Spirit flow,
   The gifts that from the Spirit flow.

O God of Loveliness

1. O God of loveliness, O Lord of Heav'n above,
   How worthy to possess my heart's devoted love!
   So sweet Thy Countenance, so gracious to behold,
   That one, and only glance to me were bliss untold.

2. Thou are blest Three in One, yet undivided still;
   Thou art that One alone whose love my heart can fill,
   The heav'ns and earth below, were fashioned by Thy
   Word;
   How amiable art Thou, my ever dearest Lord!

3. O loveliness supreme, and beauty infinite
   O everflowing Stream, and Ocean of delight;
   O life by which I live, my truest life above,
   To You alone I give my undivided love.

68 — O Jesus, Joy of Loving Hearts

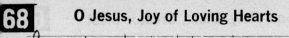

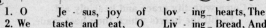

1. O Je - sus, joy of lov - ing_ hearts, The
2. We taste and eat, O Liv - ing_ Bread, And
3. Your truth un - changed has ev - er __ stood, You

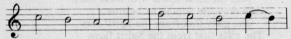

fount of life, the joy of men, From
long to feast up - on you still; We
save all them who on you call; To

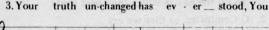

all the plea - sures earth im - parts, We__
drink of you, the Foun - tain - head Our__
them that seek, You are all good To__

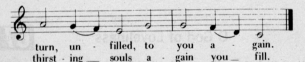

turn, un - filled, to you a - gain.
thirst - ing_ souls a - gain you_ fill.
them that__ find, you are their_ all.

69

Jesus, Highest Heaven's Completeness

1. Jesus, highest heaven's completeness,
   Name of music to the ear,
   To the lips surpassing sweetness,
   Wine the fainting heart to cheer.

2. Eating thee (you) the soul may hunger,
   Drinking still a thirst may be,
   But for earthly food no longer
   Nor for any stream but thee (you).

3. Jesus, all delight exceeding,
   Only hope of hearts distressed,
   Weeping eyes and spirits bleeding
   Find in thee a place to rest.

When Morning Gilds the Skies

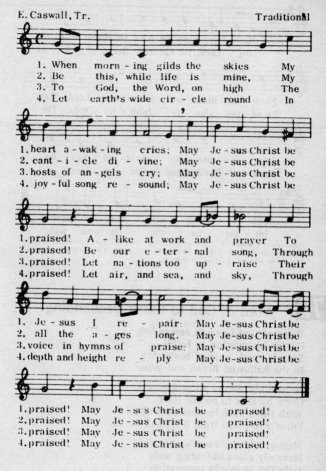

E. Caswall, Tr.

Traditional

1. When morn - ing gilds the skies My
2. Be this, while life is mine, My
3. To God, the Word, on high The
4. Let earth's wide cir - cle round In

1. heart a - wak - ing cries; May Je - sus Christ be
2. cant - i - cle di - vine; May Je - sus Christ be
3. hosts of an - gels cry; May Je - sus Christ be
4. joy - ful song re - sound; May Je - sus Christ be

1. praised! A - like at work and prayer To
2. praised! Be our e - ter - nal song, Through
3. praised! Let na - tions too up - raise Their
4. praised! Let air, and sea, and sky, Through

1. Je - sus I re - pair; May Je - sus Christ be
2. all the a - ges long. May Je - sus Christ be
3. voice in hymns of praise: May Je - sus Christ be
4. depth and height re - ply May Je - sus Christ be

1. praised! May Je - sus Christ be praised!
2. praised! May Je - sus Christ be praised!
3. praised! May Je - sus Christ be praised!
4. praised! May Je - sus Christ be praised!

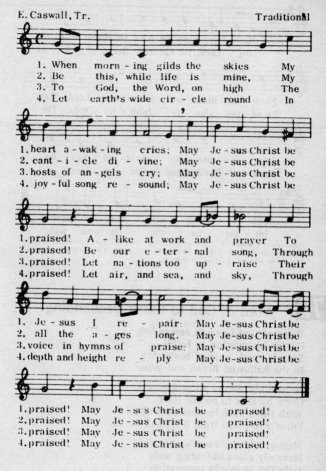

623

71 How Blessed We Are

How bless'd are we who share this Bread, the
Oh Lord, we eat this Bread of Life, the

Flesh and Blood of Christ our Lord. May
Bread you give to faith-ful sons. The

love u-nite us grate-ful-ly, As
peace of Christ, your Son is ours u-

sons of God who live in peace.
nit-ing us who do your will.

72 Word of God to Earth Descending

Word of God to earth descending
Hastes his mission to fulfill
See his hands himself bestowing
In the hallowed Bread and Wine.

Holy Body, Blood all precious
Giv'n by Him to be our food
With them both he doth refresh us
Form'd like him from flesh and blood.

Mighty Victim, earth's salvation
Heav'nly gates unfolding wide
Help thy people in temptation,
Feed them from thy bleeding side.

Loving Shepherd of Your Sheep

1. Lov - ing Shep - herd of your sheep,
2. Lov - ing Shep - herd you did give,
3. Lov - ing Shep - herd ev - er near,

Keep us Lord in safe - ty keep;
Your own life that we might live;
Teach us still your voice to hear;

Noth - ing can your pow'r with - stand,
May we love you day by day,
Suf - fer not our steps to stray

None can pluck us from your hand.
Glad - ly your sweet Will o - bey.
From the straight and nar - row way.

Good Shep - herd, shield us.
Good Shep - herd, lead us.
Good Shep - herd, guide us.

In the Lord's Atoning Grief

1. In the Lord's atoning grief
   Be our rest and sweet relief;
   Deep within our hearts we'll store
   Those dear pains and wrongs he bore.

2. Thorns and cross and nail and spear,
   Wounds that faithful hearts revere,
   Vinegar and gall and reed.
   And the pang his soul that freed.

3. Crucified we thee adore,
   Thee with all our hearts implore;
   With the saints our soul unite.
   In the realms of heav'nly light.

Let All Mortal Flesh Keep Silence

Gerald Moultrie

French, Traditional

1. Let all mortal flesh keep silence, and with fear and trembling stand; Ponder nothing earthly-minded for with blessing in his hand Christ, our God, to earth descend-eth, our full homage to demand.

2. King of kings, yet born of Mary, as of old on earth he stood, Lord of lords in human vesture in the Body and the Blood He will give to all the faithful his own self for heav'nly food.

3. Rank on rank the host of heaven spreads its van-guard on the way, As the Light of Light descends from the realms of endless day, That the powers of hell may vanish as the darkness clears away.

4. At his feet the six-winged seraph, cherubim with sleepless eye, Veil their faces to the Presence, as with ceaseless voice they cry, "Alleluia, alleluia, alleluia, alleluia, Lord Most High!"

626

O Lord, I Am Not Worthy

1. O Lord, I am not worthy,
   That thou should come to me,
   But speak the word of comfort
   My spirit healed shall be.

2. And humbly I'll receive thee,
   The bridegroom of my soul,
   No more by sin to grieve thee
   Or fly thy sweet control.

3. O Sacrament most holy,
   O Sacrament divine,
   All praise and all thanksgiving
   Be every moment thine.

To Christ the Prince of Peace

J. S. Bach

Arr. Cyr de Brant

E. Caswell, Tr.

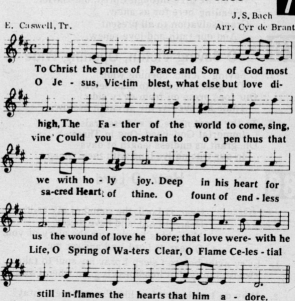

To Christ the prince of Peace and Son of God most
O Je - sus, Vic-tim blest, what else but love di-

high, The Fa - ther of the world to come, sing,
vine Could you con-strain to o - pen thus that

we with ho - ly joy. Deep in his heart for
sa-cred Heart of thine. O fount of end - less

us the wound of love he bore; that love were- with he
Life, O Spring of Wa-ters Clear, O Flame Ce-les - tial

still in-flames the hearts that him a - dore.
cleans-ing all who un - to you draw near.

78 Lord, Accept the Gifts

1. Lord, accept the gifts we offer
   At this Eucharistic Feast.
   Bread and wine to be transformed now
   Through the action of thy priest.
   Take us, too, O Lord, transform us;
   Be thy grace in us increased.

2. May our souls be pure and spotless
   As the Hosts of wheat so fine;
   May all stain of sin be crushed out
   Like the grape that form the wine:
   As we, too, become partakers
   In this sacrifice divine.

3. Take our gifts, almighty Father,
   Living God, eternal, true,
   Which we give through Christ, our Savior,
   Pleading here for us anew.
   Grant salvation to all present
   And our faith and love renew.

79 O Saving Victim, Opening Wide

1. O Saving Victim, opening wide
   The gate of heav'n to man below!
   Our foes press on from ev'ry side:
   Thine aid supply, thy strength bestow.

2. To thy great name be endless praise,
   Immortal God-head, One in Three;
   Oh, grant us endless length of days
   In our true native land with thee. Amen.

80 Hear, O Lord

Refrain: Hear, O Lord, the sound of my call;
Hear, O Lord, and have mercy.
My soul is longing for the glory of you.
O hear, O Lord, and answer me.

1. Ev'ry night before I sleep I pray my soul to take,
   Or else I pray that loneliness is gone when I awake.

2. Why do I no longer feel like I've a place to stay?
   O take me where someone will care, so fear will go
   away.

Sing My Tongue the Savior's Glory

1. Sing my tongue, the Savior's glory,
   Of his flesh the mystr'y sing;
   Of the Blood all price exceeding,
   Shed by our immortal King,
   Destined for the world's redemption,
   From a noble womb to spring.

2. Of a pure and spotless Virgin
   Born for us on earth below,
   He, as Man, with man conversing,
   Stayed, the seeds of truth to sow;
   Then he closed in solemn order
   Wondrously his life of woe.

3. On the night of that Last Supper,
   Seated with his chosen band,
   He the Paschal victim eating,
   First fulfils the Law's command;
   Then as food to his Apostles
   Give himself with his own Hand.

4. Word made flesh the bread of nature
   By his word to Flesh he turns;
   Wine into his blood he changes
   What though sense no change discerns?
   Only he the heart in earnest,
   Faith her lesson quickly learns.

(Tantum ergo)

5. Down in adoration falling
   Lo! the sacred Host we hail
   Lo! o'er ancient forms departing,
   Newer rites of grace prevail;
   Faith for all defects supplying,
   Where the feeble senses fail.

6. To the Everlasting Father,
   And the Son who reigns on high,
   With the Holy Ghost proceeding
   Forth from each eternally
   Be salvation honor, blessing,
   Might, and endless majesty. Amen.

Sing of Mary, Pure and Lowly

Trier, 1695

1. Sing of Ma - ry, pure and low - ly,
   Vir - gin - moth - er un - de - filed,
   Sing of God's own Son most ho - ly,
   Who be - came her lit - tle child.
   Fair - est child of fair - est moth - er,
   God the Lord who came to earth,
   Word made flesh, our ve - ry broth - er,

2. Sing of Je - sus; son of Ma - ry,
   In the home at Na - za - reth.
   Toil and la - bor can - not wea - ry
   Love en - dur - ing un - to death.
   Con - stant was the love he gave her,
   Though he went forth from her side,
   Forth to preach, and heal, and suf - fer,

3. Glo - ry be to God the Fa - ther,
   Glo - ry be to God the Son;
   Glo - ry be to God the Spir - it;
   Glo - ry to the Three in One.
   From the heart of bless - ed Ma - ry,
   From all saints the song as - cends,
   And the Church the strain re - ec - hoes

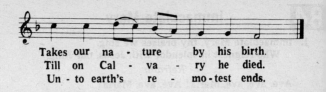

Takes our na - ture by his birth.
Till on Cal - va - ry he died.
Un - to earth's re - mo - test ends.

The God Whom Earth and Sea and Sky 83

Tr. J. M. Neale, alt.   J. S. Bach

1. The God whom earth and sea and sky   A-
2. O Moth-er blest! the chos - en shrine, Where-
3. Blest in the mes- sage Gab -riel brought; Blest
4. O Lord, the Vir - gin born, to thee   E-

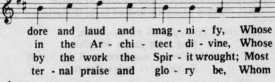

dore and laud and mag - ni - fy, Whose
in the Ar - chi - tect di - vine, Whose
by the work the Spir - it wrought; Most
ter - nal praise and glo - ry be, Whom

might they own, whose praise they tell, In
hand con - tains the earth and sky, Vouch-
blest, to bring to hu - man birth The
with the Fa - ther we a - dore And

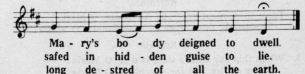

Ma - ry's bo - dy deigned to dwell.
safed in hid - den guise to lie.
long de - sired of all the earth.
Ho - ly Ghost for ev - er - more.

84   Immaculate Mary

1. Immaculate Mary, thy praises we sing,
   Who reignest in splendor with Jesus, our King.

   Refrain:
   Ave, ave, ave, Maria! Ave, ave, Maria!

2. In heaven, the blessed thy glory proclaim,
   On earth, we thy children invoke thy fair name.

   Refrain:

3. Thy name is our power, thy virtues our light,
   Thy love is our comfort, thy pleading our might.

   Refrain:

4. We pray for our mother, the Church upon earth;
   And bless, dearest Lady, the land of our birth.

   Refrain:

85   Hail, Holy Queen Enthroned Above

Hail, holy Queen enthroned above, O Maria!
Hail, Mother of mercy and of love, O Maria!

Refrain: Triumph, all ye cherubim,
          Sing with us, ye seraphim,
          Heav'n and earth resound the hymn.
          Salve, salve, salve Regina.

2. Our life, our sweetness here below, O Maria!
   Our hope in sorrow and in woe, O Maria!

   Refrain:

3. To thee we cry, poor sons of Eve, O Maria!
   To thee we sigh, we mourn, we grieve, O Maria!

   Refrain:

4. Turn, then, most gracious Advocate, O Maria!
   Toward us thine eyes compassionate, O Maria!

   Refrain:

5. When this our exile's time is o'er, O Maria!
   Show us thy Son for evermore, O Maria!

   Refrain:

632

Joseph, Be Our Guide

1. Jo - seph, be our guide and pat - tern,
2. Faith - ful to the guid - ing vi - sion,
3. Lead - ing them through man - y dan - gers
4. Work - man skilled with saw and ham - mer,
5. Train - ing Christ, the grow - ing Mas - ter,

1. Faith - ful to your sa - cred trust,
2. Lis - t'ning to the an - gel's word;
3. To the home in Na - za - reth,
4. Strong to earn the dai - ly bread,
5. In the skill - ful use of tools;

1. Strong pro - tec - tor of the Vir - gin
2. Shield - ing Mar - y from all slan - der,
3. Hum - bly for their needs pro - vid - ing
4. From the gifts of God cre - at - ing
5. Teach - ing him, the world's Re - deem - er,

1. And the in - fant, Je - sus Christ.
2. Guard - ing Christ, the lit - tle Lord.
3. In your wise and stead - fast faith.
4. Use - ful things to meet man's need.
5. Craft - man's love of wood and nails.

1. Jo - seph, firm and faith - ful; guide us,
2. Jo - seph, true and trust - ing, guide us,
3. Jo - seph, brave, o - be - dient, guide us,
4. Jo - seph, strong and stead - fast, guide us,
5. Jo - seph, hum - ble, help - ful, guide us,

1. Jo - seph, walk the way with us.

633

Ye Watchers and Ye Holy Ones

Athelstan Riley, 1858-1945

Cologne, 1623

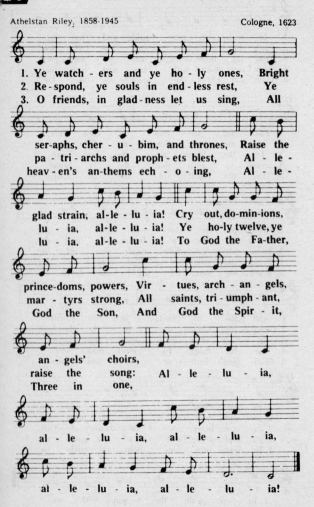

1. Ye watch - ers and ye ho - ly ones, Bright ser-aphs, cher - u - bim, and thrones, Raise the glad strain, al - le - lu - ia! Cry out, do-min-ions, prince-doms, powers, Vir - tues, arch - an - gels, an - gels' choirs,

2. Re - spond, ye souls in end - less rest, Ye pa - tri - archs and proph - ets blest, Al - le - lu - ia, al - le - lu - ia! Ye ho-ly twelve, ye mar - tyrs strong, All saints, tri - umph - ant, raise the song: Al - le - lu - ia,

3. O friends, in glad-ness let us sing, All heav - en's an-thems ech - o - ing, Al - le - lu - ia, al - le - lu - ia! To God the Fa-ther, God the Son, And God the Spir - it, Three in one,

al - le - lu - ia, al - le - lu - ia,

al - le - lu - ia, al - le - lu - ia!

For All the Saints

William W. How
Moderately, in unison

R. Vaughan Williams, 1872-1958

1. For all the saints,
   who from their labors rest,
   Who Thee by faith
   before the world confessed,
   Thy Name, O Jesus, be for ever blest.
   Alleluia, alleluia!

2. O blest communion!
   fellowship divine!
   We feebly struggle,
   they in glory shine;
   Yet all are one in Thee, for all are Thine.
   Alleluia, alleluia!

3. From earth's wide bounds,
   from ocean's farthest coast,
   Through gates of pearl streams
   in the countless host,
   Singing to Father, Son and Holy Ghost.
   Alleluia, alleluia!

Within Thy Sacred Heart

1. With - in Thy Sa - cred Heart, dear Lord, My
2. Say on - ly Thou hast par - doned me, Say

anx - ious thoughts shall rest. I
on - ly I am Thine. In

nei - ther ask for life nor death, Thou
all things else dis - pose of me, Thy

know - est what is best.
Ho - ly Will is mine.

90

My God, How Wonderful Thou Art

Frederick W. Faber

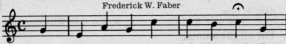

1. My God, how won-der - ful Thou art! Thy
2. How dread are Thine e - ter - nal years, O
3. How won-der-ful, how beau-ti - ful The
4. Oh, how I fear Thee, liv - ing God, With

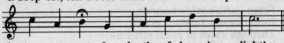

1. Maj - es - ty how bright! How beau - ti - ful Thy
2. ev - er - last-ing Lord, By pros-trate spir-its
3. sight of Thee must be, Thine end-less wis-dom
4. deep-est, ten-d'rest fears And wor-ship Thee with

1. mer - cy - seat In depths of burn-ing light!
2. day and night Un - ceas-ing - ly a - dored!
3. bound-less power And shin - ing pur - i - ty!
4. trem-bling hope And pen - i - ten - tial tears!

91

Peace Prayer of St. Francis

Make me a channel of your peace
Where there is hatred, let me bring you love.
Where there is injury, your pardon, Lord.
And where there's doubt, true faith in you.

Make me a channel of your peace.
Where there's despair in life, let me bring hope.
Where there is darkness only light.
And where there's sadness ever joy.

O Master, grant that I may never seek,
So much to be consoled as to console.
To be understood as to understand.
To be loved, as to love, with all my soul.

Make me a channel of your peace.
It is in pardoning that we are pardoned.
In giving to all men that we receive.
And in dying that we're born to eternal life.

© 1967 Franciscan Communications Center. Reprinted with permission.

For All the Love

92

(Use the same melody as "For All the Saints")

For all the love that in our life abounds,
For all the beauty that this world surrounds,
For music which so joyfully resounds,
Alleluia, Alleluia.

For all the love of family and friends,
And for the love which God in mercy sends,
For all the love toward other he intends,
Alleluia, Alleluia.

For all God's love to bless their vows today,
For all the love to guide them on their way,
For all his love and joy and peace we pray,
Alleluia, Alleluia.

Creighton Lacey

Copyright, 1975, Hymn Society of America

Accept, O Lord

93

Mrs. A. C. Marshall, 1973

Charlotte Hayr

1. Ac - cept, O Lord from grate - ful hearts Our
2. We join our hands, our voi - ces raise, Be -
3. On high the host of an - gels song, Both

thanks for gifts_ thy love im - parts; For
fore thy throng_ to sing thy praise; One
heav'n and earth_ with joy now ring. From

this good life we with thee share, And
fam - i - ly whom thou hast made, Thy
Par - a - dise thy saints give hymn, With

broth - er man, for whom we care.
whole cre - a - tion, here ar - ranged.
love that time nor space can dim.

Copyright, 1966, Hymn Society of America
Text Copyright, 1973, Hymn Society of America

94   With Hearts Renewed

1. With hearts renewed by living faith,
   We lift our thoughts in grateful prayer
   To God our gracious Father.
   Whose plan it was to make us sons
   Through His own Son's redemptive death
   That rescued us from darkness.

   Refrain: Lord God, Savior, gives us strength
            To mould our hearts in your true lifeness.
            Sons and servants of our Father.

2. So rich God's grace in Jesus Christ,
   That we are called as sons of light
   To bear the pledge of glory.
   Through Him in Whom all fullness dwells.
   We offer God our gift of self
   In union with the spirit.

   Refrain: Lord God, Savior, gives us strength . . .

95   Praise the Lord

Praise the Lord for He is glorious,
never shall His promise fail.
God has made His saints victorious,
sin and death shall not prevail.
Praise the God of our salvation;
Hosts on high His power proclaim;
Heav'n and earth and all creation,
Praise and magnify His name.

Worship, honor, glory, blessing,
Lord, we offer unto Thee;
Young and old Thy praise expressing,
In glad homage bend the knee.
All the saints in heaven adore Thee,
We would bow before Thy throne;
As thine angels serve before Thee,
so on earth Thy will be done.

(Public domain)

That All Be One

S. Somerville - J. Ritchie

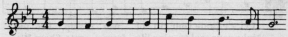

1. That all be one in you, O Lord, we pray,
2. When we are gath-ered for the Eu - char -ist,

That Christ-ians all be joined in one true fold; O
Re - mind us of the words you ut-tered then-Your

heal the sad di - vis- ions in your Church, Re-
prayer of u - ni - ty and peace and love, The

store the Faith kept.. by your saints of old, Good
one-ness sym - bo - lized by bread and wine. So

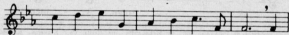

Shep-herd of the sheep, re-make us one, All
may we all one bread, one Bod - y be, Through

broth-ers born for you, God's on - ly Son.
this blest sac -ra- ment of u - ni - ty. A-men.

3. Let charity direct our thoughts and deeds,
Let your love for all men be in our heart;
So Shall we truly your disciples be,
So for our sep'rate brethren do our part.
Teach us our common Father all to own.
Your holy people in one only home.

97 Celebrate Your Gift of Worship

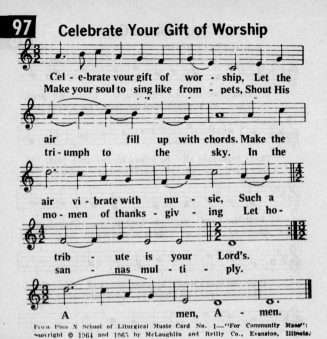

Cel - e-brate your gift of wor - ship, Let the
Make your soul to sing like from - pets, Shout His

air fill up with chords. Make the
tri - umph to the sky. In the

air vi - brate with mu - sic, Such a
mo - men of thanks - giv - ing Let ho -

trib - ute is your Lord's.
san - nas mul - ti - ply.

A men, A - men.

From Pius X School of Liturgical Music Card No. 1—"For Community Mass":
copyright © 1964 and 1965 by McLaughlin and Reilly Co., Evanston, Illinois.

98 America the Beautiful

O beautiful for spacious skies,
For amber wave of grain,
For purple mountain majesties
Above the fruited plain.
America! America! God shed his grace on thee.
And crown thy good with brotherhood
From sea to shining sea.

2. O beautiful for pilgrim feet
Whose stern impassioned stress
A thoroughfare for freedom beat
Across the wilderness.
America America! God mend thy ev'ry flaw,
Confirm thy soul in self control,
Thy liberty in law.

America

1.

My country, 'tis of thee,
Sweet land of liberty,
Of thee I sing;
Land where my fathers died,
Land of the pilgrim's pride
From ev'ry mountainside
Let freedom ring.

My native country, thee,
Land of the noble free,
Thy name I love;
I love thy rocks and rills,
Thy woods and templed hills;
My heart with rapture thrills
Like that above.

3.

Our father's God, to thee,
Author of liberty,
To thee we sing;
Long may our land be bright
With freedom's holy light,
Protect us by thy might,
Great God, our King.

Battle Hymn of the Republic

1. Mine eyes have seen the glory of the coming of the Lord;

He is trampling out the vintage where the grapes of wrath are stored;

He hath loosed the fateful lightning of his terrible swift sword:

His truth is marching on.

Refrain:

Glory, Glory, hallelujah! Glory, glory, hallelujah!
Glory, glory, hallelujah! His truth is marching on.

2. He has sounded forth the trumpet that shall never call retreat;

He is sifting out the hearts of men before his judgment seat;

O be swift my soul to answer him; be jubilant, my feet!
Our God is marching on! —*Refrain*

3. In the beauty of the lilies Christ was born across the sea,

With a glory in his bosom that transfigures you and me;

As he died to make men holy, let us die to make men free,

While God is marching on. —*Refrain*

Amazing Grace

1. Amazing grace! how sweet the sound
   That saved a wretch like me!
   I once was lost, but now am found,
   Was blind, but now I see.

2. 'Twas grace that taught my heart to fear,
   And grace my fears relieved;
   How precious did that grace appear
   The hour I first believed!

3. Through many dangers, toils, and snares,
   I have already come;
   'Tis grace hath brought me safe thus far,
   And grace will lead me home.

4. The Lord has promised good to me,
   His word my hope secures;
   He will my shield and portion be,
   As long as life endures.

5. Yea, when this flesh and heart shall fail,
   And mortal life shall cease,
   I shall possess, within the veil,
   A life of joy and peace.

Lord Who at Cana's Wedding Feast

1. Lord who at Cana's wedding feast
   Did as a guest appear,
   Though dearer far than earthly guest,
   We ask thy presence here,
   For holy you indeed did prove
   This sacrament to be,
   Proclaim it as a bond of love
   For all mankind to see.

2. This holy vow that man can make,
   The golden thread of life,
   The bond that none should dare to break,
   The bond of man and wife;
   Which blest by you whate'er befalls
   No evil can destroy,
   This blessing, Lord, when one recalls,
   Can heighten every joy.

Gift of Finest Wheat

Omer Westendorf   Robert E. Kreutz

Refrain: You satisfy the hungry heart
With gift of finest wheat;
Come give to us, O saving Lord,
The bread of life to eat.

1. As when the shepherd calls his sheep,
They know and hear his voice;
So when you call your fam'ly, Lord,
We follow and rejoice.

2. When joyful lips we sing to you
Our praise and gratitude,
That you should count us worthy, Lord,
To share this heav'nly food.

3. Is not the cup we bless and share
The blood of Christ out-poured?
Do not one cup, one loaf, declare
Our oneness in the Lord?

4. The myst'ry of your presence, Lord,
No mortal tongue can tell:
Who all the world cannot contain
Comes in our hearts to dwell.

5. You give yourself to us, O Lord;
Then selfless let us be,
To serve each other in your name,
In truth and charity.

Christ Our Victor

Refrain: Christ our Victor,
Christ our Ruler,
Christ our Lord and Savior.

May good and blessed times come to us;
May Christ's peace be upon us;
May the kingdom of Christ come!

To Thee O Christ Eternal King;
To Thee O blest Redeemer
Let us sing our endless praises.

Praise be to the Father and to the Son
And to the holy Spirit
Let our praises be forever.

Whatsoever You Do

Refrain:
Whatsoever yo do to the least of my brothers
That you do unto me.

When I was hungry you gave me to eat.
When I was thirsty you gave me to drink.
Now enter into the home of my Father.

When I was homeless you opened your door.
Whn I was naked you gave me your coat.
Now enter into the home of my Father.

When I was weary you helped me find rest.
When I was anxious you calmed all my fears.
Now enter into the home of my Father.

When in prison you came to my cell.
When on a sick bed you cared for my needs.
Now enter into the home of my Father.

In a strange country you made me at home.
Seeking employment you found me a job.
Now enter into the home of my Father.

Hurt in a battle you bound up my wounds.
Searching for kindness you held out your hands.
Now enter into the home of my Father.

When I was aged you bothered to smile.
When I was resless you listened and cared.
Now enter into the home of my Father.

When I was laughed at you stood by my side.
When I was happy you shared in my joy.
Now enter into the home of my Father.

Blest Are the Pure in Heart

Blest are the pure in heart,
For they shall see our God;
The secret of the Lord is theirs,
Their soul is Christ's abode.

2. The Lord, who left the heav'ns
Our life and peace to bring,
To dwell in lowliness with men,
Their pattern and their King.

TREASURY OF PRAYERS

MORNING PRAYERS

Most holy and adorable Trinity, one God in three Persons, I praise you and give you thanks for all the favors you have bestowed upon me. Your goodness has preserved me until now. I offer you my whole being and in particular all my thoughts, words and deeds, together with all the trials I may undergo this day. Give them your blessing. May your Divine Love animate them and may they serve your greater glory.

I make this morning offering in union with the Divine intentions of Jesus Christ who offers himself daily in the holy Sacrifice of the Mass, and in union with Mary, his Virgin Mother and our Mother, who was always the faithful handmaid of the Lord.

Glory be to the Father, and to the Son, and to the Holy Spirit. Amen.

Prayer for Divine Guidance through the Day

Partial indulgence (No. 21) *

Lord, God Almighty, you have brought us safely to the beginning of this day. Defend us today by your mighty power, that we may not fall into any sin, but that all our words may so proceed and all our thoughts and actions be so directed, as to be always just in your sight. Through Christ our Lord. Amen.

* The indulgences quoted in this Missal are taken from the 1968 Vatican edition of the "Enchiridion Indulgentiarum" (published by Catholic Book Publishing Co.).

Partial indulgence (No. 1)

Direct, we beg you, O Lord, our actions by your holy inspirations, and carry them on by your gracious assistance, that every prayer and work of ours may begin always with you, and through you be happily ended. Amen.

NIGHT PRAYERS

I adore you, my God, and thank you for having created me, for having made me a Christian and preserved me this day. I love you with all my heart and I am sorry for having sinned against you, because you are infinite Love and infinite Goodness. Protect me during my rest and may your love be always with me. Amen.

Eternal Father, I offer you the Precious Blood of Jesus Christ in atonement for my sins and for all the intentions of our Holy Church.

Holy Spirit, Love of the Father and the Son, purify my heart and fill it with the fire of your Love, so that I may be a chaste Temple of the Holy Trinity and be always pleasing to you in all things. Amen.

Plea for Divine Help

Partial indulgence (No. 24)

Hear us, Lord, holy Father, almighty and eternal God; and graciously send your holy angel from heaven to watch over, to cherish, to protect, to abide with, and to defend all who dwell in this house. Through Christ our Lord. Amen.

PRAYERS BEFORE HOLY COMMUNION

Act of Faith

Lord Jesus Christ, I firmly believe that you are present in this Blessed Sacrament as true God and true Man, with your Body and Blood, Soul and Divinity. My Redeemer and my Judge, I adore your Divine Majesty together with the angels and saints. I believe, O Lord; increase my faith.

Act of Hope

Good Jesus, in you alone I place all my hope. You are my salvation and my strength, the Source of all good. Through your mercy, through your Passion and Death, I hope to obtain the pardon of my sins, the grace of final perseverance and a happy eternity.

Act of Love

Jesus, my God, I love you with my whole heart and above all things, because you are the one supreme Good and an infinitely perfect Being. You have given your life for me, a poor sinner, and in your mercy you have even offered yourself as food for my soul. My God, I love you. Inflame my heart so that I may love you more.

Act of Contrition

O my Savior, I am truly sorry for having offended you because you are infinitely good and sin displeases you. I detest all the sins of my life and I desire to atone for them. Through the merits of your Precious Blood, wash from my soul all stain of sin, so that, cleansed in body and soul, I may worthily approach the Most Holy Sacrament of the Altar.

PRAYERS AFTER HOLY COMMUNION

Act of Faith

Jesus, I firmly believe that you are present within me as God and Man, to enrich my soul with graces and to fill my heart with the happiness of the blessed. I believe that you are Christ, the Son of the living God!

Act of Adoration

With deepest humility, I adore you, my Lord and God; you have made my soul your dwelling place. I adore you as my Creator from whose hands I came and with whom I am to be happy forever.

Act of Love

Dear Jesus, I love you with my whole heart, my whole soul, and with all my strength. May the love of your own Sacred Heart fill my soul and purify it so that I may die to the world for love of you, as you died on the Cross for love of me. My God, you are all mine; grant that I may be all yours in time and in eternity

Act of Thanksgiving

From the depths of my heart I thank you, dear Lord, for your infinite kindness in coming to me. How good you are to me! With your most holy Mother and all the angels, I praise your mercy and generosity toward me, a poor sinner. I thank you for nourishing my soul with your Sacred Body and Precious Blood. I will try to show my gratitude to you in the Sacrament of your love, by obedience to your holy commandments, by fidelity to my duties, by kindness to my neighbor and by an earnest endeavor to become more like you in my daily conduct.

Act of Offering

Jesus, you have given yourself to me, now let me give myself to you; I give you my body, that it may be chaste and pure. I give you my soul, that it may be free from sin. I give you my heart, that it may always love you. I give you every thought, word, and deed of my life, and I offer all for your honor and glory.

Prayer to Christ the King

O Christ Jesus, I acknowledge you King of the universe. All that has been created has been made for you. Exercise upon me all your rights. I renew my baptismal promises, renouncing Satan and all his works and pomps. I promise to live a good Christian life and to do all in my power to procure the triumph of the rights of God and your Church.

Divine Heart of Jesus, I offer you my poor actions in order to obtain that all hearts may acknowledge your sacred Royalty, and that thus the reign of your peace may be established throughout the universe. Amen.

Indulgenced Prayer before a Crucifix

Look down upon me, good and gentle Jesus, while before your face I humbly kneel, and with a burning soul pray and beseech you to fix deep in my heart lively sentiments of faith, hope and charity, true contrition for my sins, and a firm purpose of amendment, while I contemplate with great love and tender pity your five wounds, pondering over them within me, calling to mind the words which David, your prophet, said of you, my good Jesus: "They have pierced my hands and my feet; they have numbered all my bones" (Ps 21, 17-18).

A *plenary indulgence* is granted on each Friday of Lent and Passiontide to the faithful, who after Communion piously recite the above prayer before an image of Christ crucified; on other days of the year the indulgence is *partial.* (No. 22).

Prayer to Mary

O Jesus living in Mary, come and live in your servants, in the spirit of your holiness, in the fullness of your power, in the perfection of your ways, in the truth of your mysteries. Reign in us over all adverse powers by your Holy Spirit, and for the glory of the Father. Amen.

Anima Christi

Partial indulgence (No. 10)

Soul of Christ, sanctify me.
Body of Christ, save me.
Blood of Christ, inebriate me.
Water from the side of Christ, wash me.
Passion of Christ, strengthen me.
O good Jesus, hear me.
Within your wounds hide me.
Separated from you let me never be.
From the malignant enemy, defend me.
At the hour of death, call me.
And close to you bid me.
That with your saints I may be
Praising you, for all eternity. Amen.

THE SCRIPTURAL WAY OF THE CROSS

The Way of the Cross is a devotion in which we accompany, in spirit, our Blessed Lord in his sorrowful journey to Calvary, and devoutly meditate on his suffering and death.

A plenary indulgence *is granted to those who make the Way of the Cross. (No. 63)*

1. Jesus Is Condemned to Death — God so loved the world that he gave his only-begotten Son to save it (John 3, 16).

2. Jesus Bears His Cross— If anyone wishes to come after me, let him deny himself, and take up his cross daily (Luke 9, 23).

3. Jesus Falls the First Time—The Lord laid upon him the guilt of us all (Isaiah 53, 6).

4. Jesus Meets His Mother—Come, all you who pass by the way, look and see whether there is any suffering like my suffering (Lam. 1, 13).

5. Jesus Is Helped by Simon—As long as you did it for one of these, the least of my brethren, you did it for me (Matt. 25, 40).

6. Veronica wipes the Face of Jesus—He who sees me, sees also the Father (John 14, 9).

7. Jesus Falls a Second Time—Come to me, all you who labor and are burdened, and I will give you rest (Matt. 11, 28)

8. Jesus Speaks to the Women—Daughters of Jerusalem, do not weep for me, but weep for yourselves and for your children (Luke 23, 2).

9. Jesus Falls a Third Time—Everyone who exalts himself shall be humbled, and he who humbles himself shall be exalted (Luke 14, 11).

10. Jesus Is Stripped of His Garments — Every one of you who does not renounce all that he possesses cannot be my disciple (Luke 14, 33).

11. Jesus Is Nailed to the Cross — I have come down from heaven, not to do my own will, but the will of him who sent me (John 6, 38).

12. Jesus Dies on the Cross — He humbled himself, becoming obedient to death, even to death on a cross. Therefore God has exalted him (Phil. 2, 8-9).

13. Jesus Is Taken Down from the Cross — Did not the Christ have to suffer those things before entering into his glory? (Luke 24, 26).

14. Jesus Is Placed in the Tomb — Unless the grain of wheat falls into the ground and dies, it remains alone. But if it dies, it brings forth much fruit (John 12, 24-25).

STATIONS
of the
CROSS

1. Jesus is Condemned to Death

O Jesus, help me to appreciate Your sanctifying grace more and more.

2. Jesus Bears His Cross

O Jesus, You chose to die for me. Help me to love You always with all my heart.

3. Jesus Falls the First Time

O Jesus, make me strong to conquer my wicked passions, and to rise quickly from sin.

4. Jesus Meets His Mother

O Jesus, grant me a tender love for Your Mother, who offered You for love of me.

STATIONS
of the
CROSS

5. Jesus is Helped by Simon

O Jesus, like Simon lead me ever closer to You through my daily crosses and trials.

6. Jesus and Veronica

O Jesus, imprint Your image on my heart that I may be faithful to You all my life.

7. Jesus Falls a Second Time

O Jesus, I repent for having offended You. Grant me forgiveness of all my sins.

8. Jesus Speaks to the Women

O Jesus, grant me tears of compassion for Your sufferings and of sorrow for my sins.

STATIONS
of the
CROSS

9. Jesus Falls a Third Time

O Jesus, let me never yield to despair. Let me come to You in hardship and spiritual distress.

10. He is Stripped of His Garments

O Jesus, let me sacrifice all my attachments rather than imperil the divine life of my soul.

11. Jesus is Nailed to the Cross

O Jesus, strengthen my faith and increase my love for You. Help me to accept my crosses.

12. Jesus Dies on the Cross

O Jesus, I thank You for making me a child of God. Help me to forgive others.

STATIONS
of the
CROSS

13. Jesus is Taken down from the Cross

O Jesus, through the intercession of Your holy Mother, let me be pleasing to You.

14. Jesus is Laid in the Tomb

O Jesus, strengthen my will to live for You on earth and bring me to eternal bliss in heaven.

Prayer after the Stations

JESUS, You became an example of humility, obedience and patience, and preceded me on the way of life bearing Your Cross. Grant that, inflamed with Your love, I may cheerfully take upon myself the sweet yoke of Your Gospel together with the mortification of the Cross and follow You as a true disciple so that I may be united with You in heaven. Amen.

THE HOLY ROSARY

Prayer before the Rosary

QUEEN of the Holy Rosary, you have deigned to come to Fatima to reveal to the three shepherd children the treasures of grace hidden in the Rosary. Inspire my heart with a sincere love of this devotion, in order that by meditating on the Mysteries of our Redemption which are recalled in it, I may be enriched with its fruits and obtain peace for the world, the conversion of sinners and of Russia, and the favor which I ask of you in this Rosary. (*Here mention your request.*) I ask it for the greater glory of God, for your own honor, and for the good of souls, especially for my own. Amen.

The Five Joyful Mysteries

1. The Annunciation
For the love of humility.

2. The Visitation
For charity toward my neighbor.

4. The Presentation
For the virtue of obedience.

3. The Nativity
For the spirit of poverty.

5. Finding in the Temple
For the virtue of piety.

The Five

Sorrowful

Mysteries

3. Crowning with Thorns
For moral courage.

1. Agony in the Garden
For true contrition.

4. Carrying of the Cross
For the virtue of patience.

2. Scourging at the Pillar
For the virtue of purity.

5. The Crucifixion
For final perseverance.

The Five Glorious Mysteries

1. The Resurrection
For the virtue of faith.

2. The Ascension
For the virtue of hope.

4. Assumption of the B.V.M.
For devotion to Mary.

3. Descent of the Holy Spirit
For love of God.

5. Crowning of the B.V.M.
For eternal happiness.

PRAYER TO ST. JOSEPH

O Blessed St. Joseph, loving father and faithful guardian of Jesus, and devoted spouse of the Mother of God, I beg you to offer God the Father his divine Son, bathed in blood on the Cross. Through the holy Name of Jesus obtain for us from the Father the favor we implore.

FOR THE SICK

Father, your Son accepted our sufferings to teach us the virtue of patience in human illness. Hear the prayers we offer for our sick brothers and sisters. May all who suffer pain, illness or disease realize that they are chosen to be saints, and know that they are joined to Christ in his suffering for the salvation of the world, who lives and reigns with you and the Holy Spirit, one God, for ever and ever.

FOR RELIGIOUS VOCATIONS

Father, you call all who believe in you to grow perfect in love by following in the footsteps of Christ your Son. May those whom you have chosen to serve you as religious provide by their way of life a convincing sign of your kingdom for the Church and the whole world.

FOR THE ASSEMBLY OF NATIONAL LEADERS

Father, you guide and govern everything with order and love. Look upon the assembly of our national leaders and fill them with the spirit of your wisdom. May they always act in accordance with your will and their decisions be for the peace and well-being of all.

PRAYER OF A FAMILY

God of goodness and mercy, to your fatherly protection we commend our family, our household and all that belongs to us. We entrust all to your love and keeping. Fill our home with your blessings as you filled the holy house of Nazareth with your presence.

Above all else, keep far from us the stain of sin. We want you alone to rule over us. Help each one of us to obey your holy laws, to love you sincerely and to imitate your example, the example of Mary, your mother and ours, and the example of your holy guardian, saint Joseph.

Lord, preserve us and our home from all evils and misfortunes. May we be ever resigned to your divine will even in the crosses and sorrows which you allow to come to us.

Finally, give all of us the grace to live in perfect harmony and love toward our neighbor. Grant that every one of us may deserve by a holy life the comfort of your holy sacraments at the hour of death.

Bless this house, God the Father, who created us, God the Son, who suffered for us upon the cross, and God the Holy Spirit, who sanctified us in baptism. May the one God in three divine persons preserve our bodies, purify our minds, direct our hearts and bring us all to everlasting life.

Glory be to the Father, glory be to the Son, glory be to the Holy Spirit! Amen.

PRAYER FOR HEALTH

O Sacred Heart of Jesus, I come to ask of Your infinite mercy the gift of health and strength that I may serve You more faithfully and love You more sincerely than in the past. I wish to be well and strong if this be Your good pleasure and for Your greater glory. Filled with high resolves and determined to perform my tasks most perfectly for love of You, I wish to be enabled to go back to my duties.

PRAYER FOR PEACE AND JOY

Jesus, I want to rejoice in You always. You are near. Let me have no anxiety, but in every concern by prayer and supplication with thanksgiving I wish to let my petitions be made known in my communing with God.

May the peace of God, which surpasses all understanding, guard my heart and my thoughts in You.

PRAYER TO KNOW GOD'S WILL

God the Father of our Lord Jesus Christ, the Author of glory, grant me spiritual wisdom and revelation. Enlighten the eyes of my mind with a deep knowledge of You and Your holy will. May I understand of what nature is the hope to which You call me, what is the wealth of the splendor of Your inheritance among the Saints, and what is the surpassing greatness of Your power toward me.

PRAYER FOR CIVIL AUTHORITIES

Almighty and everlasting God, You direct the powers and laws of all nations; mercifully regard those who rule over us, that, by Your protecting right hand, the integrity of religion and the security of each country might prevail everywhere on earth. Through Christ our Lord. Amen.

PRAYER TO ST. JOSEPH

Guardian of virgins, and holy father Joseph, to whose faithful custody Christ Jesus, innocence itself, and Mary, Virgin of virgins, were committed; I beg you, by these dear pledges, Jesus and Mary, that, being preserved from all uncleanness, I may with spotless mind, pure heart and chaste body, ever serve Jesus and Mary most chastely all the days of my life. Amen.

THE TEN COMMANDMENTS

1. I, the Lord, am your God. You shall not have other gods besides Me.
2. You shall not take the Name of the Lord, your God, in vain.
3. Remember to keep holy the sabbath day.
4. Honor you father and your mother.
5. You shall not kill.
6. You shall not commit adultery.
7. You shall not steal.
8. You shall not bear false witness against your neighbor.
9. You shall not covet your neighbor's wife.
10. You shall not covet anything that belongs to your neighbor.

THE GREAT COMMANDMENT

You shall love the Lord your God with your whole heart, and with your whole soul, and with al! your mind. This is the greatest and the first commandment. And the second is like it: you shall love your neighbor as yourself.   —*Mt 22, 37*

NEW RITE OF PENANCE

(Extracted from the Rite of Penance)

Texts for the Penitent

The penitent should prepare for the celebration of the sacrament by prayer, reading of Scripture, and silent reflection. The penitent should think over and should regret all sins since the last celebration of the sacrament.

RECEPTION OF THE PENITENT

The penitent enters the confessional or other place set aside for the celebration of the sacrament of penance. After the welcoming of the priest, the penitent makes the sign of the cross saying:

In the name of the Father, and of the Son, and of the Holy Spirit. Amen.

The penitent is invited to have trust in God and replies:

Amen.

READING OF THE WORD OF GOD

The penitent then listens to a text of Scripture which tells about God's mercy and calls man to conversion.

CONFESSION OF SINS AND ACCEPTANCE OF SATISFACTION

The penitent speaks to the priest in a normal, conversational fashion. The penitent tells when he or she last celebrated the sacrament and then confesses his or her sins. The penitent then listens to any advice the priest may give and accepts the satisfaction from the priest. The penitent should ask any appropriate questions.

PRAYER OF THE PENITENT AND ABSOLUTION

Prayer

Before the absolution is given, the penitent expresses sorrow for sins in these or similar words:

My God,
I am sorry for my sins with all my heart.
In choosing to do wrong
and failing to do good,
I have sinned against you
whom I should love above all things.
I firmly intend, with your help,
to do penance,
to sin no more,
and to avoid whatever leads me to sin.
Our Savior Jesus Christ
suffered and died for us.
In his name, my God, have mercy.

OR:
> Remember, Lord, your compassion and mercy which you
>   showed long ago.
> Do not recall the sins and failings of my youth.
> In your mercy remember me, Lord, because of your
>   goodness.

OR:
> Wash me from my guilt
> and cleanse me of my sin.
> I acknowledge my offense;
> my sin is before me always.

OR:
> Father, I have sinned against you
> and am not worthy to be called your son.
> Be merciful to me, a sinner.

OR:
> Father of mercy,
> like the prodigal son
> I return to you and say:
> "I have sinned against you
> and am no longer worthy to be called your son."
> Christ Jesus, Savior of the world,
> I pray with the repentant thief
> to whom you promised Paradise:
> "Lord, remember me in your kingdom."
> Holy Spirit, fountain of love,
> I call on you with trust:
> "Purify my heart,
> and help me to walk as a child of light."

OR:
> Lord Jesus,
> you opened the eyes of the blind,
> healed the sick,
> forgave the sinful woman,
> and after Peter's denial confirmed him in your love.
> Listen to my prayer,
> forgive all my sins,
> renew your love in my heart,
> help me to live in perfect unity with my fellow Christians
> that I may proclaim your saving power to all the world.

OR:
> Lord Jesus;
> you chose to be called the friend of sinners.
> By your saving death and resurrection
> free me from my sins.
> May your peace take root in my heart

and bring forth a harvest
of love, holiness, and truth.

OR:

Lord Jesus Christ,
you are the Lamb of God;
you take away the sins of the world.
Through the grace of the Holy Spirit
restore me to friendship with your Father,
cleanse me from every stain of sin
and raise me to new life
for the glory of your name.

OR:

Lord God,
in your goodness have mercy on me:
do not look on my sins,
but take away all my guilt.
Create in me a clean heart
and renew within me an upright spirit.

OR:

Lord Jesus, Son of God,
have mercy on me, a sinner.

ABSOLUTION

*If the penitent is not kneeling, he or she bows his or her
head as the priest extends his hands (or at least extends his
right hand).*

God, the Father of mercies,
through the death and resurrection of his Son
has reconciled the world to himself
and sent the Holy Spirit among us
for the forgiveness of sins;
through the ministry of the Church
may God give you pardon and peace,
and I absolve you from your sins
in the name of the Father, and of the Son,
and of the Holy Spirit. Amen.

PROCLAMATION OF PRAISE OF GOD AND DISMISSAL

Penitent and priest give praise to God.

Priest: Give thanks to the Lord, for he is good.
Penitent: His mercy endures for ever.

Then the penitent is dismissed by the priest.

Form of Examination of Conscience

This suggested form for an examination of conscience should be completed and adapted to meet the needs of different individuals and to follow local usages.

In an examination of conscience, before the sacrament of penance, each individual should ask himself these questions in particular:

1. What is my attitude to the sacrament of penance? Do I sincerely want to be set free from sin, to turn again to God, to begin a new life, and to enter into a deeper friendship with God? Or do I look on it as a burden, to be undertaken as seldom as possible?

2. Did I forget to mention, or deliberately conceal, any grave sins in past confessions?

3. Did I perform the penance I was given? Did I make reparation for any injury to others? Have I tried to put into practice my resolution to lead a better life in keeping with the Gospel?

Each individual should examine his life in the light of God's word.

I. The Lord says: "You shall love the Lord your God with your whole heart."

1. Is my heart set on God, so that I really love him above all things and am faithful to his commandments, as a son loves his father? Or am I more concerned about the things of this world? Have I a right intention in what I do?

2. God spoke to us in his Son. Is my faith in God firm and secure? Am I wholehearted in accepting the Church's teaching? Have I been careful to grow in my understanding of the faith, to hear God's word, to listen to instructions on the faith, to avoid dangers to faith? Have I been always strong and fearless in professing my faith in God and the Church? Have I been willing to be known as a Christian in private and public life?

3. Have I prayed morning and evening? When I pray, do I really raise my mind and heart to God or is it a matter of words only? Do I offer God my difficulties, my joys, and my sorrows? Do I turn to God in time of temptation?

4. Have I love and reverence for God's name? Have I offended him in blasphemy, swearing falsely, or taking his name in vain? Have I shown disrespect for the Blessed Virgin Mary and the saints?

5. Do I keep Sundays and feast days holy by taking a full part, with attention and devotion, in the liturgy, and especially in the Mass? Have I fulfilled the precept of annual confession and of communion during the Easter season?

667

6. Are there false gods that I worship by giving them greater attention and deeper trust than I give to God: money, superstition, spiritism, or other occult practices?

II. The Lord says: "Love one another as I have loved you."

1. Have I a genuine love for my neighbors? Or do I use them for my own ends, or do to them what I would not want done to myself? Have I given grave scandal by my words or actions.?

2. In my family life, have I contributed to the well-being and happiness of the rest of the family by patience and genuine love? Have I been obedient to parents, showing them proper respect and giving them help in their spiritual and material needs? Have I been careful to give a Christian upbringing to my children, and to help them by good example and by exercising authority as a parent? Have I been faithful to my husband/wife in my heart and in my relations with others?

3. Do I share my possessions with the less fortunate? Do I do my best to help the victims of oppression, misfortune, and poverty? Or do I look down on my neighbor, especially the poor, the sick, the elderly, strangers, and people of other races?

4. Does my life reflect the mission I received in confirmation? Do I share in the apostolic and charitable works of the Church and in the life of my parish? Have I helped to meet the needs of the Church and of the world and prayed for them: for unity in the Church, for the spread of the Gospel among the nations, for peace and justice, etc.?

5. Am I concerned for the good and prosperity of the human community in which I live, or do I spend my life caring only for myself? Do I share to the best of my ability in the work of promoting justice, morality, harmony, and love in human relations? Have I done my duty as a citizen? Have I paid my taxes?

6. In my work or profession am I just, hard-working, honest, serving society out of love for others? Have I paid a fair wage to my employees? Have I been faithful to my promises and contracts?

7. Have I obeyed legitimate authority and given it due respect?

8. If I am in a position of responsibility or authority, do I use this for my own advantage or for the good of others, in a spirit of service?

9. Have I been truthful and fair, or have I injured others by deceit, calumny, detraction, rash judgment, or violation of a secret?

10. Have I done violence to others by damage to life or limb, reputation, honor, or material possessions? Have I involved them in loss? Have I been responsible for advising an abortion or procuring one? Have I kept up hatred for others? Am I estranged from others through

quarrels, enmity, insults, anger? Have I been guilty of refusing to testify to the innocence of another because of selfishness?

11. Have I stolen the property of others? Have I desired it unjustly and inordinately? Have I damaged it? Have I made restitution of other people's property and made good their loss?

12. If I have been injured, have I been ready to make peace for the love of Christ and to forgive, or do I harbor hatred and the desire for revenge?

III. Christ our Lord says: "Be perfect as your Father is perfect."

1. Where is my life really leading me? Is the hope of eternal life my inspiration? Have I tried to grow in the life of the Spirit through prayer, reading the word of God and meditating on it, receiving the sacraments, self-denial? Have I been anxious to control my vices, my bad inclinations and passions, e.g., envy, love of food and drink? Have I been proud and boastful, thinking myself better in the sight of God and despising others as less important than myself? Have I imposed my own will on others, without respecting their freedom and rights?

2. What use have I made of time, of health and strength, of the gifts God has given me to be used like the talents in the Gospel? Do I use them to become more perfect every day? Or have I been lazy and too much given to leisure?

3. Have I been patient in accepting the sorrows and disappointments of life? How have I performed mortification so as to "fill up what is wanting to the sufferings of Christ"? Have I kept the precept of fasting and abstinence?

4. Have I kept my senses and my whole body pure and chaste as a temple of the Holy Spirit consecrated for resurrection and glory, and as a sign of God's faithful love for men and women, a sign that is seen most perfectly in the sacrament of matrimony? Have I dishonored my body by fornication, impurity, unworthy conversation or thoughts, evil desires or actions? Have I given in to sensuality? Have I indulged in reading, conversation, shows, and entertainments that offend against Christian and human decency? Have I encouraged others to sin by my own failure to maintain these standards? Have I been faithful to the moral law in my married life?

5. Have I gone against my conscience out of fear or hypocrisy?

6. Have I always tried to act in the true freedom of the sons of God according to the law of the Spirit, or am I the slave of forces within me?

HYMN INDEX